Genders and Sexualities in History

Series Editors: John Arnold, Joanna Bou

Palgrave Macmillan's series *Genders an*
date and foster new approaches to hi.
and sexualities. The series will promote world-class scholarship that concentrates
upon the interconnected themes of genders, sexualities, religions/religiosity, civil
society, class formations, politics and war.

Historical studies of gender and sexuality have often been treated as disconnected
fields, while in recent years historical analyses in these two have synthesised,
creating new departures in historiography. By linking genders and sexualities
with questions of religion, civil society, politics and the contexts of war and
conflict, this series will reflect recent developments in scholarship, moving away
from the previously dominant and narrow histories of science, scientific thought,
and legal processes. The result brings together scholarship from contemporary,
modern, early modern, medieval, classical and non-Western history to provide
a diachronic forum for scholarship that incorporates new approaches to genders
and sexualities in history.

Brutality and Desire: War and Sexuality in Europe's Twentieth Century integrates military history with the histories of gender and sexuality in twentieth-century
Europe. Wartime exigencies expose the contingency of both masculine and
feminine gender roles. In a series of thoughtful essays, the authors unpick
the complex intersections between sexuality (both coerced and consensual),
war, and politics. They construct carefully historicized arguments, all of which
pay attention to the specificities of each conflict, from the Armenian genocide to the conflict in Bosnia. Innovative uses of primary sources (many of
which have rarely been used by historians before) contribute to the analytical persuasiveness of the chapters. As with all volumes in the series *Genders
and Sexualities in History*, the authors present multifaceted and subtle analyses of the past within narratives that are sophisticated methodologically and
theoretically.

Titles include:

Jessica Meyer
MEN OF WAR
Masculinity and the First World War in Britain

Jennifer D. Thibodeaux (*editor*)
NEGOTIATING CLERICAL IDENTITIES
Priests, Monks and Masculinity in the Middle Ages

H. Vaizey
SURVIVING HITLER'S WAR

C. Forth; E. Accampo
CONFRONTING MODERNITY IN FIN-DE-SIÈCLEFRANCE

Forthcoming titles include:

Matthew Cook
QUEER DOMESTICITIES
Homosexuality and Home Life in Twentieth-Century London

Jennifer Evans
RECONSTRUCTION SITES
Spaces of Sexual Encounter in Cold War Berlin

S. Brady; J. Arnold
WHAT IS MASCULINITY?

S. Toulalan; K. Fisher
BODIES, SEX AND DESIRE FROM THE RENAISSANCE TO THE PRESENT

R. Hogg
BRITISH MASCULINITY ON THE QUEENSLAND AND BRITISH COLUMBIA
FRONTIERS, 1840–70

C. Beccalossi
FEMALE SEXUAL INVERSION

M. Hollander
SEX IN TWO CITIES

Genders and Sexualities in History Series
Series Standing Order ISBN 978–0–230–55185–5 Hardback
Series Standing Order ISBN 978–0–230–55186–2 Paperback
(outside North America only)

You can receive future titles in this series as they are published by placing a standing order. Please contact your bookseller or, in case of difficulty, write to us at the address below with your name and address, the title of the series and the ISBN quoted above.

Customer Services Department, Macmillan Distribution Ltd, Houndmills, Basingstoke, Hampshire RG21 6XS, England

Brutality and Desire

War and Sexuality in Europe's Twentieth Century

Edited by

Dagmar Herzog

Professor of History, and Daniel Rose Faculty Scholar, City University of New York

palgrave
macmillan

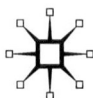

First published 2009, and in paperback 2011 by
PALGRAVE MACMILLAN

Palgrave Macmillan in the UK is an imprint of Macmillan Publishers Limited,
registered in England, company number 785998, of Houndmills, Basingstoke,
Hampshire RG21 6XS.

Palgrave Macmillan in the US is a division of St Martin's Press LLC,
175 Fifth Avenue, New York, NY 10010.

Palgrave Macmillan is the global academic imprint of the above companies
and has companies and representatives throughout the world.

Palgrave® and Macmillan® are registered trademarks in the United States,
the United Kingdom, Europe and other countries.

ISBN 978–0–230–54253–2 hardback
ISBN 978–0–230–28563–7 paperback

This book is printed on paper suitable for recycling and made from fully
managed and sustained forest sources. Logging, pulping and manufacturing
processes are expected to conform to the environmental regulations of the
country of origin.

A catalogue record for this book is available from the British Library.

Library of Congress Cataloging-in-Publication Data
Herzog, Dagmar, 1961–
    Brutality and desire : war and sexuality in Europe's twentieth
    century / Dagmar Herzog.
       p.   cm. — (Genders and sexualities in history)
    Includes bibliographical references and index.
    ISBN 978–0–230–54253–2 (alk. paper)
    1. Sex crimes—Europe—History—20th century.   2. Women—Violence
    against—Europe—History—20th century.   3. Women—Crimes against—
    Europe—History—20th century.   4. Sexual minorities—Crimes
    against—Europe—History—20th century.   5. Sexual minorities—
    Violence against—Europe—History—20th century.   6. Europe—
    History, Military—History—20th century.   I. Title.
    HV6593.E85H47 2007
    363.34'98—dc22   2008029974

10   9   8   7   6   5   4   3   2   1
20   19   18   17   16   15   14   13   12   11

Printed and bound in Great Britain by
CPI Antony Rowe, Chippenham and Eastbourne

Contents

v

List of Figures

Acknowledgments

Brutality and Desire had its origins in a conference on 'War and Sexuality in Twentieth-Century Europe' held in Esbjerg, Denmark in June 2006. The conference was organized by historians Flemming Just and Henrik Lundtofte, and was the third and final event in a sequence of conferences which addressed the non-military aspects of war. I thank Professors Just and Lundtofte for their warm hospitality, superlative organizational skills, and for the extraordinary experience of the conference itself. Papers from the conference were supplemented with commissioned pieces from experts on the histories of sex and sexual violence in wartime – not least with a view to rounding out the geographical and chronological breadth of the volume while heightening its conceptual coherence. I am grateful to Michael Strang at Palgrave Macmillan and the *Genders and Sexualities in History* series editors for accepting and shepherding the project and for their terrific suggestions for strengthening the volume. Finally, I thank the contributors for their hard work and deep seriousness of purpose, and Todd Shepard, Miriam Intrator, and Will Bishop for their particularly felicitous skills in translation and editing.

Dagmar Herzog
New York City, May 2008

List of Contributors

Matthias Bjørnlund is a historian and an independent scholar specializing in the Armenian genocide. He has researched, authored, and co-authored articles and papers on the concept of genocide, on aspects of the Rwandan genocide, and on missionary history. He is currently writing a book on Denmark and 'the Armenian Question,' 1900–1940.

Raphaëlle Branche teaches at the University of Paris 1-La Sorbonne. She is the author of *La torture et l'armée pendant la guerre d'Algérie, 1954–1962* (Paris, Gallimard, 2001) and *La guerre d'Algérie: une histoire apaisée?* (Paris, Le Seuil, 2005). She is currently working on French colonial and post-colonial history.

Richard S. Fogarty is Assistant Professor of History at the State University of New York at Albany, and is the author of *Race and War in France: Colonial Subjects in the French Army, 1914–1918* (Baltimore, MD: Johns Hopkins University Press, 2008), as well as several articles on race, colonialism, and war in twentieth-century France.

Lulu Anne Hansen is writing her PhD in Contemporary History at the University of Southern Denmark, Esbjerg. Her dissertation focuses on forms of collaboration, mechanisms of exclusion, and the social dynamics following the German occupation of Denmark 1940–1945. She has previously worked for the Archives of Danish Occupation History.

Dagmar Herzog is Professor of History and Daniel Rose Faculty Scholar at the Graduate Center, City University of New York. She is the author of *Sex in Crisis: The New Sexual Revolution and the Future of American Politics* (Basic Books, 2008), *Sex after Fascism: Memory and Morality in Twentieth-Century Germany* (Princeton, 2005), and *Intimacy and Exclusion: Religious Politics in Pre-Revolutionary Baden* (Princeton, 1996, Transaction, 2007); the co-editor of *Sexuality in Austria* (Transaction, 2007); and the editor of *Lessons and Legacies VII: The Holocaust in International Perspective* (Northwestern, 2006) and *Sexuality and German Fascism* (Berghahn Books, 2004).

Teresa Iacobelli is a doctoral candidate in the Department of History at The University of Western Ontario in London, Ontario, Canada. Her dissertation explores the application of the death penalty in the Canadian Expeditionary Force during the First World War. She also holds a Master's Degree in History from Wilfrid Laurier University and a B.A. in History and Politics from Trent University in Peterborough, Ontario, Canada.

Marie-Anne Matard-Bonucci is Professor of Contemporary History at the Université de Grenoble II. She is a specialist on fascism, antisemitism, and modern Italian history. Her publications include *Antisémythes* (Nouveau monde ed., 2005) as well as (with P. Milza) *L'homme nouveau dans les régimes fascistes* (Fayard, 2004). *L'Italie fasciste et la persécution des juifs* (Perrin, 2006).

Regina Mühlhäuser is the contact person for the working group 'War and Gender' at the Hamburg Institute for Social Research, Germany. She finished her PhD dissertation, 'Between "Racial Awareness" and Fantasies of Potency: Nazi Sexual Politics and Children of German Men and Local Women in the Occupied Territories of the Soviet Union (1941–1945)' in March 2008 (funded by the Hamburg Foundation for the Benefit of Research and Culture). She has published several articles on sexual violence in times of war, gender and sexuality under National Socialism, and German memory politics.

Na'ama Shik works at the International School for Holocaust Studies in Yad Vashem, Israel. She is a doctoral candidate in history at Tel Aviv University. Her dissertation (under the direction of Shulamit Volkov) is on Jewish women in Auschwitz-Birkenau, 1942–1945, and she has published several articles on this topic.

Robert Sommer is a doctoral candidate at the Humboldt University of Berlin and has finished his PhD dissertation on the history and role of brothels in Nazi concentration camps. In 2006 he published essays on the camp brothels of Auschwitz in the anthology *Nationalsozialistische Lager*, on oral history and SS brothels in *BIOS* (Journal for Biography and Oral History) and on the reactions of the society of Nazi camp prisoners to sexual slavery in *Theresienstädter Studien und Dokumente*. The same year, his master's thesis (completed in 2003) – on the reasons for the establishment of brothels in Nazi concentration camps and the history of the camp brothel of the Sachsenhausen concentration camp – was published on lulu.com/Morrisville (NC).

Emma Vickers is a senior teaching associate at the University of Lancaster, England. Her thesis explores military authority and homosexuality in the British armed forces during the Second World War. She has worked as a consultant for BBC Radio 4 and BBC One and she is currently working on her first monograph.

Introduction: War and Sexuality in Europe's Twentieth Century

Dagmar Herzog

The transformation of European military history from a marginal enclave into a major growth area and enormously respected subfield of the discipline of history writ large has taken place within the last dozen years. Whether the sources of the booming growth in military history and its increasing integration into the mainstream of the discipline can be found in the end of the Cold War and the resurgence in many parts of the globe of interethnic strife and 'hot wars' (and, more recently, the increasing incidents of terrorism and subsequent attempts to combat it), or in the succession of numerous anniversaries related to past wars (perhaps most significantly the 50th anniversary of the end of World War II in 1995), or in dynamics more internal to the subfield of military history which more and more opened itself to wider social historical trends (e.g. an interest in the daily lives of soldiers, the impacts of wars on home fronts, or the aftermaths of wars in military occupations and new regimes) even as social historians themselves became increasingly interested in utilizing diaries and letters produced during wars remains an open question. All these factors were consequential. What is indisputable is the richness and variety of the resulting research findings and analyses.[1]

One of the most significant pressures for integrating military history with other realms of history came – however surprising this may seem at first glance – from the subfield of women's history. Examining critically the convulsive and potentially transformative impacts of wars on gender roles and relations, as well as the often tenacious hold of pre-war conceptualizations of gender or the force of postwar attempts to restore 'traditional' gender arrangements, appeared to offer an exceptionally valuable opportunity to theorize more effectively the complex interplay of change and continuity that marked women's lives. Precisely because wars threw gender relations into disarray and thereby exposed the constructedness and contingency of gender roles more generally, the study of wars and their aftermaths provided an especially useful site for challenging the compartmentalizations and resistances to thinking critically about gender demonstrated by many professional historians.[2]

Yet also among scholars attentive to gender, there was a time lag in taking seriously the possibilities of military history for theorizing masculinity as thoroughly as scholars had begun to think about the impact of wars on women's lives and options.[3] As late as 1993, when Miriam Cooke and Angela Woollacott published *Gendering War Talk*, they were still at pains to explain that analyzing the intersections between war and gender did not only mean talking about women; it also meant talking about men. And as they pushed that case, the larger overarching objective of their collection – whose essays traversed the representations and enactments of femininity and masculinity in such diverse contexts as British involvement in World War I; Claude Lanzmann's masterpiece, *Shoah*; the experiences of Vietnam veterans returning to the United States; the 'dirty' anti-guerilla wars in Central and South America in the 1980s; the first Gulf War of 1991; and the feminist peace movement – was to stress how wars have always been conceptually and materially inseparable from the civilian societies that spawn and experience them: in their origins, in their unfolding, in their outcomes.[4]

Yet nothing was more decisive in pressing to the foreground of scholarly inquiry exactly those interconnections between civilian societies and wartime violences than the resurgence of the phenomenon of genocide in the context of the wars in the former Yugoslavia and in Rwanda in the first half of the 1990s. It was not just (though also) the haplessness of western Europe and the United States in the face of these brutal events that generated an outpouring of critical reflection on the recurrence of genocide in the second half of the twentieth century despite the West's post-1940s determination to prevent it (including renewed attention as well to prior genocidal campaigns in Cambodia in the 1970s and Guatemala in the 1980s). It was also the recognition that in the 1990s *neighbors* were slaughtering *neighbors* that prompted fresh reflection on the (theretofore undertheorized) close possible links between intimate familiarity and vicious violence, and prompted scholars to inquire into the potential connections between intimacy and massacre in previous episodes of genocide in Europe, including Armenia in the 1910s and above all in the Holocaust of the 1930s–1940s.[5]

The expansion of Holocaust studies and genocide studies alike since the 1990s, then, accounts for a great deal of the impetus for integrating military, social, and cultural history. This is not only due to the wealth of new sources made available by the opening of former Soviet and Eastern bloc archives in the postcommunist years. It is also because new questions were now posed about old topics – from the complex relationships between prejudice, ideology, and faith to the role of emotions like fear, hatred, and exhilaration in the act of killing to such matters as the intricate interconnections between civilians' homefront consumer options (and political quiescence) and the social vacuum and 'ownerless property' created by genocide.[6] In addition, ongoing research revealed the impossibility of easily separating genocide from 'normal' warfare.[7]

What further became evident in the last several years is that, for too long, scholars had mentally divided the twentieth century in half – thinking of the first half as the era of the two world wars, and the second half as a time of remarkable peace and stability. As a greater integration of eastern and western Europe followed the fall of communism, and as massive migration and globalization proceeded apace and put the multiple interconnections between western European nations and their former colonies more inescapably into view, the twentieth century in Europe became more clearly visible as actually one of continually recurring violence – a story that began with savage repression in European colonies in Africa and the Turkish genocide in Armenia, as well as World War I, found its nadir in the continent-wide carnage of World War II and the Holocaust as well as in the million fold mass killings in the Soviet Union, but then continued through brutal European anti-guerilla warfare in such places as Algeria and Kenya (including the use of torture and concentration camps), as well as Korea, Malaya, and Vietnam.[8]

Issues of sexuality – both coerced and consensual – hovered constantly around the edges of all this research into the history of wars. It was not least the mass rapes in Bosnia-Herzegovina in the early 1990s (and then also in Rwanda) – and the subsequent international recognition that these were war crimes – that gave intellectual legitimacy and ethical urgency to the study of sexual violence in other wars.[9] The 1990s saw a growing body of work both on sexual violence – including, for instance, the mass rapes of German, Austrian, and Hungarian women by the Soviet Red Army in 1945 – and on consensual cross-national sexual encounters during wartime and postwar military occupations.[10] The exposure of Japanese sexual enslavement of Korean and Chinese 'comfort women' in World War II, along with the ensuing diplomatic repercussions, put the prevalence of military brothels in almost all wars on the serious research agenda – even as it also spurred the need for far more careful delineation of the significant differences between voluntary prostitution and sexual enslavement.[11] The first years of the twenty-first century also saw sustained efforts to rethink the sexual politics of National Socialism (as well as Vichy France, Franco's Spain, and Mussolini's Italy) and to inquire into the place of sexual violence in the Holocaust.[12] At the same time, scholars became increasingly attentive to the considerable military and political relevance of patterns of fraternization both for stabilizing and for destabilizing military occupations during or after wars, as well as the frequently remarkable significance of fraternization in spurring wartime national resistance movements and/or postwar cultures of nationalist *ressentiment*.[13]

*

This volume follows the arc of violence coursing through Europe's twentieth century, from Armenia through Auschwitz and the war in Algeria to Bosnia. As the essays collected here confirm many times over, Europe in the twentieth century was indeed, as historian Mark Mazower has aptly put it, *The Dark Continent*.[14] Sexual violence accompanied warfare at almost every point, albeit always again – and this is essential to register – in quite distinct, historically and geographically specific, ways. Instances of sexual violence ranged from gang rape and genital mutilation of both women and men to forced impregnation and sexual slavery and coerced marriage for women, from spontaneous sexualized humiliations (meant to dehumanize victims and to brutalize and desensitize – or reward – perpetrators in the killing fields) to terrifyingly systematic and inventive sadisms within concentration and death camps. What becomes depressingly, horrifyingly clear is that sexual violence was simply standard operating procedure. And yet, as especially the essays by Matthias Bjørnlund, Robert Sommer, Regina Mühlhäuser, Na'ama Shik, Raphaëlle Branche, and Teresa Iacobelli explicate most carefully, the violence always served different functions. Sometimes sexual violence was a 'by-product' of war, a bribe to the perpetrators to encourage their participation in the less pleasurable activity of killing. 'You are allowed to rape but do it discreetly', one French commando leader advised his soldiers in Algeria in 1961.[15] Sometimes, sexual violence served as a means for perpetrators to entertain each other – and sometimes it was simply a gratuitous assertion of total power.[16] Sometimes, sexual violence provided a means to keep concentration camp inmates compliant. But all too often sexual violence was the war. Both in Armenia and in Bosnia – although in one case more spontaneously, in the other more deliberately – sexual violence itself became a means of implementing genocide. No volume thus far has juxtaposed chronologically and territorially diverse cases of sexual violence in twentieth-century Europe also for the purpose of advancing thoughtful comparative analysis.[17] That is one aim of this book.

However, and crucially, the volume also includes contrapuntal stories of desire and delight, of the consensual pleasures made possible by the anonymity and mass mobility of times of war and the accompanying disruptions of traditional constraints and communal and familial monitoring mechanisms. This juxtaposition of brutality with desire is deliberate. The place of sexuality in wars will never be understood adequately if we only attend to its negative manifestations. It is not just (though also) that prostitution – both coerced and consensual – almost always accompanies wars, and that we miss a huge aspect of soldiers' experiences of war if we neglect the place of visits to prostitutes in male bonding as well as rivalry (and indeed also of how cross-national and 'cross-racial' prostitution is experienced and monitored, as the essays by Richard Fogarty, Marie-Anne Matard-Bonucci, and Mühlhäuser make particularly clear). Just as important to understand is the flirting and consensual sex *among* soldiers, both heterosexual (as women increasingly joined the armed forces in various nations) and homosexual, as well as the consensual sex engaged in by soldiers with civilians – near battle fronts, in occupied lands, on home fronts. As one German lieutenant major stationed in a western European nation during World War II – and fully aware that Germany was about to suffer a shattering and comprehensive defeat – told his soldiers (as they prepared to enjoy a night of reveling and sexual intercourse with a new auxiliary service contingent of young German women), 'Enjoy the war – the peace will be awful'.[18] In many cases, talk about sexual exploits was likely to be the single most frequent subject of conversations among soldiers. As the essay by Emma Vickers on the British military during World War II recounts, one woman, arriving at a bomber station, 'was informed by a more seasoned recruit that she could "have a different boyfriend every night" if she wanted', while another woman remembered that fully 85 percent of the conversations conducted among army women concerned 'the topics of men and dances'; studies on male soldiers in other contexts have found similar levels of preoccupation with sex as 'topic number 1'.[19]

Yet as with sexual violence, so also with consensual sexual pleasures, it is imperative that we do not assume some sort of transhistorical sex drive erupting (either dangerously or happily) at those moments when constraints are removed (even as we take seriously the often heightened intensity of sexual encounters in times of war, either due to the impending separation of lovers or to the immanent threat of death). Instead, studying how individuals and cultures made sense of consensual encounters in wartime offers an unprecedented opportunity to *historicize* sexuality more generally and to note just how much assumptions about its contents and meanings have changed. What people find permissible or outrageous, what people find erotic or revolting, varies greatly over time, and the disruptions caused by wars offer an important window onto those variations. The essays on consensual sex included in this volume – especially those by Fogarty, Vickers, and Lulu Anne Hansen – all highlight the ways that wars have provided opportunities for sexual experimentation, and they emphasize the excitement and joys of transgressing boundaries of nation, color, sexual orientation, or class. They also reveal how sexual encounters in wartime, or during postwar military stationings and occupations, very frequently destabilized hierarchies of racism and homophobia as well as provided new opportunities for female sexual agency – and yet with paradoxical results, both opening up new imaginative universes with potentially positive consequences for developments in peacetime and sometimes triggering powerful backlashes. Moreover, while certainly female sexual victimization *and* agency are discussed in the essays included in this volume, one of the tasks the volume has set itself is to bring the vagaries of male sexuality (both homosexual and heterosexual) more fully into focus and thereby also to answer recent calls for a more integrated and comprehensive history of gender.

After all, the twentieth century in Europe was not only a century of extraordinary brutality. It can also usefully be thought of as 'the century of sex', arcing as it does from Sigmund Freud and the repudiation of Victorianism to the increasingly anxious debates about the depersonalization of sex in the era of Viagra and the rise of Internet pornography. What can the apparent pursuit of depersonalized sex during wars – both violent *and* voluntary – tell us about human beings' relationship to their own bodies, and to the bodies of others? At what points has the humanity of the sexual object mattered, and at what points was precisely the humanity that which needed to be erased? These questions are pursued especially in the essays by Sommer, Shik, and Branche.

*

In seeking to explicate the complexities of both violence and sex, each of the essays included in this volume stands out for its innovative use of previously untapped primary sources and for its analytic acuity. Drawing especially on a wealth of sources produced by missionaries (from Denmark, Germany, Norway, and other nations) who observed the violence and cared for survivors, Matthias Bjørnlund is able to provide the most comprehensive account to date of the pervasiveness of sexual violence in the Armenian genocide. His differentiated analysis of the divergent functions of sexual violence in the context of genocide also facilitates comparative understanding across time and space precisely because it is grounded in the particularities of the Armenian situation. 'Sexual violence was quite simply the norm on the death marches'. Yet at the same time, Bjørnlund stresses that the sexual slavery and mutilations were more an end in themselves rather than serving strategic means, serving more as occasions for dehumanizing and degrading the victims, asserting the power of the perpetrators and providing them with occasions for 'mutual demonstrations of masculinity'. Since most of the male Armenian population had already been murdered before the marches began, this was not an instance of using violence against females to send a message to the males of the enemy. In addition, Bjørnlund positions the Armenian case within the complex history of ethnoreligious hatreds which contain biologistic components but differ from biological racism, and in this way he can explain as well how some Armenian women were permitted to survive by becoming wives of Turkish Muslim men.

Shifting the focus entirely to consensual affairs, Richard S. Fogarty offers nuanced perspectives on the subversion of colonial hierarchies made possible by sexual encounters between white French women and Indochinese and Tunisian and Madagascan soldiers and workers stationed in France during World War I. Fogarty uses the remarkable source of postal censors' records in tracing the love letters and romantic and suggestive photographs revealing these affairs. Officials were aghast at the remarkably warm and sensual welcome given to males of color not just by French prostitutes but also numerous nurses and daughters of bourgeois families, and worried that if news of these affairs reached the colonies all respect not just for white women living overseas but also for the entire colonial enterprise would be lost. Expanding recent insights of colonial historians into the instabilities of colonial rule produced by intimate contacts across the color line (insights usually based on colonizing white men's relationships with women of color), Fogarty explores the even more destabilizing impact of white women's consensual sex with colonized men.

Drawing on judicial decisions and debates in the Italian press as well as fascist government records, Marie-Anne Matard-Bonucci investigates the changing regulations shaping Italian soldiers' and Italian colonial settlers' relationships with Ethiopian women during the colonial war and occupation from the mid-1930s on. Offering new insight into the still inadequately understood issue of fascist racism, Matard-Bonucci is able to show that the turn to racism within Italian fascism was partly related to the government's and ideologues' concern about sex between whites and indigenous peoples. Previously, Ethiopian women had been eroticized and exoticized, and their charms and their appeal for Italian men described in the most glowing terms. With an abruptness that was remarkable, after the declaration of the fascist empire, long-term – and most specifically loving and passionate – relationships were deemed an 'obscenity' and disgrace to Italian racial dignity, and were criminalized in 1937 (and could lead to up to five years imprisonment) – and police and the law alike attempted to distinguish between (tolerable) emotionally uninvolving, 'episodic' relations and (now utterly unacceptable) cohabitation. Prostitution per se, however, was not considered a problem; indeed, the government's preferred 'solution' was to send white prostitutes to the colony to provide services for white men.

Emma Vickers investigates the history of the British armed forces' handling of homosexuality within their ranks. Starting from the misremembering and misrepresentations of that history rampant in the present (including flat-out denials that there were any gay or lesbian servicemen and -women in the armed forces during World War II), she uncovers the conjunction of factors that both permitted a large number of homosexuals to serve in the British military during World War II – estimates range from 5 to 10 percent of servicemen and -women – and simultaneously made that service invisible to those who would have been uncomfortable with it. Drawing especially on oral historical interviews with former military personnel, Vickers notes both the ingenuity employed by homosexuals who were 'passing' as straight as well as the pragmatic need of the nation for as many competent and skilled bodies as possible. She also provides fresh perspectives on the history of sexuality more broadly by exploring such matters as how men who otherwise identified as heterosexual engaged in homosex, how lesbianism was sometimes interpreted as infantilism, as well as how loyalty within a unit often incorporated also flamboyantly gay men who were fiercely defended by their comrades.

Lulu Anne Hansen draws on the underground press and social workers' case studies of Danish teen girls who sought romance with German occupation soldiers during World War II, reading these against the grain for insights into the apparent difficulty that child welfare authorities, parents, and police alike had in disciplining adolescent female sexuality under the inverted social rules and hierarchies occasioned by the occupation. Like Fogarty, Hansen is interested in taking seriously the pleasures of fraternization for its female participants – the fun rather than any economic gain – and the feeling of power they acquired as desired sex objects. But unlike Fogarty, Hansen focuses on a case in which the military authorities were operating under the premise that Danes and Germans were racially compatible and politically congenial, even while critical local observers felt the fraternizing girls were violating Danish national honor.

Thoughtfully interpreting such sources as concentration camp brothel visitor lists and medical reports on cervical smear tests, Robert Sommer turns our attention to the highly changeable nature and content of sexual desires in the midst of mass deprivation and death and analyzes the reasons for the establishment of prisoner brothels in ten of the major Nazi concentration camps from 1942 on (in Germany, Austria, and Poland). Sommer charts as well the recruitment strategies of the SS to find sexual slave workers, the operation and supervision of the brothels, the enormous status differentials among prisoners, and the motivations of male prisoners who visited the brothels as well as the reactions of those who did not. Both the SS-run granite quarry companies and the chemical giant I.G. Farben believed they could get higher productivity out of their slave laborers if they offered them not only more food and improved piece work rates, but also brothel visits. While a few scholars have recently worked to recover the experiences of women who were forced to provide the sexual slave labor, Sommer turns to the heretofore wholly unexplored matters of the male visitors' motivations (often existential more than sexual in the conventional sense), the dystopian streamlining of their sexual activity, as well as the surveillance mechanisms and voyeurism of the guards – and some prisoners' efforts to subvert these and build something resembling relationality with the women they visited.

Regina Mühlhäuser provides a pathbreaking assessment of the Nazi Wehrmacht's attempts to regulate the sexuality of German men in the total war conditions on the Eastern front in the first half of the 1940s. Charting officials' responses not only to rape and other kinds of sexual abuse but also to consensual sexual and romantic liaisons with women in the occupied territories of the East (including those resulting in reproduction), Mühlhäuser offers a fine-grained analysis of the conflicting demands of the Nazis' racial, sexual, and military aims, and shows just how open-ended, continually evolving, and contradictory were the

Wehrmacht's efforts to channel sexual desire in racially approved paths even as military leaders were also moved by their own beliefs about the imperatives of regular heterosexual outlets for improving soldiers' military performance. Finally, however, Mühlhäuser demonstrates that – however counterintuitively nonetheless crucially – it was not the rigidity of racial ideas but rather specifically the ambiguities and flexibility of Nazi conceptions of race that permitted the regime to maintain its power.

Sensitively reading the testimonies written by Jewish female survivors of Auschwitz shortly after the war for what they can tell us about the use of sex as a survival strategy as well as about sexual violence in the death factory, Na'ama Shik navigates between the extremes that have previously characterized the discussion of sexual violence in Auschwitz: on the one hand, deliberate silence and denial, on the other, a kind of titillated fascination. Examining both verbal and physical sexual humiliation and violation from guards and other prisoners as well as the phenomenon of 'prostitution' in exchange for food, Shik documents the wide range of sexual abuses that occurred, including rapes, while also asking why the public knowledge of these abuses – in Europe, the United States, and Israel – disappeared from the 1960s on, as shame and guilt over the use of sex for survival was intensified, and as a mostly male-centered narrative of the Holocaust became ascendant. In some ways echoing the findings of Sommer about the fears of demasculinization experienced by male prisoners deprived of sexual outlet, Shik notes the fears of defeminization experienced by female prisoners, even as some found – in a world of horrific non-choices – that although their bodies no longer felt female or human at all, in the eyes of male prisoners with food to exchange they could still function as sexual objects, as 'a wide-open bodily site'.

In her book on the use of torture during the French war in Algeria from 1954 to 1962, Raphaëlle Branche, drawing on military archival records and soldiers' and anticolonial insurgents' memoirs as well as oral history interviews she conducted with former perpetrators, has analyzed the sexual elements in the torture of insurgents and civilians suspected of working for the Front de Libération Nationale (including rapes with objects and the use of electroshocks to the genitals).[20] In her essay for this volume, she particularly documents the pervasiveness (and pervasive acceptance within the French military) of rapes of Algerian women, both of women held in detention camps and of civilian women assaulted in their homes and on the streets. Unlike torture, rape was not officially permitted, nor did it serve any military purpose beyond the terrorizing of the local population. Nonetheless, rape was widespread, and Branche looks at this ubiquity of rape both from the point of view of assumptions prevailing in France at that time about 'normal' male heterosexuality and in the context of Algerian Muslim and Kabyle conceptions of female sexual honor, interpreting the significance of Islam for the Algerian communities as itself a response to decades of French colonization and repression.

Teresa Iacobelli offers yet another vantage point on rape as an aspect of warfare in her close study of the city of Foca in 1992–1993. As there has been considerable dispute over whether the mass rapes of Muslim women in Bosnia-Herzegovina were systematically 'planned' and ordered or rather 'spontaneous' and random, Iacobelli carefully combs the available evidence on Foca – an early site of systematic and organized raping – in order to make a case for the 'planned' perspective and to document not only the knowledge but also participation of high-ranking Serbian officers in systematic sexual slavery within camps. Like Bjørnlund and Branche, Iacobelli considers the multiple possible functions of rape in the context of war. Iacobelli shows that in the Bosnian case, rape was used as a deliberate tactic of warfare in the sense that by spreading terror it expedited 'ethnic cleansing' and flight, but that it also worked as a deliberate strategy of genocide via the forced impregnation of Muslim women.

*

While it is indisputably challenging, even emotionally and intellectually disorienting, to think carefully about the two profoundly different ways that war and sexuality have intersected in the twentieth century – on the one hand, the topsy-turvy border-crossing sex made possible by the increased mobility, anonymity, and intensification of daily life brought by wars and, on the other hand, the recurrent reality of grotesque sexual violence (along with the libidinal elements within violence itself) – considering the two dynamics side by side is absolutely essential if we are to make sense both of the experiences of wars and of their aftermaths (in defeats, victories, occupations, and postwar attempts at societal rebuilding) and if we are to further the larger project of historicizing human nature, as its changeable and its durable elements become apparent in moments of intensity and extremity. It is no surprise that the essays in this volume – while ranging from Armenia in 1915 to Bosnia in 1993 – cluster heavily in the century's brutal center, World War II and the Holocaust. As historian Omer Bartov has recently pointed out, it was only from the vantage point of the early twenty-first century that we even came to understand 'the Holocaust as the leitmotif of the twentieth century' and – as the essays by Sommer, Mühlhäuser, and Shik in particular show – there is far more about this event that we have yet to understand.[21] But there is no question that the Holocaust's role as a leitmotif in thinking about the twentieth century is reinforced not least because this event above all raised the most acute questions about the relationships between war, genocide, and sexual and reproductive control and invasion that are now, in the early twenty-first century, being again pressed to the fore in numerous sites around the globe.

This volume, then, not only represents a first attempt to analyze the multiple and complex intersections of war and sexuality in Europe's twentieth century. And it is not least because each essay is grounded in the chronological and geographical specificities of its subjects that the collection can recurrently provide innovative vantage points on major themes in twentieth-century Europe, including nationalism, imperialism, decolonization, migration, racism, and violence in warfare as well as changing gender dynamics and conceptions of sexuality. The interpretive challenges posed by the topics are not merely a matter of historical interest, but raise issues of great urgency at the current twenty-first-century juncture. The authors' findings are most timely, as the analyzes advanced in the collected articles echo with and provide insights into numerous matters worrying us in our own day. These matters range widely and include the kinds of sexual violence evident in Darfur and Sierra Leone as well as in Abu Ghraib, the confused and angst-ridden response of secularized European liberals to the sexual restrictions on women within neofundamentalist Islam both inside and outside Europe's borders, the peculiar ways – in the case of the United States – renewed sexual conservatism at home has coincided with military aggressiveness abroad, the fantasies and fears accompanying the proliferation of transnational romances and marriages (in which love and the desire for European citizenship are often difficult to disentangle), the incorporation of 'out' homosexuals into most European armies, the new influx of eastern European and Russian women into western Europe as sex workers, and, more generally, the at present utterly devastated dreams for advancing human rights, socioeconomic justice, and peace in the wake of the end of the Cold War. It is our hope that this volume about the past will help to inform conversations about our evolving present as well.

Notes

1. See T. Kühne and B. Ziemann, 'Militärgeschichte in der Erweiterung: Konjunkturen, Interpretationen, Konzepte', in T. Kühne and B. Ziemann, eds, *Was ist Militärgeschichte?* (Paderborn, 2000); O. Bartov, *Mirrors of Destruction: War, Genocide, and Modern Identity* (New York, 2000); M. Geyer, 'Insurrectionary Warfare: The German Debate about a Levée en Masse in October 1918', *Journal of Modern History*, 73 (September 2001); J. Bourke and A. Burke, 'Killing and Responsibility – A Dialogue', *Borderlands*, 2, no. 2 (2003); C. Merridale, *Ivan's War: Life and Death in the Red Army, 1939–1945* (New York, 2006); A. Lüdtke and B. Weisbrod, eds, *No Man's Land of Violence: Extreme Wars in the Twentieth Century* (Göttingen, 2006); as well as the Oxford Reader, L. Freedman, ed., *War* (Oxford, 1994); and the series edited for Berghahn Books by Omer Bartov, *Studies on War and Genocide*, launched in 1999.
2. See especially the keynote essay by Joan Wallach Scott, 'Rewriting History', in M. R. Higonnet et al., eds, *Behind the Lines: Gender and the Two World Wars* (New Haven, 1987).
3. See C. Enloe, *Bananas, Beaches and Bases: Making Feminist Sense of International Politics* (Berkeley, 1990); J. Bourke, *Dismembering the Male: Men's Bodies, Britain and the Great War* (Chicago, 1996); J. Bourke, *An Intimate History of Killing: Face-to-Face Killing in Twentieth-Century Warfare* (London, 1999); P. Lerner, *Hysterical Men: War, Psychiatry and the Politics of Trauma, 1890–1930* (Ithaca, 2003); T. Kühne, *Kameradschaft: Die Soldaten des nationalsozialistischen Krieges und das 20. Jahrhundert* (Göttingen, 2006); K. Hagemann, 'Military, War and the Mainstreams: Gendering Modern German Military History', in K. Hagemann and J. Quataert, eds, *Gendering Modern German History: Themes, Debates, Revisions* (New York, 2007).
4. See M. Cooke and A. Woollacott, *Gendering War Talk* (Princeton, 1993).
5. See P. Gourevitch, *We Wish to Inform You That Tomorrow We Will be Killed with Our Families: Stories from Rwanda* (New York, 1998); M. Levene and P. Roberts, eds, *The Massacre in History* (New York, 1999); J. Gross, *Neighbors: The Destruction of the Jewish Community in Jedwabne, Poland* (Princeton, 2001); M. Mamdani, *When Victims Become Killers: Colonialism, Nativism, and the Genocide in Rwanda* (Princeton, 2002); S. Powers, *'A Problem from Hell': America and the Age of Genocide* (New York, 2002); E. Weitz, *A Century of Genocide: Utopias of Race and Nation* (Princeton, 2003); G. Grandin, *The Last Colonial Massacre: Latin America in the Cold War* (Chicago, 2004).
6. See S. Aschheim, 'On Saul Friedlander', *History and Memory*, 9, nos 1–2 (Fall 1997); S. Friedlander, *Nazi Germany and the Jews. Vol. 1: The Years of Persecution, 1933–1939* (New York, 1998); M. Geyer, 'There is a Land where Everything is Pure, its Name is Land of Death', in G. Eghigian and M. P. Berg, eds, *Sacrifice and National Belonging in Twentieth-Century Germany* (Arlington, TX, 2002); J. Matthäus, 'Anti-Semitism as an Offer: The Function of Ideological Indoctrination in the SS and Police Corps During the Holocaust', in D. Herzog, ed., *Lessons and Legacies VII: The Holocaust in International Perspective* (Evanston, IL, 2006); J. Gross, *Fear: Anti-Semitism in Poland after Auschwitz* (New York, 2007); G. Aly, *Hitler's Beneficiaries: Plunder, Racial War, and the Nazi Welfare State* (New York, 2007).

7. See O. Bartov, A. Grossmann, and M. Nolan, eds, *Crimes of War: Guilt and Denial in the Twentieth Century* (New York, 2003); H. Heer and K. Naumann, eds, *War of Extermination: The German Military in World War II* (New York, 2004).

8. See P. Grosse, 'What Does German Colonialism Have to Do with National Socialism? A Conceptual Framework', in E. Ames, M. Klotz, L. Wildenthal, and S. Gilman, eds, *Germany's Colonial Pasts* (Lincoln, NE, 2005); I. Hull, *Absolute Destruction: Military Culture and the Practices of War in Imperial Germany* (Ithaca, 2005); R. Branche, *La torture et l'armée pendant la guerre d'Algérie, 1954–1962* (Paris, 2001); C. Elkins, *Imperial Reckoning: The Untold Story of Britain's Gulag in Kenya* (New York, 2004).

9. The most influential early text was A. Stiglmayer, *Mass Rape: The War against Women in Bosnia-Herzegovina* (Lincoln, NE, 1994).

10. On the Soviet army's rapes of German women at the end of World War II, see especially the pathbreaking issue of *October*, 72 (Spring 1995), guest coedited by Stuart Liebman: *Berlin 1945: War and Rape/'Liberators Take Liberties'*. See also A. Petö, 'Memory and the Narrative of Rape in Budapest and Vienna', in R. Bessel and D. Schumann, eds, *Life after Death: Approaches to a Cultural and Social History of Europe during the 1940s and 1950s* (Cambridge, UK, 2003); B. Beck, *Wehrmacht und sexuelle Gewalt: Sexualverbrechen vor Deutschen Militärgerichten 1939–1945* (Paderborn, 2004); J. Mark, 'Remembering Rape: Divided Social Memory and the Red Army in Hungary 1944–1945', *Past and Present*, 188 (August 2005). On cross-national consensual sexual relations during and after World War II, see, e.g., A. Warring, *Tyskerpiger under besættelse og retsopgør* (Copenhagen, 1994); I. Bauer, ' "Austria's Prestige Dragged into the Dirt"? The "GI-Brides" and Postwar Austrian Society (1945–1955)', in G. Bischof et al., eds, *Women in Austria* [*Contemporary Austrian Studies*, vol. 6] (New Brunswick, 1998); K. H. Adler, 'Reading National Identity: Gender and "Prostitution" during the Occupation', *Modern and Contemporary France*, 7, no. 1 (1999); as well as the recent transnational overview by Anette Warring, 'Intimate and Sexual Relations', in R. Gildea, O. Wieviorka, and A. Warring, eds, *Surviving Hitler and Mussolini: Daily Life in Occupied Europe* (Oxford, 2006).

11. See G. L. Hicks, *The Comfort Women: Japan's Brutal Regime of Enforced Prostitution in the Second World War* (New York, 1997).

12. See D. Herzog, ed., *Sexuality and German Fascism* (New York, 2004); D. Herzog, *Sex after Fascism: Memory and Morality in Twentieth-Century Germany* (Princeton, 2005); M. Sibalis, 'Homophobia, Vichy France, and the "Crime of Homosexuality": The Origins of the Ordinance of 6 August 1942', *GLQ*, 8, no. 3 (May 2002); C. Beadman, 'Abortion in 1940s Spain: The Social Context', *Journal of Gender Studies*, 11, no. 1 (2002); M. Ebner, 'The Persecution of Homosexual Men under Fascism', in P. Willson, ed., *Gender, Family, and Sexuality: The Private Sphere in Italy* (London, 2004); C. Schikorra, 'Forced Prostitution in Nazi Concentration Camps', and D. Bergen, 'Sexual Violence in the Holocaust: Unique and Typical?', both in Herzog, ed., *Lessons and Legacies VII*.

13. See J. Willoughby, 'The Sexual Behavior of American GIs during the Early Years of the Occupation of Germany', *Journal of Military History*, 62 (January 1998); M. Hoehn, *GIs and Fräuleins: The German-American Encounter in 1950s*

West Germany (Chapel Hill, 2002); A. Grossmann and M. Nolan, 'Germany Is No Model for Iraq', *Los Angeles Times*, 16 April 2003; Warring, 'Intimate and Sexual Relations'; I. Bauer and R. Huber, 'Sexual Encounters across Former Enemy Lines', in G. Bischof et al., eds, *Sexuality in Austria* [*Contemporary Austrian Studies*, vol. 15] (New Brunswick, 2007).

14. M. Mazower, *Dark Continent: Europe's Twentieth Century* (New York, 1998).

15. Quoted in Branche, this volume.

16. See Shik, this volume; see also O. Lengyel, 'Scientific Experiments', in C. Rittner and J. Roth, eds, *Different Voices: Women and the Holocaust* (New York, 1993); W. Sofsky, *The Order of Terror: The Concentration Camp* (Princeton, 1997); G. Greif, *We Wept Without Tears: Testimony of the Jewish Sonderkommando in Auschwitz* (New Haven, 2005). See in this context also the important analyses of perpetrator motivation in Joanna Bourke, *Rape: A History from 1860 to the Present Day* (London: Virago, 2007); R. Seifert, 'War and Rape: A Preliminary Analysis', in Stiglmayer, *Mass Rape*; and J. Franco, 'Rape: A Weapon of War', *Social Text*, 25, no. 2 (Summer 2007).

17. See the call for such a volume in G. Zipfel, ' "Blood, Sperm and Tears": Sexual Violence in War', *Frankfurter Allgemeine Zeitung* (20 February 2001), available at www.eurozine.com.

18. Memoirs of G. C., quoted in Herzog, *Sex after Fascism*, 61.

19. See Vickers, this volume; see also Kühne, *Kameradschaft*; F. Rouquet, F. Virgili, and D. Voldman, eds, *Amours, guerres et sexualité* (Paris, 2007); and K. Williams, *Love My Rifle More Than You: Young and Female in the U.S. Army* (New York, 2005).

20. Branche, *La Torture et l'Armee*.

21. O. Bartov, 'The Holocaust as Leitmotif of the Twentieth Century', in Herzog, ed., *Lessons and Legacies VII*.

1

'A Fate Worse Than Dying': Sexual Violence during the Armenian Genocide

Matthias Bjørnlund

All tell the same story and bear the same scars: their men were all killed on the first days' march from their cities, after which the women and girls were constantly robbed of their money, bedding, clothing, and beaten, criminally abused and abducted along the way. Their guards forced them to pay even for drinking from the springs along the way and were their worst abusers but also allowed the baser element in every village through which they passed to abduct the girls and women and abuse them. We were not only told these things but the same things occurred right here in our own city before our very eyes and openly on the streets.[1]

Introduction

The above quote, taken from a letter written 6 August 1915 by F. H. Leslie, US missionary in the Ottoman city of Urfa, to US Consul Jesse B. Jackson in Aleppo, encapsulates much of what was the Armenian genocide – the killing of 1–1.5 million Ottoman Armenians during World War I – including the fundamental gendered aspect of this event. But when it comes to massive extermination campaigns like the Armenian genocide, the Holocaust, and the Rwandan genocide, gendered aspects have usually been downplayed in scholarly works. This is perhaps understandable considering the all-encompassing nature of what has rightly been called the total genocides of the past century.[2] The Armenian genocide was the almost completely successful attempt by the Young Turk dictatorship (also known as the *Committee of Union and Progress*, CUP) at 'cleansing' from Anatolian soil not only the approximately 2 million Ottoman Armenians, but also other mainly Christian nationalities like the Ottoman Greeks and Assyrians, and it was usually secured through a number of methods of direct and indirect killings: massacres, drownings, death marches under the guise of relocations, imposed starvation and diseases, etc.[3]

So, when the ultimate goal of the perpetrators is to secure the disappearance of an entire group – men, women, and children – subjects like sexual abuse, or whether or to what extent factors like gender or age played a role in selecting the victims, may seem of secondary importance. Nevertheless, history shows that males and females have often been affected by genocide in quite different ways, whether as victims or as perpetrators, and focusing on aspects such as gender is important if one seeks to fully understand the modes, motives, dynamics, and consequences of genocide and other mass crimes.[4] This study attempts to examine gendered aspects of the Armenian genocide, in particular the ways Ottoman Armenian females were targeted for physical destruction, sexual abuse, slavery, and/or forced assimilation. As the particular fate of the Armenian females in this period has been analyzed in only a few scholarly works,[5] and because this fate is today little known by non-Armenians and non-specialists in the field of genocide studies, the aim is also to help create a larger basis for further discussion of this event, as well as for comparison of gendered aspects of the Armenian genocide with similar aspects of similar historical events; that is, to tentatively bring this material into a wider context of sexual violence during war and genocide.

Gender and the Armenian genocide: An overview

Organized, gender-selective mass killing – sometimes termed *gendercide* – is a common feature of war, ethnic cleansing, and genocide, and has in such situations of conflict primarily targeted men through history, especially younger 'battle-age' men.[6] These mass killings have either been seen as a goal in itself – the destruction of real or imagined opposition and/or reproductive powers and group coherence, a recent case in point being the 1995 Srebrenica massacre of some 8000 Bosnian Muslim men and boys[7] – or as a more or less distinctive part of a more thorough genocidal design – what Adam Jones calls 'root-and-branch extermination'.[8] The latter applies to the Armenian genocide, which was executed as what one might call two sequential, relatively distinct, but interconnected gendercides within the framework of a larger exterminatory campaign. Thus, the first victims of the Armenian genocide were almost exclusively men: the approximately 200,000 Armenian soldiers fighting in the Ottoman army who, from the beginning of 1915, were disarmed and massacred or worked to death in large numbers, followed by politicians, religious leaders, and other members of the Armenian elite who were arrested, deported, often tortured, and killed from the spring of that same year. They, in turn, were followed by those of the remaining men and older boys who had not managed to hide or escape and were massacred as a prelude to, or in the early stages of, the deportations – the death marches. Some men and older boys managed to stay alive for at least a period of time on these marches through bribery or by disguising themselves as women.[9]

There could be important similarities between the ways male and female Armenian victims were treated, especially near the Caucasian frontline where massacres tended to be total and thus less gender-selective. And, as during the Bosnian genocide,[10] the Rwandan genocide,[11] the Japanese occupation of South-East Asia during WWII,[12] and at times during the 1914 German invasion of Belgium and France,[13] both males and females were from early on often subjected to sexually charged mutilations as part of what seems to be humiliating or dehumanizing rituals connected to the actual killings, perhaps aimed at showing the omnipotence of the perpetrators and the impotence of the victims. In late May 1915, an American missionary in Harput, Henry H. Riggs, encountered the bodies of two almost naked elderly Armenian men, noting that they

> ... were laid in such a position as to expose their persons to the ridicule of passers by, and on the abdomen of each was cast a large stone. They had evidently been murdered there at the noon hour and then the brutal guards had stopped to leave behind them the signs not only of violence but of mockery and insult.[14]

According to a German source,

> [f]or a whole month [during the summer of 1915, MB] corpses were observed floating down the River Euphrates nearly every day, often in batches of from two to six corpses bound together. The male corpses are in many cases hideously mutilated (sexual organs cut off, and so on), the female corpses are ripped open.[15]

Armenian refugees from Ottoman-occupied parts of Persia reported in early 1915 that

[t]he 750 Armenians that have reached Salmast from Urmia are completely stripped, the women, abducted. In Dilman there is also the same amount of murdered Armenians, whose martyrdom was carried out in the most horrific manner. They cut off the feet of living people with saws, they cut their wrists in the same way, they cut noses, cheeks, and lips off with scissors. They burned those parts of the body which are most sensitive. Both the elderly and the young were killed by frightful tortures, without regard to gender. We saw the traces of boundless brutality, glowing skewers were run through the genitals of both women and men, and they were put to death this way.[16]

But as a rule the Armenian population had been brutally and largely successfully emasculated before victims as well as missionaries and other Western observers came to consider the fate of the survivors to be even crueler.[17] This happened when it was learned what was meant by the government-approved deportations or relocations, operations orchestrated and executed by the Ministry of Interior's *Directorate for the Settlement of Tribes and Immigrants*, and supposedly dictated by what was officially deemed to be military necessity.[18] From the summer of 1915, after the Ottoman Armenians had been deprived by the CUP government of most potential means of organized armed or political resistance, as well as of the traditional breadwinners of families,[19] Armenian women and children were the next major group to be targeted.[20] Hundreds of thousands were given short notice, from weeks to mere hours, by the authorities to leave their homes and possessions and march toward the Syrian desert to be 'relocated'.

Yet though there were exceptions, usually depending on the individual attitudes of escorting gendarmes or local administrators, the general purpose of the deportations was to kill all or most of the deportees by outright massacre, individual acts of violence, attrition, starvation, dehydration, or disease before they reached the alleged relocation areas in the desert.[21] This is testified to by covert governmental instructions,[22] as well as by reports by Armenian survivors and by Ottoman and neutral or Ottoman-allied observers.[23] As for reports by neutral observers, Carl Ellis Wandel, Danish diplomatic minister at Constantinople (Istanbul), stated on 4 September 1915 that it was certain that the intention of the CUP policy of massacre and deportation was to 'exterminate the Armenian people'.[24] And Danish missionary nurse Maria Jacobsen, stationed in the Central Anatolian town of Harput, stated in her diary 26 June 1915 that if the destination of the deportees really was to be the Syrian desert, 'it is quite obvious that the purpose of their departure is the extermination of the Armenian people'.[25] At that point, few believed the promises made by the authorities to protect the deportees. In an eyewitness report by Ottoman Lieutenant Sayied Ahmed Moukhtar Baas (who like many other Muslim Ottoman citizens was against the genocide or even tried to save Armenian lives, although it was punishable by death),[26] it was stated that

> When the first batches of the deported Armenians arrived at Gumush-Khana all able-bodied men were sorted out with the excuse that they were going to be given work. The women and children were sent ahead under escort with the assurance by the Turkish authorities that their final destination was Mosul and that no harm will befall them. The men kept behind were taken out of town in batches of 15 or 20, lined up on the edge of ditches prepared beforehand, shot and thrown into the ditches. Hundreds of men were shot every day in a similar manner. The women and children were attacked on their way by the ('Shotas') the armed bands organised by the Turkish Government who attacked them and seized a certain number. After plundering and committing the most dastardly outrages on the women and children they massacred them in cold blood. These attacks were a daily occurence until every woman and child had been got rid of. The military escorts had strict orders not to interfere with the 'Shotas'. [...] In July 1915 I was ordered to accompany a convoy of deported Armenians. It was the last batch from Trebizond [Trabzon, MB] [...] I fell ill and wanted to go back, but I was told that as long as the Armenians in my charge were alive I would be sent from one place to the other.[27]

Another eyewitness, Mushegh Hakobian, born 1890 in Nicomedia, also reported that Armenians were marched back and forth or in circles: 'They were so pitiless that they made us return and walk the same road through hills and valleys anew so as to exhaust us completely. We had already no bread and no water ... '[28] Deportees were often told by escorting gendarmes that they would all be killed, and, as a rule, anyone who fell behind was shot or left to die.[29] This typical and seemingly pointless procedure can be explained not only with the need to carry out the destruction of the remaining Armenians near remote rivers and gorges suited for the killing and disposal of bodies,[30] at a safe distance from (Western) eyewitnesses, and from the general Muslim population due to fear of diseases,[31] but also with keeping deportees away from sources of food and water and minimizing the possibility of escape. It can also be explained with hatred toward Armenians as a group, as revenge for perceived transgressions, and, perhaps, with an attempt to overcome possible resistance from gendarmes or soldiers toward outright massacre of women and children. When asked by missionaries why they did not just kill women and children in their villages instead of exposing them to the miseries of the marches, a Turkish gendarme gave an answer that reveals a combination of rationalizations: 'It is right so, they must be miserable. And – what would we do with the corpses? They would stink!!!'[32] Khanum Palootzian, who had been deported from the Erzerum region in May 1915, stated that the gendarmes escorting her convoy had received outright orders 'not to kill women with sword or bullet, only in another way', i.e., through starvation, abuse, and exhaustion. Whether such an order had in fact been given or not, the escort on this march, as well as on most other marches, did not abstain from outright massacre of women and children.[33]

Often whole convoys were massacred and plundered by the specialized, uninhibited killer units, by soldiers, by Muslim villagers, or by Kurdish militias, either under supervision by, or in close cooperation with, the authorities.[34] But the death marches were no less designed to kill by various means of attrition (i.e., without anyone necessarily having to do any direct killing), and those same means would brutalize the escort and ensure that surviving Armenians would eventually become thoroughly dehumanized.[35] And although abuse and brutalization were integral parts of the training of the Ottoman soldier and gendarme,[36] some guards needed to be further brutalized to be able to kill women and children as they were ordered to. Missionaries Thora von Wedel-Jarlsberg and Eva Elvers, from neutral Norway and Ottoman-allied Germany, respectively, reported on conversations they had in June 1915 with young Turkish soldiers escorting, abusing, and massacring deportees from Erzinjan, and the missionaries had to conclude that they deeply pitied not only the deportees, but also the poor boys ('armen Jungen') who were being systematically made into devils ('systematisch zu Teufeln gemacht werden').[37] A Turkish policeman who had participated in the killing of a group of Armenian men who had tried to resist being caught, including the father and brother of a girl he had taken as his wife, gave the well-known reason or excuse for his actions that if he had not obeyed he would have been killed himself.[38]

It is not surprising that many executors (i.e., direct perpetrators) of genocide – mainly those 'ordinary men' who are not already brutalized through warfare, violent crime, or ideological or religious commitment to a radical cause – initially need some amount of brutalization and a dehumanization of the enemy in order to be able to kill, especially when the victims are non-combatant women and children.[39] A typical example of this apparently universal need for some perpetrators to (let themselves) be brutalized is given by a survivor of the Rwandan genocide who had been driven out of town with a number of other Tutsis after a massacre, now barely making a living on a hill nearby while still being chased by Hutu *genocidaires*: '…I think that for the Hutus, to see us so, living like the lowest of the lowest wildlife, it made the work easier. Especially for those who were not spurred to massacre out of hatred'.[40] That some of the executors of the Armenian genocide were indeed 'ordinary men' is hinted at by a British POW in Yozgat, Lieutenant E. H. Jones:

> The butchery had taken place in a valley some dozen miles outside the town […]. Amongst our sentries were men who had slain men, women and children till their arms were too tired to strike. They boasted of it among themselves. And yet, in many ways, they were pleasant enough fellows.[41]

As described below, Armenians had been systematically dehumanized by being designated as disloyal, greedy, etc., by politicians and by the state-controlled media for months, even years, prior to WWI.[42] Also, it is worth considering whether earlier massacres of Armenians in the 1890s[43] and 1909[44] had fostered indifference to Armenian suffering, creating a situation where massacre led to dehumanization that ultimately helped pave the way for genocide.[45] But in 1915, dehumanization was seen as a very tangible result of the death marches. Observers noted that the very appearance of the Armenian deportees had become less-than-human, which, in turn, is likely to have worked to convince escorting gendarmes that they were in fact justified in the first place to treat Armenians as 'cattle' or 'sheep to the slaughter', common contemporary descriptions of the state and fate of the deportees.[46] Leslie Davis, US Consul at Harput in the Mamouret-ul-Aziz region, described just how dehumanized they had become, the tens of thousands of deportees who passed through his consular region, a major artery of the deportation routes to the deserts of Syria:

> There were parties of exiles arriving from time to time throughout the summer of 1915, some of them numbering several thousand. The first one, who arrived in July, camped in a large open field on the

outskirts of the town, where they were exposed to the burning sun. All of them were in rags and many of them were almost naked. They were emaciated, sick, diseased, filthy, covered with dirt and vermin, resembling animals far more than human beings. They had been driven along for many weeks like herds of cattle, with little to eat, and most of them had nothing except the rags on their backs. When the scant rations which the Government furnished were brought for distribution the guards were obliged to beat them back with clubs, so ravenous were they. There were few men among them, most of the men having been killed by the Kurds before their arrival in Harput. Many of the women and children also had been killed and very many others had died on the way from sickness and exhaustion. Of those who had started, only a small portion were still alive and they were rapidly dying.[47]

This was confirmed by Maria Jacobsen, who writes that one could smell those same sick, dead, and dying deportees from a far distance, and that 'these poor people did not look like humans any more, not even animals could be found in this state, people would be merciful and kill them'.[48] A survivor described how female deportees at such temporary camps were examined before rape and abduction, and compared it with the way a butcher would examine animals before slaughtering them.[49] Harput and nearby Mezreh were among the several towns and cities along the deportation routes that became centers for the systematic distribution of Armenian girls and women among the local populations.[50] Other sources confirm that outside Mezreh, Armenian women and children camped under atrocious conditions. This camp turned into a well-organized slave market where the most desirable females, first and foremost women of wealthy families, were searched for by local Muslims and checked by doctors for diseases, etc. If a woman refused to follow her new 'owner', she was detained by the local authorities until she accepted a life in slavery.[51] According to the Turkish post-war Military Tribunals, the systematic distribution and abuse of Armenian females was not restricted to the lower levels of Ottoman society. For instance, Nuri, chief police officer of Trabzon, brought young girls to Constantinople as gifts from the Governor-General to members of the CUP Central Committee, and the Trabzon Red Crescent Hospital was made into a 'pleasuredome' where high-ranking officials indulged in orgies.[52] Indeed, selecting girls and women to distribute among leading Muslims seems to have been a common occurrence.[53]

Sexual violence on the death marches

Like in the Nazi death camps and concentration camps, everything was permitted or accepted in the Eastern provinces and on the death marches; the marches in particular became, to use Hannah Arendt's description of the Nazi camps, laboratories in total domination.[54] In describing the official license granted to Serbians to transgress legal and moral barriers during the 1990s war and genocide in Bosnia, Slavoj Zizek and Christopher Hanlon describe a 'carnivalistic' situation comparable to that of the moral collapse that was the Armenian genocide: '...it's not simply some kind of "dark terror", but a kind of false, explosive liberation'.[55] In a letter dated 15 September 1915 to British Minister of Munitions David Lloyd George, Philip P. Graves, at the Intelligence Department of the British War Office, stated regarding the Armenian genocide that '[m]aking all allowance for exaggeration there can be no doubt that there has been a carnival of murder and rape in many parts of the interior...',[56] while Raphael de Nogales, a Venezuelan mercenary serving with the Ottoman army on the Caucasian and Persian fronts, used phrases like 'orgy' and 'bacchanal of barbarity' to describe the extermination of Armenians he witnessed in the Van region.[57]

In return for such 'liberation', i.e., the license to kill, plunder, and rape, loyalty to the CUP dictatorship and its genocidal scheme was expected. Jackson, American Consul at Aleppo, stated 12 May 1915 regarding the deportations from Zeitun, Marash, and surrounding areas: 'According to reports from reliable sources the accompanying gendarmes are told that they may do as they wish with the women and girls'.[58] And most of them did. The Danish relief worker and League of Nations Commissionary Karen Jeppe, who was working from her base in Aleppo to secure the release of the tens of thousands of Armenian women and children from Muslim households who had been forcibly abducted during the genocide, stated in 1926 that out of the thousands of Armenian females she had come into contact with, all but one had been sexually abused.[59] It is clear that in addition to starvation, diseases, beatings, and general exhaustion, Armenian females were subjected to a deliberate pattern of constant, systematic sexual abuse and humiliations for weeks, sometimes months.

In some areas of the empire, especially in Eastern Anatolia, the collapse of moral values happened so fast and was so complete that the abuse took place openly. This was probably as a consequence of a combination of factors, like the closeness to the frontline; brutalization through warfare; vengeance for atrocities committed against Muslim civilians and for (perceived) Armenian resistance and revolutionary activity; and the officially sanctioned view of all Armenians as being inner representatives of the main outer enemy, the Russians. Examples of atrocities committed include a case where government officials in Trabzon were reported to have picked up 'some of the prettiest Armenian women of the best families. After committing the worst outrages on them they had them killed. Cases of rape of women and girls even publicly are very numerous. They were systematically murdered after the outrage'.[60] A report from Mush stated that female relatives of male torture victims were raped in front of their husbands or brothers as part of the punishment.[61] In that same region, 'good-looking' Armenian women and children were abducted to be Turkified or adopted into Kurdish households (thus securing the loyalty of tribesmen and villagers by allowing them to accept Armenians as 'payment'), but the rest were burned alive rather than deported.[62]

But most of the gender-specific abuse took place during the deportations, far removed from the frontline. The deportations constituted what was widely regarded as a particularly prolonged, grueling, and humiliating way of killing, a fate that was 'worse than dying', i.e., worse than immediate killing.[63] As the marches could drag on for months, so could the suffering. The deportees, walking barefoot over mountain passes and through deserts, were regularly clubbed, beaten, whipped, robbed, sold, abducted, or sexually abused by their guards or by 'the ruffians of every village through which they passed as the former allowed the latter to enter the camp of the exiles at night and even distributed the girls among the villagers for the night'.[64] An Armenian woman from Mush told that 8 to 10-year-old girls were raped in front of the other deportees and subsequently shot since they could not walk as a consequence of the abuse.[65] Sexual violence was quite simply the norm on the death marches. Still, whether the individual woman or girl was raped, killed, abducted, or (temporarily) left unmolested could sometimes, as it has been put, depend on 'the whim of the moment'.[66] Knowing this, mothers would intentionally keep the faces of their daughters dirty to make them unattractive and thereby hopefully keep them from being raped.[67] For that same reason, Armenian women, like German women in 1945 when facing the Soviet Army[68] or women in Japanese POW camps during WWII,[69] would apply strategies like cutting their own hair, wearing ragged clothing and veils, and putting medicine in their eyes to appear blind.[70]

Other gender-specific violations on the death marches include the numerous examples of women giving birth and having to leave their infants to die, whether out of exhaustion or desperation, or because they were ordered to do so by the escorting gendarmes, and the women themselves often died of hemorrhages as a consequence of not being allowed rest or treatment after giving birth.[71] A typical report by a German source on the 'convoys of exiles' states that

> [t]he girls were abducted almost without exception by the soldiers and their Arab hangers-on. [...] The children left behind by the Armenians on their journey are past counting. Women whose pains came upon them on the way had to continue their journey without respite. A woman bore twins in the neighbourhood of Aintab; next morning she had to go on again. She very soon had to leave the children under a bush, and a little while after she collapsed herself. Another, whose pains came upon her during the march, was compelled to go on at once and fell down dead almost immediately. There were several more incidents of the same kind between Marash and Aleppo.[72]

As has been the case with other instances of mass crime,[73] there are also several examples of pregnant women having their wombs opened to cut out unborn children.[74] Helen Fein, paraphrasing Roger W. Smith, notes on such atrocities that in the history of genocide '[c]utting open pregnant women was a recurrent form of terrorizing display...'.[75] Such 'displays' are perhaps not only meant to terrorize, but also to symbolize the complete destruction of the victim group, including the most defenseless and vulnerable. That 'complete destruction' was desired by the CUP was expressed by Interior Minister Talaat Pasha, one of the main architects behind the genocide: 'We have been reproached for making no distinction between innocent Armenians and the guilty, but that was utterly impossible, in view of the fact that those who were innocent today might be guilty tomorrow.'[76]

Also, since bribing guards or villagers was often the only way to survive – by acquiring food and water, and avoiding or, more likely, postponing physical abuse or murder[77] – Armenian women who had not been robbed completely before being deported were at times forced to hide gold coins or other valuables inside their body as a means of survival.[78] A US report based on survivor accounts relates how the existence of such 'protection money' was both necessary and, at the same time, another potential source of danger and humiliation:

> When they came near an Arab village, in that naked state, the Arabs pitied them and gave them old pieces of clothes, to be covered with.

Some of the exiles who had money left, bought some clothes. But there were still some left, who came in that naked state up to the city of Haleb [Aleppo, MB]. The poor women could not walk for shame, they were all bent forward. In this naked state they had found some ways to keep the little money they had. Some kept it in their hair, some in their mouths and some in their wombs. And when the robbers attacked them, some were clever enough to search for the money in those secret places and that in a very beastly manner, of course.[79]

Amidst the horrors and the humiliations, this shows that even though deportees were fair game, and escape or actual physical resistance was rarely possible, some still managed to be resourceful by hiding money in order to be able to buy means of survival for their children or themselves. Under the circumstances, it can be argued that resourcefulness could even include suicide, an option many Armenian women chose by drowning themselves individually or collectively in rivers. This seems usually to have been done out of despair, fear, and exhaustion, after sexual abuse, or after having witnessed the murder of relatives.[80] According to Sevart Mikaelian, a deportee from Erzerum, her aunt's four children were killed on the march, and when the deportees came to a stream her aunt could not stand it any longer and managed to drown herself despite efforts to save her.[81] The women often also faced impossible choices before or during the marches, like having to choose between keeping a child that would almost certainly die, or selling or giving it to a Muslim.[82] An example is given by Surpurhi and Diuhi Stefanian, two sisters from Ismid who were deported on 26 June 1915. Nineteen-year old Diuhi had a three-year old son, Magreditz, who at some point was unable to walk any further, and since the mother could no longer carry or feed him, she tried sell him to local Arabs. As Magreditz clung to his mother and pleaded not to be sold, Diuhi decided to try to keep him anyway. But he died after a few days on the road from Osmanieh, while the other four of the two sisters' five children died within the next ten days.[83]

There are also plenty of examples of altruistic behavior by the deportees, including examples of 'altruistic suicide', as when mothers or grandmothers gave whatever food or water they had to the children, or when mothers decided to stay and die with their children, rather than abandoning them.[84] But suicide – sometimes mass suicide – could also be what at least partly seem to be acts of defiance, that is, resistance by denying the perpetrators the right to decide over body and life of the victim.[85] In such cases the traditional religious notion of suicide as 'sinful death' seems to have been replaced by the notion of suicide as an heroic act[86] – 'defiant suicide'.[87] This ethos of 'death before dishonour' is even described (and honored) in some of the many songs about the genocidal experience sung by Armenian survivors in exile:

> Armenian girls going, going!
> One day death will come upon us,
> Before becoming the enemy's wife,
> Let us find our death in the Euphrates.[88]

Such songs are comparable to songs or stories celebrating the instances of armed Armenian resistance or of post-genocidal revenge acts[89] in that they seek to deny or modify the sense of powerlessness of the genocide survivor, instill a sense of personal or national pride, and give some meaning to a basically meaningless experience. And instead of risking that violated women would stand as a lone metaphor for not only the women themselves, but for the 'ravaged' or 'ravished' Armenian nation as such (as in the 1919 US motion picture *Ravished Armenia* based on genocide survivor Aurora Mardiganian's account), celebrating or commemorating acts of defiance or resistance have resulted in the creation of a 'counter-metaphor'.[90]

Sexual violence on the death marches could take forms in which the violent elements of the abuse were less direct, and where the victim managed to preserve some measure of bargaining power. An example is given by Vahram Touryan who lost most of his family on a death march from the village of Darman in Eastern Anatolia. As was the rule, Ibosh, the Turkish gendarme leading the caravan, had orchestrated murderous attacks *en route*, in this case by Kurds, but Ibosh was also the person who ended up rescuing Vahram and his older sister Siroun. When the caravan reached Palu in the Mamouret-ul-Aziz region, Ibosh was about to be replaced, and he had decided to abduct Siroun to his father's house in the mountains near Harput. Siroun had no choice but to follow, even though she was engaged to be married. But she strongly insisted that Vahram should go with them, and the gendarme, wanting to win her favor, accepted it. The rest of what was left of their family continued with the caravan and were never seen again.[91]

Sexual violence – means or end?

Western eyewitnesses like Bergfeld, German consul at Trabzon, did state that the rapes of Armenian females were part of a plan to exterminate the Armenian people.[92] This is not unlikely, but contrary to other genocidal campaigns of the twentieth century, the pattern of sexual violence and other atrocities before and during the death marches seems generally to have had relatively little 'practical', i.e., tactical or strategical, purpose. It is difficult to state with certainty what the goal(s) were, as little is known of the overall, local, or individual motives for the sexual violence during the Armenian genocide. But considering the evidence at hand, and assuming that the executors were generally no different from executors of other mass crimes, the main purposes on a local and individual level are likely to have been sadism;[93] gratification by total domination; symbolic purification (the exorcizing of 'evil' through rituals of degradation);[94] 'mutual demonstrations of masculinity' in the cases of gang rape;[95] and humiliation, intimidation, and dehumanization of the immediate victim, the victim's male relatives, and of the Armenians as a group (the rape of women as the symbolic rape of a whole community),[96] as most of the women and girls were killed after the abuse, committed suicide, died, or were at least expected to die during or after the deportations.

To put it another way, sexual violence during the Armenian genocide can at least partly be seen as a result of a thoroughly brutalized environment that left room for local initiatives when it came to the methods of killing and humiliation, initiatives that satisfied individual needs, not only for self-gratification but also for variation. Killing and abuse can become routine, and one way of breaking the monotony, showing off, or distancing oneself from the act is to invent 'games',[97] like during the Japanese massacre at Nanjing and surrounding areas in 1937, where killing and gang rape could be viewed as a sport.[98] Hagop Der-Garabedian, a survivor of labor battalions, torture, and imprisonment, literally described the torture of Armenians by Ottoman soldiers as 'creative play'.[99] A concrete example is given by the radically pro-Turkish and anti-Armenian Danish engineer O. A. Rygaard. In 1928–1929 he was travelling through Anatolia on horseback, encountering the after-effects of the Armenian genocide. In Sarki Karahissar he had frank conversations with several of the local Turkish men about the massacres of Armenians there in August 1915: 'While laughing coarsely they remind each other about how they then tried to find out how many victims a single rifle bullet could penetrate. "We managed up till 10", says one of them, "but then the Turkish soldier's rifle is a fine gun", he adds proudly and joyfully'.[100]

Sexual violence during the Armenian genocide was probably primarily a gender-specific way of degrading and killing, and to the extent that such abuse was directly and explicitly sanctioned from local or top-level CUP leadership, it would most likely be for reasons of securing popular male participation in the extermination process. The constantly repeated rituals of violence would have helped to create bonds between the CUP and the general population that they were trying to mobilize. This would be reminiscent of how the distribution of Armenian wealth and people was used to secure loyalty. In fact, plunder and rape during wars and genocide seem in many cases to be phenomena that are inextricably linked to each other.[101] If women (as was often the case in the Ottoman Empire) are basically viewed as chattel, as male property by soldiers, gangs, or the general population who have been given more or less explicit permission to live off the land during war and genocide, sexual violence can be seen as a right, as a natural extension of the right to plunder – rape as 'the most extreme violation of the domestic interior', as it has been put.[102]

But since most of the battle-age male Ottoman Armenian population at the time had been killed, and the survivors offered little organized resistance, it seems less likely that the CUP leadership would be using sexual violence against Armenian females with a main motive of 'sending a message' to a designated enemy, although this rationale as well as the other rationales mentioned below could have been motivating factors on a regional and local level.[103] Sexual violence seems rather to have been a completely accepted, often encouraged, 'by-product' of the overall genocidal program. Regardless of whether the Ottoman government or the CUP directly authorized the sexual abuse as a separate policy or not, it was an integral part of the widespread and systematic attacks against a civilian population with the aim of destroying this population, thus making the sexual abuse genocidal as such. It is not unlikely, though, that rape, together with the other abuses and the deprivations of the marches, in some cases was a conscious means of weakening young women and children, thus preparing them for absorption into Muslim households (see discussion of the forced assimilation below).[104] But this is still somewhat different from the frequent use of organized rape as a political strategy and a military weapon in other, less total, genocidal campaigns, where the ultimate goal is not (or has not yet developed into) annihilation, but rather the submission, partial destruction, and/or forced emigration of a group.

The aim of organized rape in such instances is to destroy family ties and group solidarity; to undermine military morale by inflicting trauma, humiliation, and fear; to block procreation of the group; and to impregnate women in order to affect the ethnic composition of populations.

Such crimes are therefore rightly included in the UN Genocide Convention as part of what can constitute the crime of genocide.[105] As Ruth Seifert expresses it, 'rape is not an aggressive manifestation of sexuality, but rather a sexual manifestation of aggression', and when occurring in a systematic, organized fashion during genocidal campaigns, rape becomes an integrated part of the arsenal of destruction.[106] Examples include the Serbian rape camps during the Bosnian genocide,[107] the 1971 massive killings and abuses committed by Pakistani forces against the Bengali population of Bangladesh,[108] and the 1914 attempted 'cleansing' of Ottoman Greeks from the Aegean littoral during the pre-war phase of the CUP campaign of Turkification or 'ethnic reconfiguration'[109] of the Ottoman Empire. According to Alfred Van der Zee, Danish Consul at Smyrna (Izmir), in March 1914, the *valis* (general governors) of Smyrna and the nearby regions had made tours of inspection to the coastal towns and villages, 'advising' the local officials to force the Greek population out, first by economic boycotts, then, when this did not have the desired effect, by violent persecution: 'Armed "Bashibozuks" [state-financed gangs, MB] attacked the Greek population, raped the Greek women, killed the children, etc. Finally, the gangs also violated non-Ottoman citizens'.[110]

I must underline that the attempt to compare the ways systematic sexual violence has been rationalized, instrumentalized, and carried out by various perpetrators in various genocidal campaigns is part of an attempt to clarify the differences and similarities of conceptually related, but historically and geographically distinct events. It is not an attempt to minimize or relativize the suffering of one group or individual compared to that of another group or individual. Such an attempt would be morally dubious, and the measuring of suffering would be practically impossible as well as irrelevant for scholarly purposes. What tie these instances of organized sexual abuse together is that innocent individuals were systematically violated within the context of larger campaigns of destruction. For instance, in both the Armenian and Bosnian cases, the abuse happened after or during a period of what has in a Bosnian context been called a social production of fear and vengefulness directed against a victim group,[111] and during wars of conquest that were aimed not only at acquiring territory, but also at creating an ethnically pure *Lebensraum* for the preferred group.[112] Also, mass violence during these campaigns was systematically directed against members of groups, a large proportion of whom shared what one might call traditional, conservative values and lifestyles. In such groups, sexual violence against women carries a comparatively large stigma, as virginity before, and chastity after, marriage is not only highly valued, but is a matter of personal, family, and national honor.[113] Thus, all victims from all groups had to suffer the trauma of not only the personal violations and of the attempted destruction of their group, but often also of the added trauma of being ostracized by surviving family members or other members of the group.[114]

'Relocation': The end of the death marches

The remnants of the death marches that actually managed to reach the area of the Syrian desert found none of the settlements promised by the government, only enormous, chaotic concentration camps on open fields,[115] and those who were not forcibly assimilated or managed to escape suffered further persecution, killings, and exposure to diseases and starvation that killed approximately 400,000, culminating with the outright massacre of some 200,000 survivors in 1916.[116] Late in July 1915, Jackson, American Consul at Aleppo, was informed of the arrival in the Diarbekir region of a group of more than 1000 Armenian women and children from Harput. There they were handed over to a band of Kurds who rode among them, selecting what were deemed to be the most attractive women, young girls, and children. Some terrified women tried to resist, thereby agitating the Kurds who killed a number of the women on the spot. Before carrying off the selected Armenians, they stripped most of the 300 remaining Armenians and forced them to continue the march for the next six days through the desert until they reached Ras-el-Ain in northern Syria, 'burned to the color of a green olive, the skin peeling off in great blotches, and many of them carrying gashes on the head and wounds on the body', as witnessed by Jackson himself.[117] Practically no subsistence was furnished by the authorities, which meant that unless surviving deportees could get illegal assistance from local Muslims or Westerners, or from Armenians in Aleppo who had not yet been deported,[118] they were left to die of fatigue, hunger, or diseases, or, as was frequently the case, to sell their children to prevent starvation for themselves and their offspring.[119] By then, slave trade of Armenian women, young girls, and children had become a lucrative business for Bedouin and Kurdish tribes in the Arab regions of the empire.[120]

Dr Martin Niepage, a German teacher at the German technical school in Aleppo, witnessed how thousands of deported Armenians, almost exclusively women and children, were lying dead or dying in the streets and backyards of the city, or were hidden in the houses of Christians or of Muslims opposed to the genocide. The deportees did not receive any aid from the authorities, and, like other observers, Niepage concluded that the aim was to destroy the Armenians completely. He and his colleagues desperately tried to save as many as possible, but the need was overwhelming, and Niepage felt that reading fairy tales to his mainly Armenian pupils or trying to teach them to conjugate verbs was a slap in the face of true morality and a mockery of human compassion when the children's compatriots were starving to death in the near vicinity of the school.[121] Some Armenian females were bought by Europeans from Turkish soldiers who had raped or gang raped them, and the women and girls were now all showing signs of severe trauma, like speechlessness or delirium, because of the abuse and because they had had to watch relatives getting their throats cut.[122] Gertrude Bell – British traveller, archeologist, and government official – after having interrogated captured Turkish soldiers about the massacres and abuse of Armenians at Ras-el-Ain, wrote on the fate of Armenian women that '[n]o man can ever think of a woman's body except as a matter of horror, instead of attraction, after Ras al-Ain'.[123] The abuse was indeed so frequent and systematic that H. Hoffmann-Fölkersamb, German Consul at Aleppo, by late 1915 concluded that rape had become official policy, a fact the authorities did not even bother to hide.[124]

Genocide by forced assimilation: Background and rationale

But another fate worse than death had, on the basis of a gender- and age-specific calculus, been decided for some Armenian children and women of child-bearing age, in common with other cases of genocide. In fact, Roger W. Smith contends that genocide has generally affected women differently from men in at least three ways:

> Women have seldom participated directly in genocide, though this has begun to change in the twentieth century (e.g., in Nazi Germany and Cambodia); women have been victimized in ways different from men to a large extent (rape and enslavement); and the consequences of genocide (incorporation into the perpetrator's society; or ostracism of victims of rape, as in Bangladesh) have often been different as well. All these differences can be explained in terms of: (1) the specific biological attributes of women (sexuality, reproductive capacity, and maternity) that historically made them both vulnerable and valuable; and (2) the assumptions of patriarchal society that women are weak, dependent, and the sexual property of males, who may appropriate their bodies, labor, and reproductive power.[125]

In the case of the Armenian genocide, a significant number of women and children – all in all an estimated 100,000–200,000, or between 5 and 10 percent of the whole Ottoman Armenian population – were, because of their biological attributes, deemed fit to be incorporated into what would now be Turkish, not Ottoman, society. As it has been put, Armenian men were the bearers of ethnicity, while Armenian women and children were susceptible to assimilation.[126] This was not only a consequence of individual abductions, forced marriages, etc., but of official CUP policy, and was, as Ara Sarafian states, part of the same genocidal calculus as the massacres, rapes, and death marches,[127] making the Armenian genocide a 'differentiated program'.[128] Contemporary Western observers, whether neutral, allied, or at war with the Ottoman Empire, also concluded that this policy of forced conversion was one of the methods used to secure the disappearance of the Ottoman Armenians.[129] According to W. Spieker, a German employee at the Baghdad railway, a Turkish commissioner had related to him in July of 1915 that the authorities no longer had any survey of the number of women and girls who had been abducted either, as expressed by the commissioner, 'by force' (i.e., without explicit official consent and cooperation) or in agreement with the government. The commissioner saw this as the fulfillment of a long-desired plan that had left nine out of ten Armenians dead.[130] But even the limited number of converted Armenians worried CUP leader Talaat, and was at times being further 'restricted'.[131] Thus, many converted Armenians, including some of those who had been forcibly converted after the large-scale 1894–1896 massacres of Armenians during the reign of sultan Abdul-Hamid II,[132] as well as thousands of orphaned Armenians originally designated for Turkification, were killed.[133]

Sarafian operates with four categories of how Armenians were transferred, forcibly converted, and absorbed into Muslim households in the course of 1915–1916:

1) 'Voluntary' conversions of individuals in the initial stages of the 1915 persecutions.
2) Selection of individual Armenians by individual Muslim hosts for absorption into Muslim households.
3) Distribution of Armenians to Muslim families by government agencies.
4) The use of Ottoman government–sponsored orphanages as a direct means of assimilating Armenian children.[134]

The fact that the disappearance of what was commonly known at the time as 'the Armenian race' was achieved partly by an official policy of absorption of Armenians into the Muslim population is a clear indication that the widespread anti-Armenian sentiments among CUP leaders and the general population (and, for that matter, among many contemporary Western observers) were generally not based on a notion of biological racism, as was the case with the anti-Semitism of the Nazis.[135] There are many similarities between anti-Armenian sentiments and anti-Semitism – Armenians were even believed by some to be 'Jews of the East', which was not meant as a compliment.[136] But although hatred of Armenians and other Christians based on the relatively modern concept of eliminatory biological racism did exist among some influential Young Turks,[137] the prevalent variant of racism in the Ottoman Empire was based mainly on ethno-religious hatred: Armenians were believed to be subversive, disloyal, greedy, cunning, infidel, etc., an 'ethno-religious anomaly'.[138] According to Carl Ellis Wandel, the Danish diplomat at Constantinople, anti-Armenianism was the main ingredient of the general nationalist xenophobia that the CUP had since 1913 made their leading political principle.[139]

This hatred or distrust of 'cunning' and 'treacherous' Armenians was a necessary, but not sufficient factor leading to genocide. One also has to take into consideration the related fact that in 1915, when the World War was raging, Ottoman Armenians had become completely identified with the main outer enemy, Russia. As US doctor William S. Dodd reported from Konia, 15 August 1915:

> The Turks here are saying, 'The Armenians must die and we are sending them down there for that purpose'. The Turks of Konia have been noted for their mildness and opposition to such measures, but their temper we can see is changing. The papers are publishing articles against the Armenians as traitors, as revolutionists, telling of atrocities committed by them in Van, 60,000 Turks killed by them etc, everything to inflame their minds and poison their thoughts. It is the same course that I saw at the time of the massacres twenty years ago [the 1894–96 massacres of Ottoman Armenians, MB].[140]

Furthermore, *Jihad* had been declared against 'infidels', further inflaming anti-Christian sentiments in the empire,[141] and it was also widely believed that the Turkish nation and Turkish individuals would reap economical, political, and territorial benefits by getting rid of Armenian competition, and the war proved to be the perfect opportunity for such a project.

These factors were sufficient to mobilize a large portion of the Muslim population for participation in the elimination of the Armenians. But since 'Armenianness' was generally not considered to be based on biology, elimination could be partly achieved by forced assimilation. Ethnicity and religion were the principal markers of difference, making 'Armenianness' to the Turks less indelibly fixed than 'Jewishness' would be to the profoundly racist Nazis.[142] Both the CUP and the Nazi genocidal regimes worked toward securing the complete disappearance of an unwanted group. But for the CUP, annihilation was directed at all visible traces of Ottoman Armenians and their 3000-year history in Anatolia and Cilicia, including churches, names of persons and cities, etc.; they wanted to 'destroy the Armenian name' and leave Turkey for the Turks, as a Turkish official told W. Spieker.[143] The Nazis, on the other hand, wanted even the invisible traces – the allegedly dangerous blood and genes of first and foremost Jews – to disappear. This also explains the fact that while it was legally forbidden in Nazi Germany for an 'Aryan' to have sexual intercourse with a Jew, there were seemingly no restrictions against a Turkish man having sexual intercourse with and even impregnating an Armenian woman.[144]

In other words, by changing religion and forgetting or ignoring language, cultural background, upbringing, and experiences, including the extermination of most of one's fellow Armenians, a limited number of Armenian females (but generally no Armenian males above the age of 10–15 years) could, at least theoretically, become Turkish in every sense of the word. As it has been put, 'Traditional society in the Middle East still looked upon women and children as chattel, persons lacking political personality and of transmutable ethnic identity. The cultural values of children and females could be erased or reprogrammed. Genetic continuity was a male proposition'.[145] In a society and a time where the more or less rudimentary concepts of 'race', nation, ethnicity, and culture were so closely linked to the concept of religion, it made sense to many that one could change 'race' by changing religion.[146]

For example, Yeghsa Khayadjanian from Harput, 15 years old in 1915, recalled that when she and a group of other young Armenians were given the choice between conversion or death, they were not asked whether they wanted to become Muslims, but whether they would 'become Turks or not?'[147] Likewise, Khanum Palootzian tells how Turkish gendarmes prior to a massacre told Armenian women that 'those who want to be Turks can go to the 3 houses on the road and be saved'.[148] What had to be formally changed as well as violently and systematically suppressed, then, was not only religion, but also expressions of Armenian language, culture, and even the personal names of the survivors, whether in private homes, government-run orphanages, or the public sphere, leaving only the biological 'raw material' to be systematically Turkified. This is one of the ways in which the forced assimilations correspond with the more direct sexual violence of the death marches: in the minds of the perpetrators, neither assimilation nor rape was a matter of encounters between persons, but rather of encounters between the person of the perpetrator and the body of the victim. But the first and most important step of the forced assimilation process was the conversion to Islam, which, for women, could only be ratified by immediate marriage to a Muslim and by the surrender of Armenian children to be brought up as 'true Muslims', with Muslim names in Muslim families.[149] Thereby these Muslim families, by participating in the forced conversions and by controlling the faith and actions of the converted afterward, became crucial agents for what amounted to a centrally organized program of forced assimilation within the grander genocidal design.[150] The Young Turk leaders themselves were often secularists, even atheists, but they believed that successful Turkification could only be built on Islamization.

For Armenian boys, the forced conversions could be followed by public circumcisions performed by local Muslim clerics.[151] Supposedly, this often-painful and humiliating ritual marked a 'point of no return' in the conversion from being a Christian Armenian to becoming a Muslim Turk. Sarkis Saroyan, four years of age in 1915, even remembered that the 'excised piece of flesh' was dried in the sun and kept as a proof of his becoming a Muslim and a Turk.[152] Naturally, conversion to avoid persecution or destruction was not a desirable option as it evoked fears of divine punishment and social exclusion among the usually very religious Armenians, where martyrdom, not surrender, was highly valued.[153] But as the examples show, they had little choice. That choice, however, was far from always offered; in fact, the authorities often turned down desperate requests to convert, preferring to have the Armenians killed.[154] Missionaries Wedel-Jarlsberg and Elvers witnessed and describes just how desperate the situation was for the surviving Armenian women in Erzinjan, telling about a woman shouting to them in the street that, 'We want to become Muslims. We want to become Germans, whatever you want, just save us, they are about to take us to Kemagh and slit our throats'.[155] Dr Niepage relates that in some instances, Armenian adults were allowed, as a means of saving their lives, to apply to local administrations for the right to convert, only to see the application being rejected by officials who answered that 'religion is not something to be toyed with'. They preferred to have the applicants killed, but according to Niepage they first wanted to humiliate the Armenians and their European benefactors.[156] On the other hand, when a sincere choice was offered of applying for an *erzuhal*, a petition for religious conversion,[157] many other Armenians chose death rather than conversion.[158]

According to some contemporary Western observers, one of the reasons that the CUP in some instances preferred conversion to murder was that some of the perceived 'racial' traits of Armenians were deemed desirable if somehow disassociated from any actual 'Armenianness', i.e., from any visible manifestation of anything 'Armenian'. Henry Morgenthau, US ambassador at Constantinople, stated regarding the forced assimilation of Armenian females that,

> [t]he most beautiful and healthy Armenian girls could be taken, converted forcibly to Mohammedanism, and made the wives or concubines of devout followers of the Prophet. Their children would then automatically become Moslims and so strengthen the Empire, as the Janissaries had strengthened it formerly. These Armenian girls represent a high type of womanhood and the Young Turks, in their crude, intuitive way, recognized that the mingling of their blood with the Turkish population would exert a eugenic influence upon the whole.[159]

That the often Western-educated Young Turks, according to Morgenthau, were thinking in rudimentary terms of eugenics could indicate that they were not foreign to the modern ideas of human beings as divided into a hierarchy of biologically defined races, and of 'certain social behaviors as reflective of a transgenerational, immutable biological or cultural constitution, either of a superior or a degenerate nature'.[160] The view that the Turkish authorities somehow appreciated the Armenian 'gene pool' is also expressed by an Armenian survivor and by US missionary Mary Graffam.[161]

Whatever the reason, the authorities did organize special orphanages for the direct assimilation of Armenian children.[162] Also, on a local level, it was sometimes realized that in times of war, with many Muslim men serving in the army, the local population needed cheap or free labor – shepherds, servants, farmhands – which could be provided by Armenian women and children distributed by the authorities.[163] Danish missionary Hansine Marcher stated in a 1916 testimony that

> [i]n the Turkish villages agricultural work was being largely carried on by the Armenian women and children, who had been handed over to the Moslem peasants by the authorities. Sister [Marcher, MB] saw quantities of them everywhere, practically in the condition of slaves. They were never allowed to rest in peace, but were constantly chivied about from one village to another.[164]

In Diarbekir, in the early spring of 1916, Marcher encountered some of the few surviving Armenians of the city, a number of children living as servants and slaves, with Turkish names and speaking only Turkish.[165] But generally, the CUP were reluctant to accept exemptions from physical destruction, even though the economy, the international prestige, and the war effort suffered severely as a consequence.[166]

There is nothing unique in the way religion and ethnicity or 'race' could become interchangeable in the Ottoman Empire. When compared to the Holocaust, where a modern, dominant ideology of extreme biological anti-Semitism ruled out conversion or assimilation as a means of survival, in the case of the Armenian as well as the Bosnian genocide, ideologies based on ethno-religious hatred both incited murder and, to a limited extent, also provided paths of survival, even where ethno-religious affiliation had started to be viewed as a modern 'racial' marker. As Michael Sells describes it, in the Balkans, Croat and Serb nationalists to this day still refer to Bosniaks – Slavic Muslims – as Turks, even though they share language, tribal descent, and cultural and physical traits with their Christian neighbors. The idea behind the notion of Slavs changing 'race' and becoming Turks is that conversion to Islam is actually Turkification, a 'racial' or ethno-religious transformation. In this view, Slavs are not and cannot be Muslims, and conversion, whether voluntary or not, equals betrayal of not only religion, but of 'race' and culture.[167] Also, in the imagination of some Serbs and Bosniaks, women, whether Christian or Muslim, are basically incubators who secure the reproduction of male genes, meaning that through rape, Muslim and Serbian women could give birth to 'pure' Serbian and Muslim children, respectively.[168]

Forced assimilation as a practical experience

In reality, for an Armenian to go through the required motions of becoming a Turk did not mean that he or she at any point of time truly accepted 'reprogramming'. That depended on various factors, age being seemingly the most important one: younger children tended to completely forget about native tongue, religion, and national or ethnic identity, while older Armenians tended to maintain at least parts of their 'Armenianness' and to remember the murder of their close relatives. Often, older children also tried to escape.[169] Nor was this 'reprogramming' necessarily truly accepted by ethnic Turks, Kurds, or Arabs. Many who were forcibly converted and placed in Muslim households were not being assimilated or treated as equals at all, but as servants or slaves. The story of the Armenian girl, Hansa, illustrates this. She lost all her relatives in 1915 when she was six, and was abducted by Bedouins where she was not treated as 'one of their own', but was abused and had to steal bread from the Beduin children she was looking after. She escaped several times, only to fall into the hands of other abusers.[170] Many converts did not even speak Turkish, and were still considered to be *gâvur*, i.e., infidel, as was the case with another young Armenian girl:

> Initially I was with a Turkish family where the man had two wives. One of them had children and the other did not. The wife without children used to take care of me, but the other was envious, saying that she was taking care of a *gâvur*, taking the food away from her own children. The man being the cause of the strife between them [the two women] took me to another house. Here the woman was paralyzed and very thin. She had a child and couldn't take care of her. So I was to do all the chores around her. I was so young myself and didn't understand her language [Turkish].[171]

It is also in the survivor testimonies that one can get an idea of the organized nature of the assimilations, with Ottoman bureaucracy, police, judiciary, and clergy being involved in the approval of forced marriage, conversion, and adoption, keeping accounts of these official acts, compiling lists of those who were to be deported, adopted, or converted, etc.[172] In Sivas, nine-year old Henry Vartinian, his widowed mother, and his four siblings had survived 1915 by being protected by an influential Turkish friend, Ali Effendi, who eventually had to tell the family that he could no longer hide them as he would be hanged if the authorities learned about his actions. He advised the Vartinians that they could only survive by converting, which the mother, a devout Christian, refused at first; but Ali told her that the alternative would be that her children would be killed in front of her and that she would be forced to marry a Turk. Left with such a choice, she decided to convert, but only 'externally', remaining Christian in secret. Conversion required that they all went to a judge in the city council, denounced their faith, and declared their adherence to Islam. They were then given new names (Henry Vartanian became Abdul Rahman oghlu Assad) and outward symbols (fez and turban), got registered with the authorities, and were issued new identity papers. The boys were circumcised by a Muslim cleric and went to a Turkish school, but were still harassed by ethnic Turkish boys who called them *dönme*, 'turncoats'.[173]

Concluding remarks

Early in 1916 US missionary Frederick W. MacCallum wrote a letter from Tiflis (now Tbilisi, Georgia) describing the conditions and experiences of Armenian refugees in the area:

> I heard a great many stories of individual suffering – men flayed alive, hacked to pieces with axes, starved to death, buried alive, burned to death, starved to death in holes of indescribable filth, of women outraged in the most cruel and disgusting manner, pregnant women ripped open, breasts cut off, delicate, refined young women compelled to travel day after day perfectly naked, innumerable cases of women being forced into Moslem harems; of children also tortured and killed in the most brutal manner. But all I have seen myself are some of the effects of this treatment, scars, sickness, insanity, fright, desperation, hatred, desire for revenge on the Turks, etc.[174]

Niall Ferguson states that '[i]t would certainly be simplistic to regard raping women as a form of violence indistinguishable in its intent from shooting men.'[175] As this study has aimed to show, this is true regarding the Armenian genocide. There is ample evidence that the destruction of the Ottoman Armenians was characterized by distinct gendered aspects, not least the particular timing and the methods of killing women and children, that females were subjected to massive, systematic sexual abuse, and that a number of women and children were allowed to survive as Muslim Turks. Also, while the context and exact execution of the violence against Armenian females makes this case in some ways a particular phenomenon in the history of sexual abuse during mass violence, the experiences – separation of families, rape, starvation, dehumanization, forced assimilation, etc., all within the context of an exterminatory scheme carried out during a war – are of profoundly universal importance. The violence against Armenian women during WWI, as well as the immediate and long-term effects of this violence (subjects that fall outside the scope of this paper), is a phenomenon that deserves far more attention than it has already received, not least because it can in meaningful, illuminating ways be compared to other instances of large-scale, systematic sexual violence during war and genocide, and used in conceptual discussions aimed at analyzing causes, modes, and, ideally, prevention of such events.

Notes

1. A. Sarafian, comp., *United States Official Documents on the Armenian Genocide 1915–1917* (Princeton and London, 2004), p. 199.
2. M. Levene, 'Creating a Modern "Zone of Genocide": The Impact of Nation- and State-Formation on Eastern Anatolia', *Holocaust and Genocide Studies*, XII, no. 3 (Winter 1998), 395; R. F. Melson, *Revolution and Genocide: On the Origins of the Armenian Genocide and the Holocaust* (Chicago, 1992); A. Destexhe, *Rwanda and Genocide in the 20th Century* (New York, 1995). C. P. Scherrer, 'Comparing Total Genocide in the 20th Century: A 22-Point Comparison', *Paper Prepared for the Workshop on Comparative Research on Genocide and Mass Murder*, Hiroshima (March 2004), adds the Cambodian genocide 1975–1979 to the Armenian genocide, the Holocaust, and the Rwandan genocide in his category of 'total genocides'.
3. Recent monographs on the Armenian genocide include: T. Akcam, *A Shameful Act: The Armenian Genocide and the Question of Turkish Responsibility* (New York, 2006); T. Akcam, *From Empire to Republic: Turkish Nationalism and the Armenian Genocide* (London and New York, 2004); D. Bloxham, *The Great Game of Genocide: Imperialism, Nationalism, and the Destruction of the Ottoman Armenians* (Oxford, 2005); V. N. Dadrian, *The History of the Armenian Genocide – Ethnic Conflict from the Balkans to Anatolia to the Caucasus* (Oxford, 1997). On the Assyrian and Armenian genocides: D. Gaunt, *Massacres, Resistance, Protectors: Muslim-Christian Relations in Eastern Anatolia During World War I* (New Jersey, 2006).
4. R. W. Smith, 'Women and Genocide: Notes on an Unwritten History', *Holocaust and Genocide Studies*, VIII, no. 3 (Winter 1994), 315–334; D. E. Miller and L. T. Miller, *Survivors: An Oral History of the Armenian Genocide* (Los Angeles, 1993), p. 94; C. Card, 'Genocide and Social Death', in C. Card and A. T. Marsoobian, eds, *Genocide's Aftermath: Responsibility and Repair* (Malden, MA, 2007), pp. 10–11.
5. For a notable exception: K. Derderian, 'Common Fate, Different Experience: Gender-Specific Aspects of the Armenian Genocide, 1915–1917', *Holocaust and Genocide Studies*, XIX, no. 1 (Spring 2005), 1–25.

6. On the concept of 'gendercide', A. Jones, ed., *Gendercide and Genocide* (Nashville, 2004). For what I believe to be relevant critiques of this often arbitrarily applied and perhaps not very accurate or illuminating concept, see S. Stein, 'Geno and Other Cides: A Cautionary Note on Knowledge Accumulation', ibid., pp. 196–229; R. C. Carpenter, 'Beyond "Gendercide": Operationalizing Gender in Comparative Genocide Studies', ibid., pp. 230–256.

7. See, e.g., J. Hagan, *Justice in the Balkans: Prosecuting War Crimes in the Hague Tribunal* (Chicago and London, 2003), pp. 85–88.

8. A. Jones, 'Gendercide and Genocide', *Journal of Genocide Research*, II, no. 2 (June 2000), 185, 193. Online version: www.gendercide.org/gendercide_and_genocide_2.html.

9. See, e.g., the testimonies of Sevart Mikaelian and Khanum Palutian (Palootzian), *Rigsarkivet* [Danish National Archives], *Kvindelige Missions Arbejdere* [Women Missionary Workers, hereafter: KMA], 10.360, no. 15, 'Armenier-Missionen, Diverse Skildringer vedr. Arminierne [*sic*] 1906–1927'; V. M. Garougian, *Destiny of the Dzidzernag* (Princeton and London, 2005), pp. 205, 292–293, n. 22. For a man to disguise himself as a woman was made easier by the fact that it was common for Armenian peasant women to have veiled faces.

10. R. Hukanovic, *The Tenth Circle of Hell: A Memoir of Life in the Death Camps of Bosnia* (London, 1998), pp. 35, 75–76; A. Cavelius, *Leila, En Bosnisk Flicka*, trans. M. Hoelstad (Stockholm, 2002), pp. 86–87.

11. See, e.g., R. Dallaire, *Shake Hands with the Devil: The Failure of Humanity in Rwanda* (London, 2004), p. 430; Ø. Kyrø, *Godmorgen, Rwanda – er I begyndt at arbejde* (Copenhagen, 2004), pp. 116–117.

12. G. Daws, *Prisoners of the Japanese: POWs of the Second World War in the Pacific* (London, 2007 [1994]), p. 363.

13. J. Horne and A. Kramer, *German Atrocities, 1914: A History of Denial* (New Haven and London, 2001), e.g., pp. 34, 185–187, 232–234.

14. H. H. Riggs, *Days of Tragedy in Armenia: Personal Experiences in Harpoot, 1915–1917* (Ann Arbor, 1997), pp. 57–58.

15. Quoted in J. Bryce and A. Toynbee, *The Treatment of Armenians in the Ottoman Empire, 1915–1916*, Uncensored Edition, ed. by A. Sarafian (Princeton, NJ, 2000 [1916]), p. 67. See also Miller and Miller, 1993, p. 85; Sarafian, comp., 2004, p. 158; C. D. Ussher, *An American Physician in Turkey: A Narrative of Adventures in Peace and War* (Boston and New York, 1917), pp. 238, 283.

16. Quoted from a contemporary Russian-Armenian newspaper article, in E. G. Danielyan, *The Armenian Genocide of 1894–1922 and the Accountability of the Turkish State* (Yerevan, 2005), p. 32. On the massacre and mutilations of Christians in the Urmia region, see also Gaunt, 2006, pp. 81–120. On mutilations of Armenian women and men in and around Bitlis and Diarbekir witnessed by Myrtle O. Shane and Floyd O. Smith, J. L. Barton, comp., *Turkish Atrocities: Statements of American Missionaries on the Destruction of Christian Communities in Ottoman Turkey, 1915–1917* (Ann Arbor, MI, 1998), pp. 9, 12, 92–93. For an example of male genital mutilation during the Armenian genocide, see also H. L. Larsen, *Fra Blodets og Taarernes Land i Europa. En Orientrejse 1922* (1922), p. 40. On the emasculation and

dismemberment of male corpses, see also A. Ter Minassian, 'Van 1915', in R. G. Hovannisian, ed., *Armenian Van/Vaspurakan* (Costa Mesa, CA, 2000), p. 218. For comparable examples of rape, mutilations (e.g., the cutting off of ears and noses), and the use of young sex slaves in Wehrmacht officers' brothels on the Eastern front during WWII, K. C. Berkhoff, *Harvest of Despair: Life and Death in Ukraine Under Nazi Rule* (Cambridge, MA and London, 2004), pp. 114–115, 217, 222, 302. On mutilations of Muslims during the 1912 Balkan War, see, e.g., S. Cagaptay, *Islam, Secularism, and Nationalism in Modern Turkey* (London and New York, 2006), p. 7.

17. See, e.g., W. Gust, ed., *Der Völkermord an den Armeniern 1915/16: Dokumente aus dem Politischen Archiv des deutschen Auswärtigen Amts* (Springe, 2005), p. 181; H. Morgenthau, *Ambassador Morgenthau's Story* (Detroit, MI, 2003 [1918]), p. 209. Some Armenian soldiers were (temporarily) left alive to fight for the Ottoman Empire while their families were being massacred or deported: e.g., Larsen, 1922, pp. 32–33, 55; E. J. Zürcher, 'Ottoman Labour Battalions in World War I', in H.-L. Kieser and D. J. Schaller, eds, *Der Völkermord an den Armeniern und die Shoah/The Armenian Genocide and the Shoah* (Zürich, 2002), p. 192; Sarafian, comp., 2004, pp. 27–28, 249, 255.

18. L. Kuper, *Genocide: Its Political Use in the Twentieth Century* (London, 1981), p. 111; M. Niepage, *Rædslerne i Aleppo. Sete af et Tysk Øjenvidne* (London, 1917), pp. 3–4; Sarafian, comp., 2004, p. 51. According to Bastendorff, a German engineer working at the Baghdad railway, Sükrü Bey, the director of the Directorate, was an actual racist in the modern, biological sense who believed that the end result of the anti-Armenian policies 'had to be the extermination of the Armenian race. It is the eternal battle between Muslims and Armenians, which is now being fought to the end. The weakest must disappear'. In Gust, ed., 2005, p. 421. For a similar view expressed by a German diplomat, see Morgenthau, 2003, p. 257. For a contemporary official Turkish view of the deportations and of the 'Armenian Question' in general, see, e.g., A. Djemal Pascha, *Erinnerungen eines Türkischen Staatsmannes* (München, 1922), pp. 313ff.

19. On the generally strongly patriarchal social organization of the Ottoman Armenians, especially in rural areas, S. H. Villa and M. K. Matossian, *Armenian Village Life Before 1914* (Detroit, 1982), e.g., pp. 24, 26–27, 71–72.

20. Armenian women did, however, participate alongside men in resistance activities, like in the attempted defense of the Armenian quarter in Urfa, October 1915: Miller and Miller, 1993, p. 75.

21. See, e.g., Miller and Miller, 1993, p. 78; A. Ohandjanian, *1915: Irrefutable Evidence. The Austrian Documents on the Armenian Genocide* (Yerevan, 2004), e.g., pp. 95, 103. It is estimated that an average of no more than 20–25 percent of deportees reached the Arabian provinces alive: R. P. Adalian, 'The Armenian Genocide', in S. Totten, W. S. Parsons, and I. W. Charny, eds, *Century of Genocide: Eyewitness Accounts and Critical Views* (New York and London, 1997), p. 43; Å. M. Benedictsen, *Armenien – Et folks Liv og Kamp gennem to Aartusinder* (Copenhagen, 1925), p. 254. German eyewitness Niepage estimated that 90 percent of deportees were killed before reaching Aleppo from Anatolia: Niepage, 1917, p. 5. Deportees from Western Anatolia had a higher rate of survival as they were generally not massacred *en route* and were often transported by train. This was

only a slightly less inhumane way of 'relocation' than the death marches: Armenians had to pay to be cramped in cattle carts, with little or no food and water, and, once in the desert, they usually met the same fate as other Armenians: H. Kaiser, *At the Crossroads of Der Zor: Death, Suvival, and Humanitarian Resistance in Aleppo, 1915–1917* (Princeton and London, 2002), pp. 9–13. See also Y. Auron, *The Banality of Indifference: Zionism and the Armenian Genocide* (New Brunswick and London, 2003), pp. 177–178.

22. See, e.g., V. N. Dadrian, 'The Turkish Military Tribunal's Prosecution of the Authors of the Armenian Genocide: Four Major Court-Martial Series', *Holocaust and Genocide Studies*, XI, no. 1 (Spring 1997), 35, 41; A. Sarafian and E. Avebury, eds, *British Parliamentary Debates on the Armenian Genocide, 1915–1918* (Princeton and London, 2003), Appendix III, p. 91.

23. See, e.g., Dadrian, HGS, 1997, 33; P. Balakian, *The Burning Tigris: The Armenian Genocide and America's Response* (New York, 2003), p. 272; H. Stürmer, *Two War Years in Constantinople: Sketches of German and Young Turkish Ethics and Politics*, annot., rev., and intr. by H. Kaiser (London, 2004 [1917]), pp. 41ff; R. Kloian, comp., *The Armenian Genocide: News Accounts From the American Press: 1915–1922* (Richmond, CA, 2005).

24. *Rigsarkivet* [Danish National Archives], *Udenrigsministeriets Arkiver* [Archives of the Foreign Ministry, hereafter: UM], 139. D. 1., 'Tyrkiet – Indre Forhold', Pk. 1, til 31 December 1916, nr. CXIII, 4/9 1915 (20/9). On Wandel, Denmark, and the Armenian genocide, see M. Bjørnlund, ' "When the Cannons Talk, the Diplomats Must Be Silent": A Danish Diplomat in Constantinople During the Armenian Genocide', *Genocide Studies and Prevention*, I, no. 2 (Fall 2006), 197–223.

25. M. Jacobsen, *Maria Jacobsen's Diary 1907–1919, Kharput – Turkey* (Antelias, 1979), pp. 210–211. A facsimile of the original, handwritten Danish-language diaries is included in this volume. For an English translation: M. Jacobsen, *Diaries of a Danish Missionary: Harpoot, 1907–1919* (Princeton and London, 2001).

26. There are numerous testimonies re. Muslims as protectors and re. the death penalty for such acts: e.g., A. Lange, *Et Blad af Armeniens Historie: K.M.A. 1910–1920* (Copenhagen, 1920), p. 51.

27. Sarafian and Avebury, eds, 2003, Appendix III, pp. 91–92. See also report by Lt. Maaroue, ibid., pp. 93–94. The *Shotas*, or *Chetes*, were parts of the Special Organization, a secret organization created by the CUP leadership in order to wage guerilla warfare behind enemy lines, as well as to act as the main killer units massacring Armenians in Eastern Anatolia. The *Chetes* were usually made up of released convicts and/or Muslim tribesmen and refugees, and were led by officers or by CUP officials: Bloxham, 2005, pp. 69–70, 78–79, 86–87; Akcam, 2004, pp. 158–166.

28. V. Svazlian, *The Armenian Genocide and Historical Memory* (Yerevan, 2004), p. 58. See also Riggs, 1997, p. 140. The same method of marching deportees back and forth or in circles as a method of mass killing was also used against Ottoman Greeks by Kemalists in the early 1920s: Telegram no. 201, British High Commissioner Sir H. Rumbold to the British Government, 10 May 1922, quoted in H. Tsirkinidis, *At last we Uprooted Them ... : The Genocide of the Greeks of Pontos, Thrace and Asia Minor through the French Archives* (Thessaloniki, 1999), pp. 241–242.

29. See, e.g., Sevart Mikaelian's testimony, in KMA, 10.360, Pk. 15, 'Armenier-Missionen, Diverse Skildringer vedr. Arminierne [*sic*] 1906–1927'; Barton, comp., 1998, p. 17.
30. H. Kaiser, ed. and intr., *Eberhard Count Wolffskeel Von Reichenberg, Zeitoun, Mousa Dagh, Ourfa: Letters on the Armenian Genocide* (Princeton and London, 2004 [2nd. edn]), p. ix.
31. See, e.g., V. N. Dadrian, 'The Role of Turkish Physicians in the World War I Genocide of Ottoman Armenians', *Holocaust and Genocide Studies*, I, no. 2 (1986), 175, 185, n. 15.
32. Gust, ed., 2005, p. 262. See also ibid., p. 289.
33. Khanum Palutian's [Palootzian] testimony, KMA, 10.360, Pk. 15, 'Armenier-Missionen, Diverse Skildringer vedr. Arminierne [*sic*] 1906–1927'. See also 1920 testimony given by Palaidzu Captanian under oath at the office of the British High Commission in Constantinople, quoted in G. S. Graber, *Caravans to Oblivion: The Armenian Genocide, 1915* (New York, 1996), pp. 102–104.
34. H. Kaiser, ' "A Scene from the Inferno." The Armenians of Erzerum and the Genocide, 1915–1916', in Kieser and Schaller, eds, 2002, p. 129; L. A. Davis, *The Slaughterhouse Province: An American Diplomat's Report on the Armenian Genocide, 1915–1917* (New York, 1989), pp. 79–87.
35. See, e.g., Miller and Miller, 1993, p. 83. W. Litten, German Consul at Tärbis, believed that an advantage of the marches was that it was hard to determine the actual killer: Gust, ed., 2005, p. 446.
36. See, e.g., Riggs, 1997, especially chapter, 'The Turkish Soldier's Woes', as well as pp. 127–128.
37. Gust, ed., 2005, p. 259. On the charges of mass rapes of 250 Armenian women and children around Erzinjan by Captain Mehmed Hassan and his men: Dadrian, 1986, 174.
38. T. Atkinson, '*The German, the Turk and the Devil Made a Triple Alliance': Harpoot Diaries, 1908–1917* (Princeton, NJ, 2000), p. 88. On a related note, Governor Faik at Merzifun (Marsovan) told Greek professor Xenidhis, when confronted with the reality of the deportation and literal butchery of Armenians in the area, that he and the commandant of the gendarmes were only following orders: Dadrian, 1986, 180.
39. See, e.g., Lt. Col. D. Grossman, *On Killing: The Psychological Cost of Learning to Kill in War and Society* (Boston, New York, and London, 1996), pp. 209–210.
40. J. Hatzfeld, *Into the Quick of Life. The Rwandan Genocide: The Survivors Speak* (London, 2005), p. 72. See also T. Longman, 'Placing Genocide in Context: Research Priorities for the Rwandan Genocide', *Journal of Genocide Research*, VI, no. 1 (March 2004), 35. On brutalization of Nazi perpetrators, T. Jørgensen, *Stiftelsen – Bødlerne fra Aktion Reinhardt* (2003), pp. 124–127.
41. E. H. Jones, *The Road to En-Dor* (London, 1973 [1920]), p. 83; quoted in R. Fisk, *The Great War for Civilization: The Conquest of the Middle East* (London, New York, Toronto, Sydney, 2006 [2005]), p. 403. On the Yozgad massacres, see also Vahram Dadrian, *To the Desert: Pages from My Diary* (Princeton and London, 2003), p. 23; Gust, ed., 2005, pp. 323, 455. For discussions of 'ordinary men' as perpetrators, C. R. Browning, *Ordinary Men: Reserve Police Battalion 101 and the Final Solution in Poland* (1998 [1992]),

passim; M. Mann, *The Dark Side of Democracy: Explaining Ethnic Cleansing* (Cambridge, 2005), pp. 26–30. For a conceptual discussion of the Armenian genocide, ibid., pp. 111–179.

42. UM, 139. D. 1., 'Politiske Begivenheder i Tyrkiet i 1914', indsendt af Gesandtskabet i Konstantinopel 26/1 1915, p. 2; UM, 139. D. 1., 'Tyrkiet – Indre forhold', Pk. 1, til 31 December 1916, nr. LXXI, 7/6 1915 (21/6); H.-L. Kieser, 'Dr Mehmed Reshid (1873–1919): A Political Doctor', in Kieser and Schaller, eds, 2002, p. 257.

43. See, e.g., A. J. Kirakossian, ed., *The Armenian Massacres 1894–1896: U.S. Media Testimony* (Detroit, 2004).

44. See, e.g., N. Saupp, *Das Deutsche Reich und die Armenische Frage 1878–1914* (Köln, 1990), pp. 167ff.

45. N. M. Naimark, *Fires of Hatred: Ethnic Cleansing in Twentieth-Century Europe* (Cambridge, Mass., 2002), p. 23. See also Balakian, 2003, p. 157: 'As the concept of Armenian massacre was hammered deeper and deeper into the social psychology of Turkish society, the Armenian Question was inculcated as an issue that could only be solved by unmitigated state-sponsored and state-sanctioned violence.'

46. See, e.g., Jacobsen, 1979, p. 229; Garougian, 2005, pp. 205, 243; Riggs, 1997, p. 125; C. A. Krethlow, 'Colmar Freiherr von der Goltz und der Genozid an den Armeniern 1915–1916', *Sozial. Geschichte*, XXI, no. 3 (2006), 64.

47. Quoted in A. Sarafian, 'The Absorption of Armenian Women and Children into Muslim Households as a Structural Component of the Armenian Genocide', in O. Bartov and P. Mack, eds, *In God's Name: Genocide and Religion in the Twentieth Century* (New York and Oxford, 2001), p. 214. See also Miller and Miller, 1993, p. 174; R. A. Parmalee, *A Pioneer in the Euphrates Valley* (Princeton and London, 2002), p. 24.

48. Jacobsen, 1979, p. 270. Another Danish missionary in Harput, Karen Marie Petersen, describes the deportees in a similar way: E. Bockelund, *En Tjenergerning blandt Martyrfolket. Kvindelige Missions Arbejdere 1900–1930* (1932), pp. 36–37. See also Atkinson, 2000, pp. 40, 53; Riggs, 1997, pp. 146–147; Barton, comp., 1998, p. 68.

49. Khanum Palutian's [Palootzian] testimony, KMA, 10.360, Pk. 15, 'Armenier-Missionen, Diverse Skildringer vedr. Arminierne [sic] 1906–1927'.

50. On the Malatia slave market, see Kaiser, in Kieser and Schaller, eds, 2002, pp. 160, 165. On a slave market in Erzinjan, see Gust, ed., 2005, p. 260.

51. Sarafian, in Bartov and Mack, eds, 2001, p. 215; Kaiser, in Kieser and Schaller, eds, 2002, p. 166; Riggs, 1997, pp. 148–149; Barton, comp., 1998, p. 42. It is possible that the doctors also checked if the girls were virgins as the price could then be four times higher than the price of a raped girl: Benedictsen, 1925, p. 254. According to Villa and Matossian, 1982, p. 73, Turks valued Armenian virgins rather than non-virgins, so one reason that prepubescent Armenian girls sometimes married was to protect them from violation: 'Generally speaking, the more physically or politically insecure the villagers felt, the younger the age for marriage'. On an incident in 1922 where a deported Greek girl in Harput married a Greek man to avoid abduction, Garougian, 2005, p. 200. On the connections between rape, abductions, looting, and forcible conversions of Armenians before and during WWI, J. J. Reid, 'Total War, the Annihilation Ethic, and the

Armenian Genocide, 1870–1918', in R. G. Hovannisian, ed., *The Armenian Genocide: History, Politics, Ethics* (Hampshire and New York, 1992), p. 39ff.

52. V. N. Dadrian, 'The Armenian Genocide: An Interpretation', in J. Winter, ed., *America and the Armenian Genocide of 1915* (Cambridge, 2003), pp. 83–84. Armenian survivors at the Yozgat Tribunal in 1919 testified that '[w]ith very few exceptions, young Armenian females were [...] the victims of rape, often serial rape': A. Höss, 'The Trial of Perpetrators by the Turkish Military Tribunals: The Case of Yozgat', in Hovannisian, ed., 1992, p. 217. At a similar post-war tribunal at Kayseri (Cesarea), leading local officials were charged with rape and serial rape: V. N. Dadrian, 'The Agency of "Triggering Mechanisms" as a Factor in the Organization of the Genocide Against the Armenians of Kayseri District', *Genocide Studies and Prevention*, I, no. 2 (Fall 2006), 120–121.

53. See, e.g., Kaiser, 2002, pp. 91–92, n. 102; Derderian, 2005, 7–8; E. Mugerditchian, *I Tyrkernes Kløer: En Beretning om en Armenisk Families Flugt* (London, 1918), p. 20; D. E. Miller and L. T. Miller, 'Women and Children of the Armenian Genocide', in Hovannisian, ed., 1992, p. 160. There are also reports that Armenian boys were distributed for sexual abuse: J. Künzler, *Im Lande des Blutes und der Tränen. Erlebnisse in Mesopotamien Während des Weltkrieges* (Berlin-Potsdam, 1921), pp. 77, 87. See also V. N. Dadrian, 'Children as Victims of Genocide: The Armenian Case', on http://myweb.tiscali.co.uk/cragsite/Children.htm.

54. H. Arendt, *Essays in Understanding – 1930–1954* (New York, 1994), p. 304.

55. S. Zizek and C. Hanlon, 'Psychoanalysis and the Post-Political. An interview with Slavoj Zizek', *New Literary History*, XXXII, 1 (2001), 19. Quoted in B. Diken and C. B. Laustsen, *Becoming Abject: Rape As a Weapon of War* (Aalborg, 2004), p. 19. On mass violence and sexual abuse as 'carnival', see also W. W. Hagen, 'The Moral Economy of Popular Violence: The Pogrom in Lwów, November 1918', in R. Blobaum, ed., *Antisemitism and Its Opponents in Modern Poland* (Ithaca and London, 2005), p. 125ff.

56. Quoted in A. Nassibian, *Britain and the Armenian Question 1915–1923* (London, Sydney, and New York, 1985), p. 72. For a poetical treatment of the 'carnivalistic' atmosphere that could characterize the killings of Armenians in the empire, Siamanto (A. Yarjanian), *Bloody News from My Friend*, trans. P. Balakian and N. Yaghlian (Detroit, 1996). This collection of poetry, originally published in 1911, was directly inspired by the massacre of some 20,000 Armenians in and around the Cilician town of Adana in 1909. An excerpt from the poem 'Grief', p. 38, reads: '...what a mob, what dances, what joy / and what feasts everywhere..../Our red shrouds are victory flags./ The bones of our pure brothers are flutes... / with them others are making strange music.' Siamanto was one of the Armenian intellectuals killed 24 April 1915.

57. R. de Nogales, *Four Years Beneath the Crescent*, trans. M. Lee (London, 2003 [1924]), pp. 59ff.

58. Sarafian, comp., 2004, p. 41. See also letter from Dr Shepard, Aintab, 20 June 1915, in Bryce and Toynbee, 2000 (1916), p. 483; Dadrian, in Winter, ed., 2003, p. 83; Riggs, 1997, pp. 120–121.

59. K. Jeppe, *Armeniervennen*, VI, nos 7–8 (July–August 1926), 28. Considering (a) the amount of evidence that points to the fact that sexual abuse was the

norm on death marches, and, (b) that Armenian females who were released by Jeppe's organization were released from Muslim households where they would most likely have been sexually abused, Jeppe's statement does not seem unlikely. On Jeppe's experiences as eyewitness and rescue worker during and after the genocide, see M. Bjørnlund, 'Karen Jeppe, Aage Meyer Benedictsen, and the Ottoman Armenians, National survival in imperial and colonial settings', Paper presented at *Nordic Perspectives on Colonialism*. Conference arranged by Netværk for Global Kulturhistorie (Network for Global Cultural History), University of Aarhus, in Höör, Sweden 11–12 January 2007.

60. Sarafian and Avebury, eds, 2003, Appendix III, Report by Lt. Baas, p. 92. F. H. Leslie reported 6 August 1915:

> There must be no less than five hundred abducted now in the homes of the Moslems in this city [Urfa, MB] and as many more have been sexually abused and turned out on the streets again. They have even abused these girls openly on the streets and before the eyes of the foreigners.

In Sarafian, comp., 2004, p 199. See also G. H. Knapp, *The Tragedy of Bitlis* (London, 2002 [1919]), pp. 42ff.; Ter Minassian, 'Van 1915', in Hovannisian, ed., 2000, p. 218.

61. Quoted in Bryce and Toynbee, 2000, p. 121. For a description of a comparable incident during the Armenian genocide, Fisk, 2006, pp. 391–392. For a similar occurence during the Bosnian genocide, A. Stiglmayer, 'The Rapes in Bosnia-Herzegovina', in A. Stiglmayer, ed., *Mass Rape: The War against Women in Bosnia-Herzegovina* (Lincoln and London, 1994), p. 82. For similar occurences during the German WWI-occupation of Belgium and parts of France, Horne and Kramer, 2001, pp. 196–204.

62. See, e.g., Svazlian, 2004, pp. 49–50; Balakian, 2003, pp. 273–274; de Nogales, 2003, pp. 116–117.

63. See, e.g., Bryce and Toynbee, 2000, p. 356; D. Jensen, *Et Hjemløst Folk: Spredte Træk fra min Rejse i Orienten* (1929), p. 37.

64. F. H. Leslie, Urfa, 28 June 1915, report on deportation from Zeitun: Sarafian, comp., 2004, p. 85. See also Svazlian, 2004, p. 57; Miller and Miller, 1993, pp. 88–89; Gust, ed., 2005, e.g., pp. 217, 287, 406–407, 420; Atkinson, 2000, p. 39; Fisk, 2006, p. 433; Garougian, 2005, pp. 23–24; Fâiz El-Ghusein, *Martyred Armenia* (London, 1917), pp. 12–17; Barton, comp., 1998, passim.

65. Bryce and Toynbee, 2000, p. 128. See also Miller and Miller, 1993, pp. 102–103.

66. Bryce and Toynbee, 2000, p. 640. On how '[t]he variants in the systematic rape presumably reflected the predilections of local commanders or their political bosses' during the Bosnian genocide: Gutman, 'Foreword', in Stiglmayer, ed., 1994, pp. x–xi.

67. Miller and Miller, 1993, p. 101; Atkinson, 2000, p. 51; Riggs, 1997, p. 126.

68. A. Nesaule, *A Woman in Amber* (New York, 1995), p. 26.

69. L. Warner and J. Sandilands, *Women beyond the Wire* (1997), p. 95; N. Lillelund, *En Brutal Bagage: Barndom i en japansk fangelejr* (Copenhagen, 2004), p. 60.
70. Testimonies of Sevart Mikaelin and Khanum Palutian [Palootzian], KMA, 10.360, Pk. 15, 'Armenier-Missionen, Diverse Skildringer vedr. Arminierne [*sic*] 1906–1927'. See also Derderian, 2005, 1718, n. 16; Atkinson, 2000, pp. 46–47; Garougian, 2005, pp. 293–294, n. 30; Riggs, 1997, p. 126; Barton, comp., 1998, pp. 30, 68–69; Naimark, 2002, p. 31.
71. See, e.g., despatch from Jackson, Aleppo, 8 June 1915, in Sarafian, comp., 2004, p. 60; statement by Merrill, Marash, ibid., pp. 68–69; statement by US Consul General at Beirut, Hollis, ibid., p. 118; letter from Dr Shepard, Aintab, 20 June 1915, in Bryce and Toynbee, 2000, p. 482; Report by Hunecke, July 1915, in Sarafian and Avebury, eds, 2003, p. 67; Miller and Miller, 1993, p. 102; Kaiser, 2002, p. 25; Gust, ed., 2005, p. 255; Atkinson, 2000, p. 47; El-Ghusein, 1917, p. 14; L. Einstein, *Inside Constantinople* (London, 1917), p. 126.
72. Quoted in Bryce and Toynbee, 2000, pp. 68, 160.
73. A. Jones, 'Gender and Genocide in Rwanda', in Jones, ed., 2004, pp. 118–119; C. A. MacKinnon, 'Turning Rape into Pornography: Postmodern Genocide', in Stiglmayer, ed., 1994, p. 80; R. Seifert, 'War and Rape: A Preliminary Analysis', ibid., p. 65; G. Grandin, 'History, Motive, Law, Intent: Combining Historical and Legal Methods in Understanding Guatemala's 1981–1983 Genocide', in R. Gellately and B. Kiernan, eds, *The Specter of Genocide: Mass Murder in Historical Perspective*, (Cambridge, 2003), p. 350; J. Nevins, *A Not-So-Distant Horror: Mass Violence in East Timor* (Ithaca and London, 2005), p. 109. On pregnant Jewish women being shot in the belly 'for fun': E. Klee, W. Dressen, and V. Riess, eds, *'The Good Old Days': The Holocaust As Seen by Its Perpetrators and Bystanders* (1991 [1988]), p. 179. Some may claim that such acts are myths or symbols, but there seem to be too many confirmed occurences during war and genocide to dismiss the phenomenon as fabrication, although some occurrences may be categorized as such. On the fabrication of 'atrocity myths', Horne and Kramer, 2001, pp. 196–225.
74. Derderian, 2005, 9; Kaiser, in Kieser and Schaller, eds, 2002, p. 162; R. G. Hovannisian, 'Bitter-Sweet Memories: The Last Generation of Ottoman Armenians', in R. G. Hovannisian, ed., *Looking Backward, Moving Forward: Confronting the Armenian Genocide* (New Brunswick and London, 2003), p. 120; Bryce and Toynbee, 2000, p. 319; M. D. Peterson, *'Starving Armenians': America and the Armenian Genocide, 1915–1930 and after* (Charlottesville and London, 2004), p. 55.
75. H. Fein, 'Genocide and Gender: The Uses of Women and Group Destiny', *Journal of Genocide Research*, I, no. 1 (March 1999), 45.
76. Quoted in D. G. Dutton et al., 'Extreme Mass Homicide: From Military Massacre to Genocide', *Aggression and Violent Behaviour*, X (2005), 443.
77. e.g., 'En Redegørelse for Dr Khosrov Krikorians Oplevelser i Ørkenen fra 1915–1918', KMA, 10.360, Pk. 15, 'Armenier-Missionen, Diverse Skildringer vedr. Arminierne [*sic*] 1906–1927', 1.
78. Miller and Miller, 1993, p. 89; Kaiser, in Kieser and Schaller, eds, 2002, pp. 157–158, 161.

79. Sarafian, comp., 2004, p. 331. See also Gust, ed., 2005, pp. 217, 284–285; Larsen, 1922, p. 32; Riggs, 1997, p. 142; Vahram Dadrian, 2003, p. 78.
80. See, e.g., Svazlian, 2004, p. 84; Miller and Miller, 1993, pp. 80, 96, 103–105; Gust, ed., 2005, p. 281; B. Nercessian, *I Walked through the Valley of Death* (New York, 2003), p. 25; Atkinson, 2000, p. 40; Knapp, 2002, p. 47; Riggs, 1997, pp. 136–137; K. Meyer, *Armenien und die Schweiz* (Bern, 1974), p. 96; Ussher, 1917, p. 312. Collective suicide to avoid sexual abuse also occurred in Eastern Germany in WWII when whole female populations of villages threw themselves in rivers to avoid being raped by Russian soldiers: Gellately and Kiernan, 'Introduction', in Gellately and Kiernan, eds, 2003, p. 14.
81. Sevart Mikaelian's testimony, KMA, 10.360, Pk. 15, 'Armenier-Missionen, Diverse Skildringer vedr. Arminierne [sic] 1906–1927'.
82. Miller and Miller, 1993, pp. 97–103; Kaiser, 2002, p. 12; Gust, ed., 2005, pp. 214, 264.
83. Larsen, 1922, pp. 55–56.
84. Miller and Miller, 1993, p. 104. For examples of more general altruistic behaviour, see, e.g., S. B. Harper, 'Mary Louise Graffam: Witness to genocide', in Winter, ed., 2003, p. 231.
85. Re. resistance to genocide as a broader concept than, say, taking up arms, see C. Tatz, *With Intent to Destroy: Reflecting on Genocide* (London and New York, 2003), p. 24, who quotes Yehuda Bauer for stating that resistance to Nazi decrees during the Holocaust was 'any group action consciously taken in opposition' to such decrees.
86. On the subject of the existence from the early modern period of the discourses of suicide as 'sinful', as 'a medical condition' ('the product of an unsound mind'), and as 'heroic', respectively, and of what is described as the post-WWI decriminalization of acts of suicide, R. M. Brown, *The Art of Suicide* (London, 2001), e.g., pp. 13–14, 147.
87. Miller and Miller, in Hovannisian, ed., 1992, p. 170.
88. Svazlian, 2004, p. 83. See also Miller and Miller, 1993, pp. 103–105; Gust, ed., 2005, p. 253; Kaiser, in Kieser and Schaller, eds, 2002, pp. 160, 163; Knapp, 2002, p. 47; El-Ghusein, 1917, pp. 14, 17; Meyer, 1974, p. 95.
89. See, e.g., Svazlian, 2004, pp. 106, 108; R. Peroomian, 'Armenian Literary Responses to Genocide: The Artistic Struggle to Comprehend and Survive', in Hovannisian, ed., 1992, pp. 224–226.
90. For a discussion of collective Armenian victimhood and attempts at redressing this, R. Panossian, *The Armenians: From Kings and Priests to Merchants and Commissars* (London, 2006), pp. 236ff.
91. Miller and Miller, 1993, pp. 11–13. It must be noted that in such instances where there seems to be no physical violence involved in the abduction of a woman, it is in my opinion still an act of gender-specific violence, and intercourse during forced marriages and/or slavery are still acts of rape. The Trial Chamber at *The International Criminal Tribunal for Rwanda* used what I believe is a sensible definition of rape as 'a physical invasion of a sexual nature, committed on a person under circumstances which are coercive', and sexual violence, including rape, as 'any act of a sexual nature which is committed on a person under circumstances which are coercive'. Quoted in N. Pillay, 'Sexual Violence in Times of Conflict: The Jurisprudence of

the International Criminal Tribunal for Rwanda', in S. Chesterman, ed., *Civilians in War* (London, 2001), p. 173. For a further discussion of rape as genocide, C. Eboe-Osuji, 'Rape as Genocide: Some Questions Arising', *Journal of Genocide Research*, IX, no. 2 (2007), 251–273. For an illustrative description of life as an Armenian woman in a forced marriage, testimony of Digin Versjin, KMA, 10.360, Pk. 15, 'Armenier-Missionen, Diverse Skildringer vedr. Arminierne [*sic*] 1906–1927'. The fate of Digin ('Lady', 'Mrs') Versjin (here spelled 'Vergene') is also mentioned in Atkinson, 2000, p. 72.

92. Dadrian, in Winter, ed., 2003, p. 83.
93. See, e.g., B. A. Valentino, *Final Solutions: Mass Killing and Genocide in the 20th Century* (Ithaca and London, 2004), pp. 40–43; Dutton et al., 2005, 470.
94. Mark Levene, 'Introduction', in M. Levene and P. Roberts, eds, *The Massacre in History* (New York and Oxford, 1999), p. 17.
95. R. Seifert, 'War and Rape: A Preliminary Analysis', in Stiglmayer, ed., 1994, p. 56.
96. See, e.g., Fein, 1999, 43–44; Horne and Kramer, 2001, pp. 199–200; D. Baro, 'Children Witnessing Atrocities against Parents or Caregivers, a Human Rights Perspective', *Torture – Journal on Rehabilitation of Torture Victims and Prevention of Torture*, XVI, no. 3 (2006), 194–196; K. Weis and S. Weis, 'Victimology and the Justification of Rape', in I. Drapkin and E. Viano, eds, *Victimology: A New Focus. Vol. V. Exploiters and Exploited: The Dynamics of Victimization* (Lexington, Toronto, and London, 1975), p. 14.
97. See discussion in R. F. Baumeister, *Evil: Inside Human Violence and Cruelty* (New York, 2001), chapter 7.
98. H. Katsuichi, *The Nanjing Massacre* (2000), passim. The arrest of a group of Armenian women in Bitlis was described as 'a sport' by an American eyewitness: Barton, comp., 1998, p. 11. On killing as 'sport' during the Holocaust, see, e.g., Browning, 1998, pp. 101, 134.
99. H. S. Der-Garabedian, *Jail to Jail: Autobiography of a Survivor of the 1915 Armenian Genocide*, trans A. H. Der-Karabetian (New York, Lincoln, Shanghai, 2004 [1957]), pp. 76–77.
100. O. A. Rygaard, *Mellem Tyrker og Kurder. En Dansk Ingeniørs Oplevelser i Lilleasien* (1935), p. 165. For a description of a similar occurrence in the course of the destruction of Assyrian and Armenian populations in Persia's Urmia region in 1915, Gaunt, 2006, p. 113. For a description of a similar occurrence during the 1894–1896 massacres of Armenians, Balakian, 2003, p. 65. On killings of Armenians as 'a sport', see also Einstein, 1917, p. 231. On the massacre of Armenians in Sarki Karahissar (Shabin Karahissar), Nercessian, 2003, pp. 8–13; *New York Times*, 18 August 1915. For a description of what appears to be ritualized mass killings of Muslim Arabs by Ottoman regular cavalry, including the sexualized mutilation and killing of a pregnant woman, T. E. Lawrence, *Seven Pillars of Wisdom* (1983), p. 652, quoted in J. J. Reid, 'The Concept of War and Genocidal Impulses in the Ottoman Empire, 1821–1918', *Holocaust and Genocide Studies*, IV, no. 2 (1989), 187. On the rape of Armenian and Jewish women by Ottoman forces in Ottoman Palestine: H. V. F. Winstone, *The Illicit Adventure: The Story of Political and Military Intelligence in the Middle East from 1898 to 1926* (London, 1982), p. 234.

101. See, e.g., N. J. Mitchell, *Agents of Atrocity: Leaders, Followers, and the Violation of Human Rights in Civil War* (2004), pp. 9–10, 48–50. See also E. K. Jernazian, *Judgment unto Truth: Witnessing the Armenian Genocide* (New Brunswick and London, 1990), p. 65.
102. Horne and Kramer, 2001, p. 198. See also Katsuichi, 2000, p. xx, on the Nanjing (Nanking) massacre: '[To] most men in Japan's peasant army, women were chattels, to be used at a man's convenience. This was especially true of Chinese women – who, according to many of their officers, were a subrace. Once looting was allowed, rape was sure to follow'.
103. See, e.g., Derderian, 2005, 5, who contends that 'physical abuse and rape of female relatives was also used to intimidate the Armenian leadership and dampen its will to resist'.
104. Sarafian, in Bartov and Mack, eds, 2001, p. 210.
105. Diken and Laustsen, 2004, pp. 1, 5. For an introduction to the ICTR judgment of Jean-Paul Akayesu, mayor of a Rwandan commune, who was convicted of counts relating to rape and sexual violence as genocide, A. Stiglmayer, 'Sexual Violence: Systematic Rape', in R. Gutman and D. Rieff, eds, *Crimes of War: What the Public Should Know* (New York and London, 1999), p. 327.
106. Seifert, in Stiglmayer, ed., 1994, p. 55.
107. See, e.g., Stiglmayer, ed., 1994; T. Shanker, 'Sexual Violence', in Gutman and Rieff, eds, 1999, pp. 323–326; G. Rodrigue, 'Sexual Violence: Enslavement and Forced Prostitution', ibid., pp. 328–329.
108. See R. Jahan, 'Genocide in Bangladesh', in Totten, Parsons, and Charny, eds, 1997, p. 298: '[S]ystematic and organized rape was the special weapon of war used by the Pakistani army during the second phase of the liberation struggle. While during the first phase, young able-bodied males were the victims of indiscriminate killings, during the second phase, girls and women became the special targets of Pakistani aggression. During army operations, girls and women were raped in front of close family members in order to terrorize and inflict racial slander. Girls and women were also abducted and repeatedly raped and gang-raped in special camps run by the army near army barracks. Many of the rape victims either were killed or committed suicide. Altogether, it is estimated that approximately 200,000 girls and women were raped during the 1971 genocide'. See also K. K. Roy, 'Feelings and Attitudes of Raped Women of Bangladesh towards Military Personnel of Pakistan', in Drapkin and Viano, eds, 1975, pp. 65–72.
109. Cagaptay, 2006, p. 9.
110. UM, 5. L. 15., 'Grækenland-Tyrkiet: Politiske Forhold', Pk. 1, Juni 1914–31/12 1945, nr. 31, 23/6 1914.
111. P. Parin, 'Open Wounds: Ethnopsychological Reflections on the Wars in the Former Yugoslavia', in Stiglmayer, ed., 1994, p. 42.
112. On the relations between expansionism and genocide – the attempts by genocidal regimes to purify a territory rather than, or combined with, purifying a 'race': B. Kiernan, 'Twentieth-Century Genocides: Underlying Ideological Themes from Armenia to East Timor', in Gellately and Kiernan, eds, 2003, pp. 33–37. On the 'purification' of Anatolia, M. Bjørnlund, 'The 1914 Cleansing of Aegean Greeks As a Case of Violent

Turkification', *Journal of Genocide Research*, X, 1 (2008), 41–58; Stürmer, 2000, pp. 48, 93; H. Kaiser, 'The Ottoman Government and the End of the Ottoman Social Formation, 1915–1917' (2001), http://www.hist.net/kieser/ aghet/Essays/EssayKaiser.html; N. Seker, 'Demographic Engineering in the Late Ottoman Empire and the Armenians', *Middle Eastern Studies*, XLIII, no. 3 (May 2007), 463.

113. On Bosnia, see, e.g., R. Gutman, 'Foreword', in Stiglmayer, ed., 1994, p. x; on Armenia, Villa and Matossian, 1982, p. 124.

114. Seifert, in Stiglmayer, ed., 1994, p. 59; J. Hagan, *Justice in the Balkans: Prosecuting War Crimes in the Hague Tribunal* (Chicago, 2003), p. 186; A. Gram, *Blandt Armeniske Flygtninge i Grækenland. Med Erindringer af den tidligere Armeniermissionær Margrethe Jepsen* (1953), p. 18; *Industrimissionens Blad*, I, no. 4 (December 1922), 49.

115. See, e.g., Vahram Dadrian, 2003, pp. 51ff.

116. See, e.g., Kaiser, 2002, pp. 10–12, 66–68; M. Levene, 'The Experience of Genocide: Armenia 1915–16 and Romania 1941–42', in Kieser and Schaller, eds, 2002, pp. 436–37; R. H. Kevorkian, 'Ahmed Djémal Pacha et le sort des déportés armeniéns de Syrie-Palestine', ibid., 206–207; V. N. Dadrian, HGS, 45; Larsen, 1922, p. 36. For an eyewitness testimony of the 1916 Der Zor massacres by the Armenian deportee Sanduk Gorjaslian, *7 Gamle Koner* (Lemvig, 1927), pp. 9–10. These massacres could be preceded by mass rape, as testified in Sarafian, comp., 2004, p. 550: 'I am reliably informed that the Mutessarif [local CUP official Zekki/Zeki Bey, MB] of Der-el-Zor has arranged and carried out the massacre of all the remaining Armenians that were there, some 12,000 in all, having gone personally to superintend the work. That before the end all the presentable women and girls were outraged by the "Chachames" of the Arab tribes there, whose participation was at the invitation or command of the Mutessarif'. See also 'En Redegørelse for Dr Khosrov Krikorians Oplevelser i Ørkenen fra 1915–1918', KMA, 10.360, Pk. 15, 'Armenier-Missionen, Diverse Skildringer vedr. Arminierne [*sic*] 1906–1927', 2–4.

117. Quoted in Miller and Miller, 1993, p. 19. See also Riggs, 1997, pp. 137–138.

118. Kaiser, 2002, passim; Ohandjanian, 2004, p. 118.

119. Sarafian, comp., 2004, p. 169.

120. V. Tachjian and R. H. Kévorkian, 'Reconstructing the Nation with Women and Children Kidnapped During the Genocide', trans. M. R. Appel, *Ararat*, XLV, no. 185 (Winter 2006), 5–14. See also Auron, 2003, p. 191.

121. Niepage, 1917, pp. 3–7. See also Kaiser, 2002, pp. 13–18.

122. Niepage, 1917, pp. 13–14.

123. H. V. F. Winstone, *Gertrude Bell* (London, 2004), pp. 276–277, quoted in Fisk, 2006, p. 402. On the large-scale massacre and abuse of Armenians at Ras-el-Ain, see also testimony of an Armenian woman deported from Bitlis with her family, in Jensen, 1929, p. 37; Auron, 2003, p. 182.

124. Kaiser, 2002, p. 27.

125. Smith, 1994, p. 316.

126. Derderian, 2005, 4.

127. Sarafian, in Bartov and Mack, eds, 2001, p. 210. On the number of assimilations, see also E. G. Danielyan, *The Armenian Genocide of 1894–1922 and the Accountability of the Turkish State* (Yerevan, 2005), p. 27.

128. Kaiser, 2002, p. 1. See also Morgenthau, 2003, pp. 200–201; Tachjian and Kévorkian, 2006, 5; Derderian, 2005, 2; A. Baum et al., 'Review of Mass Homicides of Intelligentsia As a Marker for Genocide', *The Forensic Examiner*, XVI, no. 3 (Fall 2007), 34–41. On the continuation of the policy of forced assimilation of Armenian and Greek women in the early 1920s during Kemalist rule, see, e.g., H. J. Psomiades, 'The American Near East Relief (NER) and the *Megali Catastrophe* in 1922', *Journal of Modern Hellenism*, XIX–XX (Winter 2002–2003), 135–150.

129. Sarafian, in Bartov and Mack, eds, 2001, p. 211. See also Kaiser, 2002, p. 1.

130. Gust, ed., 2005, p. 217.

131. Kaiser, in Kieser and Schaller, eds, 2002, p. 151. See also Derderian, 2005, 4; T. Hofmann, ed., *Der Völkermord an den Armeniern vor Gericht: Der Prozess Talaat Pascha* (Göttingen and Wien, 1985 [1921]), pp. 133–136; Riggs, 1997, p. 97; U. Ü. Üngör, 'Center and Periphery in the Armenian Genocide: The Case of Diyarbekir Province', in H.-L. Kieser and E. Plozza, eds, *Der Völkermord an den Armeniern, die Türkei und Europa/The Armenian Genocide, Turkey and Europe* (Zürich, 2006), p. 80.

132. Bryce and Toynbee, 2000, p. 297; Kieser and Schaller, 'Einleitung', in Kieser and Schaller, eds, 2002, p. 31; Kaiser, ibid., p. 159; Sarafian, comp., 2004, p. 154.

133. Jacobsen, 1979, pp. 284, 288, 316; Bryce and Toynbee, 2000, p. 288; Davis, 1989, pp. 64, 169; Gust, ed., 2005, p. 236.

134. Sarafian, in Bartov and Mack, eds, 2001, pp. 210–211. On government-run orphanages as part of the genocidal calculus, see also Benedictsen, 1925, p. 257; Barton, comp., 1998, pp. 164–165.

135. On (proto-)racist prejudice, Turkish and Western, against Armenians, W. Gust, 'Die Verdrängung des Völkermords an den Armeniern – ein Signal für die Shoah', in Kieser and Schaller, eds, 2002, pp. 463–480; S. H. Astourian, 'Modern Turkish Identity and the Armenian Genocide: From Prejudice to Racist Nationalism', in R. G. Hovannisian, ed., *Remembrance and Denial: The Case of the Armenian Genocide* (Detroit, 1998), pp. 23–50; Bjørnlund, 'Karen Jeppe, Aage Meyer Benedictsen...', 2007; M. L. Anderson, '"Down in Turkey, Far Away": Human Rights, the Armenian Massacres, and Orientalism in Wilhelmine Germany', *Journal of Modern History*, LXXIX (2007), 80–111; C. E. Bechhofer, *In Denikin's Russia and the Caucasus, 1919–1920* (1992 [1921]), pp. 257ff.

136. Gust, ed., 2005, p. 227. For comparisons between anti-Armenianism and anti-Semitism, see also Raphael Lemkin, quoted in D. J. Schaller, '"La question arménienne n'existe plus": Der Völkermord an den Armeniern während des Ersten Weltkriegs und seine Darstellung in der Historiographie', in Fritz Bauer Institut, ed., *Völkermord und Kriegsverbrechen in der ersten Hälfte des 20. Jahrhunderts* (Frankfurt and New York, 2004), p. 113; S. H. Astourian, 'Genocidal Process: Reflections on the Armeno-Turkish Polarization', in Hovannisian, ed., 1992, p. 59. US diplomatic minister at Copenhagen during WWI, Maurice Francis Egan, stated that his Turkish colleagues looked upon Armenians as 'deadly parasites', and he compared their views on Armenians with the way Russian noblemen viewed 'inferior Jews': M. F. Egan, *Ten Years Near the German Frontier: A Retrospect and a Warning* (New York, 1919), p. 312. On one of these diplomats in Copenhagen

during WWI, Djevad Bey, and, e.g., his insistence on a 'Turkey for the Turks', see Bjørnlund, ' "When the Cannons…" ', 2006, 205.

137. See especially Kieser, 'Dr Mehmed Reshid…', in Kieser and Schaller, eds, 2002, pp. 245–280.

138. Adalian, in Totten, Parsons, Charny, eds, 1997, p. 46. See also, e.g., Seker, 2007, 463.

139. UM, 139. D. 1., 'Tyrkiet – Indre Forhold', Pk. 1, til 31 December 1916, nr. CXXV, 22/9 1915 (5/10); UM, 139. D. 1., 'Tyrkiet – Indre Forhold', Pk. 1, til 31 December 1916, nr. XCVII, 14/8 1915 (25/8).

140. Quoted in Sarafian, comp., 2004, p. 194. See also ibid., p. 446. On the discussion of Armenian resistance/rebellion at Van, see, e.g., Ter Minassian, 'Van 1915', in Hovannisian, ed., 2000, pp. 209–244.

141. See, e.g., R. Bonney, *Jihad: From Qur'an to bin Laden* (Hampshire and New York, 2004), pp. 150–153.

142. R. G. Suny, 'Religion, Ethnicity, and Nationalism: Armenians, Turks, and the End of the Ottoman Empire', in Bartov and Mack, eds, 2001, pp. 53–54.

143. Gust, ed., 2005, p. 291. Re. the CUP principle of 'Turkey for the Turks', see also O. L. von Sanders, *Fünf Jahre Türkei* (Berlin, 1920), p. 200.

144. On the Nazi race laws, etc., see I. Kershaw, *The Nazi Dictatorship* (London, 1993 [3rd edn]), pp. 92–93; Fein, 1999, 52–53. Despite the race laws, many Jewish women were still subjected to rape, sexual humiliation, slavery, and mutilation during the Holocaust: e.g., A. L. Gold, *Fiet's Vase and Other Stories of Survival, Europe 1939–1945* (New York, 2003), p. 108; M. Gilbert, *The Holocaust: A History of the Jews of Europe during the Second World War* (New York, 1987), p. 301; E. Schloss, *Eva's Story* (New York, 1990), pp. 76–77; Browning, 1998, pp. 152–153.

145. Adalian, in Totten, Parsons and Charny, eds, 1997, p. 52. See also Diken and Laustsen, 2004, pp. 7–8.

146. That such a linkage between 'race' and religion could exist in the eyes of Turkish authorities is expressed in a quote related by Garougian, 2005, pp. 134–135. Around 1921, when Pontian Greeks were being massacred or deported from the Black Sea coast to the interior, Armenian survivors in Harput inquired with Turkish officials about feeding what were described as the wretched and sick deportees. According to Garougian, the response was that '[t]hey're part of your own race. You help them!' Here, the fact that both Greeks and Armenians are generally Christian seems to have been interpreted as meaning that both groups were belonging to the same 'race'.

147. Svazlian, 2004, p. 81. See also Miller and Miller, 1993, pp. 71, 108, 183; Adalian, in Totten, Parsons, Charny, eds, 1997, p. 72; Garougian, 2005, p. 215; B. Morley, *Marsovan 1915: The Diaries of Bertha B. Morley* (Ann Arbor, MI, 2000), pp. 16, 23; A. I. Elkus, *The Memoirs of Abram Elkus: Lawyer, Ambassador, Statesman* (Princeton and London, 2004), p. 68.

148. Khanum Palutian's [Palootzian] testimony, KMA, 10.360, Pk. 15, 'Armenier-Missionen, Diverse Skildringer vedr. Arminierne [*sic*] 1906–1927'. See also R. G. Hovannisian, 'Intervention and Shades of Altruism during the Armenian Genocide', in Hovannisian, ed., 1992, p. 181, 191–192. For a pre-CUP example, see *The Friend of Armenia*, no. 25 (Spring 1906), 'Orphans of Diarbekir', 154, about a widowed Armenian mother, wounded during the 1890s massacres, who 'in her misery, turned Turk', i.e., converted to Islam.

The same principle seems to have been applied in one of the rare cases where a Muslim Turk converted to Christianity. According to Maria Jacobsen, the young woman in question who had voluntarily (and, considering this was an offence punishable by death, most likely secretly) converted to Christianity, was thus not only no longer a Muslim, she was no longer a Turk: KMA, 10.360, no. 15, 'Armeniermissionen, Korrespondance til og fra Frk. Marie [*sic*] Jacobsen (1912–1919), "1914", letter from Jacobsen to KMA, Harput 19 March 1914.

149. Kuper, 1981, p. 111. 'Taking another name' or 'changing name' were in fact used as expressions denoting forced conversion and assimilation: Larsen, 1922, p. 35; Barton, comp., 1998, p. 83.

150. Sarafian, in Bartov and Mack, eds, 2001, p. 217.

151. See, e.g., Kaiser, 2002, p. 51; Sarafian, comp., 2004, p. 256; Dadrian, 'Children As Victims...'. See also Barton, comp., 1998, p. 127.

152. Svazlian, 2004, p. 82.

153. O. Bartov and P. Mack, 'Introduction', in Bartov and Mack, eds, 2001, p. 8.

154. See, e.g., Kaiser, in Kieser and Schaller, eds, 2002, p. 159.

155. Gust, ed., 2005, p. 260. On the massacres at the Kemakh Gorge, south of Erzinjan on the Euphrates, see, e.g., S. Payaslian, 'The Death of Armenian Karin/Erzerum', in R. G. Hovannisian, ed., *Armenian Karin/Erzerum* (Costa Mesa, Ca., 2003), pp. 353–355; I. K. Hassiotis, 'The Armenian Genocide and the Greeks: Response and Records (1915–23)', in Hovannisian, ed., 1992, pp. 146–147.

156. Niepage, 1917, pp. 14–15. On rejections of such applications, see also Morley, 2000, pp. 36–37; T. Hofmann and M. Pehlivanian, '"Der Schlimmsten Orte Einer..."': Malatia 1915 bis 1918' (1998), http://www.aga-online.org/de/texte/malatia/index.php#1.

157. Morley, 2000, pp. 50, 83.

158. See, e.g., Gust, ed., 2005, p. 263.

159. Morgenthau, 2003, pp. 200–201. On Islamization and 'mingling of blood' (here called 'amalgamating races') as means of forced assimilation and Turkification of Ottoman Greeks, as well as on sexual abuse of Armenian women, see H. Morgenthau, *United States Diplomacy on the Bosphorus: The Diaries of Ambassador Morgenthau, 1913–1916* (Princeton and London, 2004), p. 275. On the Islamization and sexual abuse of Armenian women, see also ibid., e.g., p. 322.

160. E. D. Weitz, 'The Modernity of Genocides: War, Race, and Revolution in the Twentieth Century', in Gellately and Kiernan, eds, 2003, p. 56.

161. Svazlian, 2004, p. 83; S. E. Moranian, 'Bearing Witness: The Missionary Archives as Evidence of the Armenian Genocide', in Hovannisian, ed., 1992, p. 115. See also Dadrian, 1986, 184.

162. Sarafian, in Bartov and Mack, eds, 2001, p. 216.

163. Dadrian, in Winter, ed., 2003, p. 85; Kaiser, in Kieser and Schaller, eds, 2002, p. 167. According to J. Winter, 'Under Cover of War: The Armenian Genocide in the Context of Total War', in Gellately and Kiernan, eds, 2003, p. 194, 50–60 percent of the adult male population of the Ottoman Empire were mobilized during WWI.

164. Bryce and Toynbee, 2000 (1916), p. 289.

165. H. Marcher, *Oplevelser Derovrefra* (1919), p. 16.

166. Kaiser, in Kieser and Schaller, eds, 2003, p. 142; Zürcher, ibid., p. 193.
167. M. Sells, 'Kosovo Mythology and the Bosnian Genocide', in Bartov and Mack, 2001, pp. 182–83, 189. See also Hukanovic, 1998, p. 31; L. Jones, *Then They Started Shooting: Growing up in Wartime Bosnia* (2004), e.g., pp. 46–47, 75–77.
168. Diken and Laustsen, 2004, pp. 4–5.
169. See, e.g., Miller and Miller, 1993, p. 122; Bockelund, 1932, pp. 46–47.
170. J. Svanenskjold and U. Fugl, eds, *K.M.A.s Arbejde gennem Femogtyve Aar, 1900–1925* (Copenhagen, 1925), pp. 42–43.
171. Quoted in Miller and Miller, 1993, p. 113.
172. Sarafian, in Bartov and Mack, eds, 2001, pp. 212–214; Miller and Miller, 1993, p. 110; Jacobsen, 1979, pp. 235–236; H. M. Chitjian, *A Hair's Breadth from Death* (London and Reading, 2003), pp. 100–101.
173. Miller and Miller, 1993, pp. 145–146.
174. Quoted in Peterson, 2004, p. 55.
175. N. Ferguson, *The War of the World: History's Age of Hatred* (London, 2007), p. 1.

2
Race and Sex, Fear and Loathing in France during the Great War

Richard S. Fogarty

In April 1916 Sergeant Hao, an Indochinese soldier serving in the French army on the Western Front, wrote, 'On Sundays, we go strolling with [French] women, as we would do in Indochina, with our own women at home'.[1] Sergeant Hao may have been surprised by the very ordinariness with which some French people treated such interracial contacts, and even more intimate relationships, between non-white soldiers (colonial subjects in the French army, known as *troupes indigènes*) and white French women, but these contacts were anything but ordinary. They ranged from simple strolls in the park to sexual liaisons of more or less short duration, to friendships, even to pregnancies and marriages. The women with whom these men became involved ranged from prostitutes, to nurses, to daughters of respectable bourgeois families. For many in France, particularly those in positions of authority, these relationships were deeply troubling, challenging 'the prestige of the European woman', as one military censor put it, by transgressing sexual mores and racial and colonial hierarchies.[2] The attitude of this official, and that of many other French military, political, and colonial authorities, confirms Benedict Anderson's description of the racist imagination, which 'dreams of eternal contaminations, transmitted from the origins of time through an endless sequence of loathsome copulations'.[3] These 'loathsome copulations' across the racial divide, the thinking went, threatened to undermine French authority, blur the distinctions that underpinned French national identity, and contaminate the French population – both through the simple fact of contact and through the even more disconcerting possibility of mixed-race offspring. Ultimately, these relationships raised an ominous question about the future of French colonial rule: What if these relationships encouraged the men who engaged in them to demand recognition not as colonial subjects but as Frenchmen, not as racial inferiors but as equals?[4]

Authorities, in France and in the colonies, feared both the effect that these relationships would have on the *indigènes'* respect for white women and the society they lived in, and the corresponding destabilizing effect upon colonial rule. This constituted a potentially large problem, as more than 500,000 *troupes indigènes* from North and West Africa, Indochina, and Madagascar served in the French army during the war, but French officials also worried about the indigenous populations in general, as soldiers returning home might spread tales of easy conquests and French women of dubious morals. In addition, postal censorship showed that the soldiers also sent home revealing letters and thousands of photographs of French women. Censors were particularly concerned about these photographs, which featured simple portraits of purported girlfriends or mistresses, or pictures of soldiers with their beloved, or, worse yet, photos of nude women in suggestive poses. Though these soldiers might have thought that, by defending the French nation, they had earned the right to interact with French people on a basis of some equality and familiarity, racial and colonial hierarchies required the maintenance of a strict separation between the white colonizers and the non-white colonized. Making these men soldiers had already called into question this separation, rendering it more difficult to maintain, and relationships between white women and non-white men presented an even more profound and intimate (in the most literal sense of the term) challenge to the racial and colonial order.

Numerous studies have elucidated the importance of intertwined ideas about race and gender in the construction and maintenance of European colonial rule, but what transpired during the war years differed in crucial respects from what usually took place in the colonies both before 1914 and after 1918.[5] Scholars have long recognized women's more general role in defining, through reproduction, the boundaries of culture, ethnicity, and nationality within modern states.[6] In the colonies, as Ann Laura Stoler argues, 'Creating and securing the European community's borders took on special significance when cultural, political, and sexual contagions were conjured everywhere – where European and native sensibilities and desires brushed against one another as they were borrowed and blurred'.[7] How much more important would it be to create and secure these borders in France itself? During the early part of the twentieth century, the state began to promote the settlement of European women in the colonies as vectors of civilization, domesticity, bourgeois morality, and racial purity, but what to do now that colonial men had arrived in Europe and were interacting with French women who seemed stubbornly resistant to their roles as guardians of the culture and race?[8] Perhaps most disconcerting, love and sex in France occurred between men from the colonies and white French women, reversing the more frequent pairing of white men and indigenous women overseas. Thus, male authorities faced not only a colonial, political, and racial threat as authorities, but a sexual threat as men. They were menaced with the betrayal of formerly loyal colonial subjects and soldiers, on the one hand, and of wives and daughters on the other. This was an era in which modern European states and the male elites who governed them were increasingly concerned with power over people's bodies, what Michel Foucault called 'a certain mode of detailed political investment of the body', a 'new micro-physics of power'.[9] As part of this process, states focused on sexuality in particular as a 'dense transfer point for relations of power', a privileged site of state intervention, seeking to establish and wield new technologies of 'bio-power' over individuals and societies.[10] Stoler's work has shown how important the colonial context was for the emergence of these concerns, and how instrumental racialist categorization through sexual proscription and prescription in the colonies was to the emergence of the European bourgeois order and European identity.[11] The concerns of the French state and military, and their attempts to investigate and regulate the sexual behavior both of colonial men and French women, fall neatly into this story, but power and control proved more difficult to exercise in the metropole in a time of war than in the colonies. Officials often found themselves in a position of what one might call 'bio-powerlessness', concerned with but largely unable to stop love and sex across racial lines, or to prevent the ominous effects they feared would result from such unions.

One can perceive this anxiety in a multitude of archival sources. Official communications, both in the field and at the Ministry of War, among the various officers responsible for colonial subjects in uniform reveal that interactions with the French civilian population, especially French women, were a constant concern. Inspection reports and the comments of French *officiers interprètes*, medical personnel, and colonial administrators show that the authorities believed that the effects of these interactions went beyond questions of discipline, morale, and health to encompass larger concerns about racial hierarchies and empire. The richest sources by far, though, are the reports of military censors charged with reading and, if necessary, confiscating the mail of *troupes indigènes*. These reports provide a glimpse into the lives of the soldiers themselves through their words – even though these words were filtered through the concerns of the censors, who provided extracts that reflected what the censors were interested in, not necessarily what the letter writers thought most important. However, it is precisely the views of the censors – army officers (though perhaps pulled from civilian life by the nationwide wartime call-up), with a knowledge of indigenous languages often derived from administrative or military service in the colonies – that expose most clearly official views and anxieties about interracial relationships. Various branches of the *Contrôle Postal* responsible for correspondence to and from particular colonies operated independently, and censorship of mail between France and North Africa, Madagascar, and Indochina – the latter in particular – was quite active and thorough. Though one can sometimes perceive distinct attitudes toward *indigènes* from different parts of the French empire, the commentary of the censors is consistent with a broader discourse within military and political circles that viewed all relationships between non-white men and white French women as equally subversive and alarming.

Wartime relationships across the racial divide, then, provide an important window into the experience and attitudes of both *troupes indigènes* and French officials, and the role sex and race played more generally in the structure of white predominance and empire.[12] These men's status as soldiers fighting for France and their presence on French soil opened up many possibilities for the destabilization of hierarchies that were virtually immutable back in the colonies. These colonial subjects observed a certain 'desacralization' of one of the tenets of imperial rule – white superiority – both as they observed France as an often nearly prostrate victim of German aggression and as they discovered that women in France were not as aloof and untouchable as their counterparts at home in the colonies. As officials watched the behavior of these soldiers, and of French women and their families as they welcomed colonial subjects into their lives and homes, and particularly as censors read the correspondence of *troupes indigènes*, acute anxieties emerged. It seemed to them that these relationships were creating significant weaknesses and fissures that had the potential to undermine imperial rule.

Crossing the color line

Colonial subjects serving in France wrote a great deal about their relationships with French women.[13] A censor's report for November 1917 noted that though Madagascans in France expressed opinions on a variety of issues, such as the quality of army food, leave policy, life in hospitals, and rumors of military operations, the 'greatest part' of their correspondence dealt 'with their adventures in the company of white women'.[14] Workers imported from the colonies, of which there were over 200,000 by the end of the war, also had opportunities to engage in these relationships, given their placement among the civilian population and their integration into an increasingly sexually diverse wartime work place. Relationships developed despite official attempts at segregation, though such attempts no doubt seriously restricted some men's ability to interact freely with native French people.[15] Soldiers, subject to military discipline and spending most of their time in the all-male environment of the army, faced hurdles as well. Yet the army employed many *troupes indigènes* as staging troops behind the lines, performing labor such as construction, resupply, and guard duty, where they came into contact with French civilians. Even combat troops had such opportunities. As one censor noted of soldiers from Indochina, '[t]he soldiers themselves make conquests in the villages where they are encamped'.[16] As all West African soldiers and some Indochinese soldiers spent the winter months away from the cold, wet north of France, encamped near Bordeaux or the Mediterranean, they often had extensive interaction with nearby populations. Lucie Cousturier's experiences bringing Senegalese soldiers into her home in the south of France and teaching them French is probably the most well-known of these interactions.[17] Stays in the hospital were also an occasion for soldiers to meet French women: nurses on their wards as well as other women in the surrounding communities. In short, it was difficult to prevent *troupes indigènes* from interacting with the French civilian population, or even from having relationships with the women whose homes they had traveled thousands of miles to defend.

Many of these relationships were of a distinctly impermanent nature. Soldiers' letters made clear that they paid for many of their 'conquests'. A Madagascan soldier wrote in September 1917, 'Once one arrives and walks upon French soil, one is obliged to partake of or one is attracted by something: it is prostitution'.[18] In the Mediterranean city of Fréjus, near a hospital and the largest winter camp for *troupes indigènes*, prostitution became a major health concern. In the summer of 1915, the Ministry of war instructed the commandant of the camp to prevent Senegalese troops from frequenting 'houses of ill-repute', though 'it would be prudent to tolerate certain establishments where prostitution, regulated and supervised, would be less dangerous for the health of the men than illicit prostitution'.[19] Yet despite this tolerance of (properly regulated) interaction between African men and French prostitutes, authorities recognized the danger of even commercial sex for the reputation of French women overall. As one report noted of the letters of Madagascan soldiers, '[i]t does not appear, in general, that Madagascans make a distinction between women of the night and white women in general'.[20] The fear was that *indigènes* would present prostitution to their correspondents as evidence of a general attraction French women felt toward colonial subjects in uniform. In August 1918, an Indochinese sergeant noted this habit among his countrymen, warning a friend at home not to give credence to stories others told of their amorous conquests over French women: 'Do not believe that French women have any passion for the Indochinese; just like the women of our country going for European men, they care only about money'.[21]

Yet prostitution was not the only means through which *troupes indigènes* and French women had contact, and the authorities had to admit as much. 'Our Indochinese', one censor observed, 'receive, in fact, letters which indicate that their correspondents sometimes belong to the best society'.[22] Moreover, each month brought reports of dozens of new engagements, marriages, and even births stemming from such liaisons. This presented a particular problem for the authorities, given their assumptions about the dangerous sexuality of colonial men. Europeans traditionally viewed non-whites as especially sexually active, potent, and depraved, and censors clearly had such stereotypes in mind when they noted that the easy availability of prostitutes exacerbated the 'natural lubricity' of the Indochinese.[23] An early censor's report on Madagascans, intended as a guide to the 'general characteristics of the race', observed that a Madagascan man rarely attained an advanced age because, '[t]he tendency to promiscuity which he often abuses, even from childhood, is for him a cause of degeneration and shortens his days'. This promiscuity also had as a consequence widespread syphilis among the island's population, the report claimed.[24] Observers judged North Africans, too, according to the prevailing sexual stereotype. The practice of polygamy and the ease of divorce under Muslim law (involving a simple declaration by a husband to his wife before the man could take another wife) served for many as proof of North Africans' uncontrollable desires. Commenting on a legislative proposal that would require Muslim soldiers to renounce such customs in order to acquire French citizenship, the French Resident General of Tunisia wrote that such a sacrifice was out of the question for such men, given their limited ability to control their desire for more than one woman. The *indigène* who renounced such prerogatives as polygamy and easy divorce would make 'a sacrifice beyond his strength'.[25]

Concerns over polygamy of a somewhat different sort plagued French authorities. Now that hundreds of thousands of non-white men were present in the metropole, bringing with them their dangerously active sexual drives, French women were in danger of being duped by soldiers with wives back in the colonies. Censors in Tunis noted that many French women wrote letters to men they had met in France describing their disappointment and anger upon discovering that the soldiers had made promises of marriage despite having a family in Tunisia. Such duplicity was often explicitly calculated, as was evident from the words a Tunisian soldier in the artillery addressed to a friend back in the colony. Not only did he write that he was happy to be in France, 'where pretty women are plentiful', but he advised his friend not to forget, in the event he also came to France, to say that he was a bachelor.[26] The serial adultery, dishonesty, and potential bigamy of Indochinese interpreter Pham Van Khuong was even more troubling to censors reading his mail. He received several letters from his fiancé, Ninon, in Toulouse, who professed her love and her desire to accompany him to Indochina after the war. However, Khuong was also receiving letters from another young French woman, who reproached him bitterly for having earlier promised marriage to her, only to admit later that he already had a wife back home in the colony.[27]

Also alarming to authorities were the motives of some of the *troupes indigènes*, quite apart from their sexual appetites. Some were quite open about the ultimate goal of marriage to a French woman, which would bring with it French citizenship and economic stability. Corporal Trong wrote home to his parents in August 1917, informing them that '[b]y seeking to marry a French woman, I intend to obtain the naturalization which will permit me to set myself up in a job later'.[28] Other soldiers' motives were less ambitious, but no less threatening to the elevated status French women were supposed to enjoy. Jacques Ngon, a nurse in Montpellier, described his girlfriend (or perhaps wife, as he referred to her as 'ma femme'), the daughter of an artillery captain, to his parents and sisters, but told them he had no intention of bringing her home to Saigon with him because he was using her to take care of him in case of illness during his stay in France. Ngon's colleague, Theo, claimed that he had taken up with a French woman for the duration of the war only, and she did his washing.[29] This was of course a dramatic inversion of the colonial order, in which indigenous women would often serve as concubines and perform domestic tasks, like washing, for white European men in the colonies.[30]

Such opportunism at the expense of French womanhood was troublesome enough to French authorities, but some soldiers expressed even more threatening motives for their pursuit of white women. As the head of the office charged with reading the mail of Indochinese soldiers characterized it, France was now paying for the sins of its sons, who had built the colonial empire and had often taken native women as concubines. Sex with white women in France was for the *indigènes* 'like a revenge on the European, the Frenchman who down there causes old Indochina to blush and incites jealousy'.[31] Some soldiers' letters did indeed invoke revenge as a motive for many of their 'conquests'. One wrote that he was proud to see that now there were mixed-race (*métis*) children produced by the union of Indochinese men and French women, as well as those produced in the colony by French men and Indochinese women.[32] But the *indigènes* did not merely seek revenge upon French men, but also French women, specifically those who lived in the colonies. A December 1917 report noted that to have sex with a white woman was for Madagascan men 'not only a pleasure not to be scorned, but also a form of vengeance'. These intimate encounters were 'a payback' which makes it 'possible today to repay all the contempt in which European women, in Madagascar, hold the *indigène*'. As one soldier wrote, women in the colonies 'regard us rather like lepers, well then, come on today, don't deprive yourself, take as much as possible'.[33] Another Madagascan put it even more bluntly: 'What to tell you of white women? Down there, we fear them. Here they come to us and solicit us by the attraction of their charm ... What delights in their smooches ... I am forgetting about Madagascar because of them'.[34] It was clear, too, that Madagascans were not the only soldiers with such attitudes, as an Indochinese soldier wrote, 'In our country, the women of this race are very difficult to approach, but us being here, two francs is enough for us to have fun with them'.[35] Such statements made clear the potential effect of interracial relationships upon the status of French women in the colonies. If these women were supposed to be pillars of the community there, embodying French ideas about civilization and domesticity and defining the boundaries that separated colonizers from colonized, *indigènes* with such attitudes, many of whom would eventually return to their homes, presented a significant potential threat to the colonial order.

Blurring the color line

Yet transgression was a two-way street, and authorities felt that native French people – women and their families – were often at least partially to blame for encouraging *indigènes* in their indiscretions. French citizens of the metropole, ignorant of the imperative and impermeable nature of boundaries between colonizers and colonized, were guilty of blurring the color line, and officials felt they faced a threat to the social order at home in France as a result of interracial relationships. This stemmed largely from what officials regarded as the ignorance of French civilians about the realities of colonial hierarchies and the 'special mentality' of *indigènes*, a mentality at once primitive and duplicitous, childlike and naïve, and potentially unpredictable and dangerous. Colonial administrators and army officers, possessed of long experience, could take this mentality into account when interacting with *indigènes*, but civilians living in the metropole could not. Typical of this supposed lack of understanding was a letter from Mme Baudin to Larbi Arboui, an Algerian soldier convalescing in the hospital. The French *officier interprète* who intercepted the letter reported that, 'The author of this letter is assuredly a courageous person, but ignorant of the mentality of our *indigènes*, she uses with her protégé a language he cannot possibly understand' (whether Mme Baudin used romantic language or merely conversed with the soldier as a racial and cultural equal is not clear, though censors would no doubt disapprove either way).[36] But it was not merely the use of inappropriate language that posed a problem. From the letters of the soldiers it was clear that many of them had found acceptance within respectable families, and as the censors in Tunis argued, French families failed to take into sufficient account the social rank of the *indigènes* whom they invited into their homes. One Tunisian, mobilized as a driver in the engineering corps at Montpellier, married the daughter of a lawyer in that city.[37] Jacques Ngon, the Indochinese nurse who had taken up with the daughter of a captain in the artillery, wrote that he ate lunch each day at the home of the father, who also provided the couple with an allowance of 60 francs per month.[38] Indochinese soldier Dinh also benefited from parental benevolence, as he paid frequent visits to a young, 22-year-old widow, 'in full view of her father and mother'.[39] Lawyers, army officers, and other self-respecting parents, the thinking went, ought to have known better and to have shown greater discretion than to allow their daughters to consort with colonial subjects serving as truck drivers, nurses, or common soldiers – with men, in short, who were racially and socially beneath them.

Even more subversive of racial and social hierarchies, given his motives, was the case of the recently naturalized Adjutant Victor Tru. He had become dissatisfied with girlfriends in Tourane and Champagne, as they did not possess the kind of fortune he was seeking.

Happily for him, a wealthy grocer in St. Dié had recently agreed to the engagement of his daughter to Tru. As of November 1917, Tru was working with a friend in Indochina, a functionary in the colonial administration who apparently had greater facility in written French, to craft a letter that would provide the now wavering father with sufficient reassurance to allow the marriage to go forward.[40] The case of Khamaci Mohamed, a Tunisian soldier who impressed a family with his knowledge of French over dinner, illustrated the dangers of inviting *indigènes* into French homes. The family, he wrote, took him 'for a Frenchman' and considered him 'as a true child of the family'. This disregard of racial and social conventions through inappropriate intimacy ran the very grave risk of inflating the soldier's opinion of himself through excessive praise.[41] Military and colonial authorities feared this sort of acceptance, along with what they regarded as gullibility and naïveté on the part of metropolitan French people, would inevitably raise the expectations of the *indigènes* and cause them to regard the more strictly segregated society of the colonies in an unfavorable comparative light.

In this respect, French families, and especially French women, were damaging the colonial order while bringing disorder to metropolitan society as well. When one officer claimed that Algerians were apprehensive about 'contact with our women, who in their eyes are all prostitutes and whose conduct unfortunately, in many cases, only confirms them in their opinion', he was voicing not only his concern over the effect of French women's behavior upon the mentality of colonial subjects, but also his disappointment as a French male with the failure of these women to conform to sexual mores and social expectations.[42] This is unsurprising, given that this period saw an intense debate about traditional gender roles and the place of women in society, and heightened anxieties about the behavior of French women.[43] Even more disturbing to officials and disruptive of the social order were the children of mixed race who began to appear with increasing frequency as the war wore on. The existence of *métis*, the product of unions between French men and non-white women, in the colony was one thing, but French women giving birth to such children within France was quite another. Authorities could only be stung by the wry comment of an Indochinese doctor to a friend who had also come to France: 'Like many others, you can say that you have more than served France, you are defending her and you are repopulating her'.[44] The official attitude toward this development was best illustrated by one report that referred to the new mothers as 'contaminated unfortunates'.[45] This term resonated with the discourse on *métissage* (miscegenation) as inevitably leading to the 'degeneration of the race', but also indicated that such mixed-race unions and mixed-blood offspring were, as one scholar has put it, 'sexual affronts'. Behind ostensibly biological concerns about 'contamination' lurked the larger and more unsettling questions about the permeability of political and cultural boundaries between European and 'other', between colonizers and colonized. Crossing and blurring these lines in such a dramatic way destabilized the separation of people into categories upon which colonial domination depended, and confused questions of national identity in troubling ways.[46]

If the existence of *métis* was undesired and disturbing – a 'nightmare', in fact[47] – at least that existence was not their fault, but the same could not be said of the women whose actions brought them into the world. And these actions were distressing to male French officials whether or not intimate contact produced children. One category of French women who had a great deal of contact, which could easily deepen into intimacy, with the *troupes indigènes* caused particular concern. Nurses at the various hospitals throughout France where wounded and sick men received treatment had perhaps the greatest opportunity to form relationships with soldiers, especially combat soldiers, as a prolonged period of recovery allowed sufficient time spent in one relatively confined place for men and women to get to know one another. These bonds often greatly comforted soldiers, as the experience of some West Africans demonstrated.[48] The military, however, found soldiers' extended stays away from their units and in the company of nurses especially corrosive of morale. A July 1915 report on North African soldiers in the south of France asserted that many of them had lost their soldierly qualities as a result of periods spent in the hospital. This was in large part because 'they have been treated in too benevolent a manner, especially by the female personnel'. The men had come to expect such treatment, and their newly acquired arrogance became indiscipline when they did not receive the same kind of treatment from their officers outside the hospital. Worse still, the nurses' 'benevolence' apparently extended beyond mere medical attention to

> sexual favors which have been given to the soldiers by certain of their nurses and other of our female compatriots, favors which for reasons of national pride we would like to doubt, but that the letters . . . oblige us to observe. One finds in these letters proof that French women have dared to deliver themselves up to these men and have not hesitated in their hysterical folly to commit the crime of turning these

soldiers from their military duty, advising them to avoid leaving for the front.[49]

What else but hysteria, a constitutional weakness to which women were supposedly especially prone, could explain French women simultaneously betraying their race, French men, the war effort, and their nation? Nurses, as professionals and like prostitutes, were predictable targets of official male anxiety, as they 'fell outside the colonial space to which European women were assigned: custodians of family welfare and respectability and dedicated and willing subordinates to and supporters of men'. If 'French family life and bourgeois respectability were conceived as the cultural bases for imperial patriotism and racial survival', these women were failing on many levels.[50]

These nurses' 'hysterical folly' disrupted more than military order. Naively, some of these women had given to their North African patients photographs of themselves in their Red Cross uniforms. For anyone who knew the 'boastfulness' of *indigènes* about anything to do with women, the author of the report argued, it was obvious that the soldiers would send these pictures back to friends in North Africa as evidence of their 'innumerable mistresses'. As the images and stories passed through many hands in indigenous society, they would excite 'the amusement and derision of our *indigènes*'. This would strike a blow to French prestige in its Muslim colonies, especially given their 'so particular conception of the woman – beast of burden, flesh for pleasure'.[51]

Official concerns repeatedly focused on the behavior of French women, and its effect upon the 'special mentality' of *indigènes*. The author of the July 1915 report on North Africans' interactions with French nurses admitted that these issues were not 'of a purely military order', but they did relate to 'the work of moral education of the Muslims of North Africa', the civilizing mission for which the army was partly responsible. Further upsetting the hierarchies that defined political and social relations between colonizers and colonized in France's overseas possessions, some nurses had written to their North African friends not only expressing love, but also exalting the bravery of the *troupes indigènes* to such an extent that many of the soldiers would undoubtedly suppose 'they have saved France'.[52] Another officer, faced with the same problem, claimed to have found a remedy in the forceful statement of French republican colonial ideology: 'It has been profitable to explain to them with authority, and in front of hospital personnel . . . that they were the saviors of their own African homes and that the tricolor flag is quite as much theirs as it is ours'.[53] Still, the idea that *troupes indigènes* were indispensable to the defense of the metropole went to the heart of one of the great paradoxes of the use of these troops: if France was such a powerful nation, if its moral and military superiority were such that it had every right to rule over distant lands and peoples in its colonial empire, why then did it need these peoples to save it from defeat at the hands of the Germans? This apparent need for help from the subject peoples, as well as the sight of large parts of France devastated and prostrate before the invading German army, was subtly, but deeply, destabilizing to the colonial order. Military authorities were not happy to observe French women adding to the problem by calling the *indigènes'* attention to it.

Authorities could intervene with the *indigènes* themselves, as when an Indochinese man was imprisoned for 15 days for 'daring to fall in love with a French girl'.[54] But recommendations for preventing the problems stemming from these relationships often made it clear that the primary concern was to modify the behavior of the French women in question. In 1915, a wealthy woman near Toulouse took a special interest in North African soldiers, sending food and money to the nearby hospital, hosting *tirailleurs* in her home, and listening with sympathy to their grievances. This led, an officer reported, to a 'very unjustified arrogance and a discontentment' among the *indigènes* with their treatment at the hospital. Worse, this woman had persuaded two badly wounded men to stay with her after their convalescence, one of whom had a good attitude while at the front but had now acquired 'a rebellious, arrogant, and very undisciplined spirit, having hatred for his superiors and believing that he alone saved France'. This situation, in addition to the presence of three North Africans (who had been discharged after having been disabled by wounds) already living in Toulouse with their French wives, threatened to undermine the morale of other soldiers.[55] The Ministry of War's response to this problem noted that though the soldiers had to be sent back to North Africa for processing before their formal discharge, they would be free to return to France after that. Still, the army could place the men under surveillance and deport them if they had a harmful effect upon the attitudes of their former comrades. But the measure likely to have the greatest effect was to have the intelligence service inform the woman discretely that the military authorities would not tolerate any incitement to indiscipline.[56]

Perhaps even more effective than a visit from intelligence officers would be to forbid all closed correspondence for the soldiers, requiring that they send and receive nothing but postcards. This would prevent writers from expressing the most intimate and subversive sentiments,

'Or, then, must we doubt irremediably the modesty of our women?' Officials hoped they could count on the modesty of at least some French women, and some clearly befriended their North African patients with the most innocent of motives, but it was still important to inform the nurses 'of the danger of their enthusiasm, even the most modest, for our Muslim soldiers: to enlighten [the nurses] about [the soldiers'] military qualities, but also about their moral qualities, alas deplorable'.[57] Still, it was not clear that it would be politically wise to interfere too overtly with the mail, even though wartime censorship was no secret, and in any case, soldiers and civilians often found ways around such measures. However, a more subtle campaign to educate French women about the peculiar nature of *indigènes* and the sensitivity of relationships with them did appear appropriate. A December 1915 circular from the *Service de Santé* noted the problems with the 'too maternal' behavior of the nurses, which presented 'for our *indigènes* as for our French families a true danger', and mandated that nurses were thenceforth to have periodic meetings with knowledgeable doctors and interpreters 'to inform them of the very special mentality of our indigenous soldiers'.[58]

Nonetheless, the problem did not go away. In May 1917, an *officier interprète* reported relationships between North Africans and their nurses at a military hospital in Guerche. Demonstrating the kind of 'modesty' in his language that officials hoped nurses would display in their postcards to the *indigènes*, this officer noted that the soldiers were 'having conversations with the nurses', and a letter intercepted from a Mme Laurent 'leads one to believe that these conversations have been pushed a little too far'.[59] One solution to this problem, of course, was to staff the hospitals where *troupes indigènes* would be treated with male nurses. This was the solution that one General made after inspecting several of these facilities. Noting that the soldiers 'acquire in France a morality, or rather an immorality, which does not honor us, and which they boast of in their correspondence with Algeria', he advocated forbidding closed letters and removing women from the hospitals. However, he admitted that this last measure would be difficult to accomplish.[60] The authorities did in fact stipulate that only male nurses should treat wounded or sick West African soldiers, but the relationships between these men and women in and around their hospitals indicate that the army was unable to maintain strictly this prescription.[61] The elliptical nature of authorities' descriptions of these contacts indicated their discomfort and suspicion that any interaction between West Africans and French women was inappropriate, potentially subversive, and perhaps even sexual. A report on correspondence from the large camp at

Fréjus-St. Raphael noted that 'our *indigènes* are cared for at the home of Madame Bourdieu' near their hospital. Another local woman was also implicated for having 'many connections with the Senegalese world'.[62] Officials disapproved of these kinds of relationships and did what they could to discourage them, though their continuation proved the effects of such efforts to be limited.

As these references made clear, the problem of interactions between *troupes indigènes* and French civilians stretched beyond nurses in hospitals to other women and even entire families in their homes. This expansion of contact was particularly alarming to officials, as it spread potential disorder both more broadly among more soldiers and more widely in French society and into the intimate spaces of French homes. These issues came to a head in the middle of 1915, with a proposal to allow North African soldiers, smarting under army policy that denied most of them leave to visit their families, to apply for a period of leave to visit French families willing to host the men in their homes. One Ministry-of-War official responded to the proposal by pointing out that it was unlikely that a soldier's stay with 'persons foreign to his race, his language, his mentality' would raise his morale, as a period of leave was designed to do. Such an experience would affect the *indigènes* negatively:

> The debilitating influence exercised over our indigenous soldiers by the attentive care that the female personnel of our hospitals lavish upon them suggests that their admission to the homes of French families, [and] the care and well-being with which they will be surrounded [there], will lead to the same consequences.[63]

And French families would suffer as well: 'Those of these families who are totally ignorant about the mentality and the ways of our Muslim soldiers will come to regret their generous offer'.[64] Another official also noted that it was unlikely that the results of allowing *indigènes* to associate with French families would be any better than the unfortunate results arising from contact with Red Cross nurses, such as 'often passionate correspondence'. Families of the metropole would not be familiar with the *indigènes'* mentality, and these men would search out 'indulgent' families and use the hospitality accorded them to move about freely in French cities, 'to exploit the credulity and the generosity of the public'. The soldiers would certainly have intimate encounters with French women, and this unleashed primitive and degenerate sexuality would pose a danger to public health and hygiene, 'if one considers that most of them are syphilitic'.[65]

The exploitation of the French public's hospitality and gullibility was a recurring fear for French officials trying to police the behavior of thousands of colonial subjects let loose on the streets of the metropole. One *officier interprète* cautioned his superiors about the *indigènes'* native cunning, as they sought out civilians, women in particular, who were 'naïve', unlike the Europeans of Algeria, who would never fall for their wiles. At once persistent and hypocritical, these men would seek money or sexual favors, often skillfully using promises of marriage to obtain the latter, and the army could expect all manner of indiscipline from men whose military worth had thus been spoiled.[66] Often, it seemed that officers had a difficult time deciding whose behavior they found more deplorable, their men or the naïve and fallen women who consorted with them. A nurse, who at one point drove all the way from Paris to the camp for North African soldiers at Aix in an automobile to see her paramour, persisted in sending letters which included some phrases she had learned to write in Arabic. Apparently, the officer who read them considered these unspecified phrases inappropriate, as he described her use of Arabic as 'flouting decency'. Her behavior had ruined the attitude of her correspondent, who had been punished for insubordination: he had been 'a good soldier', but 'today he appears [to have] irremediably lost [his] military spirit'.[67] Still, this soldier was probably not as far gone as another whom an *officier interprète* met on the street in Marseilles. This Algerian had adopted 'the attitude and dress of a pimp', with 'long hair, curled [and] greased, a garish scarf, hat pushed back on his head with some sort of medal on the front', all this after spending seven days on leave with a French woman in the neighborhood.[68] The anxieties such behavior raised could provoke extreme reactions. In one case, an officer reported a North African soldier for having broken the rules by spending his leave periods after being treated for wounds at the apartment of a Parisian woman, even though the officer knew full well that the woman was the soldier's wife. Despite his legitimate marriage to a French woman, the officer felt that this and similar 'deplorable practices' by other *indigènes* should be stopped.[69]

At the root of military authorities' worries was the conviction that the French women who became romantically involved with these soldiers did not adequately understand the 'indigenous mentality'. Censors noted that these women had formed 'an erroneous ideal' of the soldiers and their way of life in the colonies. One letter that illustrated particularly well the phenomenon of women 'steeped in Orientalism', the censors in Tunis asserted, was that of Mme Marthe Crozat to Tunisian soldier Salah Ben Amor. After having been posted back to his regiment at Bizerte, Ben Amor sent her a package containing a rug as a gift. Mme Crozat wrote in return,

> In fact, looking at this rug, I cannot help but think of the luxury which is laid out in your beautiful homes, so firmly closed off, of your delicious harems, so well hidden away, where the women of Africa and of all the Orient are found, so perfectly happy because they have a comfort that many French women envy, thanks to soft rugs of many colors....[70]

Several months later, another woman's correspondence revealed the dangers of being 'seduced by the mirage of the Orient'. This woman had married a Tunisian with the intention of moving to North Africa with him, but he had been posted back to Bizerte, and she had lost contact with him. Her last letter to him had been returned marked 'unknown', and she had learned that while their marriage was legal in France, at home in Tunisia her husband had the right to take up to four wives and even to repudiate her if he so chose. She admitted to suffering terribly, but wrote that she 'did not have the courage to leave him', even though with her property she could have made a better marriage. The censor noted the pathos of the situation, as here was a woman 'whom no moral consideration or material interest seemed to be able to restrain'.[71] Even some of the *indigènes* themselves expressed doubts about the understanding of some of the women who became involved in interracial relationships. One Madagascan counseled a friend who was talking of marriage to a French woman to let her know that he was poor and what life was like in Madagascar, and to be sure that she would not arrive in the colony, regret the status of other European women who live there, and kill either herself or her new husband to escape her fate.[72]

Images across the color line

These kinds of situations exemplified for authorities the destabilizing effects that interracial relationships had upon metropolitan society, as French women were apparently deluded and sometimes suffering for their transgression of racial and sexual boundaries. That they were deluded and suffered was bad enough, but it was all the more galling to male French officials that this was occurring at the hands of colonial subjects. Even more humiliating, it quickly became apparent that *indigènes* were providing friends and family in the colonies with visual proof of their transgressions in the form of photographs, and these were not always merely pictures of nurses in their Red Cross uniforms.

In many ways, the censors were more concerned about the subversive effects of these images than they were about the written and verbal testimony of the soldiers. This was in part, no doubt, because it represented another dramatic inversion of the colonial order, as 'traditional exoticism' had featured nude indigenous women for the fascinated gaze of European men.[73] In November 1916, the censors in Marseille reported that they had destroyed several postcards, bound for Indochina, which pictured 'nude French women in poses more or less academic with, on the other side, some reflections of doubtful taste'.[74] As this was fairly early in the life of formal censorship, and as the majority of Indochinese soldiers were yet to arrive in France, there were relatively few of these postcards, 13 in all. However, a few months later, the censors were alarmed to see the volume increase dramatically. By February of the next year, they were confiscating numerous 'photographs of nude women, the subjects of which decorate only rarely our museums of painting or sculpture', and, what was worse, the censors suspected that the traffic in these images had begun before the institution of regular censorship.[75] In March, they seized over 400 'nudités' along with another 100 photographs accompanied by 'libidinous or lewd comments'. Shocked, the censor noted, 'One of these is most obscene'. This state of affairs was 'absolutely disconcerting', all the more so as the Indochinese did not make any attempt to hide their 'vices' from their families, sending lewd pictures and remarks to their mothers and fathers, wives, and even their children. Often the soldiers accompanied the photos with the remark, 'There are only such marvels in France', but censors observed that 'this admiration of French beauty is not without irreverence'. Remarkably, as disconcerted as they were about the *nudités*, the censors seemed even more worried about the photographs the Indochinese sent home of themselves in the company of white women. Such proof of interracial contact was damaging to 'our prestige in the Far East', so the censors confiscated 23 of these images.[76]

That same month, Sergeant Thai Hu Tham wrote to his brother in Indochina. Tham warned his brother to be skeptical of the photos that soldiers sent home, as many had their pictures taken with prostitutes in order to present them as their fiancés or wives. He assured his brother that the 'women in the countryside' were not like these urban prostitutes, and such virtuous women were good conversationalists who sometimes let one hold their hand, 'or kiss, but not . . . '. The censors observed, however, that such laudatory remarks were rare, and 'the Indochinese repertoire has furnished some new terms for a comparative anatomy which is not at all flattering to French women'. The report noted that though many of the hundreds of pictures confiscated originated from Indochinese workers in France, many also came from soldiers, even those at the front in combat units, and a later report claimed that during September 1918 soldiers sent most of the *nudités*, 'as usual'.[77] In December 1918, censors gave a final accounting of all the photos seized from mail to Indochina during the two years of their work. Almost 10,000 images were listed according to the following categories: nudes, undressed, bathers, kissing, mixed-race children, photographs of French women, photographs of Franco-Indochinese couples.[78] These categories made it clear that French authorities considered any visual proof of interracial relationships – from suggestive or fully- or partly-nude pictures of French women, to photos of mixed-race children, to photos of French women in the company of *indigènes* – as potentially subversive. Moreover, it was not just Indochinese soldiers who sent these images home. Censors in Tunis reported that one North African sent home a photograph of a Muslim soldier with his arm around a very young French girl, along with a message in Arabic that read, 'I ask you, my brother, to tell me if this young girl pleases you, in which case I will procure one for you [and] you can then do with her what you like'. Others sent pictures of French women with obscene captions, such as, 'One can have this young thing for a few francs…'.[79]

Troupes indigènes from all of the colonies engaged in this traffic in photos between the metropole and the colonies, rendering the problem very serious in the eyes of military officials. Consequently, on 5 June 1917, the Ministry of War issued a circular formally forbidding the photographs and ordering the seizure and destruction of all obscene pictures and postcards, though this had already been de facto policy for some time.[80] Yet the effect of this circular upon the behavior of the soldiers was at first limited. A report on Indochinese correspondence for the same month in which the circular appeared observed that despite the new formal policy and severe punishments for transgressions, the number of *nudités* seized had only slightly decreased (from 480 during the previous month to 349).[81] By April, however, the strict policy seemed to have begun working, as the number had decreased further (to 216).[82] Still, in later months this number was sometimes higher, and there were other indications that the authorities were not entirely able to prevent the ill effects of these images. Some *indigènes* labored to find ways around the strictures, the most creative of which was probably that employed by Fang, a worker who wrote to a friend from the hospital that he could not get any more *nudités* as requested, because the sale of them was forbidden, but, 'In order to simplify, I will draw some myself and send them to you'.[83] Moreover, the existence of the restrictive policy itself provided possible occasions for criticizing French assumptions of racial superiority. In August 1917, an Indochinese letter writer observed that officials had forbidden *nudités* because 'the French fear ridicule'.[84] It seemed, then, that French officials faced ridicule whether they allowed the traffic in these photos to continue (the *indigènes* laughing either at the nudity of their proud colonial masters, or at the impotence of French men to prevent their women from behaving shamelessly, or both), or whether they forbade it (the French fearing their colonial subjects' laughter, or French men, unable to exercise control over their women, resorting to cracking down on *indigènes* who looked at the photographs). If, as George Orwell contended, the white man's life in the colonies 'was one long struggle not to be laughed at', then the traffic in these images and the resulting risk of ridicule presented a serious challenge to the white prestige upon which colonial rule rested.[85]

Consequences

Photographs, as visual proof of the willingness of French women to have relationships with colonial men, were indeed striking and hence prized by *indigènes* eager to inform and titillate friends and family back home, but they were not necessary, nor were they even the only form of proof. For instance, Sergeant-Major Hô sent to his brother in Indochina letters he had received from French women, and told him to save them as 'sacred things' that the Sergeant could, upon his return, show to European *colons* who did not believe his stories and who might mock him for his pretensions to relations with white women. Censors were quite candid about the ultimate consequences for public order and French rule in the colonies: examples, like Sergeant Hô, of the 'deplorable attitude' that many *troupes indigènes* had acquired during their stay in France would lead the population of Indochina to think that the French lived in a 'shameful debauchery'.[86] The sexual (mis)conduct of *indigènes* in France, and its consequences, soon became the main preoccupation of the military officials charged with reading their mail. Censors worried, often explicitly, about the effect upon the 'prestige' of white women in the colonies.[87] Put succinctly in a report on the correspondence of North Africans, 'Some of these letters are injurious to French women'.[88] And injuries to French women and their prestige were equally injuries to France and the white prestige that justified and supported European rule.

The authorities certainly did not want rumors spread in the colonies like the one Hussein el Gassem Blagui described in a letter to friends in Tunisia:

> I would like to inform you that the Minister has directed that as soon as the war is finished, each soldier must marry, whether he likes it or not, a young French girl; reservists will have the right to a virgin, and active soldiers to a young and beautiful woman. There we are then, o my brother, stuck. No matter, thank God anyway![89]

Nor was it gratifying to the officials who had brought these *indigènes* to France to see a Tunisian send home a picture of a young French woman and her younger sister, with an accompanying letter that indicated neither of these women wanted him to leave France. Of course, he wrote, he did not want to leave France either, as there were even better women than these around for the taking. Though another Tunisian complained of the cold of French winters, he was able to withstand them, he wrote, because French women helped him keep warm, and he assured his correspondent that if he too came to France, he would be 'very debauched'.[90] Far from stimulating their enthusiasm for coming to France and making war on Germany for what officials would regard as the right reasons – a sense of obligation to France for the benefits colonial rule had ostensibly brought to the colonies, even a kind of patriotism – the experiences these soldiers had in the metropole making love with French women inspired them with a desire to stay in France for very different reasons. One Madagascan, whose physical condition was so poor (from wounds or sickness) that he was slated to be sent home, obtained a period of leave to remain in France. 'I invoked', he wrote, 'my great desire to continue to serve the fatherland, but in reality, I find French women too pretty and nice and I would hate to leave them already'. Another encouraged a friend in Madagascar not to be slow in volunteering for service in France because 'the white women whom we believe haughty and disdainful at home, are here before us just like little dogs, they lick the soles of our feet... Some of them are as pretty as angels [there followed, the censor noted, "obscene details," which he did not specify]... each Madagascan has his own'.[91] One exasperated officer asked how one could expect to maintain the loyalty of North Africans when they were 'obsessed by the *idée fixe* of satisfying their violent passions and the image of defending the *Patrie* is erased entirely from their mind'.[92]

Eventually, officials began to suspect that their efforts to discourage and prevent 'liaisons' between *indigènes* and French women could not stop contact altogether, and despite what authorities often wanted to believe, many of these relationships were of a genuinely romantic and serious nature. By 1918, for example, at least 250 Indochinese men had married French women and 231 such couples were living together in the metropole, with these and other relationships producing dozens of mixed-race children.[93] More interracial couples, including men from other colonies, no doubt escaped the officials' accounting, and some French women had certainly emigrated to the colonies to be with their beloved. Such circumstances caused officials to reflect upon the consequences of these relationships and to consider their own role in policing them. In March 1917, censors admitted that the problem of the liaisons between Indochinese men and French women was not going to go away and that officials were confronting not merely overactive libidos and duplicity, but (sometimes, at least) real affection and commitment. When men returned home to their colony of origin, whole families were left desolate in France, especially when the union produced children, and the army received urgent requests for the return of the man to the metropole. 'Should we', the report asked, 'respect these consensual unions, especially when they are consecrated by a birth?' The obligation the state owed to the children seemed to indicate that the answer was yes. As for young mothers, their situation was desperate. Should the authorities condone in certain cases the regularization of the union by marriage? Here the report seemed to espouse a liberal view on the matter of integrating these (admittedly few) men into French society: 'Assimilation increases day by day, to such an extent that this stage could be easily reached by a rather large number of *indigènes*, if their stay in France is prolonged for many more months'.[94] In other words, perhaps these unions would perform the ideological work of French imperialism, civilizing colonial subjects.

Nevertheless, just as voices touted the benefits of *métissage* to bring the French and subject 'races' closer together only occasionally during certain periods of French imperial history, there was never any doubt about the overall negative official attitude toward these wartime unions.[95] As the war continued and the stay of Indochinese men in France grew longer and longer, bringing evidence of more and more relationships and, especially, births of *métis* children, alarmed censors admitted that there was little or nothing authorities could do to 'prevent the liaisons and the consequences which result from them'.[96] In November 1917, a report summed up at length the predicament facing authorities. The number and sincerity of 'amorous letters' was beginning to give the censors pause. Whole families were evidently embracing Indochinese men who courted their daughters. The most intelligent letter writers were aware of official censorship of the mails, and found alternative ways to correspond, while the less perceptive grew angry and bitter over the perceived failure of their beloved to respond. 'What can we do?...To protect the French woman for us is an urgent duty, but stopping a few letters is a palliative which loses all of its value when the writer remains in the country'. Intrusive censorship might be too grave a restriction on individual liberty, as well as providing a new source of complaint against the government for both French people and *indigènes*. The Indochinese chafed at being treated 'as little boys'. Letters often indicated that these men found French women in the metropole more approachable and likeable than those in the colonies, but, '[w]hile waiting for them to change their opinion of our female compatriots in the Far East, is it a good idea to spoil, in a certain measure, that which they have of us all here?' As a more practical matter, too draconian a surveillance of this correspondence risked exposing the preventative efforts of authorities to ridicule, because despite censorship there were many 'unfortunate French women led astray in obviously grotesque liaisons' which were clearly a form of revenge for mixed unions between European men and indigenous women in the colonies. In the end, the report recommended discretely warning women and families of the risks they were running by welcoming colonial men into their homes, beds, and hearts.[97]

Ultimately, however, officials were concerned about the effects of these interracial relationships not only upon French metropolitan society, but also upon the social and political order in the colonies. The problems overseas were potentially more destructive over the long term. Within weeks after the war ended in November 1918, the French began repatriating the *troupes indigènes* who had helped bring about the recent victory over Germany. By 1920 many of these men were home. Now the problem was no longer the stories and pictures that they sent home in envelopes, but those that they brought home with their own persons, and there was no form of censorship that could effectively prevent these men from telling of their experiences. Moreover, these men had gained the kind of experience, skills, and in some cases education that would make them leaders in their societies in the postwar years. With their newfound perspective on the prestige of European women and white superiority, bulwarks of the colonial order, such men would in all probability be more difficult to rule. After the war, one official articulated this concern explicitly, worrying that some Indochinese men who had served in France would return to the colony with new ideas and be less 'submissive' to 'their traditional discipline'.[98] The colonial administration in Indochina was a few steps ahead on this issue, having already instructed regional officials in June 1918 to interrogate and maintain close surveillance on returning soldiers.[99]

It would be difficult to determine whether French officials were correct about the effect of these relationships, as that would entail identifying colonial subjects who were involved with European women and then tracking their behavior as they spread out over the vast French colonial empire during the postwar period – a large, complicated, and perhaps impossible task. However, there are indications that military and colonial officials did observe the behavior of some of these men, and that, at the very least, authorities believed their wartime anxieties to be justified. To take one example, an official in Tunisia claimed in 1921 that, 'All the *tirailleurs* are coming back ... with ideas clearly turned around as far as French prestige, and European prestige in general, are concerned'. Those who served in France during the war 'were welcomed too warmly into French families, where it was too often repeated to them that they were the saviors of the country'. Unhappily, these men had now become aware of 'their importance and their strength', and worse, 'the license of certain *milieux* and the impropriety of too many women have succeeded in destroying the respect they had for us, and all of the countryside (*le bled*) now knows about the amusing adventures' these soldiers had in French society.[100] Circumstances like these demonstrated how much, in the words of one historian, 'the First World War was experienced by colonial authorities as traumatic experiment'.[101]

In official French eyes, soldiers' changed attitudes did not bode well for the future of the French colonial empire. In this respect, though historians debate the significance of the experiences of *troupes indigènes* in raising political consciousness among colonized peoples and in stimulating nationalist and independence movements, the use of these troops and their experiences moving (and loving) across the color line did provoke significant fears about the stability of the colonial order.[102] The high point of French imperialism in the postwar years, which saw the addition of former Ottoman territories in the Middle East to the French colonial empire, and the hyperbole of imperial propaganda that culminated in the celebratory Colonial Exposition of 1931 in Paris, then, perhaps masked a deeper fear that the Great War had produced circumstances that would doom European colonial empires. Indeed, as one historian has put it, the postwar years saw a 'double movement of pride and worry, of pride in the work accomplished but also of fear for the fate that history might have in store for it'.[103] In short, in a postwar context that saw a shift toward stricter notions of racial hierarchies in the justification of colonial rule, French officials worried that *indigènes'* less exalted view of white French people, whom they had visited, loved, and even seen naked, set the stage for challenges to that rule.[104]

Conclusion

At the beginning of the period of decolonization that would bring about an end to European colonial empires, the Tunisian writer Albert Memmi observed of the colonial order, 'It is essential that this order not be questioned by others, and especially not by the colonized'.[105] French authorities recognized this as well, but the participation of *troupes indigènes* in the war effort in France after 1914 raised numerous unsettling questions. Many of these arose out of contacts between colonial subjects in uniform and white French women. These contacts, especially when intimate, violated the rigid separation between white and nonwhite that prevailed in the colonies. Such crossing over the color line threatened white prestige at a point French officials considered most vulnerable and sensitive, a point loaded with sexual and racial significance. The behavior of French civilians, especially women, was a concern as they too seemed to be questioning, or at least inspiring *indigènes* to question, the restrictions and boundaries of the colonial order. Citizens of the metropole blurred the color line by failing to observe strictures upon interracial mixing that were much more vigorously, and much more easily, enforced in the colonies themselves. *Métis* offspring of interracial couples constituted the most spectacular and disturbing visual proof of grave moral, social, and racial transgressions. Visual proof also came in the form of pictures and postcards of the unrestrained sexuality of French women and the access that *indigènes* had to that sexuality, either as partners or as voyeurs. This too caused French officials no end of trouble, as they feared the spread of these photographs into indigenous societies, and thus the amplification of a wartime metropolitan problem into a postwar, empire-wide concern.

The overriding fear that all of this activity provoked was the undermining of white prestige, and thus of French power, in the colonies.

Colonial subjects who had had sexual contact across the color line, or had seen it in photographs, or had heard about it from reliable sources, might be less willing to subject themselves to colonial and racial hierarchies. Sex and love between colonial men and French women was an intimate challenge to a racial order that was indispensable to the entire colonial system, for, as Memmi put it, 'Racism appears then, not as an incidental detail, but as a consubstantial part of colonialism... Not only does it establish a fundamental discrimination between colonizer and colonized, a *sine qua non* of colonial life, but it also lays the foundation for the immutability of that life'.[106] Interracial relationships disproved both sides of the equation, demonstrating that discrimination did not have to be universal and showing that the relationship between colonizer and colonized was mutable, could change and take different, less restrictive forms.

Official reactions to these relationships demonstrated at least an instinctive awareness of just these sorts of dangers. Much like the existence of *métis* in the colony (almost always the offspring of a European man and indigenous woman), relationships between indigenous soldiers and white women provided 'living proof of the impossibility of sustaining the very basis of colonial domination' because they violated the dualistic racial and cultural oppositions upon which colonialism depended.[107] This was 'the fundamental contradiction of imperial domination: the tension between a form of authority simultaneously predicated on incorporation and distancing'.[108] Colonial subjects, especially those in uniform fighting for France, were in theory part of the nation, but were also distanced from it by their racial identity. If that distance disappeared, then so would colonialism, the French empire, power, prestige, and much else that mattered very much to French officials. Their anxieties about these matters became more acute as they recognized, to a certain extent, their powerlessness to stop much of this activity.[109] Colonial authorities had always been interested in extending bio-power into the area 'where they had equivocal control – in the home'.[110] Now, ironically, at home in the metropole and in the homes of French civilians, military and political officials found that their control was even more equivocal, because of the social and administrative disorder war brought with it; because of the greater freedoms and liberality of the social order of the metropole, at least when compared with the colonies; and because of the political and cultural terrain created by the leaders of the French army and state themselves, asking men to wear a uniform, to be a part of the nation and perhaps die in its defense.[111]

Notes

The author wishes to thank Alice Conklin, Jean Pedersen, Alice Bullard, and Matt Matsuda for their helpful comments on various versions of this essay. The essay also appears in Richard S. Fogarty, *Race and War in France: Colonial Subjects in the French Army, 1914–1918* (Baltimore, MD, 2008), and in condensed form in *Historical Reflections/Réflexions Historiques* 34, 1 (Spring 2008), 50–72.

1. *Service Historique de l'Armée de Terre* (SHAT) 7N995: Commission de Contrôle Postal (CP) Marseille, 'Annamites en France', 2 janvier 1917.
2. *Centre des Archives d'Outre-Mer* (CAOM) Service de liaison avec les orginaires des territoires français d'Outre-mer (SLOTFOM) III, 143: M. Lacombe, Contrôle Postal Annamite, 12 février 1917.
3. B. Anderson, *Imagined Communities: Reflections on the Origin and Spread of Nationalism*, Revised Edition (New York, 1991), p. 149.
4. As Frantz Fanon put it, 'I wish to be acknowledged not as *black* but as *white*. Now ... who but a white woman can do this for me? By loving me she proves that I am worthy of white love. I am loved like a white man. I am a white man ....' *Black Skin, White Masks* (New York, 1967), p. 63.
5. On race and gender in the imperial context, see A. L. Stoler and F. Cooper, 'Between Metropole and Colony: Rethinking a Research Agenda', in their edited collection, *Tensions of Empire: Colonial Cultures in a Bourgeois World* (Berkeley, 1997); M. Strobel, 'Gender, Sex, and Empire', in M. Adas, ed., *Islamic and European Expansion: The Forging of a Global Order* (Philadelphia, 1993), pp. 345–375; N. Chaudhuri and M. Strobel, eds, *Western Women and Imperialism: Complicity and Resistance* (Bloomington, 1992); R. J. C. Young, *Colonial Desire: Hybridity in Theory, Culture and Race* (New York, 1995); J. Clancy-Smith and F. Gouda, eds, *Domesticating the Empire: Race, Gender, and Family Life in French and Dutch Colonialism* (Charlottesville, 1998).
6. N. Yuval-Davis and F. Anthias, eds, *Woman-Nation-State* (New York, 1989).
7. A. L. Stoler, *Carnal Knowledge and Imperial Power: Race and the Intimate in Colonial Rule* (Berkeley, 2002), p. 6.
8. On European women's changing roles in the colonies, see T. Stovall, 'Love, Labor, and Race: Colonial Men and White Women in France during the Great War', in T. Stovall and G. Van Den Abbeele, eds, *French Civilization and Its Discontents: Nationalism, Colonialism, Race* (Lanham, 2003), pp. 299, 301–302; Stoler, *Carnal Knowledge*; and A. Conklin, 'Redefining "Frenchness": Citizenship, Race Regeneration, and Imperial Motherhood in France and West Africa, 1914–1940', in Clancy-Smith and Gouda, eds, *Domesticating the Empire*, pp. 65–83.
9. M. Foucault, *Discipline and Punish: The Birth of the Prison* (New York, 1979), p. 139.
10. M. Foucault, *The History of Sexuality, Volume I: An Introduction* (New York, 1990), pp. 103, 143.
11. A. L. Stoler, *Race and the Education of Desire: Foucault's History of Sexuality and the Colonial Order of Things* (Durham, 1995). See also *Carnal Knowledge*, chapter 6, 'A Colonial Reading of Foucault: Bourgeois Bodies and Racial Selves', pp. 140–161.

12. The main concern here is with men, both *troupes indigènes* and French offi-
    cials, though these relationships also provide at least an indirect view of the
    experiences of the French women who were the objects of, on the one hand,
    desire and love, and on the other, concern and dismay.
13. The term 'the color line' figured prominently in the context of American
    race relations because of Frederick Douglass's and W. E. B. Du Bois's use of the
    term, but it is also useful in describing the rigid racial boundaries imposed by
    French colonialism. See T. Stovall, 'The Color Line behind the Lines: Racial
    Violence in France during the Great War', *American Historical Review*, 103, 3
    (June 1998), 737–769. On 'love across the color line', see his 'Love, Labor,
    and Race', as well as B. A. Berliner, *Ambivalent Desire: The Exotic Black Other
    in Jazz-Age France* (Amherst, 2002), chapter 2, 'Love and the Color Line',
    pp. 37–70.
14. SHAT 7N997: CP Malgache, Novembre 1917. On wartime postal censor-
    ship in France, see M. Rajsfus, *La Censure militaire et policière (1914–1918)*
    (Paris, 1999); and G. Liens, 'La Commission de censure et la Commis-
    sion de contrôle postal à Marseille pendant la première guerre mon-
    diale', *Revue d'Histoire moderne et contemporaine* 18 (October–December
    1971).
15. On colonial workers in France during the war, see B. Nogaro and L. Weil, *La
    Main-d'Oeuvre Étrangère et Colonial pendant la Guerre* (Paris, 1926); J. Horne,
    'Immigrant Workers in France during World War I', *French Historical Studies*,
    15, 1 (Spring 1985), 57–88; and T. Stovall, 'Colour-blind France? Colonial
    Workers during the First World War', *Race and Class*, 35, 2 (October–
    December 1993), 35–55. On women in the World-War-One labor force, see
    J. F. McMillan, *Housewife or Harlot: The Place of Women in French Society, 1870–
    1940* (New York, 1981), pp. 131–162; M. H. Darrow, *French Women and the
    First World War: War Stories of the Home Front* (Oxford, 2000), pp. 169–228.
16. SHAT 7N997: CP Indochinois, septembre 1917.
17. Lucie Cousturier, *Des inconnus chez moi* (Paris, 1920).
18. SHAT 7N997: CP Malgache, septembre 1917.
19. SHAT 9N691 (Supplément): Direction des Troupes Coloniales to Comman-
    dant of Fréjus, 'AS dépôt de convalescents Sénégalais à Menton', 14 juillet
    1915.
20. SHAT 7N997: CP Malgache, septembre 1917.
21. CAOM SLOTFOM I, 8: CP Indochinois, août 1918.
22. SHAT 7N997: CP Indochinois, septembre 1917.
23. Ibid. On perceptions of black Africans' sexual potency and depravity, see
    W. B. Cohen, *The French Encounter with Africans: White Responses to Blacks,
    1530–1880* (Bloomington, 1980). Similar perceptions prevailed for other
    non-whites in the colonial empire; see Stovall, 'Love, Labor, and Race',
    pp. 300, 310.
24. SHAT 7N997: CP Marseille, juillet-août 1917, 'Les soldats malgaches en
    France'.
25. *Archives du Ministère des Affaires Étrangers* (AMAE) G1665: Résident General
    (RG) Alapetite to Ministre des Affaires Étrangères (MAE), 'Naturalisation des
    indigènes musulmans', 16 mai 1915.
26. SHAT 7N2107: CP Tunis, décembre 1916. For more on duplicitous roman-
    tic behavior by Indochinese men in France during this period, see K. Hill,

'A Westward Journey, An Enlightened Path: Vietnamese Linh Tho, 1915–1930' (Ph.D. Dissertation, University of Oregon, 2001), pp. 165–166.
27. SHAT 7N997: CP Indochinois, août 1917.
28. Ibid.
29. Ibid.
30. A. L. Stoler, 'Making Empire Respectable: The Politics of Race and Sexual Morality in Twentieth-Century Colonial Cultures', *American Ethnologist*, 16, 4 (November 1989), 636–639.
31. CAOM SLOTFOM III, 143: M. Lacombe, CP Annamite, 12 février 1917.
32. CAOM SLOTFOM I, 8: CP Indochinois, octobre 1917.
33. CAOM SLOTFOM I, 8: CP Malgache, décembre 1917.
34. SHAT 7N997: CP Malgache, septembre 1917.
35. M. Favre-Le Van Ho, 'Un milieu porteur de modernisation: travailleurs et tirailleurs vietnamiens en France pendant la première guerre mondiale' (Thèse de doctorat, École national des chartes, 1986), p. 539.
36. CAOM DSM5: L'Officier Interprète Dijan, Rapport Hebdomadaire, 9 mai 1917.
37. SHAT 7N2107: CP Tunis, janvier 1917.
38. SHAT 7N997: CP Indochinois, août 1917.
39. Ibid.
40. SHAT 7N997: CP Indochinois, novembre 1917.
41. SHAT 7N2107: Commission Militaire de Contrôle Postal, Tunis, février 1917.
42. CAOM DSM6: Observations de M. Reymond Officier Interprète Principal, 28 novembre 1917.
43. See M. L. Roberts, *Civilization without Sexes: Reconstructing Gender in Postwar France, 1917–1927* (Chicago, 1994), and J. McMillan, 'The Great War and Gender Relations: The Case of French Women and the First World War Revisited', in G. Braybon, ed., *Evidence, History and the Great War: Historians and the Impact of 1914–1918* (New York, 2003), pp. 135–153.
44. Favre, 'Un milieu porteur', pp. 539–540
45. CAOM SLOTFOM I, 8: CP Indochinois, octobre 1917.
46. Stoler, *Carnal Knowledge*, chapter 4, 'Sexual Affronts and Racial Frontiers: Cultural Competence and the Dangers of Métissage', pp. 79–111. See also O. White, *Children of the Empire: Miscegenation and Colonial Society in French West Africa, 1895–1960* (Oxford, 1999); E. Saada, 'Race and Sociological Reason in the Republic: Inquiries on the *Métis* in the French Empire (1908–37)', *International Sociology*, 17, 3 (September 2002), 361–391; A. Bullard, *Exile to Paradise: Savagery and Civilization in Paris and the South Pacific, 1790–1900* (Stanford, 2000), pp. 210–233; F. Vergès, *Monsters and Revolutionaries: Colonial Family Romance and Métissage* (Durham, 1999); R. Harris, 'The "Child of the Barbarian": Rape, Race, and Nationalism in France during the First World War', *Past and Present*, 141 (November 1993), 170–206.
47. J. Yee, '*Métissage* in France: A Postmodern Fantasy and Its Forgotten Precedents', *Modern & Contemporary France*, 11, 4 (2003), 411–425.
48. See J. Lunn, *Memoirs of the Maelstrom: A Senegalese Oral History of the First World War* (Portsmouth, 1999), p. 172.
49. SHAT 7N2103: Rapport de l'Officier Interprète Reymond, 14 juillet 1915.
50. Stoler, *Carnal Knowledge*, p. 61. On suspicions about nurses and their sexuality, see Darrow, *French Women*, pp. 142–151; For more general suspicions

of working women, see McMillan, *Housewife or Harlot?*; Roberts, *Civilization without Sexes*, pp. 188–196; Stovall, 'Love, Labor, and Race', pp. 300–301.

51. SHAT 7N2103: Rapport de l'Officier Interprète Reymond, 14 juillet 1915.
52. Ibid.
53. SHAT 7N2112: L'Officier Interprète Galtier, Rapport Hebdomadaire no. 41, 11 september 1915.
54. Hill, 'A Westward Journey', p. 166.
55. SHAT 7N2112: L'Officier interprète Brudo to Gen Cdt 17ᵉ Region, 14 décember 1915.
56. SHAT 7N2112: Ministre de la Guerre (MG) to Gen Cdt 17ᵉ Region, 28 décembre 1915.
57. SHAT 7N2103: Rapport de l'Officier Interprète Reymond, 14 juillet 1915.
58. CAOM DSM5: Sous-Secrétariat d'Etat du Service de Santé, AS de l'état d'esprit des militaires indigènes musulmans, 7 décembre 1915.
59. CAOM DSM5: L'Officier Interprète Benhazera, Rapport Hebdomadaire no. 42, 26 mai 1917.
60. SHAT 7N2107: Inspection Générale des Régions, Général Menestrel, no. 126, 2 septembre 1915.
61. SHAT 7N144: Service de Santé circular, 'Hospitalisation des militaires indigènes sénégalais', 27 mars 1916; Lunn, *Memoirs*, p. 172.
62. CAOM DSM5: Camps de Fréjus-St. Raphael, Interprète Stagiaire Denant, Contrôle de correspondance, 25 janvier 1918.
63. SHAT 7N2111: MG, 1 juin 1915.
64. Ibid.
65. SHAT 7N 2111: SA, 'Note pour Monsieur le Ministre au sujet de l'hébergement dans les familles françaises des militaires indigènes', 8 juin 1915.
66. SHAT 7N2112: L'Officier interprète Galtier, Rapport Hebdomadaire no. 41, 11 septembre 1915.
67. SHAT 7N2111: L'Officier interprète Galtier, Rapport Hebdomadaire no. 60, 22 janvier 1916.
68. SHAT 7N2111: L'Officier interprète Galtier, Rapport Hebdomadaire no. 32, 10 juillet 1915.
69. SHAT 7N2111: Gen Pontavice to Gen Gouverneur Militaire de Paris, 14 juin 1915. The soldier was not in the end punished, as his actions were technically within the regulations in force at the time.
70. SHAT 7N1001: CP Tunis, décembre 1916.
71. SHAT 7N2107: CP Tunis, février 1917.
72. SHAT 7N997: Contrôle Postal Malgache, septembre 1917.
73. J.-Y. Le Naour, *Misères et tourments de la chair durant la Grande Guerre: les moeurs sexuelles des Français, 1914–1918* (Paris, 2002), p. 261; Stovall, 'Love, Labor, and Race', p. 312.
74. CAOM SLOTFOM I, 8: CP Marseille, 25 novembre 1916.
75. CAOM SLOTFOM III, 143: M. Lacombe, CP Annamite, 12 février 1917.
76. CAOM SLOTFOM I, 8: M. Lacombe, CP Annamite, 8 mars 1917.
77. CAOM SLOTFOM I, 8: CP Annamite, mars 1917; CP Indochinois, septembre 1918.
78. CAOM SLOTFOM I, 8: CP Indochinois, décembre 1918.
79. SHAT 7N1001: CP Tunis, juin 1917; octobre 1917.

80. CAOM SLOTFOM III, 143: Direction des Troupes Coloniales, circulaire, 5 juin 1917.
81. CAOM SLOTFOM I, 8: CP Indochinois, juin 1917.
82. CAOM SLOTFOM I, 8: CP Indochinois, avril 1917.
83. CAOM SLOTFOM I, 8: CP Indochinois, juin 1917.
84. SHAT 7N997: CP Indochinois, août 1917.
85. G. Orwell, 'Shooting an Elephant', in S. Orwell and I. Angus, eds, *The Collected Essays, Journalism and Letters of George Orwell, Volume I: An Age Like This, 1920–1940* (New York, 1968), p. 239.
86. CAOM SLOTFOM III, 143: M. Lacombe, CP Annamite, 12 février 1917.
87. SHAT 7N997: CP Indochinois, septembre 1917.
88. SHAT 7N2107: CP Tunis, février 1917.
89. AMAE G1670: Commission Interministérielle des Affaires Musulmanes (CIAM), Séance 8, 27 mai 1915.
90. SHAT 7N2107: CP Tunis, février 1917.
91. SHAT 7N997: CP Malgache, septembre 1917.
92. SHAT 7N2112: L'Officier interprète Galtier, Rapport Hebdomadaire no. 41, 11 septembre 1915.
93. Hill, 'A Westward Journey', p. 168.
94. CAOM SLOTFOM I, 8: CP Indochinois, mars 1918.
95. On the positive value sometimes attributed to miscegenation in the French colonial context, see Owen White, *Children of the French Empire: Miscegenation and Colonial Society in French West Africa, 1895–1960* (Oxford, 1999); Yee, '*Métissage* in France'; S. Belmessous, 'Assimilation and Racialism in Seventeenth and Eighteenth-Century French Colonial Policy', *American Historical Review* 110, 2 (April 2005), 322–349; S. Drescher, *From Slavery to Freedom: Comparative Studies in the Rise and Fall of Atlantic Slavery* (New York, 1999), pp. 295–299. Even the famous nineteenth-century racialist Arthur de Gobineau believed that racial mixing could provide benefits; see Young, *Colonial Desire*, pp. 102ff.; and Cohen, *French Encounter*, pp. 181, 218.
96. CAOM SLOTFOM I, 8: CP Indochinois, janvier 1918.
97. SHAT 7N997: CP Indochinois, novembre 1917.
98. CAOM SLOTFOM I, 4: 'Les indochinois en France', undated [1921].
99. CAOM 9PA13: Circulaire, 2 juin 1918.
100. SHAT 7N2305: Unattributed, 'Note sur l'état d'esprit des tirailleurs tunisiens libérés', no date [summer 1922].
101. Le Naour, *Misères et tourments*, p. 275.
102. For works that emphasize the contribution of veterans and their wartime experiences in weakening French colonial control, see Favre, 'Un milieu porteur'; Hill, 'Westward Journey'; and G. Meynier, *L'Algérie Révélée: La guerre de 1914–1918 et le premier quart du XXᵉ siècle* (Geneva, 1981). For similar arguments about the role of colonial veterans of the First World War in the British Empire, see G. Howe, *Race, War and Nationalism: A Social History of West Indians in the First World War* (Kingston, 2002); and R. Smith, *Jamaican Volunteers in the First World War: Race, Masculinity and the Development of National Consciousness* (Manchester, 2004). On the other hand, G. Mann, *Native Sons: West African Veterans and France in the Twentieth Century* (Durham, NC, 2006), shows that former *tirailleurs sénégalais* occupied an ambiguous, to say the least, position in the evolution of nationalism and independence in Mali.

103. R. Girardet, *L'idée coloniale en France, 1871–1962* (Paris, 1972), p. 136. On the expansion of the French empire as a result of the war, see C. M. Andrew and A. S. Kanya-Forstner, *The Climax of French Imperial Expansion, 1914–1924* (Stanford, 1981). D. Bouche, *Histoire de la colonisation française, Tome second: Flux et reflux (1815–1962)* (Paris, 1991), points out the way in which the 1931 Colonial Exposition in Paris masked systemic weaknesses in the empire, while H. Lebovics, *True France: The Wars over Cultural Identity, 1900–1945* (Ithaca, 1992), pp. 51–52, points to broader anxieties masked by the Exposition.

104. A. Conklin, *A Mission to Civilize: The Republican Idea of Empire in France and West Africa, 1895–1930* (Stanford, 1997) discusses this shift to more rigid notions of race in the colonial context in postwar French West Africa. See also W. Schneider, *Quality and Quantity: The Quest for Biological Regeneration in Twentieth-Century France* (Cambridge, 1990).

105. A. Memmi, *The Colonizer and the Colonized*, Expanded edition (Boston, 1991), p. 76. [Originally published in French in 1957].

106. Memmi, *Colonizer and Colonized*, p. 74.

107. White, *Children of the French Empire*, p. 182.

108. Stoler, *Carnal Knowledge*, p. 83. See also, A. L. Stoler and F. Cooper, 'Introduction', in Cooper and Stoler, eds, *Tensions of Empire*, pp. 1–56.

109. Le Naour, in *Misères et tourments*, p. 270, notes that official attempts to prevent contacts by a policy of segregation did not work. Stovall, in 'Love, Labor, and Race', though in some respects more confident in the success of official intervention (p. 298), also points out that officials succeeded 'not so much in preventing or even limiting individual interracial contacts, but rather in establishing the very idea of a color line in France, particularly one governing relations between members of the opposite sex (p. 313)'.

110. Stoler, *Carnal Knowledge*, p. 153.

111. Stovall, 'Love, Labor, and Race', pp. 310–311, notes that 'opportunities for interracial contact were largely a creation of the French government', which only intensified officials' concern.

3
Italian Fascism's Ethiopian Conquest and the Dream of a Prescribed Sexuality

Marie-Anne Matard-Bonucci

In a 9 May 1936 speech in Rome broadcast over thousands of loudspeakers throughout Italy, Mussolini announced the conquest of Ethiopia. From his Venice Palace where he was cheered on by a teeming crowd, the Duce claimed Italy was giving the world a lesson in civilization, and he celebrated Italy's combat against the 'cruel reign of the arbitrary' and 'millennial slavery' along with the triumph of justice over barbarity. The night before and in a similar atmosphere, the Duce had addressed the regime's organizations for women, and thanked them for having supported the heroism of their brothers, sons, and husbands by resisting the sanctions decreed by the League of Nations.[1] Several months earlier, for the day of 'Faith', groups of women had given up their wedding rings to symbolize the engagement of the entire nation in the colonial adventure.

This communion of genders at the altar of fascist imperialism should not hide the fact that the war in Ethiopia was a high point in the glorification of virility by a regime that had raised it to heights never before attained.[2] Marshal Rodolfo Graziani, who became viceroy of Ethiopia in June 1936, exhorted:

> Remember that the passion of the colonies is the proudest, most masculine and powerful passion an Italian can nurture; love them even more for the sacrifices they have and will continue to cost us than for the riches they will bring us. In the colonies, be ready to measure your capacity for domination and your power as *condottiere* [mercenary soldiers].[3]

A fascist and colonial war, the Ethiopian conflict was thought of as an important moment in the preparatory strategies for the creation of a 'new fascist man'.[4] The Duce, Marshal Graziani and the fascist elite invited soldiers and colonizers to be pitiless and dominating. All means were deemed suitable for squelching an adversary that was as poorly equipped as it was resolute: poison gases, bombings, civilian massacres, annihilation of the elite.[5] Ethiopia was the theater of very extreme violence. As was the case during the high times of *squadrismo* [the use of violence by fascist gangs during the period 1918–1922], soldiers and men of rank experimented with a warrior hubris, whose particular cruelty was justified by the presumed inferiority of the indigenous population. In his journal, the intellectual and fascist officer Giuseppe Bottai deplored episodes of barbarity, perpetrated mainly by officers and commanders: 'The lamb of the middle classes is becoming a little lion, confusing heroism with cruelty'.[6] Starace, the national secretary of the fascist party, hadn't hesitated to set the example by performing shooting exercises on prisoners while soldiers struck a pose close to cadavers or wielded human remains as trophies.

Despite a discourse advertising Italian-style humanism, fascist authorities did not repress the barbarian acts of their combatants, judging it more important to modify their behavior on another terrain: sexuality. Several months after the beginning of hostilities, the relations between Italian men and Ethiopian women became, in the eyes of the fascist elite, a veritable political 'question' and one of the regime's principal battlegrounds.

Ethiopian women, obscure objects of desire

The Ethiopian conquest had been prepared for by several decades of nationalist ideology and had given the Italian population great hopes. In addition to the desire of the poorest to acquire land, there were also more complex motivations in which, as in other colonial contexts, exoticism and eroticism were confusingly intertwined. The legendary beauty of the region's women certainly contributed to the seductive force of this Eldorado, and the hope of possessing them appeared as legitimate as did the claim to the appropriation of their land.

Photos of Ethiopian women that showed them, as did the majority of representations of African women up until the 1930s, stripped of their clothes, as well as popular and wide-selling novels and songs, also contributed both before and after the conquest to the spread of the stereotype of creatures of exacerbated sensuality who were available for the white man's pleasure.[7] In a puritan Italy that only authorized nudity in art, the busts of Ethiopian women nourished sexual fantasy. As Leo

Longansi later recalled, 'Italians were in a hurry to leave. To their eyes, Abyssinia had the appearance of a forest of superb mammals within their grasp'.[8] During the war, many comic drawings reproduced in the media or on post cards showed images of a people contrasting backward and savage men with seductive and forthcoming women.[9] With a tone that was trying-to-be-funny, the artist Enrico De Seta drew a soldier at a post office window in an illustration called 'Post Office'. The soldier was getting ready to send off a strange package: an Abyssinian woman wrapped up in a blanket, with head and feet sticking out![10]

In 1935, the troops had brought the song *Faccetta Nera* (Pretty little black face) along with them on the campaign. The song was first composed in Roman dialect, but the Italian version had become extremely popular.[11] The lyrics were very much in keeping with the complex feelings of the colonizers regarding African women: a desire for possession and domination, the promise of emancipation and civilization, desire and fascination. 'Facetta Nera, Beautiful Abyssinian, wait and hope, your time is coming soon. Once we are with you, we will give you another law and another king. Our law is slavery to love, our slogan is freedom and duty etc'.[12]

The imagination of novelists and lyricists was not unrelated to certain aspects of the reality of relations between men and women in Ethiopia. While restrictions on women's sexuality were still very stringent in Italy, Ethiopians, and especially the Amhara, offered women greater liberty, since relations outside of marriage were not stigmatized as they were in European Catholic countries. Not only was cohabitation practiced without any disapproval – since a local custom called the '*dämòs* marriage' allowed women to be a member of a temporary contractual union – but, as recent work has revealed, from the perspective of Ethiopian women, it could also be an element in a strategy of social elevation, and even emancipation.[13] The practice of *madamismo* was widespread in Somalia and Eritrea, even amongst civil servants and high-ranking military men.[14] In Eritrea, the civil servant Alberto Pollera, however convinced he was of the benefits of the colonization and in spite of his responsibilities, nonetheless fathered six children by two Eritrean women.[15] As Giulia Barrera has put it

> The *madamato* was a set of relationships grounded in the material basis of colonialism and shaped by colonial discourse but it was lived out by concrete individuals: by men who participated in very different ways in the colonial enterprise and by women who were not merely passive victims.[16]

Among the 300,000 pioneers and soldiers present after the conquest, some did indeed experience the 'sweet slavery' mentioned in the song. Even when fascination played no role, cohabitation was understood to be practically the only option, and it represented 'the true institution of sexual relations under colonialism'.[17] In spite of the propaganda designed to attract them, very few women came from the continent to settle in Ethiopia, fearful of insecurity and the precarious conditions of life. Shortly after the conquest, a ship with 2000 wives and fiancées on board was equipped and sent off to the Empire.[18] In 1938, 10,000 Italian women had accepted to participate in the colonial adventure, half of them in the Empire's capital. The regime had also sought to bring in white prostitutes recruited on the peninsula, but once again, the demand exceeded the supply.[19] Men continued assiduously to frequent *sciarmute*, indigenous prostitutes, whose work the authorities attempted to regulate. Among the 1500 women authorized for sex work in Addis Ababa and inspected during medical check-ups, the authorities distinguished between three different categories that were identified by the color of a little flag attached to their *tucul*, the traditional hut: yellow for officers, green for soldiers and workers, black for colonial troops. This institutionalized prostitution and its hierarchy were apparently not enough to satisfy the needs of troops, and certain military officials grew indignant over the long lines stretching in front of indigenous brothels. Moreover, across the territory, occasional or clandestine prostitutes continued to operate.

Between the sexual exploitation of the indigenous population and chastity, there existed a wide range of behavior. Cohabitation, or *concubinage*, was one of these, and it presented several advantages for the colonizers before it was outlawed. Before the Ethiopian conquest, in the Italian colonies of Somalia and Eritrea, it was frequent for colonial administrators, civil servants and military officers to live with African women. The Italians' companions were known as *madames* and cohabitation was known as *madamismo*. These unions often saw the birth of mixed-race children, or *meticci*, who, starting in 1933 and by virtue of the 'Organic Law for Eritrea and Somalia', were given the possibility of obtaining Italian nationality.[20] In 1935 there was a count of 1000 *meticci* in Eritrea out of a population of 3500 Italians.[21] For the colonists, motivations behind moving in with Ethiopian women could have been several, sometimes concomitant ones that didn't exclude being in love: having a companion to share daily life and household chores, having a stable sexual partner who was safer than prostitutes. Indro Montanelli, a journalist who signed up as a volunteer in Ethiopia at age 23, was named head of a squad of indigenous Eritrean men. He claims to have 'bought' a young 12-year-old girl from her father for 500 lira. Though this practice was reprehensible on the continent, it was widespread in the colonies and was justified in the following terms: 'but at age twelve [in Africa], young girls are already women'. When he left Ethiopia, he sold the young girl, 'a docile little animal', to a high-ranking officer who already had a 'little harem' at his disposition.[22]

Before racism became fascism's official doctrine, perspectives on mixed unions were ambivalent. Lidio Cipriani was alarmed by *meticciato*, while the demographer Corrado Gini saw in it an occasion for regenerating European populations, and Domenico Simoncelli, a means of populating the colonies.[23] In the colonial press, mixed unions were not yet being condemned.[24] In the *Illustrazione coloniale* of February 1936, Lorenzo Ratto contrasted the racist attitude of British colonizers with the 'Roman' tradition of fraternization with defeated populations. Condemning relations with 'negroes', he admitted the possibility of mixed unions with Ethiopian women who were considered racially superior: 'the most beautiful girls of the Semitic-Ethiopian race are easily selected on Ethiopian tableland and can be chosen by the pioneers of the rural military engineers to become a part of our colonies as legitimate spouses [...]'.[25]

The specter of *meticciato*

The proclamation of the Empire represented a turning point in the history of racism and of fascist doctrine. Until then, Italian domination of colonial populations had been translated into a fairly banal form of colonial racism. In Libya, there was no legislation on the subject of *meticciato*, and Arabs were allowed to visit European brothels. In addition to the racist economy that valorized Arab populations in relation to the inhabitants of Black Africa, one also finds objective factors that limited the risks of mixed couples procreating: Italian women were there in greater numbers and the institution of 'short-term' marriages did not exist.[26]

It is difficult to decide whether the sexual question functioned as a catalyst or as a revelator of the racist radicalization in the summer of 1936. Mussolini had long been appalled by the very idea of mixed couples. In April 1934, he had ordered that the novel *Black Love* be removed from circulation: 'It's the story of an Italian man's affairs with a negress. Inadmissible on the part of a nation seeking to create an Empire'.[27] Two days after the Empire was declared, the head of the government ordered

Badoglio and Graziani not to authorize any Italian civilian or military official to stay in Ethiopia without a white woman for more than six months so as to avoid 'the terrible and predictable effects of *meticciato*'.[28] At work on setting vast projects for the Empire's economic expansion in place during this same period, Mussolini had explained to Baron Aloisi, the head of the cabinet of the Ministry of Foreign Affairs, his intention to send many Italians, 'but with the obligation that they bring their wives, because the danger of a race of *meticci*, who would become our worst enemies, must be avoided at all costs'.[29] In June 1936, *Facetta Nera* fell into disgrace not long after having been the target of attacks by the successful journalist Paolo Monelli. In an article called '*Donne e buoi dei paesi tuoi*' – an Italian proverb that literally means 'women and cows from home' – and possibly written under dictation, he challenged the song's author to spend some days with a '*facetta nera*':

> one of those filthy Abyssinians, with ancestral stench that stinks of rotten butter dripping in little drops on her neck; already destroyed at age twenty by an age-old tradition of amorous servitude and rendered cold and inert in a man's arms; for one beauty with a noble face, a hundred are sticky-eyed and have hard, masculine features on pockmarked skin.[30]

The journalist's vitriolic pen railed against the song's sentimentality and denounced its incitation to frequent 'stinking little negresses' who led to *meticciato* and to 'infractions against the race'. Breaking with the light-hearted and libertine atmosphere that had marked the conquest of Ethiopia, the article was in synch with the period's ideological evolution. Addressing the Great Council of fascism in November 1936, Mussolini affirmed the necessity of 'confronting the racial problem and introducing it into fascist literature and doctrine'.[31]

When he gave this address, the constitution of a corpus of racist literature and propaganda was already well underway. For several months, the adventure novel of colonial conquest occupied the pages of the newspapers. Starting in May 1936, the scarecrow figure of the *meticcio* began appearing in fascist newspapers and magazines both on the continent and in the colonies.[32] Not only did *meticciato* threaten the prestige of the race, but the *meticcio* was presented as either a potential delinquent or a hopeless person. A high-ranking civil servant in the Ministry of Africa painted a somber portrait:

> In Eritrea and in Somalia, we have often seen officers and state employees, sometimes of very high rank, live as if in matrimony with

indigenous women and give birth to a category of poor wretches. Their Italian paternity did not stop them, once the father returned to the continent and if the missionaries did not intervene, from living out their adolescence among the maternal race. These poor souls were avoided by Whites and scorned by the Indigenous.[33]

In the battle for the race, appeals were made to patent racists such as Lidio Cipriani, who had been railing against *meticciato* between superior and inferior races since the beginning of the 1930s.[34] His multiple trips 'from the Cap to Cairo' had made him the 'specialist' on African populations through investigations published in widely distributed papers and in *l'Illustrazione italiana*.[35] In 1937, he became the director of the Anthropological Institute and Museum in Florence, one of the most renowned in all of Italy. He also became one of the major actors in the crusade against *meticciato* by playing an important role in the publication of the main journal for militant racism, *La Difesa della Razza*, launched in the summer of 1938.[36] He gave the journal free access to his collections of photos of African populations.[37]

La Difesa della Razza excelled in the invention of techniques of photomontage meant to give visual evidence of *meticciato*. A quarter of its covers appealed to readers based on this theme. One of them displayed a combination of the faces of a white woman and a black man, resulting in a grotesque mask. Another combined a white woman's head with an African's: from this strange Janus-head emerged a toothless skull. Two hands, one white and the other black, were clasped and dropping a wilted flower. More classical in aspect, a May 1940 cover staged an African Eve offering the forbidden fruit to an 'Aryan'. A cactus in the foreground was yet another symbol of the danger of the fusion of the races.[38] The Fascist Party inspired its own literature on the subject. In 1939 *The Meticcio Problem* appeared under the aegis of the Fascist Institute of Italian Africa.[39] The introductory quote read, 'God created white people and the Devil mulattoes'.[40] In Africa, the Fascist Party campaigned for a change in mentality. Guido Cortese, secretary of the *fascio* of Addis Ababa, interpreted the new political current faithfully:

> The folklore of nudes, full moons, long caravans and ardent sunsets, of mad love with the faithful and humble indigenous woman all represent outdated things that are more suited to a third-rank novel. It is high time to destroy any novel, illustration and little song of this type in order to avoid allowing them to give birth to a mentality that is absolutely not fascist.[41]

Reforming the sexual practices of Italians in the empire

On 19 April 1937, a law-decree was passed that outlawed relations 'of a conjugal nature' between Italian citizens and the subjects of the Empire and made them punishable by one to five years in prison.[42] The law targeted only Italians and not the Africans who were defined as subjects of the Empire – a situation that would soon be deemed unjust by some fascists who would call for the law to be strengthened.[43] In the fall-1938 measures for the defense of the race that established the State's official anti-Semitism, the question was addressed in the context of the division between citizens, or not, of Italian race. Like the subjects of the Empire, Jews did not belong to the Italian race. In this context, marriages between individuals of different races were forbidden: even if the law applied to the Empire, its principal target was the very frequent mixed unions involving Jews, although these unions were extremely rarely the prolongation of a *madamismo* situation.

In the Empire, the occupation troops and colonists were able to continue their visits to brothels and to the many African prostitutes known as *sciarmute*.[44] In June 1939, a new law made the previous law more precise and more extreme, integrating the repression of mixed couples and of *meticciato* into a broader text in defense of the prestige of the race.[45] Any offence, whatever its nature, was punishable by a fourth to a third heavier sentence if there were an attack on the prestige of the Italian race, or whenever it was committed in the presence of an indigenous person or with an indigenous person's complicity. The law reaffirmed the 1937 provisions punishing relations of a conjugal nature between Italians and subjects of the Empire, but a novel element indicated that an additional threshold had been crossed in the struggle against *meticciato*. Article 11, '*Inchiesta relative ai meticci*,' invited prosecutors confronted with the presence of a *meticcio* child to request an inquiry since the child could have been probably conceived after the April 1937 law went into effect. The text announced (art 20, *Meticci*) future norms concerning the position of the *meticci* in the Empire. In May 1940, new provisions assimilated *meticci* into the category of African subjects and forbade Italian fathers from recognizing them. Like the anti-Semitic measures, the colonial laws willfully ignored the *meticci* and gave them no official status, no doubt for fear that the invention of a new juridical category would make the phenomenon last.

Repression was carried out in several ways. Several officers were repatriated to the continent and sometimes were expelled from the ranks of the army.[46] As for civilians, the police and the courts were called upon to put an end to behavior qualified by the Duce as 'scandalous' and 'criminal'. A 'police' for *madamismo* was given the power to distribute 'yellow cards' of warning.[47]

Several trials were carried out against Italians as a way of repressing the crime of *madamismo*.[48] The first decision was rendered in September 1937. Dozens of other trials followed in the courts of Addis Ababa, Asmara, Gondar, and Harar. The evidence offered by a small number of trials may seem anecdotal in comparison with a phenomenon that concerned several thousand individuals. The texts of the courts' decisions are nonetheless replete with lessons concerning judges' interpretations of the law. The difficulty lay in establishing the crime, with all that this presupposed of intrusions into the private life of individuals. Confronted with a first trial for *madamismo* in November 1938, the Court of Gondar noted the difficulty of carrying out a judgment given how recent the constituted jurisprudence was. It efficiently summarized the line of behavior followed by judges in the majority of these cases:

> Given the decisions rendered by other Courts in the Empire, this Court intends to lead its enquiry into a search for material proof, such as a life lived in common over a certain amount of time and characterized by repeated sexual relations; it is also a question of determining elements, on the moral or psychical level, that attest to a particular spiritual bond that would look in some way or another like our *affection maritalis*.[49]

Apparently, the fact of having sexual relations with African women was not the problem. Several decisions illustrate the judges' understanding of the 'sexual needs' of expatriates, of the necessity for a 'physiological outlet'. Occasional sexual relations with a domestic servant, as long as she did not live under the same roof, were not condemned.[50]

Sex with indigenous women was tolerated as long as it was lacking in all affect. In one affair of *madamismo*, judges estimated that the accused – charged for his manifest attachment to the woman – would not have been guilty 'if he had used the woman only as a prostitute by paying her the price for occasional couplings then dismissing her after having satisfied his sexual needs'.[51] In spite of such an open display of cynicism, some judges claimed to be imposing morality onto sexual commerce between white men and black women, sometimes growing indignant about the practices of certain colonizers.[52] This led two Italians to be condemned for offending the prestige of the race by sharing a bedroom with two Ethiopian women.

> Without a doubt, the sexual act having been carried out in the presence of a third is an offence to modesty and denotes a modesty inferior to that of civilized peoples, and in particular to that of the Italian people in whom one finds the felicitous conjunction of the principles of fascism and the moral lessons of Catholicism. This is all the more reprehensible if one takes into account the noted reserve of indigenous women in terms of sexuality.[53]

How were judges to pronounce upon the existence of sexual relations once they were no longer 'simple exchanges destined to satisfy a physical need'?[54] How were they to establish the reality of a relation of a conjugal nature? Prolonged cohabitation constituted an important presumption that was not always considered sufficient proof of guilt. The passionate character of certain relations was, however, frequently considered as proof of guilt. Several trials had been motivated by complaints from women about the violence they had been subjected to.[55] Yet violence against women did not interest the judges in and of itself, but in so far as it revealed the affective dependency of spouses who were subject to jealousy. Several affairs revealed the Italians' lack of trust in their companions, and thus worked in favor of the accused.[56] Proof of sexual fidelity was taken as confessions of guilty emotions. Gifts were considered as incriminating evidence: the useful nature of certain presents might be pleaded, but those that were obviously destined only to procure pleasure worsened the case against the accused.[57] All these 'incriminating' elements came together in a case judged in September 1939. An African woman had been hired as a servant for 150 lira a month by a man with whom she shared both table and bed. The man was so subjugated by this woman that he bragged about her with his entourage and gave her perfumes. He had gone to look for her after she had left him to marry a 'man of her race'. For the judges, the guilty verdict was clear: 'Cohabitation, common table, trust and tenderness, reciprocal jealousy, frivolous and useless gifts make a life's companion of this little servant, which is precisely what a spouse is'.[58] Marks of tenderness or of particular attention towards indigenous women were particularly suspicious: accompanying a woman home at night, referring to her as one's wife,[59] or visiting her if she is sick.[60]

'Affection' and passion, sometimes referred to as 'intoxication', were obviously reprehensible. The word 'love' was never used; so improbable or inconvenient did judges consider its very possibility. In January 1939, a man was condemned to a year and a half in prison for *madamismo*. The fact that the man had confessed to loving the indigenous woman was an aggravating factor.[61] He admitted to having given gifts both to her and to her mother. Hoping to start a family, he had prepared a letter to the King asking for permission to marry her. The judges diagnosed a 'macroscopic case of being sanded',[62]

> for in this case, the white man does not simply show his desire for the black Venus by keeping her by his side, but the soul of the Italian man is itself disturbed; he is entirely devoted to the young Black woman who he wants to raise to the rank of life companion and whose association he seeks in all the events of his life, even those outside of sexuality.[63]

On the juridical level, the struggle against *meticciato* provided a starting point for establishing a biological racism based on the principle of purity of blood. In this sense, it marked a radical change in the conceptions that had prevailed up until then in terms of citizenship and identity, both in the Empire and on the continent. Yet these measures were adopted to respond to a question of local colonial governance: it was not yet a question of a global politics of race – at no moment were analogous measures considered to prevent alliances between Arabs and Italians in Libya, the other major colony for Italian populations, nor were there any measures targeting Jews.[64]

The stakes in Ethiopia concerned Italy as much as they did the Horn of Africa. The pioneer front of the Empire brought projects for anthropological revolution and for the construction of a new man into sharp focus, along with the difficulties of seeing them through.

Sex, race and fascist totalitarianism

Once the Empire was proclaimed, the colonial dream and the fascist utopia of a new man became contradictory projects, not in the realm of violence but in the realm of sexuality. 'Black Venuses' were quickly transformed from objects of desire and instruments of propaganda into diabolical figures, and their company was authorized only in the context of a relation outside of all affect. By organizing prostitution on colonial lands, fascism disturbed the reigning morality of the peninsula, inspired disapproval on the part of the Vatican, but behaved as did most colonial powers when confronted with the sexual needs of campaigning troops.[65]

Yet by elevating the battle against *madamismo* to a concern of the State, fascism showed its originality in a process that fused racism and totalitarianism thanks to a racial doctrine that gave support to the regime's project for anthropological revolution. On the one hand, by policing the cohabitation of Italian men and African women, fascist officials sought to avoid *meticciato* in the name of racist conceptions that were hardly original in colonial contexts.[66] But the regime was also pursuing other demons, the purported 'weaknesses' of a people that the Duce sought to transform: sentimentalism, a certain humanism and behavior deemed to be the opposite of fascist virility.

On the continent, the desire to orient affective and sexual behavior had been an active project for several years. Family and procreation were supposed to provide the limit on the horizon of Italian love. In this perspective, male homosexuality, though never an explicit target of the penal code, was discouraged through other methods. In December 1926, a tax on celibacy was adopted, and bachelors were subsequently repeatedly pointed out and penalized, for example in their career when they were civil servants. Paolo Orano, an intellectual close to the powers in place, assimilated celibacy to a form of civil and social *fuoruscitismo*.[67]

In terms of the couple, there was hardly a need to legislate on the relations between men and women, so much was male domination taken for granted. Some fascists nonetheless dreamed of branding relationships of love with the seal of fascist totalitarianism. Already in 1915, in his work *Maschilità*, the nationalist Giovanni Papini, one of the sources of inspiration for fascism, recommended emancipation from the family, romanticism and love, opposing women to men, honey to stone, and condemning love as a form of slavery.[68] For a regime that considered the family an absolute value and that relied on the Church for its political power, it became difficult to subscribe to the totality of this program after 1922. Paolo Orano proposed a compromise, given the fact that under fascism '[t]he State methodically and energetically enters into the heart of individual and domestic morality, for it is the master of social life'. It was enough to be liberated of the bourgeois idea according to which love had to precede marriage, and to get rid of the romantic and egotistical illusions of love as an end in itself. The couple became a form of association that tended towards procreation and any love between partners was a consequence and not a preliminary.[69]

This philosophy of the relations between men and women, defended in Italy by a number of fascist ideologues in the name of their particular idea of totalitarianism, inspired fascist politics in Ethiopia. Distance and stronger constraints for men in the context of war and subsequent occupation at least theoretically allowed for a more effective control of amorous behavior. In the licit economy of sexual practices, two solutions were available for fascist colonial soldiers who were always bachelors: chastity, in which the colonizer became a kind of soldier-monk, or a sexual practice disconnected from all affect.

Those who chose the first solution were in the minority. Some married men staked their honor on resisting the temptations of sex, something 'that was at the center of everyone's mind'.[70] Actively declaring their fidelity to marriage, they justified the obligation of chastity and sexual frustration with morality, the values of Catholicism, fascist law, and repulsion of a racist nature.[71] Having left wife and child on the peninsula, Nicola Gattari had come to Ethiopia as a soldier, and had stayed there to have a career as the head of a trucking business. In some of the letters to his beloved wife, he addresses this delicate subject:

I am a young man full of desires, but who can satisfy them? Those smelly black women that thousands of soldiers of all ages get infections from? No, dearest, your Nicola will come back just as he left, I swear to you [...] Think of when we will see each other again, how beautiful our embrace will be!

Answering his wife, who had asked, without really believing it, whether he had fallen in love with a little black woman, he reaffirmed his fidelity:

Yes, I may look like an imbecile compared to others and I must admit that my desire to stay faithful to the sacred bond of marriage must be the case for one resident out of a thousand in Africa. Have I fallen in love with a little negress? I can reply that there's no need to be in love to conquer one of those fleabags, because these are easy girls: 5 lira is enough and the deal is done.[72]

Prostitution was therefore a common outlet. This was not necessarily enough to diminish the appeal of cohabitation, and the change from the condition of *sciarmutta* to that of *madama* was frequent for Ethiopian women.[73] By going to inspect bedrooms and by inciting intimate confessions over the course of court trials, the State had indeed penetrated 'into the heart of individual and domestic morality'. On the continent, the effort was compromised by too many boundaries. In the Empire and in the name of the battle against *meticciato*, an attempt at it was made. In their recommendations concerning commerce with the indigenous, judges invented the ideal of a sexuality emancipated from all sentiment, ultimately participating in the 'masculinity' exalted by Papini.

What was the impact of these trials and the sentences they rendered? The judiciary treatment of the question allowed judges to show their fascist zeal. The sentencing of the trials provided lessons, directed perhaps in particular as examples in racism and fascism for men of modest social background.[74] By issuing a year and a half prison sentence for a culprit who was manifestly in love with an Ethiopian woman, the judge claimed he was 'setting him straight'.[75] The repression brought with it an atmosphere of fear for certain colonizers, if one judges by the behavior of certain couples who hid and of lovers who met each other only once night had fallen.[76]

In January 1939, the racist anthropologist Lidio Cipriani was only moderately optimistic:

> Unfortunately, the obscenity of sexual relations between white men and the indigenous continues, but it would seem that the racist measures have brought about a perceptible decrease in cases of undesirable fecundation [...] It is likely that the white man has begun to realize the inconvenience of shamelessly giving himself up to a colored woman.[77]

Most accounts, however, lead us to think that the law against *madamismo* was hardly respected, even by those who were supposed to be imposing fascist order, and in particular by the police.[78] In Eritrea, 10,000 African women were counted as living with Italians in 1935, and 15,000 in 1940.[79]

Like other measures that aimed at deep behavioral reforms, the question of sex and *meticciato* marked the limits of the fascist hold on the mind and of its ability to shape social customs.

–Translated by Will Bishop

Notes

1. 'Eloge des femmes italiennes', speech delivered on 8 May 1936, in B. Mussolini, *Edition définitive des oeuvres de B. Mussolini, vol. XI* (Paris, 1938), pp. 69–71.
2. See G. L. Mosse, *L'image de l'homme. L'invention de la virilité moderne* (Paris, 1999), pp. 179–203. B. Spackman, *Fascist Virilities: Rhetoric, Ideology, and Social Fantasy in Italy* (Minneapolis, 1996).
3. Cited in F. Le Houérou, *L'épopée des soldats de Mussolini en Abyssinie. 1936–1938. Les ensablés* (Paris, 1994), p. 50.
4. M.-A. Matard-Bonucci and P. Milza, *L'Homme nouveau entre dictature et totalitarisme* (Paris, 2004).
5. A. Sbacchi, *Legacy of Bitterness: Ethiopia and Fascist Italy, 1935–1941* (Lawrenceville, 1997). See in particular the chapter, 'Poison gas and atrocities in the Italo-Ethiopian War, 1935–1936', pp. 55–85; A. Del Boca

(ed.), *I gas di Mussolini: Il fascismo e la guerra d'Etiopia* (Roma, 1996); G. Rochat, 'L'attentato a Graziani e la repressione italiana in Etiopia 1936–1937', in *Italia contemporanea*, 118 (1975), pp. 3–38. More generally see the impressive work of A. Del Boca and R. Pankhurst. See also A. Mockler, *Haile Selassie's War: The Italian Ethiopian campaign, 1936–41* (London, 1987).

6. G. Bottai, *Diario 1935–1944* (Milan, 2001), p. 102, note from 16 May 1936.
7. On the subject of colonial literature, see G. Tomasello, *La letteratura coloniale italiana dalle avanguardie al fascismo* (Palermo, 1984). R. Bonavita, 'Lo sguardo dall'alto. Le forme della razzizzazione nei romanzi coloniali nella narrativa esotica', in *La menzogna della razza. Documenti e immagini del razzismo e dell'antisemitismo fascista* (Bologne, Grafis, 1994), pp. 53–62.
8. Cited in A. Petacco, *Faccetta nera* (Milan, 2008), p. 191.
9. See the vignettes reproduced in the catalogue *La Menzogna della Razza*, pp. 156–157. On colonial iconography, see A. Mignemi, *Immagine coordinata per un impero* (Novara, 1984); G. Campassi and M.-T. Sega, 'Uomo bianco, donna nera. L'immagine della donna nella fotografia coloniale', in *Rivista di storia e teoria della fotografia*, 4, 5 (1983), pp. 54–62.
10. L. Goglia, 'Le cartoline illustrate italiane della guerra etiopica 1935–1936: il negro nemico selvaggio e il trionfo della civiltà di Rome', in the catalogue for the exhibit *La menzogna della Razza*, pp. 27–40. Image p. 175.
11. S. Pivato, *Bella ciao. Canto e politica nella storia d'Italia* (Rome, 2007), pp. 161–162.
12. The song lyrics are published in A. Petacco, 2008, pp. 189–190.
13. Relations between men and women, after having been ignored in their racist and sexist aspects, have since been analyzed with an emphasis on the importance of colonial oppression and gender. See G. Campassi, 'Il madamato in Africa orientale: relazioni tra italiani e indigene come forma di agressione coloniale', in *Miscellanea di storia delle esplorazioni* (Genova, Bozzi, 1987), pp. 219–260. In a pioneering study, Giulia Barrera positions herself as an Eritrean woman and from that perspective affords a more complex view of gender relations in this context. G. Barrera, *Dangerous Liaisons, Colonial Concubinage in Eritrea, 1890–1941* (Evanston, 1996).
14. C. Rossetti, 'Razze e religioni nei territori dell'Impero', *L'impero (A.O.I). Studi e documenti raccolti e ordinati da T. Sillani*, La Rassegna italiana, XVI (Rome, 1938), p. 76. The author was the head of the Office of Studies of the Ministry of Italian Africa.
15. B. Sorgoni, *Etnografia e colonialismo. L'Eritrea e l'Etiopia di Alberto Pollera 1873–1939* (Torino, 2001).
16. G. Barrera, 1996, p. 6.
17. See A. Gauthier, 'Femmes et colonialisme', in M. Ferro (ed.), *Le livre noir du colonialisme. XVIe-XXIe siècle: de l'extermination à la repentance* (Paris, 2006), pp. 759–811. The quotation is on p. 802. See also A. L. Stoler, *Carnal Knowledge and Imperial Power: Race and the Intimate in Colonial Rule* (Berkeley, 2002).
18. Carlo Rossetti, 1938, p. 76.
19. On prostitution, see A. Del Boca, *Gli Italiani in Africa orientale, La caduta dell'Impero* (Rome, 1982), pp. 244–245. R. Pankhurst, 'The history of prostitution in Ethiopia', *Journal of Ethiopian Studies*, Addis Abeba university, 12, 2, pp. 159–178.

20. The text of the law stipulated the condition that the interested parties had to 'prove themselves worthy of Italian nationality through their education, culture, and level of living'. Law of 6 July 1933, no. 999.
21. This statistic is cited in A. Del Boca, 1982, p. 248.
22. I. Montanelli's account is cited by E. Biagi, in *1935 e dintorni* (Milan, Mondadori, 1982), pp. 58–61. According to his account, the young girl was Muslim.
23. On C. Gini, see M.-A. Matard-Bonucci, *L'Italie fasciste et la persécution des juifs* (Paris, 2007), pp. 74–75; D. Simoncelli, *La demografia dei meticci* (Sora, 1929).
24. Before the Ethiopian War, not one text in the colonial press denounces the damaging effects of *meticciato*. See O. Dumoulin's unpublished master's thesis, *La vision des Ethiopiens sous le fascisme: étude de quatre revues coloniales italiennes* (Université de Rouen, September–October 2001).
25. 'Metodo romano per colonizzare l'Etiopia', *Illustrazione coloniale* 2 February, 1936.
26. C. Ipsen, *Demografia totalitaria* (Bologna, 1997), p. 256.
27. Cited by the Baron Pompeo Aloisi, head of the cabinet of the Ministry of Foreign Affairs started in July 1932: *Journal (25 juillet 1932–14 juin 1936)* (Paris, 1957), p. 185.
28. Telegram from Mussolini to Badoglio and Graziani, in *La menzogna* 1994, p. 20.
29. B. Aloisi, 1957, p. 382. The conversation is dated 8 May.
30. The article appeared in Torino's *La Gazzetta del popolo* on 13 June 1936.
31. G. Bottai, 2001, p. 115 (19 November1936). Nothing proves that at the time Mussolini was also thinking of anti-Semitism.
32. The colonial press was particularly mobilized: in January 1940, *Africana italiana* came out with a special number devoted to 'Discipline and supervision of the races in the Empire'. A month later, the same magazine dealt with the question of the role of the Italian woman in the Empire.
33. C. Rossetti, 1938.
34. L. Cipriani, *Considerazioni sopra il passato e l'avvenire delle popolazioni africane* (Firenze, 1932). On the man himself, see R. Maiocchi, *Scienza italiana e razzismo fascista* (Florence, 1999), pp. 161–163.
35. *In Africa, dal Capo al cairo* is the title of the book published in Florence, 1932.
36. On the role of this journal in the racist propoganda apparatus, see M. A. Bonucci, 2007.
37. P. Chiozzi, 'Autoritratto del razzismo: le fotografie di Lidio Cipriani', in Grafis (ed.), *La menzogna* (Bologna, Grafis, 1994), pp. 91–94.
38. The covers discussed are, respectively, A. III, 14-20/05/40; A. III, 11-5/04/40; A. IV, 3-5/12/40; A. III, 8-20/02/1940.
39. G. Masucci, *Il problema dei meticci* (Rome1939).
40. An account can be found in *Razza e Civiltà*, A. I, n. 1, 23 March 1940, p. 107.
41. G. Cortese, *Problemi dell'Impero* (Rome, 1937). Cited in F. Le Houérou, 1994, p. 95.
42. Law-decree (RDL) of 19 April 1937, no. 880, 'Sanzioni per i rapporti d'indole coniugale fra cittadini e sudditi'.
43. See Giovanni Rosso's position, 'Il reato di madamismo nei confronti dell'indigena che abbia una relazione di indole coniugale con un cittadino italiano', in *Razza e Civiltà*, An I, n. 1, pp. 131–139.

44. See A. Del Boca, 1982, pp. 243–245.
45. RDL n. 1004 of 29 June 1939.
46. One finds several cases mentioned in A. Del Boca, 1982, pp. 246–247.
47. F. Le Houérou, 1994, p. 95.
48. The journal *Razza e Civiltà* started publication in March 1940. It was an organ of the High Council and of the General Direction for Demography and the Race. Under the heading 'Giurisprudenza e legislazione razziale' many extracts form judicial decisions were published. The analyses presented below are founded on the analysis of 28 cases presented by the journal. Half of the cases were convictions of the crime of *madamismo* or of offenses to racial dignity.
49. 19 November 1938 decision of the Court of Gondar, Spano accused, Maistro presiding, RC, An I, n. 1 pp. 128–131.
50. 7 February 1939 decision, Venturiello accused, Carnaroli presiding, RC, A. I, nn. 5–7, p. 549.
51. 19 November 1938 decision, Spano accused, Maistro presiding, RC, An I, n. 1, pp. 1, 130.
52. See the 4 April 1939 decision of the Appeals Court of Addis Ababa, Isella accused, Carnaroli presiding, RC, A. I, nn. 5–7, p. 552.
53. 21 December 1939 decision of the Appeals Court of Addis Ababa, Lauria and Ciulla accused, Morando presiding, RC, A. I, nn. 5–7, p. 548.
54. 3 January 1939 decision of the Appeals Court of Addis Ababa, Melchionne accused, Carnaroli presiding, RC, A. I, nn. 5–7, p. 548. 'I congressi carnali perdono il carattere d'incontro a mero sfogo fisiologico'.
55. This was the case in the trial against G. Spano, which was begun after a complaint was filed by his concubine with the police. 19 November 1938 decision of the Court of Gondar, RC, An I, n. 1, p. 128.
56. Appeals Court of Addis Ababa, Decisions of 31 January 1939, Seneca accused, Guerrazzi presiding; 3 January 1939, Marca accused, Guerrazzi presiding, RC, A. I, nn. 5–7, pp. 548–551.
57. Gifts are mentioned in several of the cases.
58. 5 September 1939 decision, Appeals Court of Addis Ababa, Fagà accused, Carnaroli presiding, RC, A. I, nn. 5–7, p. 547.
59. 14 February 1939 decision, Appeals Court of Addis Ababa, Autieri accused, Carnaroli presiding, RC, A. I, nn. 5–7, p. 549.
60. 3 January 1939 decision, Appeals Court of Addis Ababa, Giuliano accused, Carnaroli presiding, RC, A. I, nn. 5–7, p. 550.
61. The expression used was '*volerle bene*'.
62. '*Insabbiati*', or 'sanded', was the term used to describe men who stayed in Ethiopia to live, often, with an African woman.
63. 31 January 1939 decision, Appeals Court of Addis Ababa, Seneca accused, Guerrazzi presiding, RC, A. I, nn. 5–7, pp. 548–549.
64. Besides the fact that *meticciato* inspired less fear concerning Arabs than it did with populations of Black Africa, reasons specific to the Libyan context explain this choice: greater presence of Italian women in Libya; a different statute for marriage in this country compared to Ethiopia. Cf. C. Ipsen, 1997, p. 256.
65. Actually, on the continent, fascism also had a politics that aimed at a regulation of prostitution without forbidding it entirely. On the Italian

government's duplicity, which discouraged the presence of prostitutes on the street but tolerated it in brothels subject to controls by police and health authorities, see V. De Grazia, *Le donne nel regime fascista* (Rome, 1993), pp. 73–74.

66. V. Joly writes: 'Exotic loves must be ephemeral. Indigenous women are only substitutes imposed by solitude and the distance from the fiancée waiting on the continent, sometimes nothing but a dream. They must also not be sentimental, so strong is the fear of *métissage*, a weakening of the victor's race', in 'Sexe, guerre et désir colonial', in F. Rouquet, F. Virgili, and D. Voldman, eds, *Amours, guerres et sexualité 1914–1945* (Paris, 2007), pp. 62–69.

67. Paolo Orano uses this expression in 'Famiglia, razza, potenza', *Il fascismo*, II: XVIII (Rome, 1940), pp. 391–429. *Fuoruscitismo* referred to anti-fascist exile.

68. G. Papini, *Maschilità* (Firenze, 1915).

69. P. Orano, 1940.

70. A. Del Boca, 1982, p. 243.

71. A. Del Boca, 1982 gives several examples, amongst which is that of the resident of Bacco, or the account of a military council member, p. 250.

72. These letters were published by S. Luzzatto, *La strada per Adis Abeba. Lettere di un camionista dall'Impero (1936–1941)* (Paravia, 2000). The citations are on pp. 85, 144.

73. G. Barrera, 1996, p. 26.

74. The sentences of the trials do not always allow us to know the professions of the accused. The overriding impression is nonetheless one of trials carried out against men of modest condition and who came either from the proletariat or from the lower middle class. For a sociology of the Ethiopian colonizers, see F. Le Houérou, 1994, pp. 115–135.

75. 31 January 1939 decision, Appeals Court of Addis Ababa, Seneca accused, Guerrazzi presiding, RC, A. I, nn. 5–7, pp. 548–549.

76. This can be deduced from allusions in certain decisions to the fear of nighttime police investigations in order to establish the offence.

77. Archivio Centrale dello Stato (Rome) MCP, Gab., b. 151, letter dated 18 January 1939. In another letter written in the winter of 1939, at a time when he was offering his services as 'consulente razziale nell'Impero', Cipriani considers the issue yet again. (31 January 1939 letter from Cipriani to Landra in ACS, MCP, Gab., b. 151).

78. F. Le Houérou gathered 35 accounts, mostly from 'sanded' Italians who had stayed on site, often after having lived with a *madama*. The very nature of the population interviewed perhaps exaggerates the reality of the phenomenon. See in particular, Le Houérou, 1994, pp. 97–105.

79. These numbers are cited by G. Barrera, 1996, p. 43.

4
'The Good Fellow': Negotiation, Remembrance, and Recollection – Homosexuality in the British Armed Forces, 1939–1945

Emma Vickers

Background

The year 1967 marked a watershed in English law. Twenty-two years after the end of the Second World War, homosexuality was decriminalised in England and Wales by the Sexual Offences Act.[1] Prior to the introduction of the new legislation, the hero of Alamein, Field Marshall Bernard Montgomery, urged the House of Lords not to sanction the legislation.

> Our task is to build a bulwark which will defy the evil influences seeking to undermine the very foundations of our national character. I know it is said this is allowed in France and some other countries. We are not French, we are not from other nations, we are British – thank God.[2]

While Montgomery could not slow the momentum of the civil law nor the rumours that he himself was a homosexual, his concerns were shared by policy-makers within the Armed Forces. Indeed military chiefs and the Wolfenden committee agreed that decriminalising homosexual acts in the forces would affect discipline and threaten the safety of low-ranking servicemen.[3] As a result, homosexual acts remained punishable by military law even though they were made legal for civilian men over the age of 21.

By the middle of the 1990s, gay human rights campaigns spearheaded by *Stonewall, Outrage!* and *Rank Outsiders* were increasing their pressure on the government to overturn the ban.[4] Within the government, debate was furious. In 1995, Harry Cohen, Labour MP for Leyton, rationalised the inclusion of gays and lesbians in the Armed Forces by referring back to the Second World War.

> This year is the 50th anniversary of the end of the last war. The Minister [MP Roger Freedman] should remember that then the country was happy for many people of homosexual orientation to fight and to lay down their lives for it. Their orientation was not held against them by the country then, so why is the Minister adopting such a backward attitude now?[5]

Some of the most tangible and poignant arguments for equal inclusion came not from campaigners and politicians but from heterosexual veterans of the Second World War. Their letters to the national press helped to inform the debate, revealing not only the existence of the homosexual serviceman, but his unquestionable value to an institution which pursued an ambivalent policy in the name of efficiency. As one veteran recalled,

> In 1943 I had a Divisional Officer, a captain of Marines, who was overtly gay. He was also a heavily decorated hero. He was the first of many gay servicemen and women I met during four years in the Navy and later the R.A.F. I did not see or hear of any trouble [or] loss of discipline.[6]

These sentiments were echoed by Peter Tatchell when he argued that 'vast numbers of gay people were allowed to serve in combat units, some quite openly'.[7] Despite the attempts of Tatchell and others, in 1996 the ban was retained after the government reviewed its policies towards the intake of gays and lesbians in the Armed Forces. The official report of the Ministry of Defence's Homosexual Policy Assessment Team concluded that the ruling was in place because of three fundamental concerns: the potentially disruptive influence of 'homosexual practices', the desire to prevent the abuse of authority by those in charge of junior personnel, and the security risk implied by the presence of gays and lesbians, namely the threat of blackmail.[8]

The ban was finally lifted in 2000 after three gay servicemen and a former nurse took the Ministry of Defence (henceforth MoD) to the European Court of Human Rights. They had been dismissed for being gay, and alleged that the investigations into their private lives and subsequent dismissal violated their human rights. It was subsequently ruled that the bar on entry into the Armed Forces was illegal under the European Convention on Human Rights, given that the professional skills required of gay service personnel were no different from those expected of heterosexual servicemen and women.[9]

In addition to lifting the ban, the Armed Forces introduced a new code of conduct, which remains in place today, for all personnel and their relationships based on the concept of acceptable and unacceptable behaviour. If the conduct of a person undermines 'trust … cohesion and damage[s] the morale or discipline of a unit', it will be punished.[10] There is an evident historical parallel here. During the Second World War, as we shall see, sexual orientation was overwhelmingly regarded as a private issue, unless it encroached upon discipline and efficiency. There would appear to be little difference between the current code of conduct and the unofficial policy of forbearance that operated during the War. As one former major in the Army commented, 'one was either, within that military context, a good fellow or not. All other considerations were irrelevant'.[11]

The modern-day military in Britain is keen to support the current drive towards the recruitment of gays and lesbians. In February 2005, the Royal Navy began a partnership with *Stonewall* to facilitate the recruitment of gay, lesbian and bisexual personnel. In August of the same year, the Army and the Royal Air Force could be seen recruiting at Manchester's Gay Pride weekend with an oversized cockpit and a banner proudly proclaiming 'RAF rise above the rest'. At the Army recruitment stall, men in uniform were reportedly 'mingl[ing] with eager would-be recruits, one dressed in tight leather shorts and a pink cowboy hat'.[12] Lieutenant-Colonel Leanda Pitt, Commander of Regional Recruiting for the North West, was said to be 'delighted' to be taking part. 'As far as the Army is concerned, sexual orientation is a private matter'.[13]

The difference between this recent approach and the social and legal position of queer men and women in 1939 is stark. In 1939 homosexual acts between men were illegal both in the Armed Forces and under civil law. Lesbian acts were not legislated against in either context although, as we shall see, the services recognised that the presence of lesbians could have disciplinary implications. In the male services and under section 18 sub-section 5, all homosexual acts could be punished by up to two years imprisonment.[14] In civil law, the term 'indecency' was used as a catch-all term to encompass sodomy and indecent acts between men, although in the 1940s, the law made a number of distinctions.

Gross indecency, or the performance or encouragement of a sexual act between males, could be punished with two years' imprisonment, as could indecent exposure. Indecent assault on a male person involving the use of threat or force to commit a sexual act carried a maximum sentence of ten years in prison. Buggery could be punished by imprisonment for life.[15]

It is this sense of criminality and unacceptability which has surfaced most frequently in the correspondence that I have received from veterans of the war in reaction to my research. In 2005, my request for both gay and heterosexual veterans of the Second World War to share their memories reached the head of the Monte Cassino veterans association, John Clarke. Upon reading the appeal, Clarke reported the story to a journalist at the tabloid newspaper *The Sun* who in turn branded the request for respondents an 'insult'.[16] Clarke was explicit about his reasons for contacting the paper.

> In our day homosexuality was a crime – and I don't know of any gay men I saw service with. She wanted me to contact members of my association. After I spoke to one or two of them they went berserk...wouldn't the money be better spent elsewhere? They would be better off finding someone to do a write up about the trauma of combat.[17]

Clarke also constructed homosexuality as un-British; that is, inconceivable in the British Armed Forces yet prevalent in the German army, a conclusion he came to in an earlier letter to me in which he claimed to have discovered dead German soldiers wearing make-up.[18] However, the real root of Clarke's argument was that he did not serve with gay soldiers because it was illegal. This is proof, in the words of my gay interviewee Dennis Campbell, who kept a low profile during the war, that 'the veteran wasn't aware what was going on, which means that we were successful'.[19]

This divergence between the 'hidden' narratives of my queer interviewees and the 'non-existent' narratives of veterans like Clarke has been reiterated continuously by those who have opposed my research. For instance, another veteran believed that I was 'inventing false stories', and framed his objections around the perception of the Second World War in Britain as a sacred and moral battle. In my highlighting of the existence of homosexuals in the Armed Forces, the veteran believed that I was denigrating the sacredness of the war, its dead and the contribution of himself and his wife.

I recommend you study what true history you can find and do not think of inventing false stories. There were virtually none for you to find because we treated such nonsense at best as a stupid joke or at worst as not worth wasting time on.[20]

This veteran constructed a very clear dichotomy between true and false versions of the past and, moreover, between the clear and somehow 'true' heterosexuality of his marriage and the 'nonsense' of same-sex relationships. His anger was so powerful that it prompted me to write to him and justify my research.

It is not in my interests, nor those of my department or my discipline to invent history. Furthermore, it is not my intention to misrepresent your service or rake up scandal. The virtue of my work is that it allows me to examine identities, prejudices, sexuality and institutions, and how individuals respond to each of these.[21]

The veteran's subsequent reply is revealing:

It is so difficult for oldies like me to get on the same wavelength after so much life has passed us by. Truly though, I never knowingly met a 'gay' person during the whole of my service and always believed they did not then get into any of the services. But I gladly accept that I must be wrong.[22]

He testified that he had never 'knowingly met' a gay or lesbian during his service and was sure that none had ever entered the Armed Forces. He was, though, willing to accept an alternative interpretation. Others, however, remained less open. By far the most offensive tirade was written by an elderly male correspondent who in the absence of a convincing argument, reverted to personal insults, alleging that I was a 'corrupted tart' and a 'PC milky liberal'. The veteran also viewed homosexuality as a greater threat than global warming and asserted 'we never even thought of homosexuals in our day. (Or poofters as we would have called them!)'[23]

As cutting as these responses were, they represent a small proportion of the veterans with whom I have made contact. Indeed, as the evidence to be discussed below shows, many more self-described heterosexual veterans have written in support of my research – and in support of their former gay comrades. However, the underlying motivations behind the negative reactions remain telling. It could be surmised that they are rooted in recent concerns about the intake of gays, lesbians and women into the services as well as the increased visibility of the gay community in modern society. Some veterans reverted to the dichotomous and wildly stereotypical incompatibility between gay sexuality and military masculinity. Others reacted against the perceived predatory, penetrative sexuality ascribed to active queer men and therefore expressed by association their concerns about the supposed vulnerability of the heterosexual soldier in communal environments. Such arguments resonate with the homophobic and clichéd opinions often expressed by the MoD to justify the retention of the ban in the decades following the decriminalisation of homosexual acts in 1967.

> [If] heterosexuals...have to live (and not simply work) in very close, inescapable proximity for unremittingly long periods alongside known homosexuals...this would mean heterosexuals unable to escape the sexualized gazes of others who might see potential objects of physical desire rather than simply the often naked bodies of comrades. It would often also mean unwillingly colluding in potentially erotic situations through touching, lying alongside or having constantly to brush past homosexuals...[24]

The report concluded that queer men and women would damage military cohesion and operational effectiveness. Although this particular line of reasoning was frequently invoked by the MoD, it amounts to nothing more than – as one scholar put it – unqualified assumptions about 'homosexual voyeurism and heterosexual scopophobia [the fear of being looked at]'.[25] Indeed, the Ministry believed that introducing a strong homosexual element into the Forces would be tantamount to institutional suicide. As the former general Sir Anthony Farrar-Hockley said in 1999, while discussing the lifting of the ban on gays and lesbians in the Armed Forces, 'This decision will strike at morale and discipline. Comradeship is a binding factor. Sexual squabbles will be disruptive; perhaps fatally so'.[26]

In reality, there is little evidence to suggest that the recruitment of gays and lesbians and their open inclusion in the Armed Forces has fulfilled Farrar-Hockley's ominous prophecy. Indeed, research by Aaron Belkin and R. L. Evans at the University of California discovered that the lifting of the British ban has had a minimal impact on discipline and cohesion.[27] Officially, the MoD has acknowledged that the lifting of the ban has barely affected morale.[28]

Negotiating homosexuality in the Second World War

Until shortly before the Second World War began for Britain in 1939, Britain and its Armed Forces were largely unprepared for war. Economic austerity caused by the economic downturn of 1929 and public pacifism in the aftermath of the First World War had limited the wholesale modernisation of the Armed Forces and rendered at least the Army precariously under-strength.[29] It was only thanks to a rapid and desperate process of rearmament and mobilisation that Britain was able to face the prospect of war at least partially prepared. This mobilisation of people was an often indiscriminate process that drew together people from a wide range of ages and classes as well as different sexual identities. Gays and lesbians were a sexual and social minority in peacetime but they were absorbed into the British Armed Forces both as volunteers and as conscripts.

Peter Tatchell has estimated that 250,000 gay men served in the British Armed Forces during the Second World War.[30] Tatchell made this assessment based on estimates from the 1990–1991 National Survey of Sexual Attitudes and Lifestyles which found that 6 percent of the survey's respondents had had homosexual experiences.[31] Tatchell's estimation does not incorporate women, nor does it consider those who experienced same-sex love or intimacy but defined themselves as heterosexual. In 1999, the figure was recalculated by the gay human rights organisation *Outrage!* to 500,000 to include lesbians as well as bisexual men and women.[32]

Such estimates stand in contrast to court-martial figures for the Army which indicate that 790 'other ranks', that is, non-officers, were court-martialled for indecency during the course of the war.[33] (An unrecorded number of lesbians were separated from their partners or, more rarely, discharged from the auxiliary services.) It has been stated by Alkarim Jivani in *It's Not Unusual* and more recently by 'UKTV History' that there were more courts-martial for homosexuality than any other category of offence.[34] On the contrary, 790 courts-martial for indecency between men in the Army alone is remarkably few if we posit that between 6 and 12 percent of service personnel in the Second World War were gay (out of a total of 6,508,000).[35] Furthermore in comparison to courts-martial for other offences the figures are low. For instance, there were 13,927 courts-martial of men in the Army for losing property by neglect and 75,157 cases of absence without leave.[36]

There are complex and multiple reasons for this apparent lack of official disciplinary activity against homosexuality, many of which hinge upon the issue of pragmatism. In the first instance, pragmatism was necessitated by the urgent need to encourage or coerce men and women into joining the forces. The Second World War demanded mobilisation on an unprecedented scale. Indeed, as the war continued, the shortage of labour became a crucial consideration. The Military Training Act of May 1939 invoked conscription for men aged 20 and 21. In September 1939 conscription was extended by the National Service (Armed Forces) Act which made all men between 18 and 41 and all unmarried women between the ages of 20 and 30 liable to call up. The last extension of conscription for men occurred in December 1941 when the upper age limit was set at 51.[37] In 1942, the age limit was extended to include 19-year-old women. These demands were accompanied by frequent revisions in the criteria of selection, and standards were continually modified and interpreted with increasing sub-categories and increasing degrees of leniency.

Under wartime conditions, the services were under great pressure. Their aim was to recruit and conscript as many bodies as possible, and they did so with little focus on sexual preference. In fact, the need for manpower was so acute that it drowned out any debates about the capabilities of queer men and women. There is no conclusive evidence that gays and lesbians were screened out of the services on account of their sexuality. On the contrary, it would seem that many gays and lesbians entered the services and were able to express their sexuality quite openly.

Once recruited, it was difficult for the Armed Forces to identify and prosecute gays and lesbians for four important reasons. The first relates to the ingenuity of the gays and lesbians who chose or were forced to mask their homosexuality under the guise of heterosexuality.

'Playing it cool': passing and performance

Although some queer men and women were unable or unwilling to compromise their queerness, the vast majority chose or were forced to perform as heterosexuals in order to fit into their units.[38] Albert Robinson was conscripted into the Army when he was 28 as a cook in the Pioneer Corps and later in the Army Catering Corps. Much of his free time was spent alone, cruising for other men. However, on returning to his unit, Robinson was, to all intents and purposes, a heterosexual serviceman who 'went along with it [the heterosexual culture] and made out you were the same as they were'.[39] Termed by Elaine Ginsberg and many other scholars as 'passing', such impersonations helped to facilitate social blending in contexts where outright honesty might have jeopardised an individual and his or her place within a group.[40] In the context of this paper, to 'pass' is to imitate heterosexual (and heteronormative) society. The imitation that emerges is a complex cultural construction, influenced in this case by the queer community, heterosexual society and specific notions of acceptable and unacceptable gender identities.

Service life for queer servicemen and women was an intricate matrix of regulatory regimes and a spectrum of performance ranging from passing to open self-declaration.[41] First, at the level of the individual, queer men and women regulated their behaviour based on their own sexual identity, character and personal preference. Second, this internalised response was in turn influenced by the reaction of a serviceman or -woman's peers. The third regulatory entity was represented by the authorities, both those at unit level and those in the higher echelons of the military establishment. All three levels of regulation coalesced into an individualised code of moral behaviour which regulated the performance and the behaviour of queer men and women.

The environment created by the services was heavily dominated by heterosexuality. Since conformity to heterosexual values and standards of performance granted acceptance, it was crucial that recruits adhered to as many of the markers of heteronormativity as possible. For men, these markers were hyper-masculine extensions of peacetime benchmarks which included honour, courage, physical strength and sexual virility.[42] Women were judged somewhat differently, that is, by their efficiency as workers but also their adherence to accepted off-duty sartorial conventions such as hairstyle and make-up, and most importantly, their success with the opposite sex.

As we might expect, the topics of sex, romance and dating seemed to dominate conversation. Take for instance the soldier W. A. Hill who described having 'a very enjoyable and laughable evening on a topic, "My first girl" '.[43] More evidence comes from the soldier J. H. Witte, who served in Egypt. Witte's memoirs reveal the deeply heterosexist nature of life in the services. With his mates Mick and George, Witte visited a brothel in Jaffa and unable to 'raise a gallop' he felt forced to lie.

> Mick and George were waiting for me when I came out. They were eager for details. I supplied most of them and made up the rest. I dwelt at some length on the Spaniard's anatomy and how she had her pubic hair shaved off. 'Cor', said Mick, 'they're not like that in Leeds'.[44]

Similar discussions took place in the women's services. Almost immediately after she arrived at a bomber station, Pip Beck was informed by a more seasoned recruit that she could 'have a different boyfriend every night' if she wanted.[45] Similarly, one woman believed that 85 percent of the conversations held between herself and her friends were on the topics of men and dances.[46]

References to heterosexual relationships formed the backbone of group solidarity in the services because it was assumed that the topic had a universal appeal; with few exceptions, sex and romance were experienced or hankered after by everyone.[47] Indeed, for both sexes, visible success in the field of dating, romance and sexual activity contributed to the maintenance of hegemonic masculinity and femininity.[48] However, there can be no doubt that this emphasis on heterosexuality could be deeply stifling and exclusionary. From beautification rituals for women to conversations about desirable members of the opposite sex, markers of heteronormativity were everywhere and virtually impossible to avoid. Queer recruits attempting to pass faced a barrage of normative discourses on a daily basis, and most were forced to stifle any outward displays of their sexuality lest they jeopardise their position. 'Straight' mannerisms, fictional sweethearts and heterosexual banter with comrades were all faked in the name of personal discretion. Passing as a heterosexual was particularly important at training camp when servicemen and women were first attempting to fit in with their comrades and identify their potential friends and enemies. John Saunders recalled the small metal lockers in his hut at Catterick. While his friends were pasting pictures of scantily clad girls on the inside of their lockers, Saunders was more interested in cars and men. To compromise, he found a picture of a car that he liked with a semi-naked girl draped over the bonnet, thereby avoiding any questions about his sexuality.[49]

Bert Bartley took his performance very seriously.

> You've got to be as you would say, normal. You're facing a situation, your life has altered completely and you've got to sort of cope with it. It's no good going on about it and saying 'Oh I'm gay...take pity on me' because I'd have probably got my papers straight away and been working down a coalmine or something...you find that you make friends and they're straight and you've got to be straight with them and that's the point.[50]

Frank Smith never gave himself away either. 'I was terrified of being found out when I was 18. You are brought up in a heterosexual culture and either adapt or you go under'.[51]

For the queer men who chose to pass, it was crucial to maintain the façade of the heterosexual. Discretion was the order of the day; most straight-acting servicemen were careful to distinguish and separate themselves from 'queans', 'poufs' and 'pansies'[52] simply because the latter attracted too much attention. Such men could pose a threat to homosexual men attempting to pass because even the briefest of associations could lead to accusations of queerness. Bert Bartley for instance, himself a homosexual, described a man in his unit called Frank who made his sexuality obvious to everyone. 'You have very little to do with them'.[53]

Dennis Campbell was never indiscreet about his sexuality, but he was unwilling to maintain a complete silence about it either. He mastered the art of telegraphing his availability to other queer men while to all intents and purposes acting as a heterosexual serviceman. 'We pretty well behaved normally. I was just myself...but I didn't go around advertising it...you didn't brag about the gay stuff'.[54] Although Campbell did not brag about 'the gay stuff', he never lied about his marital status. Whenever he was asked, he always told people that he did not have a girlfriend, thereby obliquely confirming the suspicions of other queer men he encountered during his service in the Royal Air Force. This process of compartmentalisation in which wartime life was separated into service life and sexual life was certainly more common than obvious performances of queer sexuality. It was a separation that ensured that queer men and women could protect their sexuality from those who might choose to expose it.

'Passing' is one reason that helps to explain the limited prosecutions of gays and lesbians by the military authorities. The second reason is the authorities' ignorance (as opposed to ignoring) of homosexuality in as much as there was little understanding of it. In the 1940s, homosexuality in males was chiefly associated with effeminacy. This was, however, a stereotype cultivated by the queer community in the late nineteenth and early twentieth centuries and perpetuated by heterosexual society beyond its shelf life. By the 1940s the homosexual community had begun to diversify, developing a more discreet and masculine homosexuality. Despite this shift, effeminacy was still viewed by the heterosexual community as the principal marker of homosexuality, just as masculinity was viewed as the principal signifier of lesbianism in women. Indeed, the 'quean'[55] and the 'butch' were prevailing stereotypes that denoted two elements of a queer community which was naturally much more nuanced.[56] In the absence of other visible stereotypes, the Armed Forces tended to identify gays and lesbians using these two types alone and thus were only ever able to identify a small fraction of the queer community.

The 'good fellow'

The value and character of an individual is the third factor that explains why the Armed Forces sometimes chose to turn a blind eye to queers within their ranks. Perhaps the best example of this comes from Richard Briar. Briar conducted a number of relationships with higher-ranking officers during the war. On one occasion, he was seen by his commanding officer in a compromising position with his company's sergeant major, Ted. Briar was only partially hidden from view by a bush and found himself staring directly at his commanding officer, who promptly looked away and walked on. Upon questioning Ted about the officer's lack of reaction, Ted commented, 'Billy Boy never does see anything that is inconvenient to see'.[57] Ted was a valuable member of Briar's training battalion. If the commanding officer had chosen to 'see' the men, as opposed to ignoring them, he would have been forced to undertake costly, time-consuming, morale-deflating and publicly damaging disciplinary proceedings against two men who possessed skills which overrode their homosexuality.

This concept of 'the good fellow' ensured that many openly queer homosexuals were fiercely protected by the units, often because they possessed valuable skills or personalities. John Beardmore was gay, and served within the Navy during the war. The coder on his ship, whose name was Freddie, was also gay, and would defuse the tension of battle by calling out 'open fire, dear' and breaking into impersonations of Gracie Fields and Vera Lynn. Terry Gardener, who served as a cook in the Navy, was similarly well-liked because of his skill as an entertainer. It was a skill that allowed him to be unapologetically brazen about his sexuality. 'Everybody loves to laugh whatever the circumstances and ... there were some dreadful, dreadful circumstances especially on the Western approaches. People were just thankful to get through the day and if I was there to give them a laugh, it was a bonus, wasn't it?'[58] Jo Denith had two such entertainers in his company. Immediately before his men disembarked from their carriers during the D-Day landings, one of these men began to daub his lips with lipstick, and when asked to explain himself said 'I must look pretty for the Germans'. Denith recalled that everybody collapsed in fits of laughter. 'You couldn't help but laugh at them not because they were inadequate but because they had the bloody courage to laugh...they had this amazing capacity to see the ridiculous part of life'.[59]

The same sense of toleration can also be found in the women's services. Elizabeth Reid Simpson served in the Women's Auxiliary Air Force until 1942, during which time she encountered a lesbian couple at her station who slept together. After complaining about the noise to 'Mary...a good old East Ender', she was told, 'Where were you brought up? Don't you know anything? They're lesbians and they always manage to get posted together...they don't fancy you so get back to bed and go back to sleep and don't bother about them'.[60] In fact, Reid Simpson admitted, 'people just ignored it'. If the lesbian couple were consistently posted together, they were clearly efficient workers whose sexuality was not a threat to other women because it was expressed within the confines of a committed relationship.

Anecdotes such as these refute the claim that the presence of homosexuals in the Armed Forces has a detrimental impact on morale. This claim was one of the major premises of the report by the Homosexual Policy Assessment Team which was used to retain the ban on homosexuals in the 1990s. The report's monochrome vision of morale denies the complexities of group membership and neglects to acknowledge the existence of what Derek McGhee terms the 'compatible and non-disruptive' gay personnel; the invisible 'others' who chose to pass; as well as those who were accepted without question.[61] However, acceptance invariably depended on the qualities that individuals brought to their units.

With regard to queer men in the Navy, A. W. Weekes believed in 'accept[ing] the chap as he was. If he was a good messenger or a good pal.'[62] W. H. Bell held a similar attitude towards his ship's commander.

> [He]was a good seaman. [He wore] silk stockings. Whenever he did entertain anybody aboard it was always a man, never a woman. You can [sense] these things when you're not in direct contact with it...when we got to sea he was there and when we were under attack he took over...we never got hit.[63]

Bell also knew a steward who was queer, and 'as he didn't carry out anything on board ship, [they] let him get away with it. What he did ashore was his business'.[64] Bell's acceptance of both men rests on their effectiveness as workers and in the case of the steward, the man's separation of work and play. It was a separation which played a crucially important role in facilitating the steward's integration into his unit.

In this sense, there were various elements ensconced in the concept of being a good fellow which included whether a serviceman or woman carried out their role effectively, their character and the extent of their contribution to the maintenance of group morale. Once a queer recruit was accepted into a group, they could begin to test the boundaries of their integration. Some of the most audacious and challenging responses came from those who were unable or unwilling to hide their queerness. If Terry Gardener was met with hostility on his ship, he would respond with ' "What goes up my fucking arse won't give you a headache". I had the cheek not to let anybody take advantage of me so if anyone said "Are you queer?" I would say, "Yes! So what?" '[65] The verbal interplay between Gardener and his comrades represents a process of negotiation; in replying with his aggressive and humorous retorts, Gardener was making an assertion about his queer identity and claiming a space on board his ship. As we have seen, he found acceptance not only because of his honesty but also because he was a cook and an entertainer and was therefore a valuable asset to the rest of his crew.

Like Gardener, Charles Pether initially faced similar hostility in his unit. As a young effeminate male, Pether felt exposed and decidedly vulnerable, feelings compounded by what might be regarded as good natured 'ragging', dished out by the cook in his unit:

> I was being dolloped the porridge onto my plate. The cook said to me 'Hi beautiful. How about it?' I just dropped my plate and ran out... [I thought] I've got to stand up to this so the following morning the same thing happened and when he said 'oh, good morning beautiful. How about it?' I said, 'well, there will be others before you but if you want to queue up, be my guest.'[66]

As the antitheses of military masculinity and the most obvious and unapologetic queer men in their units, Gardener and Pether were exceptionally vulnerable to verbal and physical hostility, something that could be avoided by queer men who adopted passing performances. However, the presence, integration and effectiveness of these effeminate men are a powerful rebuttal of the opinion expressed most frequently by heterosexual veterans of the war that openly homosexual men did not serve in the Forces. Indeed, as Higate suggests, 'the notion that there exists a uniform culture of (hetero)sexuality in the British and other militaries functions at the level of rhetoric rather than reality'.[67] By necessity, the Armed Forces absorbed a significant plurality of masculinities into their ranks during the Second World War, a fact which confirms that hegemonic military masculinity represented little more than an unrealistic and unattainable model.

Moreover, while military masculinity is constructed in relation to the 'other', in which the effeminate homosexual man, the conscientious objector or the civilian are constructed as the 'other', such gendered prescriptions were effaced by the reality of the Second World War, at least in relation to queer men. Some heterosexual recruits might have used queer men to confirm and demarcate their own heterosexuality, but this was not always the case. Indeed there are numerous examples of gay men who became models of queer military masculinity, effectively helping to re-fashion the attitudes of their comrades towards homosexuality by proving their effectiveness within an institutional framework that privileged heterosexual (and hegemonic) military masculinity.

Rank and queerness

The fourth, and final, reason why some queer men and women were protected relates to their rank. Aside from military effectiveness and good character, rank was crucial to the censure of and yet also the expression of homosexuality. In the right circumstances it could even grant a certain level of immunity from the law. Oral testimony held in the Sound Archive at the Imperial War Museum in London has revealed two particularly important cases. The first is that of Crank Dyer,[68] described by one of his battalion as a 'heck of a soldier'.[69] William Brown recalled that when Dyer moved to the 14th Battalion Light Infantry Division

> one of the sergeants said 'Oh, we'll have to get him a lad fixed up.' He had to have a boy, this fella. He was a very peculiar man. Great soldier and wonderful on parade but...that was one of his things...we had to provide this young lad to be his batman, for him to use.[70]

In this context, 'use' meant sex, yet Dyer was never punished; indeed, the officers within the unit were willing (whether because of his seniority or some other factor) to accommodate Dyer's sexual tastes and turn a blind eye to his activity.

Another officer, Lieutenant Colonel Peter Burke,[71] who served with the Royal Artillery in Palestine and North Africa, was notorious for propositioning the soldiers under his command, yet he was also described as 'a good officer' and 'a brilliant soldier'. Although he was later sent to a court-martial for indecency, purportedly for propositioning a member of the Royal Air Force, Burke until then had been protected not only by his status but by his unit.[72] Isolated from outsiders who might expose him, he was able to satisfy his sexual desires without fear of exposure. This is a testament not only to the pragmatism that dominated the war years but also to the ways in which that pragmatism could both benefit and disadvantage a unit. Burke may have been an effective officer but his advances were often aggressive and hard to decline, given Burke's position and the privileges he could grant or withhold. Harold Thompson described sleeping next to Burke who proceeded to touch Harold's groin. 'I nearly jumped out of my skin... I just flung my arms... he was a good officer, as brave as anybody [but] everybody was frightened'.[73] Burke's seniority and Thompson's respect for his skills as a soldier prevented him from telling anybody about what Burke had done and was doing to other men within the unit. Daphne Brock, who served in the Women's Royal Naval Service, found herself in a similar situation following an assault by a fellow Wren. She was advised by a friend not to complain about the incident because her First Officer was a well-known lesbian.[74]

There can be no doubt that the seniority of higher-ranking gay and lesbian officers gave them a greater degree of choice because they could actively request particular visits and choose particular men and women whom they could proposition in safe locations away from others. In addition, they were able to abuse the trust engendered by their seniority. What their cases also highlight is the difference between acceptable and unacceptable behaviour. The extent of acceptance was dependent not only on the behaviour and discretion of a serviceman or woman but also the nature of the relationship between a comrade and his or her unit. An effective, popular serviceman was more likely to be shielded and protected than an unpopular, lazy one. This is an exceptionally important point because during the war, whether on the homefront or the sharp end, citizenship and group acceptance were determined by contribution and character.

One extreme example which illustrates the importance of the 'good fellow' was remembered by Lawrence Harney, a heterosexual veteran of the Royal Navy who served on board the destroyer *HMS Cotswold* during the War. He recalled the suicide of a young sailor who threw himself off his ship when it was in dry dock. Shortly after the funeral of the boy, the chief bosun's mate was found dead in the bottom of the dry dock. It emerged that the senior man had been seducing the boy, a situation which motivated the younger man's suicide. His seducer had been thrown into the dock by his shipmates in what Harney termed 'rough justice'.[75] Incidences such as these suggest that unwritten codes of honour and morality held a comparable, if not higher, importance than official conventions.

Regulating homosexuality

Official responses to homosexuality by officers and officials were dominated by leniency and pragmatism. In the first instance, there was no singular and unified opinion on how homosexuality should be dealt with. In the Army, discharge was viewed as the last resort and was only invoked if behaviour was persistently disruptive or indiscreet. In a memo written in 1942, officers were requested to watch out for 'feminine types and confirmed homosexuals' because it was thought that they possessed 'psychological characteristics [that may] indicate mental defect or temperamental instability'.[76] Aside from the obvious reference to 'feminine types', the instructions that accompany the list reveal the Army's uncertainty about homosexuality and their desperation for manpower. 'Any of the following characteristics may indicate mental defect or temperamental instability... the majority (although not all) of the men showing them will make bad front-line soldiers and will be very liable to break down in action'.[77] The use of the word 'confirmed' suggests that incidences were only punished, first, if they were repeated, second, if they were obvious to a third party or a non-consenting sexual partner and, third, if they were deemed to be disruptive. It is also implied that a 'confirmation' of homosexuality involved a positive response to the question 'are you homosexual?' We can only speculate how many queer recruits answered this line of enquiry honestly. Some queer men did, however, admit their homosexuality to try and secure their own discharge.[78]

The memo also implies that homosexual incidents constructed as 'isolated' or motivated by deprivation might be ignored and, moreover, that the Army was really only concerned with monitoring 'true' homosexuals, as opposed to men having sex with one another. The distinction is important, and has been made by, amongst others, the scholar John Howard who coined the term 'homosex' to describe sexual activity that occurs between men but which does not derive from or determine sexual identity.[79] To some extent, the exigencies of the war legitimated this kind of activity. Dennis Campbell admitted that he and other queer men had sex with married men because

> [T]hey simply wanted their rocks off... they had sexual feelings to satisfy... In many places there was not a woman about. What did you do? Stations were usually in isolated places where you did not have

access to a brothel or to a nearby city. There were no women available and you're growing up and you're feeling quite randy and quite
horny and you need sexual relief and in many cases it was sexual
relief rather than actual gayness.[80]

Motivated by an urge for sexual relief rather than indicative of sexual
orientation more generally, such liaisons could be justified because they
were deemed to be safer than those with local girls. During his service in
the Army, Richard Briar had two relationships with married heterosexual
men. Both of his partners preferred to have sex with other men because
of the expense of local prostitutes and the threat of venereal disease.
It was a system that seemed to work effectively and is a clear example
of how some senior soldiers did not merely ignore homosexuality but
actually engineered relationships in what Briar termed a 'practical and
pragmatic way'.[81]

Publicly, venereal disease was viewed as the predominant factor in
prompting homosexual acts between men. The Public Morality Council
believed that 'men may be turning to these practices [homosexuality]
to avoid the scourge of V.D., of which so much is being made in the
Press'.[82] This was also the view of the popular sex advisor George Ryley
Scott who in 1940 wrote

> In men, the contraceptive element is not so strong a motive for
> perversion, although it has undoubtedly its effects. Here the fear is
> concerned with the risk of having either to marry against one's will
> or to be burdened with the cost of supporting a baby. A far stronger
> motivation for homosexualism [sic] in males is the fear of contracting
> venereal disease...[83]

While personal testimony would suggest that some of the same-sex
activity that occurred during the war might have been motivated by the
urge to avoid disease and pregnancy, Ryley Scott's emphasis on same-
sex activity as merely a resourceful means of avoiding venereal disease
and pregnancy constructs same-sex intimacy as a wartime aberration,
thereby depicting such men as 'victims of the war' who would return
to their wives and girlfriends once the war was over. Ryley Scott also
side-steps the issue of love. Indeed, the absence of any reference to emotional attachment between same-sex pairings suggests that homosexual
acts were still being viewed through a lens of criminality. In reality, there
were a number of reasons why men and women chose to become sexually intimate with their comrades, reasons which included convenience

and desire. What Ryley Scott demonstrates is the mismatch between the multi-faceted nature of sexual expression and the binary nature of the law.

The very last sentence of the Army's 1942 memo arguably reveals the most about the service's attitude towards homosexuality. It states that 'the majority [although not all] of the men showing them – that is, the characteristics described – will make bad front-line soldiers and will be very liable to break down in action'.[84] In stating that homosexuality 'may indicate mental defect or temperamental instability', and that effeminate men and confirmed homosexuals would be 'very liable to break down', the memo does not suggest that homosexuals should be exempt from front-line soldiering, nor from service in the Army. It would seem therefore that homosexuality per se was not a primary concern, but whether that homosexuality manifested itself or led to other problems such as mental disorders or disciplinary problems. Thus, if sexual orientation became incompatible with military effectiveness, it was dealt with. In this sense, the Armed Forces were reactive rather than pro-active. They were also surprisingly practical when it came to dealing with homosexual personnel. One unnamed British psychiatrist admitted that during the war

> the conservation of manpower was an essential priority...it was often considered practical and realistic to post known homosexuals of good intelligence and proved ability to large towns, where their private indulgences were less likely to be inimical to the best interests of their service.[85]

In the long term, it was easier, more cost-efficient and less embarrassing to move queer men into the cities or simply to ignore their behaviour than it was to prosecute them by courts-martial.[86] Serious or persistent offenders could be discharged medically or administratively. The latter did not leave a paper trail and avoided the humiliation, on the part of both the offender and the military, of parading a homosexual offender in front of the general public. It is for this reason alone that the threat of a court-martial was a valuable deterrent.

Even after a court-martial and prosecution, however, some homosexual offenders were accepted back into the service. C. S. M. Firminger joined the Army in 1934. In 1939, he was found guilty by General Court-Martial of attempted buggery, and he attempted suicide. Firminger had his rank reduced, was imprisoned for two years and was discharged from the Army with ignominy, or disgrace. However, his unexpired sentence was later remitted and he was re-commissioned in 1942 after his psychiatrist assured the War Office that 'Firminger had been suffering from a disease [homosexuality] and was now practically cured'.[87]

The Air Ministry was prepared to be lenient in cases of indecency between males in the Royal Air Force 'if the offender is young and there seems to be a reasonable prospect that he will respond to punishment [in a later revision, this last word is crossed out and replaced by 'corrective treatment'] and not repeat the offence'. Moreover, a comment in the minutes concludes: 'I am prepared to consider individually those in category A (ii) (a) [homosexuals], provided that they are the passive parties and not the active'.[88] This is very interesting, for evidently in the eyes of the officials at the Air Ministry passive participants were viewed as less threatening than active ones. However, whilst the Air Ministry were willing to retain passive partners, in army culture it was often the active or penetrative male who was elsewhere in the services viewed as the more excusable party, because his active role was seen to mimic heterosexual intercourse. In wartime, such active behaviour could easily be passed off as an aberration motivated by heterosexual desperation. What is most interesting about the Air Ministry is their reversal of this construction. Presumably, they hoped to retain the younger, passive partner in the hope that their homosexuality was merely a stage of their development and that they could be 'straightened out' by physical training and military discipline.[89] It is also possible that the Air Ministry retained the young, passive offender because they viewed him as the defenceless victim who could not possibly have consented to buggery nor derived any pleasure from the act. In this sense, the age of an airman was crucial in determining the extent of his punishment.

This was also the case in the Women's Auxiliary Air Force which infantilised lesbianism in its efforts to understand it. This is clear from the following extract taken from a memo written by the director of the organisation, Dame Katherine Trefusis Forbes, in 1941:

> In approaching an airwoman or officer who we are fairly convinced is a Lesbian...we should point out to her that her behaviour is that of a schoolgirl and that these sentimental attachments are not what we expect from airwomen who must necessarily always set a good example to others. That unless she can behave herself as a sensible adult we consider that she will have a detrimental effect on discipline generally...unless she does pull herself together after a talk or two it is obvious that we would have to dispense with her services.[90]

In the 1940s, lesbianism was even less understood than homosexuality between males, hence the optimism of Trefusis Forbes in thinking that the sexual tastes of these 'misfits' could be remedied by 'a talk or two'. However, it is clear from the passage that the presence of lesbians was not a problem; it was the active lesbian who was 'causing difficulty' and affecting discipline who should be dealt with. The official policy of the Women's Auxiliary Air Force during the Second World War was to turn a blind eye to non-disruptive lesbians 'because it was expedient to do so, in the interests of maintaining maximum womanpower in the Women's Services'.[91]

Conclusion

During the Second World War, disciplinary regulations relating to homosexual acts were applied flexibly, and sometimes sensibly, in response to higher priorities. This is not to say that bodies were not regulated; they were – by queer personnel themselves, their comrades, commanding officers, the War Office and by groups such as the Royal Military Police and the Public Morality Council. However, what needs to be acknowledged is that queer men and women could, as agents, navigate around or avoid the regulations or conventional disapproval (in the case of lesbians) by how they conducted themselves. Some chose or were forced to pass; others used their discretion. A minority performed their queerness overtly. Some of these men and women were accepted because they possessed valuable qualities or skills and because the specific exigencies of war meant that those in authority were, or preferred to stay, ignorant or, pragmatically, chose to ignore homosexuality.

In this sense gays and lesbians were not the victims of a tyrannical military regime. On the contrary, they were able to navigate around military law. It is therefore not remarkable that pragmatism reigned so supremely during the conflict. What is remarkable is the extent of this pragmatism. The demand for manpower ensured that gays and lesbians were not screened out of the services during mobilisation and, moreover, that nearly all were retained. Their retention had as much to do with the ingenuity and discretion of the queer community as it had to do with the value of gay and lesbian personnel and the concept of the 'good fellow'. In this sense the war temporarily opened up a new radical possibility: that queer servicemen and women might be defined by their contribution to the war effort rather than by their sexuality.

Notes

I thank Dr Corinna Peniston-Bird, Dr Stephen Constantine and Dr Felix R. Schulz for helping me to streamline this article, and Lancaster University and the Economic and Social Research Council of Great Britain for funding the PhD research upon which the article is based.

1. Scotland did not decriminalise consensual homosexual behaviour until 1980.
2. '94–49 vote for change in homosexual law', *The Times*, 25 May 1965. See also S. Hall, 'Letters show Monty as "repressed gay"', *The Guardian Online*, 26 February 2001, http://www.guardian.co.uk/Archive/Article/0,4273, 4142165,00.html, accessed 2 January 2007 and N. Hamilton, *The Full Monty: Montgomery of Alamein, 1887–1942* [vol. 1] (London, 2002).
3. Home Office, *Report of the Committee on Homosexual Offences and Prostitution* (London, 1957), p. 53.
4. *Stonewall* was founded in 1989. It was originally conceived as a professional lobbying group. In recent years, its activities have expanded into research and legal test cases. *Outrage!* is a non-violent, direct action group famous for its controversial public campaigns.
5. Hansard Parliamentary Debates, House of Commons, 4 May 1995, p. 458. In 1996, Freeman was the Minister of State for Defence Procurement.
6. Tony Whitehead, letter to *The Guardian Weekend*, 23 March 1996.
7. P. Tatchell, 'When the Army Welcomed Gays', http://www.petertatchell. net/military/when%20the%20army.htm, accessed 18 April 2005.
8. Ministry of Defence, *Report of the Homosexuality Policy Assessment Team* (London, 1996), pp. 226–242.
9. 'Gays win military legal battle', 27 September 1999, *BBC News Online*, http://news.bbc.co.uk/1/hi/uk/458714.stm, accessed 18 October 2004.
10. The Armed Forces Code of Social Conduct, appendix 2 of the Armed Forces Bill, 8 January 2001, research paper 01/03, www.parliament.uk/commons/ lib/research/rp2001/rp01-003.pdf, accessed 1 February 2005.
11. R. C. Benge, *Confessions of a Lapsed Librarian* (London, 1984), p. 25.
12. 'Army on parade for gay recruits', *The Times Online*, 28 August 2005, http://www.timesonline.co.uk/article/0,2087-1753905,00.html,   accessed 23 October 2005.
13. 'Army marches with Pride parade', *BBC News Online*, 27 August 2005, http://news.bbc.co.uk/1/hi/engalnd/manchester/4189634.stm, accessed 23 October 2005.
14. The War Office, *Manual of Military Law* (London, 1939), p. 115.
15. Ibid., pp. 130–134.
16. G. Patrick, 'Were you only gay in army? Heroes slam quiz "insult"', *The Sun*, 13 October 2005.
17. E. Scott, 'Gay soldiers study sparks war of words', *South Manchester Reporter*, 20 October 2005.
18. Letter from J. Clarke, 10 October 2005. Three days after the article in *The Sun* was published, *The Sunday Sport* offered its comment. The observation, written by David Sullivan, the editor of the paper, self-proclaimed 'voice of common sense' and the owner of Britain's largest chain of licensed sex

shops, called my research 'an exercise in political correctness'. D. Sullivan, 'Lesbo honest. This is a waste of time!', *The Sunday Sport*, 16 October 2005.

19. Dennis Campbell (pseud.) interviewed by Emma Vickers, 22 November 2005.
20. E-mail from S. H. to Emma Vickers, 31 August 2005.
21. Letter from Emma Vickers to S. H., 31 August 2005.
22. E-mail from S. H. to Emma Vickers, 31 August 2005.
23. Letter from R. M. to Emma Vickers, 6 February 2006.
24. The Ministry of Defence, *Report of the Homosexual Policy Assessment Team* (London, 1996), p. 120.
25. D. McGhee, 'Looking and Acting the Part: Gays in the Armed Forces-A Case of Passing Masculinity', *Feminist Legal Studies*, 6 (1998), p. 210.
26. B. Summerskill, 'Save us from the armchair generals', *The Guardian Online*, 4 August 2004, http://www.guardian.co.uk/military/story/0,11816,1275547, 00.html, accessed 22 January 2005.
27. A. Belkin and R. L. Evans, 'The Effects of Including Gay and Lesbian Soldiers in the British Armed Forces: Appraising the Evidence', Centre for the Study of Sexual Minorities in the Military (Santa Barbara, 2000), p. 60.
28. B. Summerskill, 'It's official: Gays do not harm Forces', *The Observer*, 19 November 2000, and AFLaGA (Rank Outsiders), Press Release at http://www. rank-outsiders.org.uk/info/_press/001119.htm, accessed 29 January 2005.
29. C. D'Este, 'The Army and the Challenge of War 1939–1945', in D. Chandler and I. Beckett (eds) *The Oxford History of the British Army* (London, 1996), p. 272.
30. See P. Tatchell, 'When the Army Welcomed Gays', http://www.petertatchell. net/military/when%20the%20army.htm, accessed 18 April 2005. More recently, the government estimated that the current number of gays and lesbians in Britain is 3.6 million. See D. Campbell, '3.6m people in Britain are gay-official', *The Observer*, 11 December 2005, p. 13.
31. 18,876 people aged between 16 and 59 were questioned for the survey. See the UK Data Archive, survey SN3434 at http://www.data-archive.ac.uk/ findingdata/snDescription.asp?sn=3434&key=Sexual, accessed 3 January 2007 and K. Wellings, J. Field, A. Johnson and J. Wadsworth (eds) *Sexual Behaviour in Britain: The National Survey of Sexual Attitudes and Lifestyles* (London, 1994). The 1990 study was followed up in 2000 by the *National Survey of Sexual Attitudes and Lifestyles II* which conducted 12,110 interviews with men and women aged between 16 and 44. See the UK Data Archive, survey SN5223 at http://www.data-archive.ac.uk/findingdata/ snDescription.asp?sn=5223&key=Sexual, accessed 3 January 2007.
32. See 'UK Remembrance day honour', *BBC News Online*, 14 December 1999, http://news.bbc.co.uk/1/hi/uk/519408.stm, accessed 1 May 2006. This later figure still excludes those who did not define themselves as gay, lesbian or bisexual. For a fuller discussion of the statistical estimates of gays in the military, see E. L. Vickers, 'Homosexuality and Military Authority in the British Armed Forces, 1939–1945', PhD thesis, Lancaster University, 2008.
33. The War Office, *Army Discipline: 1939–1945* (London, 1950), appendix 1 (a). There are no official figures for the number of officers court-martialled for indecency, nor for the number of men tried for indecency in the Royal Navy and the Royal Air Force.

34. A. Jivani, *It's Not Unusual* (London, 1997), p. 70; UKTV History, *Love, Sex and War,* episode one: 'Sex with strangers' (Testimony Films) 6 November 2006.
35. W. F. Mellor, *History of the Second World War: United Kingdom Medical Series-Casualties and Medical Statistics* (London, 1972), p. 829. 3,780,000 men served in the Army between 1939 and 1945.
36. The War Office, *Army Discipline: 1939–1945* (London, 1950), appendix 1 (a).
37. C. M. Peniston-Bird, 'Classifying the Body in the Second World War: British Men in and out of Uniform', *Body and Society,* 9 (2003), 33.
38. Frank Bolton interviewed by Emma Vickers, 19 June 2006.
39. Albert Robinson interviewed by Emma Vickers, 5 October 2005.
40. E. K. Ginsberg (ed.), *Passing and the Fictions of Identity* (Durham, 1996), pp. 2–3.
41. See E. L. Vickers, 'Homosexuality and Military Authority', 2008.
42. T. Shefer and N. Mankayi, 'The (Hetero)Sexualization of the Military and the Militarization of (Hetero)Sex: Discourses on Male (Hetero)Sexual Practices among a Group of Young Men in the South African Military', *Sexualities,* 10 (2007), 192. See also P. Higate (ed.) *Military Masculinities: Identity and the State* (Westport, 2003) and R. W. Connell, *Masculinities* (Cambridge, 2005).
43. Imperial War Museum Department of Documents (hereafter IWM DD), W. A. Hill, accession number 28/4/42, diary entry 30 July 1942.
44. IWM DD, J. H. Witte, 87/12/1.
45. P. Beck, *Keeping Watch* (Manchester, 2004), p. 13.
46. G. Braybon and P. Summerfield, *Out of the Cage: Women's Experiences in Two World Wars* (London, 1987), p. 205.
47. It was also not uncommon for men to visit brothels together. IWM Sound Archive (hereafter IWM SA) K. C. Lovell, 13251, reel 11. During periods of free time, Lovell's company would sometimes visit the *Black Cat* brothel in Algiers.
48. T. Shefer and N. Mankayi, 'The (Hetero)Sexualization of the Military and the Militarization of (Hetero)Sex', 2007, p. 198.
49. John Saunders (pseud.) interviewed by Emma Vickers, 28 August 2006.
50. Transcript of interview with Bert Bartley, 3bmtv, *Conduct Unbecoming* (1996), p. 14. From 1943, men (the so-called Bevin Boys) could be conscripted into the coalmining industry as well as into the forces.
51. Frank Smith (pseud.) interviewed by Emma Vickers, 19 June 2006.
52. Dennis Campbell (pseud.) interviewed by Emma Vickers, 22 November 2005.
53. Transcript of interview with Bert Bartley, 3bmtv, *Conduct Unbecoming* (1996), p. 14.
54. Dennis Campbell (pseud.) interviewed by Emma Vickers, 22 November 2005.
55. According to Matt Houlbrook, 'queen' and 'quean' were used interchangeably in the first half of the twentieth century. However, in his *Dictionary of the Underworld,* Eric Partridge uses 'quean' as the standard spelling, hence, my adoption of this term. See E. Partridge, *Dictionary of the Underworld* (Hertfordshire, 1995), pp. 545–549; M. Houlbrook, *Queer London: Perils and Pleasures in the Sexual Metropolis, 1918–57* (London, 2005).

56. M. Houlbrook, ' "A Sun among Cities": Space, Identities and Queer Male Practices, London, 1918–57' (unpublished PhD dissertation, University of Essex, 2002), p. 266.
57. Richard Briar (pseud.) interviewed by Emma Vickers, 9 November 2005.
58. A. Jivani, *It's Not Unusual* (London, 1997), p. 65.
59. J. Denith, Timewatch, *Sex and War*, BBC 2 (1998).
60. IWM SA, E. Reid Simpson, 18201, reel 2.
61. D. McGhee, 'Looking and Acting the Part', 1998, p. 206; Section II of the Criminal Law Amendment Act, 1885, quoted at The Knitting Circle: Law, at South Bank University, http://myweb.lsbu.ac.uk/~stafflag/labouchere.html, accessed 3 January 2006.
62. IWM SA, A. W. Weekes, 21584, reel 3.
63. Ibid.
64. IWM SA, W. H. Bell, 22585, reel 3.
65. A. Jivani, *It's Not Unusual*, 1997, p. 65.
66. Transcript of interview with Charles Pether, *Conduct Unbecoming* (3bmtv, 1996), pp. 20–21.
67. P. Higate, 'Concluding Thoughts: Looking to the Future', in P. Higate (ed.) *Military Masculinities: Identity and the State* (London, 2003), p. 209.
68. Pseudonym.
69. IWM SA, W. P. Brown, 9951/16, reel 9.
70. Ibid.
71. Pseudonym.
72. IWM SA, H. Thompson, 12242/17, reel 7.
73. Ibid.
74. A. De Courcy, *Debs at War: How Wartime Changed Their Lives* (London, 2005), pp. 159–160.
75. Lawrence Harney interviewed by Emma Vickers, 5 October 2006.
76. Wellcome Library, John Bowlby collection, PP/BOW/C/5/213, Army memo, 1942. Bedwetters, insomniacs and nail-biters were also listed.
77. Ibid.
78. Dennis Prattley and his two friends spent much of their naval careers entertaining their matelots by 'dragging up' to impersonate women. Their success on the stage encouraged them to leave the Navy and begin full-time careers as entertainers. Unfortunately the Navy did not want to let them go. After three appointments with naval psychiatrists, three declarations of homosexuality and three out-right refusals, Dennis and his friends gave up trying and resigned themselves to the fact that the Navy would retain them until the end of the war because they were too valuable to be discharged. See Timewatch, *Love, Sex and War*, BBC 2 (1998).
79. J. Howard, *Men Like That: A Southern Queer History* (Chicago, 1999), p. xviii.
80. Dennis Campbell (pseud.) interviewed by Emma Vickers, 22 November 2005.
81. Richard Briar interviewed by Emma Vickers, 9 October 2005.
82. London Metropolitan Archives, A/PMC/41-Public Morality Council: Patrolling Officers Reports, 1941–1945, February 1944. The Public Morality Council was founded in 1899 to combat vice and indecency in London. Its members included representatives from the Church of England, Roman

Catholic and non-conformist churches, leaders of the Jewish faith and leaders in education and medicine. It had no police powers but it worked closely with the authorities and helped to prosecute amongst others, importuners, prostitutes, racketeers and pornographers.

83. G. Ryley Scott, *Sex Problems and Dangers in War-Time: A Book of Practical Advice for Men and Women on the Fighting and Home Fronts* (London, 1940), p. 76.
84. Wellcome Library, John Bowlby collection, PP/BOW/C/5/213, Army memo, 1942. My hyphenated interjection.
85. J. Costello, *Love, Sex and War: changing values, 1939–1954* (London, 1985), p. 164.
86. Traditionally, the queer community has always favoured the anonymity and sexual choice of the city. Matt Houlbrook has demonstrated that London drew thousands of migratory gay men onto its streets precisely because of its reputation as a sexual metropolis. New York was also a haven for gays and lesbians in the nineteenth and twentieth centuries. See G. Chauncey, *Gay New York: Gender, Urban Culture, and the Making of the Gay Male World, 1890–1940* (New York, 1994); M. Houlbrook, *Queer London*, 2005.
87. National Archives (hereafter NA) WO 32/1899/7, re-commissioning of Officers who have left the Service through proceedings in the civil court or for disciplinary reasons, Confidential Memo from C. J. Wallace, D.S.P, 13 November 1942, re C. S. M. Firminger.
88. NA 2/9485, Discharge of airmen for reasons of misconduct during the war-1940–1950, Air Ministry Draft Confidential Order 7A, A.92339/40/P.I., Discharges in War for Disciplinary Reasons, 1941, p. 2.
89. This line of thought was pursued by certain eminent sexologists in the inter-war period, namely Desmond Curran who in 1938 concluded that doctors should not

    conclude that the case is one of fixed or congenital inversion until at least the age of twenty-five has been reached, and sometimes, until even later...the guiding principle is perhaps that these manifestations [in adolescents] should not be taken too seriously or too tragically...many of the conflicts and fears of congenital inversion may be avoided or overcome by sensible explanation and sexual instruction.

    D. Curran, 'Homosexuality', *The Practitioner*, 141 (1938), 285–286.
90. RAF Museum, AC 72/17 Box 5, memo on lesbianism from DWAAF to DDWAAF, P and MS, 8 October 1941.
91. NA AIR 2/10673, RAF and WRAF-Homosexual offences and abnormal sexual tendencies 1950–68, 'Lesbianism in the WRAF', loose minutes from A. P. Doran, Squadron Leader, 13 October 1971.

5

'Youth Off the Rails': Teenage Girls and German Soldiers – A Case Study in Occupied Denmark, 1940–1945

Lulu Anne Hansen

Introduction

In late March 1943 the police in Esbjerg, Denmark's fifth largest town, uncovered what they considered a sex orgy involving up to six local girls between the ages of 15 and 22. The Childcare Services in Esbjerg were contacted by the police following the incident, which had taken place in an apartment where the police found four girls 'home alone' in the company of four 'half naked German soldiers'.[1] The girls were placed in a local workhouse until their parents could be contacted, and the following day they were questioned concerning the incident. One 16-year-old girl lived in the apartment and told the police that German soldiers had visited her before while her parents were present. Her father confirmed this, stating that he did not see anything wrong with having German soldiers visit and that he considered it better than having his daughter running loose in the street. It later turned out that the girl was, in fact, often present at the local train station when the German trains carrying troops rolled in. One of the other girls admitted to having had sexual relations with a German soldier since the age of 14, but insisted that she now only had sexual relations with Danes.

The case is one of many concerning intimate encounters between young Danish girls and German soldiers, documented in the journals of the Esbjerg Childcare Services (CCS). Stories like these both confirmed and at the same time helped form the foundation of contemporary perceptions of fraternization.[2] Within the CCS the cases strengthened fears of what might come of relationships between girls and soldiers, and in the underground anti-occupation propaganda stories about fraternization were generally utilized to help construct an image of soldiers'

135

girls as loose and immoral. However, for many girls the possibility of engaging in one or more relationships with representatives of the occupation forces meant new opportunities for fun, adventure, and gaining sexual experience. On the one hand, the occupation therefore spurred a certain conservatism when it came to defining acceptable gender roles and views on sexuality. On the other, it brought to light new options of sexual emancipation. The files generated by the CCS concerning girls suspected of 'going' with soldiers deliver valuable insight into this dynamic during the German occupation of Denmark.

Within the last 15 years, the subject of intimate encounters between women of the occupied countries and German soldiers during World War II has received increasing cross-national attention. Spurred on by a growing interest in women's and gender studies, and in the history of everyday life during occupation, researchers have also found motivation for their archival work in the demands made by the children resulting from such encounters who want to gain knowledge of their own history. In many countries, the fraternizing women's experiences and perspectives were suppressed for long, and only recently have begun to receive heightened public attention.

In Fabrice Virgili's study on French attitudes towards such intimate encounters, he finds inspiration in Anette Warring's categorization of Danish female fraternizers.[3] Both writers emphasize the impossibility of establishing a single profile of these women. In particular, they dismiss one stereotype – prevalent in public memory – which stamped the women as being in general 'poor', 'stupid', and 'ignorant'. While both works have contributed immensely to the breaking down of this myth, it must not be forgotten that the construction of such an image, and the imagination and fantasies attached to it, drew on actual social experiences, which then were reinterpreted and put to use within highly gendered nationalistic discourses. Concerning the Netherlands, Monika Diederichs has emphasized how relationships between Dutch girls and German soldiers were considered both a national disgrace and a social problem. For instance, a Dutch report on youth crime released after liberation pointed to relationships between Dutch girls and German soldiers as 'the most abject symptom of the degeneration of young people during the occupation'.[4] Little is still known, however, about women's and girls' own motives for entering into relationships with occupation soldiers. Young girls, in particular, were not only the targets of public condemnation but also fell within the area of formal state control, and thus there are records which offer at least traces of their self-understanding.

The subject of underage girls and German soldiers has not yet been explored as a particular phenomenon of fraternization in a Danish context, but this essay will offer some reflections based on a case study of the CCS in Esbjerg. I will attempt to offer insights on the mechanisms at work when young Danish girls, often of lower class, became intimately involved with German soldiers. Such relationships played a great part in constructing an image of fraternizing women as lacking in social and economic resources. One aim of the present study is to reflect on the construction of this image. How, for instance, were underage girls portrayed in the underground anti-occupation propaganda, and to what extent were the representatives of the CCS influenced by the disapproving position taken by that propaganda? To understand how this negative image of fraternizing women was constructed, it is necessary also to recognize the practical experiences which formed the basis of such representations. Solely focusing on the social marginalization of these women and girls does not explain the persistence of the phenomenon throughout the occupation. The second aim of the present paper is therefore to reflect on the strategies of action chosen mainly by the girls but also by their parents and by the representatives of the CCS. This will make it possible to reflect on the interplay between the perceptions developed by outsiders and the strategies of action taken by the involved parties. I will offer some suggestions to explain how different forms of relationships at certain times and in certain contexts had much to offer these young women and so sometimes counterbalanced the disciplining strategies at work on a societal level.

The CCS in Esbjerg was busy during the five years of occupation. To gain insights into the work of the institution before, during, and after the occupation around 700 cases were examined.[5] Often a case generated not only a formal report summing up the facts concerning the child or young person and his or her family, but also a variety of documents from other actors such as police reports, school statements, and so-called social reports in which the social worker dealing with the case gave his or her evaluation of the child in question. Altogether 107 cases were dealt with closely. Eighty-nine of these concerned young girls, whereas the others mainly concerned mothers whose parental skills were being doubted. Although naturally limited by the discourse in which the authorities placed themselves, such reports provide a useful view into the range of institutional and communal perceptions of fraternization. It is somewhat more difficult to find evidence for the girls' perceptions of themselves. It is possible, nevertheless, to trace some of the different self-justifying and explanatory strategies the girls used. Furthermore, the evaluative social reports often encouraged more genuine answers than might be expected from, for instance, police interrogations. In attempting to classify the young women, the social worker would engage in a confessional dialogue – one which allowed for some resistance from the girls and their parents even as it was guided by the perspective of the authorities.[6] To develop further an understanding of the social discourses at play in dealing with fraternizing girls, the propaganda of the underground press will be considered as well. The different forms of propaganda originating from the illegal press provide a basis for an understanding of (1) the tensions between fraternizing women and the surrounding society, and (2) the tensions between the surrounding society and the professional institutional context constituted by the CCS.

The sexual dynamics of occupation

Denmark since 9 April 1940 was considered a *Sonderfall* (special case) in German occupation policy.[7] This particular form of occupation became known as a so-called *peace occupation* because Denmark had – under protest – accepted German protection of Danish neutrality through occupation. Germany had promised not to interfere in Danish sovereignty and internal affairs. In return, Danish authorities had to guarantee the safety of the German forces present in the country. This meant that Denmark was never formally at war with Germany, and therefore dealings between the two countries occurred through the foreign ministries. One feature of the peace occupation was that relations between the Danish population and the occupying forces were allowed and even encouraged from both sides. (See Figure 5.1). It was not until the August Rising of 1943, when the Danish government ended its formal functions, that tensions between the Danish population and the occupying forces became dominant. The August Rising has traditionally been linked to a shift in public opinion in support of the resistance, and the last years of the occupation were marked by several confrontations resulting in public protest strikes and German reprimands. The late start of resistance activities does not mean that tensions did not exist earlier. As was the case in other occupied countries, Denmark experienced the stigmatization of those who actively collaborated with the Germans – women in particular. Shaving the hair of women who had engaged with the occupier became what has been described as 'a hallmark of Liberation' in France, and the practice has been documented as a widespread phenomenon in the western occupied territories – even in the German

Figure 5.1 The German propaganda magazine *Signal* in May 1940 referred explicitly to the good relations between German soldiers and young Danish women
Source: Archives of Danish Occupation History.

occupied British territory of the Channel Islands.[8] Harassing women who went with German soldiers was not limited to the atmosphere of liberation. In Denmark for instance, the first recorded hair cropping incident took place already in September 1940, and hair cropping later became an integral part of the August Rising and the liberation.[9]

In Anette Warring's 1994 study of female fraternization in occupied Denmark, she documents, among other things, the role of hostility to fraternizing women in the August events. In particular she emphasizes the importance of differentiating between a public and private context of fraternization as a way of understanding the different meanings inherent in such relationships. Whereas many women viewed it as a private matter if they chose to engage in relationships with one or more soldiers, such relationships immediately became politically charged in a public context. In public, they signalled sympathy with the enemy while at the same time representing low morals and lack of female virtues. In this way they posed a threat to a dignified and united front against the occupier.[10] Since Warring's study the subject has not been further elaborated on in a Danish context, leaving open questions which could and should attract further attention.

This paper takes as its frame of reference the perceived upset in power structures caused by the presence of German occupation forces. The new situation presented alternative possibilities for renegotiating values concerning gender roles and female sexuality. Pierre Bourdieu has used the concept of capital as a means to understand strategies of action within different social fields, each guided by its own rules of engagement.[11] By drawing on Bourdieu's concept, it becomes possible to illustrate further differing strategies of action at play in the various contexts. Concerning the underage girls, their sexuality in itself constituted a form of capital, a good, which they could benefit from, but which could also work against them. This was especially true in a situation where there was great demand for intimate and sexual relations.[12] I have chosen to focus primarily on two fields or contexts for dealing with the subject of fraternization: the local CCS as an institution, and the girls within the context of their peer groups. From the perspective of the CCS the girls were perceived as generally lacking in all forms of capital, but amongst peers fraternization held much potential.

Defining a controllable object

It is difficult to estimate the number of women who became involved with German soldiers during the occupation. Warring has estimated that at least 50,000 Danish women had intimate encounters with soldiers. Her estimation is based on the fact that 5000 children were registered to a Danish mother and a German father during the occupation. In the case of Norway, however, a country whose population counted around 1 million less than that of Denmark, estimates have been made of at least 10,000–12,000 children, while for the Netherlands the number of children is thought to be as high as 16,000.[13] Of course, it should be remembered that the number of German soldiers in Denmark was initially low because of the unique form of occupation, but from 1943 on, the numbers quickly rose to an estimated 250,000. Furthermore, there is clear indication that regional differences were of great importance even within a national context. Interaction with the occupier was more common where German soldiers were located in larger numbers.

It is estimated that on average around 3000–4000 German soldiers were stationed in Esbjerg from 1940 to 1945. However, this number would have been higher in the first months of the occupation, and especially during the last years when the concern for a possible Allied landing on the Danish west coast was at its highest. For the years 1944–1945 the number has been estimated as high as 25,000. In comparison, the town of Esbjerg itself grew during the same period from 32,422 citizens to around 37,382 in 1945.[14] The economic growth lay markedly above the national average. The fishing trade in particular capitalized on the enormous demand from Germany, but German military defence plans also meant an increasing demand for labour, particularly along the west coast and around Esbjerg. It is estimated that 3000–4000 Danish workers came to Esbjerg to work on the German defences. The presence of these many extra residents, particularly soldiers and single men or men away from their families, meant an abundance of money circulating in local business life, and a growth in local restaurant and bar culture. From this perspective Esbjerg, along with the rest of the west coast of Jutland, differs from the agrarian towns of less strategic importance where one would rarely see a German soldier.

On a national level the CCS had experienced a rise in cases during the late thirties, but they culminated during the occupation. The number of children removed according to section 130.1 or section 131 rose by 36 percent from around 6800 to 9291 in the years from 1938–1939 to 1945. The law allowed for unruly or neglected children to be temporarily or permanently taken into custody in order to secure their well-being. In summing up the situation in 1946 there was no doubt within the institution that this rise had been caused by the war.[15] In Esbjerg the number of children and young people who were brought under supervision or who had actually been removed from their parents followed this tendency, with the number of underage children who were placed outside their homes close to tripling from 66 in 1939 to 165 in 1945. This is not counting, of course, children under supervision or even the ones just brought into contact with the CCS. One reason for this was the rise in young boys committing petty crime, but another was an increase in cases involving 'immoral' girls. In the case of Esbjerg and probably in other large towns with a strong German presence, the concern was often caused by girls 'going' with German soldiers. This is perhaps best illustrated by the fact that the gender of children in Esbjerg who were removed and placed outside of their home, was split between 12 boys and six girls in 1938, and 29 boys and 28 girls in 1945.[16]

The date 9 April 1940 is often perceived as a turning point in trying to understand shifts in behaviour amongst children and young people. One girl, for instance, explicitly stated that this date had had a negative effect on her behaviour. She explained that she simply did not know what had happened, but since 9 April she had not been able to control herself and stay away from German soldiers. Now she feared for her own sanity. In another case, a couple explained that they had experienced problems with their daughter earlier, but on 9 April began to understand the seriousness of the matter and from then on had even used physical punishment, but to no avail.[17] Such statements – although not always as explicit – reveal how the German arrival became a point of reference for many which could help legitimize one's own failure as a parent or even as a daughter. At the same time it testifies to the uncertainties and worries amongst parents following the occupation – even though it was a peaceful one.

In the local newspapers from around 9 April a campaign aimed at deterring young girls from contacting German soldiers in the streets clearly bore nationalist undertones. Interestingly, an article appearing just weeks before discussing a prolongation of Danish soldiers' stationing in Fourfelt, at the outskirts of Esbjerg, did not envisage any problems concerning having a large number of soldiers close by. On the contrary, in this case the economic benefits of 3000 soldiers spending their money and placing orders with local businesses were discussed positively. Within days of the Germans arriving, though, the local head of police found it necessary to publish an announcement warning people not to use the blackout as an excuse for getting together in crowds or use the special circumstances as an excuse for folly. The announcement also addressed parents, asking them to discipline their children and make sure that they did not crowd the soldiers by asking for their autographs, etc.[18] Finally, underage girls were warned that the police would be particularly attentive to them, ordering them to stay away from soldiers, and stating that disciplinary steps would be taken should they choose not to act accordingly.[19] These less-than-subtle warnings were apparently not enough. Just over a week later both the social democratic and the conservative local papers reported incidents of the police stepping in and targeting underage girls in other towns. The social democratic paper was the harshest in its description of the girls. Under the headline 'Tøse i Silkeborg' (Tarts in Silkeborg) the article described how a large number of 'so-called girls' had not understood how Danish girls ought to behave under the specific conditions. For this reason they were picked up from the streets and brought in for questioning at the police station.[20]

The subject of underage girls roaming the streets and seeking contact with German soldiers was a difficult one. There were no formal rules to follow to deter girls from seeking contact with soldiers. This becomes clear in the way the newspaper announcements were phrased. There were no laws forbidding underage girls stopping and talking in the street, although there were, of course, temporary bans on group gatherings. For this reason the police had to depend on other disciplinary strategies. One was to appeal to a common sense of decency, not so much amongst the girls as amongst their parents. Young girls roaming the streets were considered a reflection of their parents' decency. Perhaps this was most clearly stated in the above-mentioned article about Silkeborg where it was made clear that only *tarts* would hang about in the streets. Such references were obviously aimed at parents. Furthermore, although the police appeals officially targeted children and young girls, it was not clearly defined when a girl was old enough to establish contact with a soldier. In a note from the town of Kolding, for instance, it was stated that the police would specifically target all girls under the age of 18. However, this age limit was not undisputed.

As it turned out, the question of what could be considered the acceptable age for engaging in flirtation and relations with German soldiers became an early cause of conflict. In May 1940 the SS-Brigadenführer Kanstein, who was in charge of the internal administration, made complaints that the police often hindered Danish girls from talking to German soldiers. In his response the Danish head of police, Thune Jacobsen, stated that this was only the case when the girls were estimated to be underage, bordering on still being children.[21] At another meeting in the Foreign Ministry in October 1940 the subject of issuing an official age limit for girls contacting German soldiers was discussed, but there was agreement that this would not be possible to enforce.[22] The conflict points to two problems concerning the girls – one which arose specifically as a consequence of the occupation and one which was intensified by it. First, the conflict demonstrates an attempt at upholding certain national standards when faced with the presence of the occupying forces. Not only did girls' relations with soldiers cause annoyance amongst the older generation in particular, but could also compromise the virtue of Danish women both in the eyes of the occupiers and in the eyes of the Allies.[23] Second, the conflict illustrates the difficulty of defining a line between childhood and adulthood. The police and certainly the CCS would attempt to draw the line at the age of 18 when the girls were legally of age, but from the German side the age of consent, which was only 15, seems to have held greater appeal.

This ambiguity concerning the girls' age continued to surface in different contexts. It was a conflict also traceable in the representations found in the illegal propaganda.

Children or tarts – girls in the illegal propaganda

The rise of the underground press marked the beginning of a more active strategy of resistance amongst certain groups in Danish society. Beginning with the communist-organized paper *Land og Folk* in October 1941 (the communist party was banned in August 1941) different groups started organizing with the purpose of turning public opinion against the policy perceived as collaborationist between the Danish government and the German authorities and of mobilizing people in favour of active resistance. Another paper, *Frit Danmark*, was established as a result of the cooperation between communist and conservative politicians. It was founded in the spring of 1942. *Land og Folk* and *Frit Danmark* were, together with the national-conservative paper *De frie Danske*, the main representatives of the underground press – with *Land og Folk* and *Frit Danmark* reaching circulation of almost 300,000 in the last months of the war. These papers developed local editions, usually based on the main paper, but adding local news and information. It is estimated that the number of illegal papers distributed during the occupation rose from around 20 titles in mid-1942 to over 200 titles in May 1945.[24]

The messages of the underground press were national and often ideological. The strategies somewhat differed and changed during the occupation. Until the August Rising in 1943, the general aim of the illegal press had been to exercise pressure on the government to limit the cooperation with the German authorities. An important part of this strategy consisted of attempts at undermining the legitimacy of the peace occupation by attacking the occupation forces at the same time as shaming any form of collaboration with the Germans. As the cooperation at government level ended, the strategy of discrediting the occupation forces was continued and the attacks on economic and social collaboration were intensified.[25] The local papers in particular were filled with concrete examples of people behaving in manners considered nationally shameful. It is usually here that we find fraternizing women named alongside economic and political collaborators. Often the papers would publish names and addresses of collaborators. In this way the illegal papers pursued a strategy of social disciplining. The efforts were partly aimed at branding people already deemed guilty of acting indecently in national terms and partly at deterring others from doing the same.

Women as part of the resistance did not play a large role in this propaganda. The mention of women usually came up in connection with general announcements calling on the whole nation to stand together. In such cases men as well as women were called upon to display a sense of national honour and an obligation to act in a dignified and worthy manner. Here the concept of womanhood was mobilized to further strengthen the idea of a common national unity. The female image was tied to the home, and the propaganda was somewhat aimed at making the housewife aware of the direct consequences of the occupation on her daily life, within the household, or calling on her to encourage her husband to join the resistance. There was a clear tendency to rely on a rather conservative representation of women as housewives.[26] The image of fraternizing women constituted a stark contrast to these traditionalist concepts. Fraternizing women were in public, out in the streets, in places of entertainment, or bringing the occupation into the private realm by entertaining German soldiers in their homes. Their fraternizing was considered, as Warring has pointed out, '...a shameless open exhibition of sexuality and it was an insult to the national honour'.[27]

Closely tied to the image of fraternizing women we often find the portrayal of the German soldier as a threat to female virtue. The German soldier was perceived as a sexual menace. As one local paper from Lolland Falster stated, 'one of the Nazi fronts is the erotic one' and 'the Germans are having too much luck in this particular area'.[28] Although some papers tried to undermine the masculinity of German soldiers by referring to possible homo- or trans-sexuality amongst them, the perception of German soldiers as sexual predators became predominant. For instance, already in March 1942 *Land og Folk* referred to Himmler's demand on German women to produce children whether married or not, as an example of Nazi barbarianism, in particular alluding to the SS journal *Das Schwarze Korps* which encouraged German SS-soldiers to impregnate at least one woman before risking their life at the front.[29] Furthermore, especially through 1944 the stories of rapes committed by German soldiers spiralled.[30]

The aim of the propaganda concerning the soldiers was to undermine a widespread image of German 'correctness'. The behaviour of the occupying forces was a matter of high priority in German circles. In fact, Hitler had himself ordered that Danish women should be treated with respect.[31] When in May 1940, for instance, a signed petition from the married women of Ringsted stated that they would not accept that they themselves and their daughters were approached in the streets by soldiers, the matter was taken very seriously by the local commander.

Issuing a set of guidelines for the soldiers he made it perfectly clear that approaching women in the evenings uninvited would cause severe disciplinary punishment. The guidelines also stated that uninvited contact with girls in the street would be considered the equivalent of seeking contact with prostitutes. The married wives of Ringsted might not have appreciated this reference to their daughters![32]

When it came to undermining the respectability of German soldiers, their relationships with underage girls could certainly be utilized. The anti-occupation propaganda included examples of German soldiers who undermined the authority of the CCS in its dealings with very young girls as well as mentions of teenage pregnancies.[33] Another theme within the same context involved soldiers' relations with girls placed in so-called 'protected homes', e.g. homes for children considered mentally disabled. An example can be found as late as January 1945, recounting how local soldiers had hidden two mentally retarded girls who had escaped a local institution. The story was used to counter the representation of the Nazi ideal soldier as '...the protector of the weak sex'.[34] In such cases young girls were portrayed as the victims of German soldiers' sexual desires.

On other occasions, however, the underage girls were themselves described as engaging in provocative or outrageous behaviour. Often the upset arose from the girls' willingness to stand up for themselves and defy their fellow Danes. An example can be found in *Vestjyden*. The paper in June 1943 ran a story about a man who was assaulted for revealing the name of a very young girl who, in the company of a German soldier, had been acting 'indecently' in a café. The article called for the CCS to step in and do something. This and other stories strongly emphasized the girls' vindictiveness.[35] The girls' willingness to challenge traditional local authorities caused particular outrage. *Aalborg Posten* in the spring of 1944 specifically played on this theme, recounting the story of a young girl who in the company of a German soldier took a walk past the very spot where a young Dane had been killed during the events of the August Risings. When criticized by a passerby, the girl allegedly turned around and shouted in a scornful and denigrating manner that he ought to 'shut up', and that the Danes were no longer in charge of the country.[36]

The portrayal of fraternizing women in the underground propaganda contained several contradictions. On the one hand, it was aimed at discrediting the image of the German soldier as honourable and knightly. On the other, in doing so, the propaganda had to recognize the existence of such an image and the appeal it held for Danish women. Moreover, in recognizing that the German soldiers *did* in fact hold a certain appeal amongst a broad range of women, the construction of *one* set image of romantic and sexual fraternizers was made complicated. In particular, the propaganda concerning underage girls was ambiguous. Here an image of German soldiers posing a threat to young girls' sexuality and an image of young girls in themselves posing a threat to a united Danish front collided. In the propaganda the idea of fraternizing girls as submissive objects of German soldiers' desires very much followed the legal limit drawn by the age of consent. As for girls between 15 and 18 years of age, they were in general classified within the overall conceptualization of fraternizing women as both loose and traitorous to the nation.

Considering the opinion-forming aims of the underground propaganda, it is of interest to ask to what extent the propaganda was reflected in an important community institution like the CCS.

Perceptions of young fraternizers at an institutional level

It is clear that the problem of underage fraternizers did not subside within the first summer, or throughout the rest of the occupation. The journals from the CCS concerning fraternizing girls in Esbjerg indicate that the number of girls being reported was more or less constant. It might have been expected that more girls would be reported at the end of the war as the resentment towards the Germans became more pronounced. On the other hand, this might have been counterbalanced by fewer girls wanting to fraternize with soldiers for the same reason. Perhaps one of the best indications, other than the CCS records, is the continuous preoccupation with the subject in the underground press throughout 1943 and 1944.

The CCS was, perhaps not surprisingly, instantly worried about the apparent prevalence of such intimate relationships. Several aspects were of concern. First, there was worry about the spread of venereal disease. Second, there was great fear of unwanted pregnancies; and finally there was worry that girls living an immoral life would be marginalized, perhaps even ending up as prostitutes. These concerns merged into an all-encompassing fear of any form of relationship between girls and soldiers. There was a perception that German soldiers posed an extraordinary threat to young women's virtue. In evaluating a young girl who, together with her older sister, had had sexual encounters with German soldiers in the local park, a social worker stated about their parents that '...they are not capable of helping her to understand what an experience with this German soldier can lead to...'.[37]

The fear was that young girls would be tempted into an idle and immoral life of drinking and roaming the streets with soldiers. From there, it would be an easy slide into extramarital pregnancy or perhaps prostitution. 'Going with soldiers' therefore became a standard category according to which girls could be classified. The question of fraternization became inherent in every new evaluation of unruly girls, either the social worker asking explicitly whether this was a problem, or parents or neighbours bringing it up as a specific character trait. Although recognizing fraternization as a particular trait of unruly girls, there is no evidence that the CCS in Esbjerg considered these girls more immoral or sexually divergent compared to the young women whom the CCS had evaluated before the occupation. Rather, the behaviour of young fraternizers was interpreted within the overall frame of troubled girls whose possibilities of straying were greatly enhanced by the occupation. For instance, reporting about a girl who stubbornly continued her relations with different soldiers and later became known as an informant for the Gestapo, a social worker wrote that she had not had an easy life and that to her 'police and authorities were things one just had to fight against'.[38]

Within the institution of the CCS much effort was put into finding out what caused this behaviour, and different ways of drawing the girls' attention away from the soldiers were attempted. The perception of young female fraternizers as just another kind of troubled teenagers seems to have been shared by some, though not all, employers. In fact, the authorities sometimes worked with employers who, to a certain extent, saw it as their obligation to offer the girls a form of guidance and thereby help bring them back onto the right track. The general problem of a girl roaming the street in the evenings and not being able to do her work properly was often considered a challenge for employers. Such cases were known before the occupation, but they were fewer and did not necessarily involve the accusation of immoral behaviour.[39] In one case an employer even arranged to have a girl walked home to avoid her stopping and talking to soldiers.[40] However, other statements from employers indicate that surrounding society, often customers, could exercise pressure and that having a girl employed who went with Germans was a bad reflection on the employer. Such perceptions must be read between the lines and were only rarely explicitly stated. The fact that only a few openly nationalistic condemnations from employers or school administrators were documented does not mean that these elements were not at play from the beginning of the occupation. During the early phase there was far less concern expressed than in later public condemnations.

When it came to underage girls the CCS's evaluation were marked by a rather pragmatic approach to the subject of intimate fraternization. Relatively few evaluations of girls can be said to fit within a nationalist discourse. When relationships between girls and soldiers were resisted it seems to have mainly been out of concern for the above-mentioned specific problems. The suspicion of the soldiers' intentions was deeply felt. For this reason any attempt at justifying the relationships were dismissed although sometimes parents – or girls – would attempt to invest the relationships with legitimacy. Claims of formal engagements were often used to prove the genuineness of the relationships. One mother, for instance, actually turned up at the door of the CCS with her daughter and the daughter's alleged German fiancé, just as many girls would argue that they were in fact engaged.[41] In the social workers' experience, such formal engagements did not last long and they were usually not taken seriously by the authorities. As mentioned above, broken engagements and pregnant unmarried girls were often made use of by the underground propaganda to counter any perceptions of legitimacy. However, for the representatives of the CCS it seems to have been the situation rather than the people who caused concern. For example, as late as March 1944 representatives of the CCS seem to have agreed with a mother who considered her daughter's fiancé, a young German officer, 'a fine young' man with whom her daughter could possibly continue romantic relations after the war. Or, in another case, the CCS concluded in the autumn of 1945 that a previously unruly girl was doing very well with her German fiancé.[42]

Most often the views of the CCS collided with the views of the parents. For the CCS to be successful in their attempts at bringing unruly girls back on track, they needed the support of the families. Much, therefore, depended on a shared frame of reference.[43] Parental views can be split into three overall categories: first, parents who seemed genuinely upset at their daughter's fraternizing and would do anything to stop it; second, parents who expressed unhappiness with their fraternizing daughter, but who did not act in order to prevent it; and finally, a small but nonetheless fascinating group of parents, who would not recognize their daughter's relations with one or more Germans as a problem, and who would be openly supportive of their daughter. Of course, sometimes parents disagreed with each other, and also viewpoints could overlap.

Usually parents would express frustration at their daughters' behaviour. Several fathers explained how they had physically beaten their daughters to get them to behave, and one had even caused an incident with a soldier when trying to pick up his daughter from the street. Some parents were more ambiguous in their views. As mentioned above, an engagement was sometimes used as a way of legitimizing the relationships. Another reason for accepting a relationship could be, as expressed in the introduction, that it was better to keep the daughter at home rather than have her straying on the streets. There was little the authorities could do if the parents did not consider their daughter's behaviour a problem. In one family the daughter was denounced by neighbours and other girls as an initiator when it came to establishing contacts with German soldiers. But the CCS immediately backed down when faced with the mother, who insisted that the girl had only had a relationship with one soldier who had been a steady boyfriend for a while. Furthermore, the mother saw nothing wrong in having Germans visiting their home, as the family was in fact German themselves. In such cases the CCS would attempt to influence the families and girls in what they considered a positive way.

The situation was somewhat different when it came to families with actual Nazi sympathies. One case concerned a lower working-class family with open Nazi sympathies. This case did not concern an underage fraternizer, but it is illustrative of how the CCS would deal with people professing Nazi convictions. The father had worked in Germany, and it was a well-known fact that the family often entertained German soldiers in their home. In this case the CCS was brought into the matter because of an incident between the husband and wife. The husband had been jealous following his wife having an affair with a German officer, and he had threatened to kill her. This family could not gather much sympathy with the CCS as 'the husband only has himself to thank' for introducing Germans into his home.[44] Interestingly, the CCS washed their hands of the family and decided to leave the supervision of the children to the wife of a leading member of the local Nazi party. However, she quickly decided to give up her position after feeling ridiculed and disrespected at the first board meeting in February 1944.

In sum, whereas the local representatives of the CCS seem to have been guided mainly by professional institutional aims, parents formed more varied strategies of interpreting their daughters' behaviour. The success of such strategies was largely determined by the social workers' perceptions of the parents' social position in relation to the CCS. However, young fraternizers and their families should not be seen as mere objects of external definitions and disciplining strategies. Girls had their own perceptions of fraternization.

The temptation of fraternization

The cases concerning fraternization brought to the attention of the CCS took many forms depending on the specific circumstances. Most of them were cases of underage girls acting on their own or with their friends. Some of them involved the girls' continuous relations with one or more soldiers, while others seem to have been more of a passing infatuation, something the contact with the authorities put an end to.

The majority of girls tried to hide or play down their relationships with Germans when confronted by the authorities. One girl, for instance, explained that she had seen several soldiers because she would end the relationship and find somebody else as soon as one became too daring in his approaches.[45] By rather cleverly turning around the suspicious circumstances of going with several soldiers and by using it as proof of her own high morals, the girl stayed within a frame of reference which seemed acceptable to the social workers. Other girls were more willing to defend their actions. These were often reported for displaying particularly indecent or provocative behaviour. An example of this attitude can be found in a case of a 14-year-old, who, in August 1940 whilst being questioned by the police, openly expressed her annoyance with the authorities, stating, according to the report, that '...she did it [went with soldiers], because that's what all girls did, now they thought it was fun, so why shouldn't they?'[46] She considered it highly unfair that she and her friend should be picked out especially, as she put it, because this might put an end to the possibility of their maintaining contact with soldiers. Such a statement would probably not be made nearer the end of the occupation.

In dealing with the CCS most girls knew what was expected and certainly tried to legitimize their actions by offering explanations which could be accepted by the social worker. However, in other contexts the aspect of intimate relations could also be used to the girls' advantage. So what was the attraction of fraternizing with German soldiers?

The economic advantages of going with soldiers were relatively limited. Denmark was throughout the occupation well provided for when it came to food, so engaging with the occupying forces was not necessary to secure provisions. The CCS's concerns centred around the perceived danger of sexual relations eventually leading to prostitution. It is thus of interest that there are no cases of underage girls admitting to having been given money by soldiers. In a few cases mother and daughter were suspected of prostitution.[47] There are some instances of girls getting a cinema ticket from their soldier boyfriend. It does not seem that the CCS considered this anything other than a gift.

The possibility existed of going to work for the Wehrmacht or other German institutions, and sometimes this was used as a form of social rebellion.[48] Most often young girls would be given jobs in kitchens etc., but in the journals we find relatively few examples of them actually holding such jobs. Instead, several girls stated that they were certainly *planning* to go to work for the Germans.[49] The common positions for young working-class girls were as house assistants. Although the wages were somewhat increasing, the position in general meant long work hours and low social status. When the girls argued that they would go to work for the Germans, they pointed to the wage difference as the main cause. This could sometimes be combined with a dream of going to Germany. The dream of going to Germany might have only prevailed during the first years of the occupation. The examples are too few to establish a clear picture, but the fascination with German soldiers amongst some girls seems to have lasted throughout the five years.[50] As we shall see below, employment with the Wehrmacht could also sometimes be used as leverage when faced with the authorities. Concerning the parents of the fraternizing girls also, there are relatively few examples of them working for the Germans, only around 15 percent. Although a connection between parents having jobs related to the occupying forces and their daughters fraternizing did in certain cases exist, it was not the rule. Therefore, economic incitement as a catalyst for fraternization does not seem to have been primary for these girls.

Instead, an aspect of novelty, excitement and self-assertiveness seems to have predominated. The Danish doctor Grethe Hartmann has pointed to certain traits which some girls found especially attractive about the German soldiers. Although problematic as a source in relation to the subject of fraternization in general, Hartmann's group of girls seems similar to the group dealt with here. When interviewed by Hartmann, half of the women who had stated that they preferred Germans over Danes claimed to have been attracted by German manners. An interesting 5–6 percent considered the Germans better lovers, as they allegedly 'showed consideration for the soul of the woman concerned...'[51] The CCS never asked the girls specifically why they went with Germans, but they would often reflect on the question in their evaluations. From the reports on the very young girls several aspects stand out.

First there is the simple aspect of curiosity. One of the things often noted by the social workers is the fact that establishing relations with

German soldiers carried the temptation of 'forbidden fruit'. Sometimes this was interpreted as a form of social rebellion and sometimes just as restlessness or search for adventure. German soldiers offered an opportunity of living out experiences in a casual manner. For instance, many of the girls had their first erotic experience with a German soldier. A certain mystery and drama surrounded the soldiers, and this was probably alluring to some girls. Perhaps this explains why a young girl of 13 boasted to her classmates that she had been locked into a room by the Germans who had given her ice cream, and why older girls would sometimes boast to their peers about their intimate relations with Germans.[52] Such stories were used to gain respect. The staff at schools and institutions certainly interpreted such boasting as the girls' attempt to stand out. Boasting about sexual experiences in this way is, of course, not unique to the occupation, but the German presence meant an added dramatic angle on the subject and offered greatly enhanced possibilities of living out the experience.

It is somewhat difficult to judge how many of the girls actually had sexual relations with soldiers. The girls were on average 16 when brought into contact with the CCS. Concerning older girls, the authorities often presupposed that they had engaged in intimate encounters, and often the reports do not state explicitly whether such relations had taken place. Nevertheless, the many cases of girls found in air raid shelters and parks with soldiers indicate that the potential for sexual encounters was great. The fact of a minimum of 5500 Danish children registered as having a German father bear witness to this.[53] At the same time we do not know the amount of illegal abortions carried out, but in Esbjerg a woman was arrested following the liberation because she had allegedly carried out abortions primarily on fraternizing women.

For many, going with soldiers served very often as a free ticket into the local cafés, bars, and restaurants. Yet the fact that sexual relations with soldiers do not seem to have involved any direct economic benefits for the girls is in itself interesting. It is obvious that the incitement for the girls to act on their own often lay in the simple fun of being around soldiers – and other girlfriends. Kjersti Ericsson has pointed to the contrast between the sad image of prostitution, often predominant in scientific works on such subjects, and young girls' intense hunt for forbidden pleasures and adventures, surfacing from the journals of a Norwegian girls' reformatory in the 1950s.[54] The same contrast appears from the journals of the CCS in Esbjerg. The contrast between the concerns of the authorities and many girls' apparent perceptions of their own actions is noteworthy. Esbjerg is a harbour town and in the journals from before the occupation there are cases of girls wandering and going on board of Danish or foreign boats. But these were individual cases and did not involve as many young girls. The phenomenon of going with soldiers seems to have appealed not only to girls already tempted by adventure, but also to girls who would normally be easier to control. The *occupation* in this way greatly enhanced the possibilities of acting outside of established norms for young girls' behaviour.

Young girls' fraternization also offered them new forms of social identification. Often girls formed casual contacts and became part of rather loose networks revolving around German soldiers. Such networks seem to have been of great importance for the recurrence of fraternization, and it is necessary to understand what social gains such relations had to offer.

By reading through the journals certain networks can be uncovered by the repetition of certain names and places. A young girl, for instance, who was caught hiding out with a German soldier in an air-raid shelter after curfew told the police that they had met other girls with *their* soldiers. She did not know their names but she had seen them with soldiers before, and they had advised her not to give her real name if discovered by a Danish patrol. In another case, the CCS discovered that a girl used a false name amongst her fraternizing friends.[55] In some cases such group identities could even form in direct opposition to other groups of low social status. In one case following the liberation, a feud between two groups of girls emerged. The girls had called each other names, – 'feltmadrasser' (field mattresses) and 'fiskertøse' (fisher tarts) respectively.[56]

The idea of being part of a larger community was probably somewhat reassuring, and it might have made it easier to act against established norms. This would have been the case whether it just involved knowing that other girls frequented the local park with soldiers or whether it meant meeting up in one of the local gathering places, perhaps accompanying somebody else or actually participating in the socializing itself. There are some cases of parents complaining that their daughter frequented homes where she would find support for her rebellious behaviour.[57]

The strength of such identification is well-illustrated by the case of a girl who had been impossible to discipline and who would not keep away from German soldiers. The CCS worker had, however, taken a liking to her. She was perceived as being a good girl who was just restless and in need of some healthy activities. For this reason it was decided to send her to a home economics school in Copenhagen. This was something which the girl had expressed a wish for, but not all girls were given such an opportunity through the CCS. Only a couple of months after she had arrived in Copenhagen the school reported back to Esbjerg with bad news. Since her arrival the young woman had gone missing twice. Both times she was later found in the Café Mokka, a well-known café in Copenhagen where German soldiers met up with their Danish girlfriends. The last time she was brought back to school she had even been infested with crab lice.[58] The superintendent expressed great frustration and stated about the girl that 'she is a sweet and mild girl, but what is the use when she cannot stay away from soldiers'.[59] In the end the girl was sent to a youth home. Further examples exist of girls going to other towns only to meet up with other fraternizing girls and soldiers there.

There is reason to think that a certain identification or perhaps cliquishness might have developed amongst the girls. This should probably not be understood as a form of solidarity, which would make the girls stick up with one another. They were quick to tell on others when in trouble. Nevertheless, the idea that a definable group of fraternizers was out there is one that can be traced throughout the journals. Forming relationships with soldiers could offer a community with other girls doing the same, at the same time as it raised one's own status within such community. This is an aspect which will need further theorizing, but indeed seems useful for deepening our understanding of risk calculation amongst young fraternizers.[60] From this perspective, girls prioritized their status in this area higher than their position in other spheres of society – although usually attempting to maintain an acceptable position everywhere using differing strategies.

Finally, a certain confidence-building or self-assertive aspect of fraternization existed. As mentioned above, the open fraternization displayed in public contact between girls and soldiers was perceived by some as rather shameful unless it took place in the context of friends meeting up or in the close vicinity of soldiers' barracks or air-raid shelters.[61] Others took open advantage of their relationships. An extreme case perhaps, but nonetheless illustrative, of the provocative potential in some girls' behaviour is found with two local girls who in September 1941 were caught in the street singing and shouting – seemingly intoxicated. In responding to the police's attempt to take them away, one girl threatened to call on her German relations, speaking in German and stating that she considered herself German rather than Danish. In another case a girl in a youth home in early 1943 was caught copying and circulating what the superintendent described as a 'dirty' poem about the

Germans which was '...a scorn to everything Danish...'.[62] The girl was reported saying that she would not stoop as low as to go out with Danish boyfriends. Such behaviour and statements could of course be put down to youth, spontaneity and excitement. But to some girls the fraternizing was part of a persistent fascination with everything German. This was not rooted in political admiration – on the contrary. One superintendent at a home stated about a young fraternizer: 'her whole outlook on life is marked by a lack of [political] positioning'.[63] The fascination with German soldiers is revealed in the habit of collecting autographs from them – for some a hobby also carried out with the Allied soldiers after the liberation. But the journals also reveal several examples of girls who, while placed in institutions, planned to go to Germany and indeed did run away to get to the nearest German barracks alone or with other girls.

Not only could establishing contact with German soldiers be used to enhance one's status amongst peers, it could also be used as a tool of empowerment both within the family and when faced with the authorities. In doing so girls, however, risked exclusion from the broader community as a result of stepping outside accepted forms of behaviour.

Channels of empowerment

Fabrice Virgili has alluded to the importance of conflicts of a private nature as catalysts for fraternization. Women were in this way offered an opportunity of turning the power balance around.[64] About half of the girls represented in the journals had backgrounds which did not follow the standards of well-adapted families as defined by the CCS. At least one-fourth of the girls came from broken homes, and often the conditions in the homes were considered unsatisfying. It could, for instance, be a case of a mother not able to keep the house tidy and clean, an alcoholic or abusive father, or just the parents' inability to deal with their roles as parents. Problems in the homes were not always a consequence of fraternizing – but this could cause an escalation of tensions. The problems could then again be perceived as a further incitement for the girls to seek interactions outside of the home. Furthermore, the intimacy involved in a flirt or a romance would offer a feeling of being appreciated – at least for a time.[65]

The perception of being wronged and finding comfort in the company of German soldiers becomes apparent in many cases. As previously mentioned there are several examples of girls escaping from institutions explicitly stating that they had gone looking for soldiers. One girl, after an argument with her mother and stepfather, threatened to commit suicide by throwing herself from the harbour quay, only to be rescued by German soldiers. A local newspaper in 1943 reported on a girl of 14 who in April 1945, after having been beaten up by her abusive father, refused to go back home. The paper reported how she then fled the youth institution where she had been temporarily placed, hurt herself in the process, and then struggled towards a German guard telling him that this was done to her by 'the Danes'.[66] In another case a family complained to the CCS that their daughter had become very difficult. She would roam the streets with her friends and go out until early hours in the morning, but when confronted by her siblings or parents she would threaten to tell on them to her German friends. Likewise a runaway girl was picked up carrying a list of the names of 15 Germans she could contact.[67]

Often mothers were suspected of fraternizing with German soldiers. When a father made contact with the CCS it was sometimes a case of the parents being divorced and the father wanting custody over the children. In some instances he would raise the issue of his former wife fraternizing to prove her unsuitability as a parent. Some of these cases were reported to stem from prostitution, but sometimes we find examples of mothers simply having German soldiers visit the home or even eloping with a soldier. Mothers could also lean on their relations with the occupying forces. One mother whose children had been forcibly removed wrote to the CCS that she expected to have her children given back to her or she would have to ' ... seek protection from the people who are now governing the country. They will surely take care of matters as I have witnesses that my children were removed because there were members of the Wehrmacht present in my apartment'.[68]

German soldiers also offered an alternative for widows or divorcees. In one case a woman had had her hair cut in the days of liberation. This happened because she had worked for the Germans and later entered into a relationship with a German officer who had supported her while her husband, a fisherman, was interned in England. The social worker dealing with the case in February 1946, expressed her understanding for what the woman had done and for her writing her husband and telling him the truth. She stated in her report that the mother could be proud of what she had achieved for her family while her husband was gone. He had almost ruined the home because of his drinking, but he would now return to a clean home, and to healthy and well-fed children.[69]

Warring has pointed to the very real fear of fraternizing women functioning as informers. This, combined with the moral and national indignation caused by the often public display of female sexuality, was reason for societies' vicious attacks on fraternizing women.[70] But another point should be made. The illegal propaganda was, as shown from the CCS records above, often based on conflicts very much present on a day-to-day level. Many of the cases presented here could certainly be perceived by contemporaries as clear evidence of a loosening of established morals and values. In 1942, for instance, Danish journalist Kate Fleron published a book which was mainly based on information from the national Childcare Services and the police. The book painted a bleak picture of slipping sexual morals amongst youths and parents mainly amongst the working-class poor. Although the book was contested, it is illustrative of perceptions in parts of the population at the time that norms and values were disintegrating.[71] The portrayal of girls who explicitly called on the Germans when disrespected or who simply used their relations with Germans to enforce their will as manipulative and vindictive, or the portrayal of mothers and sometimes daughters as prostitutes or sexual animals was not only a question of discrediting fraternizing women. By circulating such representations an aspect of social disempowerment could to a certain extent be dealt with. The concerns of husbands and boyfriends were in some communities very real. On a local level the head of police in Esbjerg for instance acknowledged that there was general outrage amongst Esbjerg's young men concerning '…the German fraternization with the young Danish women in town and the way this fraternization takes place'.[72] On a day-to-day level the option for girls and women of establishing some form of contact with representatives of the Wehrmacht was, not without reason, perceived as a realistic – and worrisome – possibility.

Virgili has, in the case of France, emphasized that an important aspect of efforts to suppress fraternization involved attempts at reasserting local male dominance. Behind the constructed image of the bad *French* fraternizing woman he also sees an image of the bad mother, wife and daughter – of a bad woman in general.[73] This image can be found in Denmark, too. In addition – and this is noteworthy in the Dutch case as well as the Danish – the phenomenon of fraternization could be inscribed in a eugenic paradigm, popular within the psychiatric profession, in which social deviance such as fraternization was seen as a symptom of intellectual and moral inferiority.[74] Still, as shown above, it is too simple to see the work of the Childcare Services as merely an extension of such efforts at suppression.

Conservation or emancipation?

Youth morals and questions of girls' sexuality were debated and negotiated independently of the occupation. But the German presence made the issues more pressing. For the girls discussed here, the occupation meant that somewhat new and alternative choices became available. Many young girls acted on these possibilities. Whether it involved using fraternizing as a key to fun and excitement which had not previously been available, or whether it involved actively using the possibility of having a boyfriend or a fiancé with authority and power, girls could capitalize on their sexuality. This situation in itself held a dynamic potential, one that was also perceived by contemporaries.

The specific experience of the younger fraternizers has probably been of great importance to later representations of fraternizing women as belonging to the margins of society. At the same time it greatly challenged available strategies of social discipline, not only because of the limited possibilities of clearly defining acceptable and unacceptable behaviour concerning girls and German soldiers, but also because the German occupation forces constituted an alternative source of power which could potentially be drawn on. This certainly left open room for manoeuvring outside of established norms at the same time as it provoked new attempts at social control and disciplining.

One such form of control was exercised through the underground propaganda. In constructing an image of fraternizing women, the underground propaganda relied heavily on the outrageous aspects of a practical day-to-day experience of relationships between girls and soldiers, and advanced a highly traditionalist approach to gender roles. The stories told in the press were often drawn from society's lower classes. Anette Warring has pointed to one main conflict of modernity as centering on women's role in society, representing at the same time an image of 'emancipation and destruction'.[75] This tendency can indeed be seen in the period of occupation when the underground propaganda often – in spite of its call for social reform – ironically, promoted an anti-modernity line when it came to gendered aspects of the resistance.

Yet while the underground propaganda pursued a strategy of one-sided condemnation of such relationships, the local representatives of the CCS in Esbjerg acted on somewhat different terms. Although sharing the interpretation of fraternizing girls as often coming from families of low social standing, the CCS worked within an institutional framework which proved relatively resistant to the disciplining discourses of the underground press. However, in identifying the girls within a larger

group of unruly young women, the CCS also contributed to later perceptions of the girls as lacking in social resources. Finally, the families
dealt with here provided a more complex image of the girls. For many
parents having a daughter categorized as fraternizer meant taking on a
label of failure. Therefore, strategies were employed which could help
legitimize such relationships.

The girls were the objects of such differing attempts at definition and
control. Most girls would, within the context of their families and the
CCS, play by the rules of established conventions and try to project an
image of conforming to expected standards, but amongst their peers
overtly sexual behaviour could be a way of gaining status and fulfilling
personal needs. Finally, some girls – just like some parents – chose to
openly defy conventions on a general societal level and thereby risked
isolation. Certainly, girls and women acting according to these new
options constituted a challenge – not only to national identity but also
to established sexual value systems.

In her doctoral thesis from 1953 on the sexual conduct of young
women, Danish doctor Kirsten Auken posed the question whether the
occupation had led to a permanent change in the sexual behaviour
of the Danish population. She concluded that this was not the case.
(Auken based her conclusion on the fall in cases of venereal disease following the liberation and on the shift in the social groups affected.
Whereas the occupation had seen a rise in cases also amongst people with relatively few sexual relationships, after the occupation, as
before, the affected were mainly made up of people having many
such encounters.)[76] But in her reliance primarily on disease statistics,
Auken ignored how the phenomenon of young fraternizers increasingly
informed the discussion of young women's sexuality and the debates on
youth delinquency.

The young fraternizers became an element in a professional and eli-
tist project of integrating young social delinquents in Danish society.
Grethe Hartmann concluded her study of the women by stating that
although their actions were reprehensible they were nonetheless best
understood as ' ... unhappy girls who by an ill fate have been flung into
the maelstrom between two belligerent forces'.[77] In the report of the
Danish Youth Commission (*Ungdomskommissionen*) from 1945 devoted
to an evaluation of how to improve social conditions for young people, the young fraternizers were also used as an example of maladjusted
youth.[78] Yet such diagnoses, although containing a large disciplining
potential concerning young women, also helped pave the way for the
program of sexual liberation yet to come.[79]

It could be said that although the public debate on youth morals amongst the lower classes was certainly moving within a very conservative discourse, the actions by some subjects were functioning independently of this. The forms and means of interaction between restrictive discourses and girls' actions and perspectives need not only additional empirical study but also a further development of theory to help us grasp these dynamics. For now, the gap between the official perceptions presented here and the private day-to-day experience of the individuals involved is well illustrated in the words of a 17-year-old girl. In 1942 she wrote her girl friend in a reformatory of the erotic and amusing pleasures she had experienced with young men (including German soldiers) in Esbjerg during her holiday from another institution. First she spent a few days in the town of Tønder with a soldier who she described as her 'future husband':

> It was wonderful days not to forget the nights. They were the best of it all. He was with me every night for the three days I was there... I was also sad when I left him but it helped when I arrived in Esbjerg. I was out having fun you bet.

In Esbjerg she then met a German mariner with whom the girls had previously had contact. After she left the other young men who had accompanied her to go away alone with this mariner, the two, by now drunk, ended up on a roof at the harbour to sober up. 'Then I say to Frits: "Yes but I am not wearing any panties". "I have them in my pocket he then said [quotation mark missing]. Wouldn't you have liked to see me then? And do you know what? I remember that I held his you know in my hand'. At another point in the letter, after stating her agreement with a cousin who, although pregnant, refused to marry the father of the baby, the girl writes her friend the exciting news about a German soldier they know getting engaged and bringing his new Danish fiancée to Esbjerg. '... then we will really let loose'. And finally, before encouraging her friend to burn the letter once it has been read in order to avoid confiscation, she offers an insight into her view of the CCS and the ways it infantilizes the girls it supervises: 'The first of November I'll be finished with the childcare and then I can seek my own employment [...] In any case I will be home when you arrive, that's for certain. Then we will have a wonderful time together. Then we will both be 18'.[80] In short, in the midst of all the conservative efforts of social workers and nationalist resistance rhetoric, the beginnings of a sexual revolution can be glimpsed.

Notes

I thank the people who have taken the time to read earlier drafts of this essay and for offering valuable comments, criticism, and support: Dagmar Herzog, Henrik Lundtofte, Anette Warring, Kjersti Ericsson and also Mona Jensen, who shared with me her insights on the material concerning the Childcare Services in Esbjerg. Thank you all.

1. Esbjerg Childcare Services (ECCS), Journal number (J.nr.), 680. The journals are kept at the *Esbjerg City Archives* (ECA). The material has still not undergone systematic registration and therefore has not been given a full registration number. In the following I will refer to the journal number.
2. I will use the word fraternization to describe any forms of romantic or intimate relations between Danish women and girls and German soldiers. Although the term is somewhat inadequate for grasping such relations in all their facets it is still, in my opinion, the term that holds the least amount of moral judgement. In Denmark the crude term *Feltmadras* was used about fraternizing women and girls. Also the expression *Tyskerpige* has been used as a more moderate term.
3. A. Warring, *Tyskerpiger – under besættelse og retsopgør* (København, 1994). Warring's results are also published in A. Warring, 'Intimate and Sexual Relations', in R. Gildea, et al., eds, *Surviving Hitler and Mussolini. Daily Life in Occupied Europe* (New York, 2006); F. Virgili, *Shorn Women: Gender and Punishment in Liberation France* (New York, 2002).
4. M. Diederichs, 'Stigma and Silence: Dutch Women, German Soldiers and Their Children', in K. Ericsson, ed., *Children of World War II: The Hidden Enemy Legacy* (Oxford, 2005), pp. 151–164, 52.
5. Unfortunately, no register exists from which it is possible to single out the relevant cases. Furthermore, the cases are only somewhat chronologically organized, which means that some cases from the occupation will have been left out. On the other hand, the necessity of reviewing each singular case made it possible to establish an overall view of the subjects and motivations at play over time. For the background on the development of the CCS in Esbjerg see J. Holst, et al., *Fra børnehjem til familie-institution. Socialpædagogiske strømninger gennem 100 år med udgangspunkt i Esbjerg Børnehjem* (Esbjerg, 1992). Also Anne Løkke's study – although dealing with the years before the World War II – provides useful insight into the development of formalized evaluations within the CCS in Denmark and it has served as a reference to compare the procedures used within the institution in Esbjerg. A. Løkke, *Vildfarne Børn – om forsømte og kriminelle børn mellem filantropi og stat 1880–1920* (Holte, 1990).
6. Michel Foucault has developed the concept of investigative, 'confessional' practices and pointed to the development of a 'confessional science'. This analytical frame provides an opening to dealing with the CCS's reports and evaluations. M. Foucault, *The History of Sexuality*, Vol. I (London, 1978), pp. 53–80. See also B. Rosenbeck, 'Care or Control. Unmarried Mothers in Denmark between 1900 and 1950', in L. G. Tedebrand, ed., *Sex, State and Society. Comparative Perspectives on the History of Sexuality* (Umeaa, 2000), pp. 181–194. The journals from Esbjerg show that the interrogators,

although guided by certain rigid categorizations, were to a large extent engaged in reaching behind the surface of each case. However, this cannot be said to have been a general trait within the whole institutional system.

7. For an overview of the political situation in Denmark during the occupation see H. Kirchhoff, *Samarbejde og modstand under besættelsen. En politisk historie* (Odense, 2001).

8. For a comparative perspective, see C. Bryld & A. Warring, *Besættelsestiden som kollektiv erindring. Historie- og traditionsforvaltning af krig og besættelse 1945–97* (Roskilde Universitetsforlag, 1998), pp. 1–561. 113ff. Also M. Bunting, *The Model Occupation. The Channel Islands under German Rule, 1940–1945* (London, 1995), pp. 252ff.

9. A. Warring, 1998, p. 94.

10. Warring refers to the female body as a 'combat zone'. For this subject in a European perspective see A. Warring, 'Intimate and Sexual Relations', 2006, pp. 97ff.

11. E.g. P. Bourdieu, 'The Forms of Capital', in J. G. Richardson, ed., *Handbook of Theory and Research for the Sociology of Education* (London, New York, 1986, Org., 1979), pp. 242–258. Also P. Bourdieu, *Outline of a Theory of Practice* (Cambridge, 1977, Org., 1972), pp. 72ff. On habitus e.g. P. Bourdieu, *Distinction: A Social Critique of the Judgement of Taste* (London, 2004, Org., 1979). The subject needs further theorization but this essay aims at some preliminary reflections regarding this material.

12. It is very important to state that this should not necessarily be perceived as a conscious calculation carried out by the girls, but rather as a form of intuitive knowledge engraved in the concept of *habitus* as elaborated by P. Bourdieu. Bourdieu, 2004, pp. 170ff.

13. Warring, 2006, pp. 94ff.; K. Olsen, 'Under the Care of Lebensborn: Norwegian War Children and their Mothers', in K. Ericsson, ed., *Children of World War II*, 2005, pp. 15–34, 24; Diederichs, 2005, p. 153.

14. This number does not consider the inclusion of the municipality of Jerne in April 1945. S. Henningsen, *Esbjerg under den anden verdenskrig 1939–45* (Esbjerg, 1955). For Esbjerg during the occupation, see Henningsen, 1955, p. 35; V. Bruhn and P. Holm, *Esbjergs Historie*, Vol. 3 (Esbjerg, 1998).

15. 'Statistisk beretning for Landsnævnet for Børneforsorg', in *Socialt Tidsskrift*, 12 (1946), 5f.

16. All numbers concerning the CCS in Esbjerg can be found in *Esbjerg Byraads Forhandlinger* (1938–1946). On a national level, the tendency to even out the gender division was not noticeable.

17. ECA, ECCS, J.nr. 577. Also J.nr. 118, 528, 536, 1031, 1105.

18. *Esbjergbladet*, 12 April 1940.

19. On the conflicts between German soldiers and young Esbjerg fishermen see M. Jensen, 'Wehrmacht and Police Authorities in Esbjerg during the Occupation of Denmark', in F. Just and H. Lundtofte, eds, *War and Society in Scandinavia* (Esbjerg, forthcoming).

20. *Esbjergbladet* also brought a note from the town of Kolding, stating that the police had made it illegal for underage girls to be outside after dark. *Esbjergbladet*, 28 April 1940.

21. This discussion took place in the Ministry of Justice in May 1940. Report from meeting in the Ministry of Foreign Affairs 24 October 1940, RA (*Danish National Archives*), Jr. nr. 84. C.2b.
22. Warring, 1994, p. 131.
23. C. B. Christensen, et al., *Danmark Besat. Krig og hverdag 1940–45*, 2nd edn (Gylling, 2006), pp. 117f.
24. For the illegal press in general see N. Hong, *Sparks of Resistance. The illegal Press in German-Occupied Denmark April 1940–August 1943* (Odense, 1996); J. T. Lauridsen, 'Undergrundspressen i Danmark 1940–45', in *Fund og Forskning*, 36 (1997), 261–388.
25. For the strategy of the illegal papers in discrediting the Germans see A. Trommer, 'Das Bild der Deutschen in der illegalen Presse Dänemarks', in W. Benz, et al., eds, *Kultur-Propaganda-Öffentlichkeit. Intentionen deutscher Besatzungspolitik und Reaktionen auf die Okkupation* (Berlin, 1998); H. Lundtofte, 'Nazis and Barbarians? Danish Popular Images and Perceptions of the Nazi Regime and the Germans 1933–45', in F. Just and H. Lundtofte, eds, *War and Society in Scandinavia*, forthcoming. There is agreement that the portrayals of the German occupying forces underwent radicalization.
26. For a somewhat more dramatic interpretation of the role of housewives during the occupation see K. Fleron, *Kvinder i modstandskampen* (Odense, 1945). Fleron presents an image of the housewives as 'men's shields' even evoking an image of women cooking with a loaded gun next to the cooker. Warring has touched upon this subject emphasizing that gender identity played a large role in determining which resistance activities were available to women. See A. Warring, 'Illegalitetens hule. Hjemmets funktion I modstandskampen', in *Aarbog for Arbejderbevægelsens Historie* (1994), 139–158, 140f.
27. Warring, 1994, p. 105. (My trans.).
28. *Tiden*, May 1943. The papers used here are kept at HSB (*Archives of Danish Occupation History 1940–45*).
29. The question of how the Third Reich's views on sexuality influenced the perceptions of the occupying forces in Denmark needs further research. Dagmar Herzog has pointed to the very liberal views (for racially approved heterosexuals) expressed in *Das Schwarze Korps*. D. Herzog, 'Hubris and Hypocrisy, Incitement and Disavowal: Sexuality and German Fascism', in D. Herzog, ed., *Sexuality and German Fascism* (New York, 2004), pp. 11f. The reference in *Land og Folk* indicates that such expressions were read and caused reactions.
30. A campaign arose in the autumn of 1944 after the Danish police had been removed. The crisis revolved around rumours of mass rapes committed by German soldiers against Danish women. This was taken seriously enough from German side to demand an investigation. The rumours could not be confirmed. Warring has treated this subject. Warring, 1994, pp. 135ff.
31. According to Friedrich Kanstein and Dr Stahlmann, both high-ranking officials within the German administration in Denmark, Hitler had given specific orders that Danish women were to be treated with consideration. Report in the Danish Foreign Ministry 7 October 1940, RA, Jr. nr. 84. C.2b. Also Warring, 1994, p. 131.

32. Letter from Colonel Badinski to the Foreign Ministry 8 November 1940, RA, Jr. nr. 84. C.2b. The letter emphasized the involvement of both German and Danish soldiers.
33. *Land og Folk*, nr. 2, October 1941, nr. 9, March, 1942. Highlighting German undermining of Danish authorities was also part of an attempt to show how Germany did not live up to its 9 April promises.
34. *Ungdommens Røst* (Aalborg), 20 January 1945.
35. Compare *Sydvestjylland*, December 1943. Here a girl was denounced because she had called on local German authorities after being slapped from behind by some harbour workers. The paper underlined that she had only had a light slap and so emphasized the girl's vindictiveness.
36. *Aalborg Posten*, March 1945.
37. ECA, ECCS, J.nr. 476.
38. ECA, ECCS, J.nr. 560.
39. Kjersti Ericsson has dealt with the Childcare Services in Norway in the post-war period. She points to research showing that the idea of wandering girls and immoral behaviour were closely linked in the eyes of the Childcare Services. K. Ericsson, *Drift og dyd. Kontrollen af jenter på femtitallet* (Oslo, 1997), pp. 52f. My research concerning Esbjerg shows a more ambiguous picture. Wandering girls were not necessarily considered immoral. However, there was concern that their wandering would lead to immoral behaviour.
40. ECA, ECCS, J.nr. 494. Also J.nr. 471, 482, 982.
41. See, for instance, ECA, ECCS, J.nr. 490, 494, 565, 982.
42. ECA, ECCS, J.nr. 1001, 528.
43. Ericsson has emphasized that the traditional family functioned as a primary support system and social safety net at the same time as exercising power and suppression. This somewhat changed in the postwar period as the family unit was individualized. The development has clear parallels in Denmark. K. Ericsson, *Barnevern som samfunnsspeil* (Oslo, 1996), pp. 19f.
44. ECA, ECCS, J.nr. 726.
45. ECA, ECCS, J.nr. 593.
46. ECA, ECCS, J.nr. 482. The idea that everybody went with soldiers was one shared by the CCS more than a year later in December 1941. J.nr. 711.
47. ECA, ECCS, J.nr. 285, 534. Furthermore, a girl who had been brought under supervision while still a minor, later turned up as a so-called loose woman, and finally at least five girls were suspected of acting as decoys for an illicit drink-shop. These cases usually arose from a family or guardian being targeted by the authorities.
48. In the case of France, Richard Vinen has alluded to a close connection between working for the Germans and establishing intimate encounters. R. Vinen, *The Unfree French. Life under the Occupation* (London, 2006), p. 163.
49. ECA, ECCS, J.nr. 283, 389, 487, 715, 760. Warring gives examples of girls working for the Wehrmacht and thereby gaining protection. Warring, 1994, p. 134.
50. For instance, complaints from the girls' homes of runaways persisted throughout the occupation. See for instance, ECA, ECCS, J.nr. 459 (February 1943), 711 (December 1943), 1031 (April 1945).
51. Of the 51 percent stating that they preferred German soldiers to Danish men, 19.1 percent gave the courtly manners of the Germans as their reason

for doing so. G. Hartmann, *The Girls They Left Behind* (Copenhagen, 1946), p. 61. For an analysis of Hartmann's results see Warring, 1994, pp. 31ff.

52. ECA, ECCS, J.nr. 494 (August 1940), 513 (July 1941), 711 (August 1943).
53. Warring, 1994, p. 25.
54. Ericsson, 1997, p. 37.
55. ECA, ECCS, J.nr. 536, 591, 609, 637, 711, 905.
56. Police report, Esbjerg, 3 August 1945, RAV (*Regional Archives,Viborg*), B 412, 1997/887, 361–496, J.nr. 442/45.
57. ECA, ECCS, J.nr. 479, 494, 513, 855.
58. In fact, Mokka was in October 1943 targeted by members of the communist-led sabotage organization BOPA killing one German and injuring several Danish girls. E. Kjeldbæk, *Sabotageorganisationen BOPA 1942–1945* (Copenhagen, 1997), pp. 181f.
59. ECA, ECCS, J.nr. 472.
60. The concept of subcultural capital has been applied in contemporary sociology to supplement Bourdieu's theory of capital. It has proven useful for understanding the strategies of action chosen by girls at the margins of the education system. See for instance E. Bullen and J. Kenway, 'Bourdieu, Subcultural Capital and Risky Girlhood', *Theory and Research in Education*, 3/1 (2005), 41–61.
61. The denial would of course also be caused by an attempt to avoid reprimands. However, as mentioned above many girls seem to have been somewhat inclined to tell the truth.
62. ECA, ECCS, J.nr. 536, 558.
63. ECA, ECCS, J.nr. 494.
64. F. Virgili, *Shorn Women: Gender and Punishment in Liberation France* (New York, 2002), pp. 201f.
65. In Warring's interviews with fraternizing women the attraction of being adored came up. Warring, 1994, p. 62.
66. ECA, ECCS, J.nr. 1042. Also Warring lists examples of girls who were released from custody through intervention by their German boyfriends. Warring, 1994, p. 134. Also Hartmann, 1946, pp. 206f.
67. ECA, ECCS, J.nr. 538, 760.
68. ECA, ECCS, J.nr. 771. Other examples include ECCS, J.nr. 407, 514, 536, 538, 759.
69. ECA, ECCS, J.nr. 709.
70. Warring, 1994, p, 105.
71. K. Fleron, *Afsporet Ungdom: En Appel til danske forældre* (København, 1942). The book has inspired the title of this Chapter.
72. Report from Børge Hebo 2 August 1940, HSB. 6C, 184. See also Warring on reasons given for cutting the women's hair. Warring, 1994, p. 94.
73. On the perceptions of masculine failure and feminine betrayal, and the limited studies on this subject, see Virgili, 2002, pp. 236ff.
74. Diederichs has pointed to the influence of the psychiatric profession in Holland. Diederichs, 2005, p. 152. In the case of Norway, an investigation was published in a Nordic psychiatric periodical in 1948. A. Rasmussen, 'Det intellektuelle Nivå hos 310 tyskertøser', *Nordisk psykiatrisk medlemsblad*, 1 (1948).

75. A. Warring, 'Med kønnet som prisme – om modernitet og antimodernitet i mellemkrigstidens Danmark', in T. Kruse, ed., *Historiske kulturstudier: Tradition – modernitet – antimodernitet* (Roskilde, 2003), pp. 181–208.
76. K. Auken, *Undersøgelser over unge Kvinders sexuelle Adfærd* (Copenhagen, 1953), p. 354.
77. Hartmann, 1946, p. 207.
78. Ungdomskommissionen, *Betænkning om den tilflyttede Ungdoms særlige Problemer* (København, 1948), p. 14. On the work of the comission see, H. S. Madsen, *Farlig Ungdom. Samfundet, ungdommen og ungdomskommissionen 1945–1970* (Gylling, 2003).
79. Although Kirsten Auken was a firm believer in the family unit as society's main base in the 1960s, she spoke strongly for compulsory sexual education in schools. Also Grethe Hartmann and Kate Fleron continued to engage in debates on gender roles and sexuality.
80. ECA, ECCS, J.nr. 459.

6
Camp Brothels: Forced Sex Labour in Nazi Concentration Camps

Robert Sommer

History of the camp brothels

When we speak of Nazi concentration camps we think of mass anni-hilation, terror, and starvation.[1] The image of piles of corpses in Bergen-Belsen and the crematories of Auschwitz has burned itself into our collective memory.[2] In the final years of the existence of the vast concentration-camp system in the 'Third Reich', the Nazis installed a system of brothels which only prisoners were allowed to attend. It is not surprising that the establishment of such prisoner brothels has for many years been almost completely ignored by historians. Books and movies have referred to brothels for SS guards in which Jewish women were raped, [3] but the notion of brothel barracks created for prisoners seems completely absurd. Since the 1990s, various scholars have begun to discover the so-called *Sonderbauten* (special constructions), which was the SS euphemism for these brothels.[4]

In this essay based on analysis of SS documents – such as orders concerning the organization of camp brothels, transport lists, brothel invoice sheets, test-tube information slips for blood and cervical smear samples, and brothel visitor lists – as well as interviews with former prisoner brothel visitors and forced sex labourers, I will explore the reasons for the establishment of the prisoner brothels in Nazi concen-tration camps, the recruitment strategies of the SS to find forced sex labourers, the operation and supervision of the *Sonderbauten*, and the reactions of male prisoners to the opening of those brothels. I will also address the motives of visitors to the brothels.

In the summer of 1941 the chief of the SS, Reichsführer-SS Heinrich Himmler, and the chief of the WVHA (*Wirtschafts- und Verwaltungshauptamt* – Economic and Administrative Main Office of

Figure 6.1   Himmler in front of Block 1 during a 1941 visit to the concentration camp Mauthausen, where the first camp brothel was later installed
Source: Archives of the Mauthausen Memorial.

the SS), [5] Oswald Pohl, visited the Mauthausen concentration camp and its sub-camp Gusen in annexed Austria (See Figure 6.1). While there, they also visited two nearby quarries where camp prisoners extracted granite for Hitler's megalomaniacal construction projects. [6] Following that visit, in October 1941, Himmler gave the order to establish two brothel barracks in those camps, which were opened in July 1942. [7] The reason for this decision can be found in the desperate need for building material to realize the Führer's plans to redesign the major German cities, such as Berlin, Hamburg, Munich, Linz and Weimar. Himmler's idea was to increase the efficiency of production by granting selected prisoners the right to frequent a brothel.

In April 1942, Himmler discussed with Kammler (head of the construction branch *Amtsgruppe C* of the *WVHA*) the productivity of prisoners used as construction workers in the *SS-Baubrigaden*, which were building brigades planned to be used to realize Himmler's construction plans in the context of the *Germanisierung* ('germanizing') of occupied Eastern Europe. Himmler did not want to accept that the efficiency of camp prisoners was only 50 percent compared to that of civilian workers and suggested to grant in a 'most free manner' (*freiesten Form*) certain privileges to hard-working camp prisoners, such as access to women in brothels (*Weiber in Bordellen*) and small piecework pay (*Akkordlohn*). In his opinion, to deny the necessity to 'provide' women to satisfy sexual needs of male camp prisoners would be 'out of touch with the world and life' (*welt-und lebensfremd*).[8]

At the same time, the IG Farben was building a gigantic chemical factory in Auschwitz-Monowitz, exploiting concentration camp prisoners. The IG Farben management complained to the SS about the low efficiency of the slave workers. Together they discussed the outlines of a bonus system (*Prämiensystem*) for the prisoners working on IG Farben premises. Such bonuses included extra food rations (*Verpflegungszulage*), the promise of an early release from the camp (*Inaussichtstellung der Freiheit*), and the possibility to visit women in brothels.[9] Soon after that they introduced a piecework system to the factory construction site. The privilege of an early release was neglected by the SS. Instead in the autumn of 1943 a prisoner brothel was built in Monowitz. In March 1943, the Reichsführer-SS visited Buchenwald, the biggest concentration camp on the territory of the pre-war German Reich, and inspected a rifle factory near the camp where camp prisoners worked. In a letter following that visit, he complained to Pohl about the absence of a prisoner brothel in the camp and demanded the design of a piecework wage system (*Akkordsystem*) which he wanted introduced into the entire concentration camp network.[10]

Such a piecework wage system was initiated by the WVHA just a few weeks later in the form of an official order called the *Prämien-Vorschrift* (Bonus Order).[11] The preface of the Bonus Order stressed that slave labour in munitions factories was necessary to win the war. Over four pages, the SS granted special premiums and privileges to hard-working prisoners, including higher letter frequencies, (military) haircuts, vouchers for cigarettes, extra food rations, and the right to frequent a brothel. These were thought to be effective incentives for boosting the prisoners' performance. According to the Bonus Order, the prisoners would receive bonus coupons if they fulfilled the work quota (see Figure 6.2). These could then be used to buy cigarettes, food at the camp canteen, or to pay for a visit to the brothel. The brothel visit, a maximum of one time per week, was however to be only for *Spitzenkräfte* (top-notch employees). To visit the brothel, they had to write a short application to the *Lagerkommandant* (camp commander) who then had to grant permission. The prisoner had to pay two *Reichsmark* in bonus coupons, out of which the forced sex worker in the brothel would receive 0.45, the guarding prisoner 0.05, and the SS, 1.50 *Reichsmark*.[12]

Figure 6.2 Prämienschein (Bonus voucher) from the Auschwitz concentration camp
Source: Archive of the State Museum Auschwitz-Birkenau.

The *Prämien-Vorschrift* became a binding order for the camp commanders as well as the companies employing prisoners. Buying bonus vouchers from the SS and distributing them to the prisoners was agreed to in contracts. In February 1944 the Bonus Order was modified and other privileges, such as visiting camp movie theatres and sports events, were granted. In addition to that, the price of a visit to the brothel was reduced to one *Reichsmark*. Despite the fact that neither the SS commanders nor the company's managements believed that the bonus system was especially effective in raising productivity, the SS gave clear orders and was adamant in enforcing the realization of the bonus system.[13] Until the end of the Third Reich camp brothels were opened in ten of the major concentration camps – Mauthausen and Gusen (July and October 1942), Flossenbürg and Buchenwald (July 1943),[14] Auschwitz-Stammlager (October 1943),[15] Auschwitz-Monowitz (November 1943),[16] Neuengamme (May 1944),[17] Dachau (April 1944),[18] Sachsenhausen (August 1944),[19] Mittelbau-Dora (February 1945).[20]

Since the end of the 1930s, the labour of prisoners in Nazi concentration camps had become an increasingly important issue for the economic system of the SS. Slave labour had been the backbone of the commercial enterprises of the SS, but also of various major state projects of the Nazis, such as the construction of monumental buildings, German settlement projects in occupied Eastern Europe, and arms production in a time of 'total war'. The low productivity of camp prisoners had become a major issue for the SS since the time frames for these projects were extremely narrow and the production plans absolutely unrealistic. The reasons for the low efficiency in the concentration camps were the inhuman conditions at the camps, the low food rations, poor hygiene, and the daily violence. High productivity was contrary to the survival strategies of prisoners, which included working as little as possible.[21] The effective solution to the productivity dilemma could have been very easy: larger food rations for the prisoners, better hygienic conditions, and abrogation of the daily terror. The *Prämien-System,* therefore, was destined for failure because it did not seriously improve living conditions. Himmler, however, saw in the Bonus System a solution to the efficiency dilemma, and until the end of the war, he ordered the opening of brothel barracks in most of the major concentration camps. Introducing the frequenting of brothels as part of an incentive system to concentration camp prisoners gave the brutal camp reality a new dimension: women were compelled to serve as forced sex labourers as an incentive and privilege for other prisoners.

Forced sex labourers and life in the Sonderbau

Beginning with the construction of the first camp brothels in Mauthausen and Gusen in 1942, the SS selected female prisoners mainly from the *Frauen-Konzentrationslager* (female concentration camps) of Ravensbrück,[22] but also – in the case of the brothels in Monowitz, Auschwitz-Stammlager, and Mittelbau-Dora – from Auschwitz-Birkenau (see Figure 6.3). The SS used two primary selection strategies. In Ravensbrück and Auschwitz, SS officers asked women who were working

Figure 6.3 Photographs of a young Polish woman, who later was sexually exploited in the camp brothels of Auschwitz I and Monowitz, taken at her arrival in Auschwitz
Source: Archive of the State Museum Auschwitz-Birkenau.

in very difficult *Kommandos* (work squads), such as surface level construction, to enroll for brothel commandos on the false promise that they would be released from the camp after six months of work there. Today we know that such promises were never kept. This 'offer' was made especially to young German women who were confined in a concentration camp as *'asozial'* ('asocial' persons), and preferably to imprisoned former prostitutes.[23] To them, the so-called *Freiwillige Meldung* (voluntary enlistment) became a decision between life and death and as such must be defined as coerced enlistment. The testimony of a Polish woman, who was recruited at the women's camp of Auschwitz-Birkenau for the camp brothel of the Stammlager Auschwitz, shows this explicitly. There, the *Lagerführer* (camp leader) Hössler asked women who were working in outdoor *Kommandos* to line up in front of him and enlist for the brothel. A young Polish woman stepped up to him and volunteered. When another prisoner asked her why she had done it, she answered: 'Winter is coming and I work in the fields!'[24] She knew that she would have never survived another winter in Auschwitz and preferred forced sex labour to the crematory. The Italian Auschwitz survivor and author, Liana Millu, explicitly defends women who chose to work as sex labourers in one of her writings by asking

> Well, I refused to be consumed and vanish like a cloud. I wanted to return to my house. I'm eighteen years old – I don't want to die... Everyone in the lager goes around picking up leftovers from the garbage. They suck bones other people spit out – and I'm supposed to refuse life because it's offered on a dirty plate?[25]

Besides recruitments for prisoner's brothels, the SS also searched in Ravensbrück for Polish women who they exploited sexually in brothels for Ukrainian SS guardsmen serving at various concentration camps.[26] According to German 'race laws', Ukrainian guardsmen were not allowed to have sexual intercourse with German women. That is why the SS established specifically for them small brothels at the concentration camp sites of Flossenbürg, Buchenwald, the sub-camp Gusen, and possibly at Sachsenhausen.[27] With the opening of these and other prisoner brothels, the SS needed more women for sexual exploitation and employed more drastic recruitment measures. During roll calls, SS officers would walk down the columns of the lined-up prisoners and pick out women they found 'suitable' for a brothel *Kommando*.[28] A German prisoner Magdalena Walter,[29] was selected in 1943 at the *Zellenbau* (camp prison)[30] of Ravensbrück for the camp brothel of Buchenwald.

One day, the SS told her and other women not to go to work. Instead the camp commander of Ravensbrück, Max Koegel, the *Oberaufseherin* (female head of guards), as well as the camp commander at Buchenwald, Hermann Pister, made the women line up, picked out those whom they found 'suitable' for a brothel and wrote down their serial numbers. The selected women were then brought to the camp infirmary, where they had to undress in front of the SS and the camp doctor.[31] After some weeks of quarantine, these women were dressed in their civilian clothes and transported to Weimar in a regular passenger train and later in military trucks. When they arrived at the Buchenwald brothel barrack, they were told by the SS that they would receive better food and not be harmed as long as they complied. Magdalena Walter was relieved that she was not abducted to a brothel for the SS and preferred being in the *Sonderbau* to starvation, physical hard work in a road construction *Kommando*, and being beaten every day by the SS.[32]

The brothel block in Buchenwald was a wooden barrack that was divided into a day room, a room for the SS guard, a medical room, small *Koberzimmer* (brothel rooms), and bedrooms, in which two forced sex labourers slept.[33] The clothing of the women in the Buchenwald brothel consisted of a white plaid skirt (under which they were allowed to wear panties) and a bra. Every morning, the women had to get up at 7:30, wash themselves, and get dressed. During the day, they were occupied with cleaning up the barracks and airing the rooms. They could also read non-political books from the camp library, explained Magdalena Walter.[34] This routine suggested a level of civilian normality inside the brothel, but this was deceptive. Instead, the daily routine was monotonous and consisted of waiting for the 'terrible two hours' ('*verfluchten zwei Stunden*')[35] in the evening, after the male prisoners had finished their daily work. Then, as if she was part of an assembly line, Magdalena Walter had to let the male prisoners use her.[36]

> Now, every night we had to let the men get on top of us, for two hours. That meant they could come into the brothel barrack, had to go to the medical room, to get an injection, could go to the number – to the prisoner, could do their thing, into the room, on top, down, out, back to the medical room, where they again got an injection. The prisoner had to leave the brothel. We had a bathroom with a certain number of water closets. It didn't lack cleanliness there. And then right away there came the next one. Non-stop. And they didn't have more than a quarter of an hour.[37]

In the beginning, Magdalena Walter tried to fight against her destiny and threatened to stab the first man she had to accept with a pair of nail scissors, but she did not have any choice other than to submit to the forced sex labour. The terror in the Ravensbrück concentration camp had broken her will to resist. Her life did not count anymore. Her reaction showed the typical concentration camp apathy. Her feelings were deadened. Magdalena Walter was released from the Buchenwald camp in the end of 1944. The reason for that release is unknown.[38]

Thanks to the detailed documents maintained on the organization of camp brothels, it is possible to make confident statements about the number, nationality, and reasons for detainment of forced sex workers in the Nazi concentration camps.[39] In total, the names of 174 forced sex workers are known: 168 of them were in prisoner brothels, 6 in brothels for Ukrainian SS guards (among whose two had already been in a prisoners' brothel). According to testimonies and SS documents, the total number of all women in brothels in Nazi concentration camps may be estimated at 210 (190 in prisoner brothels and 20 in brothels for Ukrainian SS men). Thus we have information on 82 percent of all forced sex workers in the concentration camps. Of the forced sex workers known by name, 114 (66%) had German nationality;[40] 46 women were Polish (26%), 3 others (2%) had, according to different documents, either a Polish or German citizenship. Six women (3%) were classified as 'Russian', but – considering their names or birthplaces – were in fact mostly of Ukrainian or Belorussian descent. In four other cases (2%), the names do not give precise information on the heritage, but they were surely of Slavic origin – probably Polish, Ukrainian, or Belorussian. One woman was Dutch (1%). SS documents give additional information in the case of 145 women on the reasons for their detainment. Of them 97 were 'asocials' (67%); 42 women were 'political' prisoners (29%); and 4 'criminals' (3%). There is no evidence that any of these women were of Jewish heritage.[41]

The surveillance and control of the camp brothels

The German sociologist, Wolfgang Sofsky, writes in *The Order of Terror: The Concentration Camp*: 'Every power of any duration organizes space and time. (...) Temporal and spatial orders guide social action and relations. Absolute power exploits this. (...) The concentration camp is a system of rigorous surveillance, a receptacle for violence'.[42] The prisoner brothels, being camp institutions, were also organized according to those rules of control and surveillance. When first introduced, the *Sonderbauten* were situated at the camp entrance (Mauthausen, Gusen,

Auschwitz), but later because of a general order, the brothel barracks were built in the peripheral area of the camp near the medical blocks (Flossenbürg, Buchenwald, Sachsenhausen, Neuengamme). The reasons for the relocation were practical. On the one hand, the SS did not want to have the *Sonderbau* being constantly looked at by prisoners.[43] On the other hand, the brothel was usually under the administration of the camp doctor, and a medical assistant worked inside the brothel barrack.[44] That led to the macabre situation in which the building for forced sex work was moved into the dying and killing zone of the camp.[45] In Sachsenhausen, the SS even built the brothel onto the back wall of the *Pathologie* (pathology building), on top of the cellar that hosted the mortuary.[46]

The special positioning in the zone of death and dying allowed the SS to isolate the brothel even further from the rest of the camp. Usually, the brothel barrack was fenced in, and an SS guard stood at the entrance.[47] Moreover, the interior organization of space provided a maximum of control. The *Sonderbau* was in most cases a standardized wooden barrack with a long corridor running from the entrance to the back. The highly structured internal division of the buildings meant that they were easy to control by a guard in the corridor (see Figure 6.4). Symbolic of the SS's urge for total control, the *Sonderbau* in Auschwitz-Stammlager was even designed on the basis of the architectural plans of the feared camp prison in Block 11.[48]

The only way for a male prisoner to get into the brothel was to undergo a long procedure that began with asking permission at the camp administration. The prisoner then had to enlist at the *Schreibstube* (the orderly room of prisoner's camp office) for the visit. When the camp commander gave permission, the names of the visitors were announced at the evening roll call.[49] In Flossenbürg the SS collected the permitted prisoners after roll call and marched with them to the brothel barrack in a row of two. The prisoners had to wait outside in a column until the SS decided it was their turn. Jakub Piecha,[50] a Polish survivor, was 19 years old when he was brought to Auschwitz. He worked at the SS hairdresser *Kommando* and became the personal barber of the camp commander Rudolf Höss. When the SS opened a camp brothel in Auschwitz the *Schutzhaftlagerführer* Aumeier came into the barber *Kommando* and gave his *Kapo* two coupons for the brothel. The *Kapo* kept one and gave the other to Jakub who decided to visit the brothel. The survivor explained that after the prisoners were led to the brothel, they went through a medical examination and had to line up in a row of two in the corridor.[51] The camp commander Höss and other high SS officials

Figure 6.4 View of Block 24a which housed the camp brothel for Auschwitz I from 1943 until 1945
Source: Photograph by Robert Sommer, 2006.

appeared. The military orders 'Stillgestanden! Augen rechts! Heil Hitler'! (Stand to attention! Eyes right!) were shouted. An SS man reported the official number of visitors. Jakub received a ticket with the number nine and was allocated to line up in front of that room: 'Number Nine! Second in the row'![52]

The time inside the room was limited. In Auschwitz, usually a male prisoner was allowed to stay for 15 minutes in the room.[53] Only 'normal sex' in the missionary position was allowed. It was strictly prohibited to get on the bed with shoes on. Through spy holes in the door the SS guards ensured that the prisoners obeyed the rules.[54] After the allotted time a bell rang and the man had to leave the room. If he did not leave the room fast enough, a guard would charge in and beat him out.[55] Before leaving the *Sonderbau*, the visitor had to go back to the medical room and get a prophylactic injection.[56]

The SS attempted to ensure that nothing defied their control, but the surveillance system did not work perfectly. Women resisted by covering the spy holes with tape.[57] Furthermore, women from the *Sonderbau-Kommando* tried to build closer relationships to certain prisoners in better social positions in the camp who would visit them frequently.[58] Such 'rational relationships', as the historian Anna Hájková called them, were a well-known survival strategy in ghettos such as Theresienstadt, as well as in camps where male and female prisoners could meet, especially in Auschwitz-Birkenau (see Na'ama Shik's essay in this anthology, Chapter 8, this volume). In such 'rational relationships', men would provide women with food and protection and receive in exchange sexual services. In the case of the camp brothels (not only in Auschwitz but in other camps such as Buchenwald[59]), men would, in addition to extra food rations and protection, bribe other men to not have sex with the women. The SS tried to hinder these closer contacts by making the women change rooms constantly so that the male prisoners would not know which woman they were going to get. In Auschwitz, black marketeering in the camp increased with the opening of the camp brothel because prisoners smuggled clothes and valuable items from 'Kanada', where the belongings of the gassed Jews were stored, to the brothel in Auschwitz-Stammlager to get the attention of a woman.[60] Some prisoners went and visited their 'lover' at night.[61] If the SS caught them, it usually meant their death. To prevent night visits from happening, the SS would lock the women in a dormitory room or simply replace the women in the brothel *Kommando* with others.[62]

Not only was control one of the SS men's preferred expression of power, but they never missed an opportunity to humiliate the prisoners in the *Sonderbau*. Voyeurism especially seems to have been one of the favourite games of the camp officers. A survivor of Auschwitz-Monowitz, Hermann Leonhardt, who was the block elder of the camp infirmary, stated that at the opening of the Monowitz *Sonderbau* in the end of October 1943, he saw how a group of SS officers appeared in the barrack to watch what was happening inside the single brothel rooms. It was obvious to Leonhardt that they were enjoying it because they continuously made dirty comments.[63] This was not a singular case. Voyeurism was apparent in other concentration camps as well; as a former Dachau prisoner explained, SS men as well as *SS-Helferinnen* (women working for the SS) often went to see prisoners engage in sexual intercourse. If it took the man too long, they would kick against the door with their heavy boots.[64]

Another aspect of controlling the camp brothel was through medical supervision. The women of the *Sonderbau* were not given any condoms for protection – and therefore occasionally women from the camp brothel became pregnant and were forced to abort[65] – but the SS was eager to enforce protection against venereal diseases. Not only did women have to wash themselves with lactic acid after any sexual intercourse and men were given unknown prophylactic medications against VD,[66] but SS-run laboratories analysed blood and cervical smear samples of forced sex workers regularly (see Figure 6.5). In Auschwitz, for example, the blood and cervical smear samples from the women from the camp brothels of Auschwitz-Stammlager and Monowitz were analysed at the laboratory of the camp infirmary of Monowitz or the state-run 'Staatliche Hygiene Institut' in Rajsko, which was situated only a few miles away from the main camp of Auschwitz.[67] At first, it seems ridiculous that the SS made such an effort to test prisoners for VD, but this has to be understood as part of the SS's more general fear of the spreading of epidemics in the camp and perhaps endangering civilians. This fear

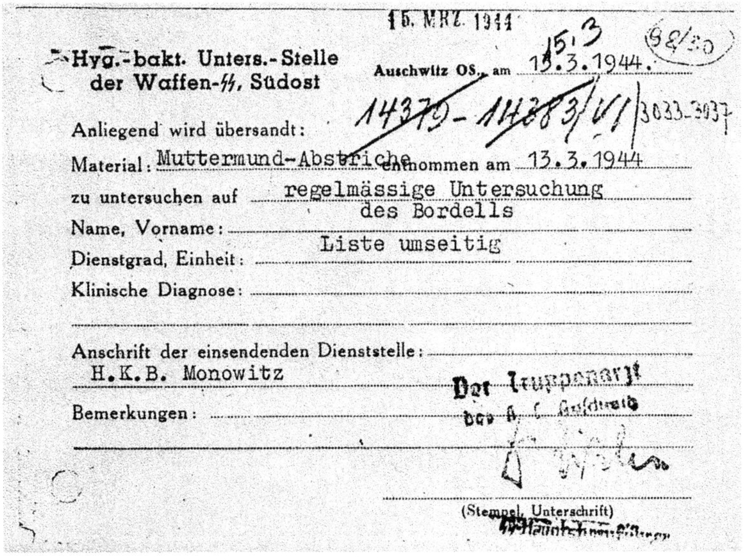

15. MRZ. 1944

Hyg.-bakt. Unters.-Stelle der Waffen-SS, Südost

Auschwitz OS., am 13.3.1944.

Anliegend wird übersandt: 14379–14383/VI

Material: Muttermund-Abstriche entnommen am 13.3.1944

zu untersuchen auf regelmässige Untersuchung des Bordells

Name, Vorname: Liste umseitig

Dienstgrad, Einheit:

Klinische Diagnose:

Anschrift der einsendenden Dienststelle: H.K.B. Monowitz

Bemerkungen:

Der Truppenarzt

(Stempel, Unterschrift)

Figure 6.5 Test tube information slip for cervical smear samples from the women of the Auschwitz-Monowitz camp brothel from March 1944

Source: Archive of the State Museum Auschwitz-Birkenau.

is evident in a *Meldung* (report slip on a prisoner's misbehaviour) from July 1943 written by the SS from the Buchenwald concentration camp in which a prisoner is reported for having tried to attend the brothel with a falsified coupon. The SS stressed the particular severity of his offense by saying that avoiding the medical examination could be a 'menace to the entire camp which (...) may not be underestimated'.[68]

In addition, Nazi concentration camps were to some degree subject to German laws since they were state-run institutions. It seems that Nazi prostitution laws, with their racial and VD-control aspects, applied in the camps as well. Adolf Hitler had already announced in *Mein Kampf* the abolition of prostitution, because he saw it as a disgrace (*Schmach*) for mankind, and in the early years of the Third Reich the Nazis fought street prostitution with drastic measures. With the onset of war in September 1939, however, the Nazis did not abolish prostitution after all, but rather took total control over it. All prostitutes in Germany and the occupied territories had to register and work in brothels which were supervised by the German police and the health authorities.[69] A confidential letter from 9 September 1939 defined rules for prostitutes, including examinations for sexually transmitted diseases that had to be done twice a week. The undergoing of sanitation procedures was a general order to all SS men as well as soldiers.[70] In addition, the SS was by law required to report on a weekly basis any cases of epidemics to the *Staatliche Gesundheitsämter* (state health authorities).[71] Fear of spreading venereal diseases became a big issue, which, in the case of the concentration camps, the *SS-Hygiene Institut* tried to solve.[72]

The society of camp prisoners and the brothel

In the following part of this chapter, I would like to discuss the question of the importance of forced sex work in brothel barracks in concentration camps to male prisoners and the motives of male prisoners behind attending the brothels. When thinking of sexuality in the concentration camp, in this case male sexuality in particular, one might wonder how any sexual desire in the *univers concentrationnaire* – the world of terror, starvation and annihilation – could exist. In an interview, Jack Terry, a survivor of the Flossenbürg concentration camp, spoke about the diminished significance of sexual desires: 'And sex was not a question. You know, survival, eating. Eating was the most important'.[73] Shortly after his liberation, Auschwitz survivor and psychologist Viktor E. Frankl recorded his experiences in the camp and stated that during his stay in Auschwitz, his sexual drive 'generally kept silent'[74] and masturbation was replaced by *Magenonanie* (stomach masturbation).[75] These accounts might represent the experiences of a large part of male concentration camp prisoners, probably the majority, but there is more to it. In 1971, the German psychiatrist Paul Matussek wrote in his study of the psychological effects of concentration camp confinement that the non-existence of sexual drives, as Frankl described it, cannot have been true for everyone. One of his interviewed survivors stated, that 'despite undernutrition, he missed sexual activity... Many [prisoners of Dachau – RS] had sexual dreams and masturbated. In silence, I had the wish to visit the camp brothel'.[76] A Buchenwald survivor, Ernst Federn, a psychologist himself, went as far as to write: 'Sexuality played a tremendous (*wahnsinnige*) role'.[77]

These accounts and statements seem at first contradictory, but they begin to make sense once one understands the different living conditions inside the camps. Considering the size of food rations and the level of terror maintained by the SS, living conditions in some camps were better than in others. In Dachau and Buchenwald the chances of surviving were much better than in Auschwitz-Birkenau, Majdanek, or Mauthausen.[78] Moreover, the social structure of the prisoner populations was a major reason for the diversity of these accounts. Sofsky describes the concentration camp as a system of extreme inequality in which countless prisoners starved in misery while others led a life of veritable luxury. To run the complex system of a concentration camp, the SS relied on giving some power to a few prisoners who organized the camp in 'Self-Management'. That gradation of power was mainly based on the racial and political ideas of the Nazi ideology and was realized though a system of classification based on taxonomy.[79]

When a person was deported to a Nazi concentration camp, from the moment of his or her arrival, his human identity was destroyed and replaced by a number. A rapid process of dehumanization began, which demanded of the prisoner to adapt completely to the laws of the camp.[80] Only a few prisoners survived that initial period.[81] An important part of the destruction of a human being is *desexualization*. The obliteration of sexuality and sexual identity becomes part of the act of terrorizing the individual. In the beginning, all body hair is shaved off and any personal belongings are taken away. After that shock, starvation makes secondary sexual characteristics disappear: women lose their menstruation, the sexual body gets reduced to a sole reservoir of energy, and in the end, it eats itself.[82] Columns of men and women pass each other in Auschwitz-Birkenau without having any sexual reactions to each other, writes Samuel Pisar.[83] Feelings of shame or loathing disappear for many prisoners. The psyche reverts to the mere will to survive. The demolition of sexuality and sexual identity happened to both women and men, but – as some female survivors testified – to women it could be even more devastating than to men.[84]

After surviving these shocks, some prisoners were able to adapt to the reality of the camp while many others died. In the process of adaptation, reconquering a sexual identity becomes a major strategy of survival. Furthermore, it shows that there is a strong connection between the social position of a prisoner in the camp's inner hierarchy and his or her sexual life. The better the *Kommando* of the prisoner, the higher the position of a prisoner in the system of prisoner-functionaries, the more food a prisoner can organize (trade), and the more important sexuality becomes in his or her life.[85]

Until the establishment of the brothel barracks, in most of the male concentration camps there were no women. In fact, many of the male prisoners, especially those who had been imprisoned already in 1933 when the Nazis took over, had not seen a woman since.[86] Therefore, seeing a woman generally caused a real sensation in the camp,[87] as did the arrival of women for the camp brothel in Auschwitz-Monowitz. There, the brothel barrack was built in the middle of the camp and the women even went out of the barrack to where the male inmates could see them.[88] In Auschwitz-Stammlager, the brothel was built into Block 24 which was situated right next to the entrance gate overlaid with the slogan *Arbeit macht frei* (see Figure 6.4). Most of the prisoners in the camp knew about the brothel, but that did not necessarily mean that details of the brothel were generally known. Knowledge of the brothel consisted mostly of rumours. In Mittelbau-Dora the brothel barrack was built into the rooms of the barrack hosting the camp library, situated right above the roll call square. During roll calls, the prisoners noticed the women in front of the barrack or at the windows where the SS made them stand in order to draw the men's attention.[89] However, to most of the prisoners the *Sonderbau* did not have any significance in their daily struggle to survive.[90] Since the prisoners for whom sexuality played a rather important role mostly occupied higher positions in the camp's social hierarchy, the camp brothel became merely an institution for the prisoner-functionaries. The number of people who frequented the *Sonderbau* was very small, almost infinitesimal. In Auschwitz-Stammlager, during the time when approximately 30,000 prisoners were interned, the estimated number of visitors was about 100. That made up only 0.33 percent of the camp's population.[91] In Buchenwald an average of 98 prisoners visited the brothel on the days it was open during its first month of operation, July 1943. That was 0.76 percent of the camp's population.[92] First of all, as we have seen, the group of prisoners to whom the 'privilege' to visit a woman in the *Sonderbau* was granted was very small. Second, a prisoner had to 'qualify racially' for a visit. Only 'Aryans' were allowed, such as Germans, Dutch, Belgians, Scandinavians, Poles, Czechs, Ukrainians, and Spaniards.[93] Jews and Soviet POWs were at all times excluded. They were brought to the camps for their own annihilation.[94] In addition, the prisoner needed to have access to bonus coupons (*Prämienscheinen*) to pay for the visit. Since in many camps those coupons were not distributed on a regular basis, a prisoner had to be able to acquire them on the black market or know someone who was in charge of their distribution.[95] In addition, the prisoner obviously needed to have the physical strength and will to visit the *Sonderbau*. Those prisoners were mainly prisoner-functionaries, such as *Lagerälteste* (senior camp prisoner), block elders, *Kapos* (*Kommando* supervisors), but also prisoners from privileged work squads such as *Lagerschutz* (camp police), *Lagerfeuerwehr* (camp fire brigade), *Küche* (kitchen *Kommando*), *Frisör* (camp barber), *Krankenbau* (camp infirmary), or *Metzgerei* (butcher). Based on accounts and testimonies as well as the *Bordellbuch* (brothel visitor book) of Block 3 of the Mauthausen concentration camp, it is possible to get a closer view of the social status of brothel visitors as well as into the frequency of their visits. The visitors could be subdivided into three different groups according to frequency and voluntariness of their visits: some of them were frequent visitors; others went there sporadically or one time only; some were even forced by the SS to go there.[96]

Frequent camp brothel visitors were an extremely small number and mainly members of the camp 'aristocracy', the upper social stratum of the prisoners.[97] Thanks to the existence of a brothel visitor book (*Bordellbuch*) from Block 3 of the Mauthausen concentration camp, we know names, camp serial numbers of visitors, and the days of their visits during the period from June to December 1942. Block 3 was the *Prominentenblock*, the barrack where most of the prisoner-functionaries slept at night. In August 1942, 90 prisoners were recorded in the *Bordellbuch*, of whom 57 visited the brothel. Looking more closely at the frequency of their visits, the book shows that some prisoners visited regularly, up to twice a week, but these were only 19 men.[98] When looking at other original documents from Mauthausen, such as a list of prisoner-functionaries who were allowed to carry a watch in the concentration camp, as well as prisoners' record cards, we are able to get an idea about the social positions in the camp hierarchy of those frequent visitors.

Some of them were *Kapos* of various working squads such as the quarry work squad, the SS garage *Kommando*, or the *Desinfikation* (disinfection *Kommando*). Among them were also a cook, a cleaner at the camp commander's office, a worker in the camp parcel post office, and a *Blockschreiber* (block scribe).[99] These work positions were highly coveted because they gave the prisoner the possibility to have access to valuable trade objects or comestibles and at the same time meant little physical labour. At the time when those men visited the camp brothel, bonus vouchers had not yet been introduced and the 'entrance fee' therefore had to be 'organized' in other ways. The *Kapos* and higher-rank prisoners were part of the *Lagerprominenz* (camp notables) who had money and valuables (both strictly forbidden to most prisoners), owned different pairs of shoes (while the mass of prisoners only had one pair), played card games on Sunday with a few thousand Reichsmark stakes, and organized sports contests as well as music evenings. They also had young men or male children as lovers, even though homosexuality was strictly forbidden in the camp.[100] Sexuality did not only play a role in their 'higher lifestyle',[101] but became a prestigious symbol of their power. The willful waste of food in front of prisoners who starved to death was equivalent to the waste of sexual energy in contrast to prisoners who could not feel anything other than hunger and fatigue.

The second group of brothel visitors was larger and can be seen as the majority group of visitors, as the Mauthausen brothel book shows. The sporadic and one-time brothel visitors belonged mainly to the camp's middle stratum. Their motives to visit the brothel were of a different character and can be better understood in the context of their vicinity to death and their desire to feel human, to feel themselves to be men through experiencing sexuality as well as emotions. In 1973 the Polish sexologists Giza and Morasiewicz published their results of a study done between 1964 and 1972 on the sexuality of male prisoners from the Auschwitz concentration camp. In that study, they discuss, among other things, the importance of masturbation to camp prisoners and find out that the test subjects masturbated very seldom (once in two or three months) and not for the purpose to satisfy any sexual needs, but rather to see whether they were still alive.[102] That was similar to female sexuality, as the sexologists found in a later study.[103] The correlation with the desire to feel like a masculine human being by having a sexual or an emotional experience can also be identified as a motive for visiting the brothel. Men wanted to see whether they were still men, in both a physical and emotional sense. Remasculinization became part of regaining one's sexual identity, which had been destroyed since the beginning of confinement in the camp.[104]

Many of the young men who were brought to a concentration camp had never had any sexual relationships with women. It was clear to them that they would never survive the *Konzentrationslager*, and so they wanted to have at least once in their life a sexual encounter. A former Auschwitz-prisoner, Johan F. B., who worked as an interpreter in the *Politische Abteilung* (Gestapo office inside the camp), received at one time a bonus coupon from his friend who worked in the butcher *Kommando*. His friend told him to visit the brothel since he had never been with a woman. He went, but regretted it the moment he entered the brothel and stated later that he only talked to the woman.[105] Another example is a Czech boy who came to Mauthausen when he was 18. There he survived only with the help and protection of a prisoner-functionary with whom he was forced to have sexual intercourse in exchange for extra food and protection. Since he had never had a sexual relationship with a woman, he wanted to see whether he was homosexual and therefore visited the camp brothel.[106] However, it seems that in many cases men were not capable of any sexual action, as various forced sex workers from camp brothels stated in interviews.[107] The reasons were not only the debilitation of the body of the prisoner, but also the reality of the context of forced sex labour in a camp, with virtually no space for sexual desire to develop, in addition to the long absence of any contact with women.[108] Many prisoners also visited *Sonderbau* simply to talk to a woman – to have personal contact with another human being.[109]

The third group of camp brothel visitors were those who did not plan to go to the *Sonderbau* but were forced by the SS to do so. This could mean that the SS wanted to reward certain prisoners, who did not want to go to the brothel, but could not refuse the offer by the SS official since that would have meant punishment. The former Monowitz prisoner Mieczysław Zając remembers such a case. The *Lagerführer* (camp leader) wanted to reward a prisoner who was a qualified worker and who because of his excellent knowledge of the German language was working for IG Farben. The prisoner was an older man, a political prisoner, and did not want to visit the brothel. Unfortunately, he did not have a choice and therefore had to follow the 'invitational order'.[110] In another instance, the *Lagerälteste* of Buchenwald, Erich Reschke, who happened also to be one of the heads of the communist resistance movement in the camp, was forced by the camp officials to 'open the brothel'. Through that act, they declared his status as the highest-ranking prisoner in the internal hierarchy to the entire camp; as such, he became the first prisoner with the right to 'live out his sexual desires'. In this way the SS authority openly revealed the award for his collaboration,[111] but at the same time exemplified their own absolute power and control, even over him. Though Reschke was the head of the prisoner hierarchy, the SS was ultimately the power that allocated the 'privilege' to attend the camp brothel.[112]

Another example of a forced brothel visit demonstrates the devastating effect it could have. A French survivor of the Mittelbau-Dora concentration camp, Jean Michel, wrote in his autobiography about his compatriot Delarouche, who, together with his work squad, one evening was returning to the camp from his shift in the tunnels of the Kohnstein, where the dreaded 'V2' missiles were produced. SS officials suddenly stopped the marching prisoners and directed them to the brothel. According to Jean Michel, Delarouche said:

> The men were stupefied. There they were marching in ranks towards the barrack which had been transformed into a house of ill-repute. The poor fellows were drunk with fatigue and only wanted to sleep after twelve hours of work. The first line was put one in front of each door and commanded to drop their trousers. The doors were still closed. The girls must have been inside. The second, order was given: 'Enter!' They went in, trousers lowered, feeling as much like making love as an ailing octogenarian. Delarouche found himself face to face with a woman who was waiting. He was worried and blushing with confusion. How could he manage it? The 'little Frenchies' were about to fail to live up to their reputation. That is how legends are destroyed![113]

The exhaustion as well as the atmosphere of the brothel would have made it impossible for the French men to fulfill their designated task. Even though the brothel visit was considered to be a privilege by the SS, it became a violation not only of the woman and her psyche and sexual body, but the male prisoner was also forced to become an agent within the forced sex labour structure and was thus forced to become a perpetrator, a rapist. At the same time, the absolute power over him humiliated him by revealing his own loss of masculinity and control. The example illustrates how in the case of forced brothel visits, sexual violence and humiliation can move in different directions: victims become perpetrators who then are themselves humiliated.

Summary

As we have seen, in 1941 Himmler decided to introduce camp brothels to a selected group of male prisoners in his concentration camps in an attempt to boost prisoner productivity to meet the unrealistic demand of the Führer's massive and diverse projects.

Female prisoners of the women's concentration camps of Ravensbrück and Auschwitz-Birkenau were selected by the SS for those brothels or asked to 'volunteer' on the basis of false promises. Since those women were usually working in very difficult Kommandos, 'volunteering' often meant deciding between forced sex labour and death. This was indisputably an act of coercion, because the SS had itself created the environment of terror and starvation. Inside the brothel barrack, women did not have any choice other than to obey and become part of the machinery of the *Sonderbau*. They were constantly under surveillance and were neither allowed to refuse a man nor to leave the brothel Kommando.[114]

The camp brothel became an institution that was severely controlled and highly regulated. The SS never purposely gave up any of their absolute control. The brothel visit was bureaucratically organized, scheduled, and monitored. The SS selected the women and gave a few men permission to satisfy their sexual needs within the structure of forced sex labour they had carefully designed. Although the SS themselves were not allowed to frequent women at the camp brothels, voyeurism became a source of amusement to them. Moreover, watching prisoners through spy holes was practiced to humiliate the prisoners even further, as was ordering prisoners to visit the brothel. The *Sonderbau* was not only subject to the severe rules of the concentration camps, but also to laws of VD-control and prostitution supervision, as records of the regular analysis of cervical smear and blood samples of forced sex labourers show.

The analysis of the motives of the brothel visitors and the frequency of their visits shows clearly the connection between power and sexuality inside the concentration camp. One's own capacity to have sexual desires and moreover to act them out was a mark of a high social position in the camp. A wasteful expulsion of sexual energy was only possible for prisoners at the uppermost levels in the prisoner hierarchy. The SS conceded extra power to these prisoners to keep the complex camp system running. With their power, the high-ranked prisoners also received the right to have controlled sexual intercourse in the camp brothel. On the other hand, the demonstration of one's loss of masculinity was used to expose those of low rank in the hierarchy and became a further occasion for humiliation.

To prisoners of the middle stratum of camp society, sexuality was less a symbol of status or prestige than a wish to have one sexual experience before 'going through the chimney', or a strategy of reconquering a sexual masculine identity and thereby feeling human again. Since in most camps it was impossible to meet women outside the *Sonderbau* and living out sexuality was strictly prohibited,[115] visiting the brothel became a part of a remasculinization strategy. Unfortunately, this created an enormous dilemma: the prisoner had to play an active part in the system of forced sex labour, a phenomenon which illuminates some of the more perfidious and vile aspects of the functioning of power within the camps. Prisoners were turned into perpetrators and yet remained victims themselves. The organized sexual exploitation in camp brothels became thus an essential piece of the structures for the elimination of humanity inside the camps. The Bonus-Order and the camp brothels were designed to enforce the functioning of the lethal concentration camp machinery and thus need to be understood as an important part of the camps' history.

Notes

I would like to express my special thanks to David Copenhafer, Adrienne Faith and Anna Hájková for their help in editing and translating this chapter.

1. I refer here to concentration camps (*Konzentrationslager*) as camps which were under the control and supervision of the *Inspektion der Konzentrationslager* and later supervised by the *SS-Wirtschafts- und Verwaltungshauptamt* (WVHA). Excluded from this definition are extermination camps (such as Chelmno, Sobibor, Belzec and Treblinka) which were under the administration of the Aktion Reinhardt and solely built between 1941 and 1943 in order to kill Jews and Gypsies from occupied Poland, the Generalgouvernement and later on from all over Europe. The camp complex Auschwitz consisting of three major camps – Stammlager (I), Birkenau (II) and Monowitz (III) – was founded as concentration camp, but served from 1943 also as principal place of the extermination of Hungarian Jews, Jews from Theresienstadt and Gypsies. Auschwitz-Birkenau, as well as Bergen-Belsen, were multi-functional camp complexes consisting of sub-camps which served different purposes, such as transit or POW camps. On the differentiation of camp types see W. Benz, 'Nationalsozialistische Zwangslager. Ein Überblick', W. Benz and others (eds), *Der Ort des Terrors. Geschichte der nationalsozialistischen Konzentrationslager. Band 1. Die Organisation des Terrors*, 1st edn (München, 2005), pp. 11–29.
2. See C. Brink, *Ikonen der Vernichtung: öffentlicher Gebrauch von Fotografien aus nationalsozialistischen Konzentrationslagern nach 1945*, 1st edn (Berlin, 1998), pp. 9–22.

3. See the most popular example, Ka-tzetnik 135633, *House of Dolls*, 1st edn (New York, 1956). Furthermore there is an entire film genre called 'SS-Sexploitation'/Sadiconazista, in which the subject of female prisoners being forced to become sex labourers for SS men is exploited in abominably distasteful manner, such as in S. Garrone's *SS Experiment Camp* and *SS Camp 5*, as well as B. Mattei's *SS Girls*. See M. Stiglegger, *Sadiconazista. Faschismus und Sexualität im Film*, 1st edn (St. Augustin, 1999). In addition to that Israeli Stalag-Comics as well as American men's adventure magazines from the 1960s and 1970s have to be mentioned. See I. Kershner, 'Israel's Unexpected Spinoff from a Holocaust Trial', *The New York Times*, 6 September 2007; M. A. Collins, G. Hagenauer, R. Oberg, and S. Heller (eds), *Men's Adventure Magazines in Postwar America*, 1st edn (Los Angeles, 2004), pp. 290–364.

4. See R. Kassing and C. Paul, 'Bordelle in deutschen Konzentrationslagern', *K(r)ampfader VI* (1/1991), pp. 26–31; C. Schulz, 'Weibliche Häftlinge aus Ravensbrück in den Bordellen der Männerkonzentrationslager', C. Füllberg–Stolberg et al. (eds), *Frauen in Konzentrationslagern. Bergen-Belsen Ravensbrück*, 1st edn (Bremen, 1994), pp. 135–146; C. Paul, *Zwangsprostitution. Staatlich errichtete Bordelle im Nationalsozialismus*, 1st edn (Berlin, 1994); H.-P. Klausch, 'Das Lagerbordell von Flossenbürg', *Beiträge zur Geschichte der Arbeiterbewegung* (4/1992), pp. 86–94; A. Baumgartner, *Die vergessenen Frauen von Mauthausen. Die weiblichen Häftlinge des Konzentrationslagers Mauthausen und ihre Geschichte*, 1st edn (Wien, 1997); K. Engelhardt, 'Frauen im Konzentrationslager Dachau', *Dachauer Hefte*, XIV (1998), pp. 218–244; P. Heigl, 'Zwangsprostitution im KZ-Lagerbordell Flossenbürg', *Geschichte Quer*, (6/1998), pp. 44f; C. Schikorra, 'Prostitution weiblicher Häftlinge als Zwangsarbeit. Zur Situation "asozialer" Häftlinge im Frauen-KZ Ravensbrück', *Dachauer Hefte*, XVI (2000), pp. 112–124; C. Wickert, 'Tabu Lagerbordell. Vom Umgang mit der Zwangsprostitution nach 1945', I. Eschenbach, S. Jacobeit, and S. Wenk (eds), *Geschlecht und Gedächtnis. Deutungsmuster in Darstellungen des nationalsozialistischen Genozids*, 1st edn (Frankfurt/Main/New York, 2002), pp. 41–58; R. Sommer, *Der Sonderbau. Die Errichtung von Bordellen in nationalsozialistischen Konzentrationslagern*. Magisterarbeit at the Humboldt-Universität zu Berlin 2003, (Morrisville/USA, 2006); H. Amesberger, K. Auer, and B. Halbmayr, *Sexualisierte Gewalt. Weibliche Erfahrungen in NS-Konzentrationslager*, 1st edn (Wien, 2004); B. Halbmayr, 'Arbeitskommando "Sonderbau". Zur Bedeutung und Funktion von Bordellen im KZ', *Dachauer Hefte*, XXI (2005); R. Sommer, 'Die Häftlingsbordelle im KZ-Komplex Auschwitz-Birkenau. Sexzwangsarbeit im Spannungsfeld von NS-"Rassenpolitik" und der Bekämpfung von Geschlechtskrankheiten', A. Jah, C. Kopke, A. Korb, and A. Stiller (eds), *Nationalsozialistische Lager. Neue Beiträge zur NS-Verfolgungs- und Vernichtungspolitik und zur Gedenkstättenpädagogik* (Ulm, 2006), pp. 81–103; B. Alakus, K. Kniefacz, and R. Vorberg (eds), *Sex-Zwangsarbeit in nationalsozialistischen Konzentrationslagern* (Wien, 2006).

5. The WVHA was the primary administrative office of all commercial and industrial enterprises of the SS including the concentration camp system.

6. See H. Marsalek, *Die Geschichte des Konzentrationslagers Mauthausen* (Wien, 1980), p. 177.

7. Entry of *Tätigkeitsbericht Nr. 2*, from 8 October 1941, in: Archives of the Mauthausen Memorial (hereafter AMM); *Bordellbuch Block 3* (visitor lists), in: AMM K2-1.

8. See Letter Himmler to Pohl from 23 April 1942, in: Archiv of the Institut für Zeitgeschichte (Munich), MA 304/0812.

9. See Weekly Report of the IG Farben for the period between 1 and 7 June 1942 (*Wochenbericht Nr. 54*), in: Archive of the State Museum Auschwitz-Birkenau (APMO), D-Au III/4/2.

10. See letter Himmler to Pohl from 23 März 1942 in: Bundesarchiv Berlin-Lichterfelde (hereafter BArch), NS 19/2065.

11. See *Dienstvorschrift für die Gewährung von Vergünstigungen an Häftlinge*. *Prämien-Vorschrift* from 15 May 1943, in: BArch, NS 3/426.

12. Ibid.

13. See *1. Nachtrag zur Dienstvorschrift für die Gewährung von Vergünstigungen an Häftlinge* from 14 February 1944, in: BArch, NS 3/427; F. Piper, *Arbeitseinsatz der Häftlinge aus dem KL Auschwitz* (Oświęcim, 1995), appendix 22; P. Setkiewicz, 'Häftlingsarbeit im KZ Auschwitz III-Monowitz. Die Frage nach der Wirtschaftlichkeit der Arbeit', U. Herbert, K. Orth, and C. Dieckmann (eds), *Die nationalsozialistischen Konzentrationslager. Entwicklung und Struktur*, 1st edn (Göttingen, 1998), pp. 598–601.

14. The brothel barrack of the KZ Flossenbürg was already planned in July 1942, but construction was delayed due to shortage of wooden barracks for about a year and was finished in July 1943. See construction plans of the *Sonderbau* of Flossenbürg, in: BArch, NS 4/Fl 183 and 185. On the history of the Flossenbürg camp brothel, see Klausch, 1992 and Heigl, 1998. In Buchenwald, the first daily financial account of the camp dates 11 July 1943. See Daily financial accounts of camp brothel, in: BArch, NS 4 BU/41.

15. The first VD-examination of 21 women of the brothel block 24a began on 4 October 1943. See test tube information slips for blood and cervical smear samples of block 24a, in: Archiv of the State Museum of Auschwitz-Birkenau (hereafter APMO), Akta HI 391/20a.

16. The first known VD-examination of eight women from the Monowitz brothel *Kommando* date 15 November 1943. See test tube information slips for blood and cervical smear samples of Monowitz, in: APMO, Akta HI 1201/23.

17. See deposition of Albin Luedtke at the second war criminals investigation committee, in Hamburg on 14. Dezember 1945, Bundesarchiv Dahlwitz-Hoppegarten, ZM 1173 A. 1.

18. See Engelhardt, 1998, p. 223.

19. See O. Nansen, *Von Tag zu Tag. Ein Tagebuch* (Hamburg 1949), pp. 187f, 187f. On the history of the Sachsenhausen brothel see Wickert, 2002 and Sommer, 2003/2006.

20. See transport list of women for the camp brothel from KZ Bergen-Belsen to Mittelbau-Dora, 18 February 1945, in: Archiv der Gedenkstätte Mittelbau-Dora (hereafter AGMD), DMD, D1b, Bd.5, p. 113.

21. See Sommer, 2003/2006, pp. 30–33.

22. Ravensbrück was the main woman's concentration camp located north of Berlin from May 1939 on. Over 130,000 female prisoners passed through the Ravensbrück camp system until the end of the war. Only 40,000 survived. Although the inmates came from every country in German-occupied

Europe, most were Jewish women from Poland and the occupied Soviet territories. On the history of Ravensbrück see B. Strebel, *Das KZ Ravensbrück. Geschichte eines Lagerkomplexes*, 1st edn (Paderborn, 2003).

23. See secret letter Himmler to Pohl from 15 November 1942 (DOKUMENT 1583-PS), in: Internationaler Militärgerichtshof Nürnberg, *Der Prozess gegen die Hauptkriegsverbrecher. Urkunden und anderes Beweismaterial, Vol. III–IX*, 1st edn (Nürnberg, 1948), p. 349.

24. Interview with the survivor of Auschwitz Romek Dubitzki (pseudonym), in: Interv. Sommer 2004-04-06 D., pt.1, 00.44.00.

25. L. Millu, *Smoke over Birkenau* (Philadelphia/New York/Jerusalem, 1999), pp. 171f.

26. Ukrainian guardsmen – also called Trawniki men – were recruited among Soviet POWs and trained at Trawniki camp. As *fremdvölkische* (foreign racial-ethnic) SS men they served as guards in extermination camps of the Aktion Reinhardt as well as in concentrations camps. See I. Gutmann (ed.), *Enzyklopädie des Holocaust. Die Verfolgung und Ermordung der europäischen Juden*, 2nd edn (München, 1998), p. 1425.

27. See C. Paul and R. Sommer, 'SS-Bordelle und Oral History. Problematische Quellen und die Existenz von Bordellen für die SS in Konzentrationslagern', *BIOS*, (1/2006), pp. 134–137; R. Sommer, *Das KZ-Bordell. Die Rolle von Sex-Zwangsarbeit in nationalsozialistischen Konzentrationslagern* (Ph.D. dissertation, in publication), pp. 62–64.

28. See testimony Henryka Obidzinska, in: Interv. Sommer 2002-03-16 O., 00.08.00.

29. The name is a pseudonym.

30. She was in the prison, because she had been caught stealing potatoes in Ravensbrück. See Paul, 1994, p. 49.

31. See interview with M. W. from 15 November 1988, in: Werkstatt der Erinnerung Hamburg (hereafter WdE), Sig. 295, p. 20. Passages from the interview are published in: Paul, 1994, pp. 51ff.

32. Ibid.

33. For images of the rooms inside the brothel see ibid.

34. See testimony of M. W., in R. Mieder and G. Schwarz, *Alles für zwei Mark. Das Häftlingsbordell von Buchenwald*. Radiofeature of MDR 2002, transcript under: http://www.mdr.de/DL/4051258.pdf (September 2007).

35. Paul, 1994, p. 56.

36. See ibid.

37. Testimony of M. W., in: Mieder and von Schwarz, 2002.

38. See Paul, 1994, pp. 54, 57; testimony M. W. in: (WdE), Sig. 295, p. 10.

39. See Robert Sommer, Database of Forced Sex Labour in Nazi Concentration Camps, updated 3/2008.

40. This number includes women from occupied Austria. One woman came from Lorraine.

41. See Sommer, 2008, pp. 342–344 and 424.

42. W. Sofsky, *The Order of Terror. The Concentration Camp*, 1st edn (Princeton, 1997), p. 48. Recently there has been a controversy on Sofsky's *Order of Terror*. I agree that Sofsky analyses a rather abstract ideal type of concentration camp, which sometimes lacks historical differentiation and dynamics in the development of the camp system. On the other hand, Sofsky manages

in a unique manner to analyse social structures inside the camps in relation to surveillance and control techniques of the SS used to destroy individual scope for action. In that way, his book is essential for understanding the terror of the SS and mechanisms of the Holocaust.

43. See order Liebehenschel to the commanders of KZ Sachsenhausen, Dachau, Neuengamme and Auschwitz from 15 Juni 1943, in: BArch, NS 3/426.

44. The exception is Mittelbau-Dora where the last camp brothel was opened just a few months before the end of the 'Third Reich'. The SS opened it on a hillside above the camp roll call square at the entrance of the camp in a barrack that used to be the camp library. The reason for that position might have been the availability of space, but perhaps also to increase the incentive for the prisoners. See R. Sommer, ' "Sonderbau" und Lagergesellschaft. Die Bedeutung von Bordellen in den KZ', J. Milotová and A. Hájková (eds), *Theresienstädter Studien und Dokumente 2006* (Prag, 2007), pp. 304–306.

45. On zoning in concentration camps see Sofsky, 1997, pp. 47–54.

46. See Sommer, 2003/2006, p. 94.

47. For example see plan of concentration camp of Flossenbürg (in: handout of the museum of Flossenbürg); plan of Monowitz, in: H. Frankenthal, *Verweigerte Rückkehr. Erfahrungen nach dem Judenmord*, 1st edn (Frankfurt/Main, 1999), pp. 150f.

48. When comparing the maps of block 11 and 24, it is remarkable that not only is the way the three brothel rooms are usually connected through a small corridor the same, but the size of the prison cells and the brothel rooms are almost identical as well.

49. See P. Matussek, *Die Konzentrationslagerhaft und ihre Folgen*, 1st edn (Berlin, 1971), p. 29.

50. The name is a pseudonym.

51. The procedure was similar in other concentration camps. Charles Dekeyer explained that in Flossenbürg, he had to go to a little room next to the entrance where a physician and two assistants examined the men for any visible venereal diseases and covered the genitals with some ointment. He did not know what it was. See testimony Dekeyser, in: Interv. Sommer 2003-07-19 Dekeyser, pp. 4f.

52. See testimony Piecha, in: Interv. Sommer 2003-03-30, pp. 1f.

53. In Auschwitz the SS thought that 15 minutes would be too little and so they increased it to 20. See testimony Piercha in: Interv. Sommer 2003-03-30, pp. 1, 6.

54. See testimonies Romek Dubitzki and Stephan Szymanski (both pseudonyms), in: Interv. Sommer 2005-01-28 S., pt.1, 00.47.00; Interv. Sommer 2004-04-06 D., pt.1, 00.52.00.

55. See testimony Romek Dubitzki, in: Interv. Sommer 2004-04-06 D., pt.2, 00.07.00.

56. See ibid., 00.41.00.

57. See Paul, 1994, p. 56.

58. See testimony of the Polish survivor of Auschwitz Zofia Bator, in: Library of the International Youth Meeting Center Auschwitz (IYMC), p. 29.

59. See Paul, *Zwangsprostitution*, p. 56.

60. That was also the case in other concentration camps: In June 1944 the Dachau brothel was searched by the SS. An investigation eventually led to the closing of the brothel at the end of 1944. See E. Kupfer-Koberwitz, *Dachauer Tagebücher. Die Aufzeichnungen des Häftlings 24814*, 1st edn (München, 1997), p. 293.

61. Stephan Szymanski (pseudonym) explained how he visited his 'lover' at the brothel of Auschwitz a few times at night. He would climb up to the first floor of block 24 and enter the block through an open window. See Interv. Sommer 2005-01-28 S., pt.1, 00.51.00-01.08.00.

62. See Sommer, 2006, pp. 97–99.

63. See Protocol of the hearing of witness Hermann Leonhardt on 23 April 1970, in: APMO, Ośw./Leonardt/1509, pp. 2f.

64. See Matussek, 1971, p. 29.

65. See testimony of an anonymous forced sex labourer from Neuengamme, in: Recording in Exhibition of the Museum of the former concentration camp Neuengamme.

66. See ibid. and Paul, 1994, pp. 54ff.

67. See E. Niedojadło, 'Der Lager-"Krankenbau in Buna"', Internationales Auschwitz Komitee (eds), *Przegląd Lekarski. Antologie*, Vol. II, Part. II (Warsaw, 1970), p. 51.

68. See *Meldung* from 21 July 1943, in: BArch, NS 4/BU 41.

69. See Sommer, 2006, pp. 82–88.

70. See *Vertrauliches Rundschreiben zur polizeilichen Behandlung der Prostitution* from 9 September 1939, in: Generallandesarchiv Karlsruhe, Abt. 330 Zug. 1991/34/Nr.136. Every member of the SS or the Police had to go through sanitation procedures (*Sanierung*) after any outside-marriage (*außerehelichen*) sex as well. See Order Himmler from 11 June 1943, in: Archive of the USHMM (AUSHMM), RG 48.004M, Reel 2.

71. See letter *Austausch der Wochennachweisungen über das Auftreten übertragbarer Krankheiten* from 24 August 1937, in: Thüringisches Hauptstaatsarchiv Weimar, Thüringisches Ministerium des Innern E-Nr. 1456.

72. A good example of the work of the SS-Hygiene Institut is the report (*Arbeitsbericht*) of the SS-Hygiene Institut in Berlin on their work inside concentration camps in 1941, in which also the fight against epidemics in concentration camps is an important point. See *Arbeitsbericht des SS-Hygiene-Instituts der Waffen-SS* from 29 January 1942, in: Archiv der Humboldt-Universität zu Berlin, Hygiene-Institut, Sig.192.

73. Testimony Terry, in: Interv. Sommer 2003-07-19 Terry, p. 7.

74. V. E. Frankl, *Ein Psycholog erlebt das Konzentrationslager*, 1st edn (Wien, 1947), p. 46.

75. He describes how prisoners continuously talked about food and mentions '*Magenonanie*' as general camp metaphor for that. See Frankl, 1947, p. 43.

76. Testimony of Dachau prisoner, in: Matussek, 1971, p. 29. Translation by Robert Sommer.

77. E. Federn, 'Eros hinter Stacheldraht. Interview-Auszug', H. Kirsten and U. Kirsten (eds), *Stimmen aus Buchenwald. Ein Lesebuch*, 1st edn (Göttingen, 2002), p. 69.

78. In fact Matussek mentions an objective labeling scale of *Lagerschwere* (camp severity), which was introduced by the Institut für Zeitgeschichte (Munich). See Matussek, 1971, p. 18.
79. See Sofsky, 1997, pp. 117–144.
80. On dehumanization see N. Shik, 'Weibliche Erfahrungen in Auschwitz-Birkenau', G. Bock (ed.), *Genozid und Geschlecht: Jüdische Frauen im nationalsozialistischen Lagersystem*, 1st edn (Frankfurt/Main, 2005), pp. 105f.
81. This process of adaptation to camp life is one of the main subjects in: L. Begov, *Mit meinen Augen. Botschaft einer Auschwitzüberlebenden*, 1st edn (Gerlingen, 1983).
82. See Frankl, 1947, pp. 43f.
83. See S. Pisar, *Das Blut der Hoffnung*, 1st edn (Frankfurt/Main, 1979), p. 77.
84. Liana Millu in particular underlined those differences. She explained in an interview that in Auschwitz-Birkenau, women would trade their last pieces of bread for a hair brush or some make-up. The loss of menstruation was devastating to women. See G. Jäger, ' "Was für ein schönes Seidenhemd ich hatte!" Liana Millu über die "Umwertung der Werte" ', *Werkstatt Geschichte*, XX (1998), pp. 100f. Grete Salus speaks of female prisoners in Auschwitz who tried to recall what it means to be a woman, because they felt completely genderless, see testimony Grete Salus in: Wiener Library, Reel 53, P III h. (General) No. 724.
85. That seems also to have been the case with female prisoners. The more a woman adapted to camp life and climbed up in the hierarchy, the greater the importance of sexuality in her life. Kielar describes how a female prisoner functionary in Birkenau gets her menstruation again and shows strong interests in men. See W. Kielar, *Anus Mundi: Fünf Jahre Auschwitz*, 9th edn (Frankfurt/Main, 2004), p. 164.
86. See Federn, 2002, p. 69.
87. A Polish survivor of Sachsenhausen, Aleksander Kulisiewicz, wrote in 1945 a poem about the arrival of 1000 women at the Sachsenhausen camp. Before that he had never seen a woman in a concentration camp. The male society of prisoners got very excited about that and felt, for a few instants, like sexual human beings again. See A. Kulisiewicz and C. Kulisiewicz (eds), *Adresse Sachsenhausen: Literarische Momentaufnahmen aus dem KZ*, 1st edn (Gerlingen, 1997), pp. 58–60.
88. See testimonies Maschkowski and König, in: Interv. Sommer 2004-03-19 2x Maschkowski, p. 15; Interv. Sommer 2004-02-05 König, p. 4.
89. See Interv. Sommer 2003-04-12 Lykianow, p. 2; Jouanin George, in: AGMD, DMD- EB/HF-51 and Paul, 1994, p. 47.
90. The Flossenbürg survivor Charles Dekeyser phrased that in the following way: 'The mass had only one aspiration. That is: to deat, to deat, to deat' (*'Die Masse hier hat nur eine Sehnsucht und das ist: fressen, fressen, fressen'*). Interv. Sommer 2003-07-19 Dekeyser, p. 10. On the importance of the camp brothels see Sommer, Lagergesllschaft, pp. 104–108.
91. Testinony Hantz, in: Interv. Sommer 2003-02-01 Hantz, p. 4.
92. See revenues accounts (Abrechnungsbögen) of the Sonderbau Buchenwald, July 1943, in: BArch, NS 4 Bu/41. For the analysis of them, see Sommer, 2008, p. 425.

93. See Paul, 1994, pp. 76ff. ('reichsdeutsche'/ethnic German visitors); Interview with Albert van Dijk in: Mieder, von Schwarz , Häftlingsbordell (Dutch); Interv. Sommer 2003-07-19 Dekeyser (Belgians); See Knop, Wickert, Weibliche Häftlinge, in: AGS, R 132/14, p. 10 (Scandinavians); Interv. Sommer 2003-05-01 Hantz 1, pt.1,00.28.00 (Poles); Interv. 2006-02-13 Hájková (Czechs); APMO, Ośw./Petrykowski/1931, p. 138 (Ukrainians); D. W. Pike, *Spaniards in the Holocaust. Mauthausen, the Horror on the Danube*, 1st edn (London, 2000), p. 72.

94. For example, see testimony Halbreich, in: APMO, Ośw/Halbreich/1939, p. 108 and APMO, Ośw/Halbreich/36, p. 202; Interv. Sommer 2004-06-15 D., 00.07.00; Interv. Sommer 2003-05-05 P. 2, p. 20.

95. Some prisoners did not even know that bonus coupons existed. For example, Willi Frohwein had never seen bonus coupons or even heard of the bonus system in Auschwitz, Auschwitz-Monowitz, or Groß-Rosen, where he was confined. See testimony Frohwein, in: Interv. Sommer 2003-05-07 Frohwein, pt.2, 00.25:55.

96. For more details see R. Sommer, 2007, p. 301.

97. In this context see also Sofsky, 1997, pp. 145–153.

98. See *Bordellbuch Block 3*, June–December 1942, in: AMM, K2-1. As regular visitors I define those who visited the brothel from August to December 1942 between 10 and 43 times. See Sommer, 2008, p. 424.

99. See list of the prisoners who were allowed to carry a watch, in: AMM, L/7/2; *Häftlingspersonalkarten* of Mauthausen; extracts form the Prisoner Entrance Book (*Häftlingszugangsbuch*), in: AMM, Y/44.

100. See H. Maršálek, *Die Geschichte des Konzentrationslagers Mauthausen. Dokumentation*, 2nd edn (Wien, 1980), p. 61.

101. Maršálek, 1980, p. 61

102. See J. Giza and W. Morasiewic, 'Z zagadnień popędów w obozach koncentracyjnych. Przyczynek do analiz tzw. KZ-syndromu', *Przegląd Lekarski* (1/1973), pp. 29–41. Translation by Anna Taborska.

103. According to Giza and Morasiewic, motives for masturbation in the camp among women as well were not so much connected to the satisfaction of sexual needs as to the fear of not being a woman anymore. See J. St. Giza and W. Morasiewic, 'Poobozowe zaburzenia seksualne u kobiet jako elemet tzw. KZ-syndromu', *Przegląd Lekarski* (1/1974), pp. 73f. Translation by Anna by Taborska.

104. In interviews this aspect appeared in different ways. Romek Dubitzki explained that he wanted to show the women in the brothel what a man he was by bragging over his sexual potential. Stephan Szymanski instead said that he instantly fell in love with the woman and continued to see her. See Interv. Sommer 2005-01-28 S., pt.1, 00.47.00 and Interv. Sommer 2004-04-06 D., pt.1, 00.52.00.

105. See testimony Johan F. B., in: Library of the International Youth Meeting Center Auschwitz (IYMC), without signature, p. 5.

106. See Interv. Sommer 2006-02-13 Hájková, 00.07.00f.

107. See testimony Ella F., in: minute of interview Christa Paul with Ella F. (Flossenbürg) in Private Archive Paul; see testimony Ms. B., in: Paul, 1994, p. 47.

108. See testimony Piecha, in: Interv. Sommer 2003-03-30 P.1, p. 3.

109. See Matussek, 1971, p. 29.
110. See testimony Mieczysław Zając, in: APMO, Ośw./Zając/2045, p. 106. Translation by Margret Kutschke.
111. The SS did not know that he was one of the heads of the resistance movement. The dilemma of the prisoner resistance movement was the necessity to collaborate in order to maintain power and create counter structures. See L. Niethammer (Hg.), *Der, gesäuberte' Antifaschismus. Die SED und die roten Kapos von Buchenwald*, 1st edn (Berlin, 1994), pp. 27–68.
112. See Niethammer, 1994, pp. 48f.
113. J. Michel, *Dora. The Nazi Concentration Camp Where Modern Space Technology Was Born and 30,000 Prisoners Died*, 1st edn (London, 1979), pp. 156f.
114. For the definition of constraints in prostitution, see N. Campagna, *Prostitution. Eine philosophische Untersuchung*, 1st edn (without place, 2005), pp. 176f.
115. One example is the *Lagerordnung* (camp regulations) of Ravensbrück, in which female homosexuality was officially forbidden. See C. Schoppmann, *Nationalsozialistische Sexualpolitik und weibliche Homosexualität*, 1st edn (Pfaffenweiler, 1997), p. 255. The list of beating punishment (*Prügel-Strafen*) for the Natzweiler concentration camp gives a detailed list on how many strikes a prisoner receives for whatever kind of sexual action. See 'P. Strafen', in: BArch, Film 1575.

7
Between 'Racial Awareness' and Fantasies of Potency: Nazi Sexual Politics in the Occupied Territories of the Soviet Union, 1942–1945

Regina Mühlhäuser

'Racial restructuring of Europe' (*Rassische Neuordnung Europas*) was the term under which the Germans envisioned the creation of a new social order in Europe based on racial criteria. The territory upon which this concept was to be realized in its most radical form was occupied Eastern Europe. German politics of colonization, extermination, and 'germanization' in Poland and the occupied territories of the Soviet Union was extremely violent. 'Racial selection' became the basic principle of the German efforts to control and organize the populations in these countries: everybody deemed 'useful' was to be separated from the 'useless'; the 'healthy' from the 'ill'; and the 'own' from the 'other'.[1]

Central to this new racial order in Eastern Europe was the attempted management of sexual encounters between occupiers and occupied. From the outset of the German invasion of the Soviet Union, various Nazi authorities were deeply concerned with the control and regulation of rape, sexual enslavement, military and civil prostitution, sexual affairs, and romantic relationships.[2] According to the logic of Nazi 'racial hygiene' (*Rassenhygiene*), associations between German men and 'ethnically alien women' (*fremdvölkische Frauen*) would endanger national health and vitality. Various Wehrmacht units urged their soldiers to exercise 'restraint towards [...] the other sex', as expressed by the commander of the 11th army Erich von Manstein in November 1942.[3] As other armies did during World War II, the Wehrmacht High Command (*Oberkommando der Wehrmacht*, OKW) aimed to control desire in order to ensure military discipline and prevent sexually transmitted disease as well as enemy espionage. To this end, leaders of the SS and police tried to ban 'undesirable sexual intercourse' (*unerwünschten Geschlechtsverkehr*), i.e., sexual contact between German soldiers and women designated as 'racially inferior'.[4]

German men at the Eastern front, however, did not pay great attention to these efforts at regulations. On 25 February 1942, eight months after the invasion of the Soviet Union, the Security Service Reichsführer-SS (*Sicherheitsdienst Reichsführer-SS*; SD) noted that Wehrmacht orders 'to ban any kind of sexual intercourse with Russian women and girls have up to now been without any noteworthy effect'.[5] Authorities documented rape and gang rape, incidents of sexual enslavement, as well as military and civil prostitution.[6] At the same time, in some regions, German soldiers were known to become engaged to non-German women, increasingly applying for marriage permits, and producing 'racially mixed children'.[7]

On 16 September 1942, the Reich Commissioner for the Strengthening of Germandom (*Reichskommissar zur Festigung des Deutschen Volkstums*, RKF), Heinrich Himmler, asserted that 'undesirable sexual intercourse' in 'the East' must be 'prevented if possible'. Implicitly he conceded the impossibility of gaining complete control over the desire of the individual man. At a conference in the Ukraine, he advised leaders of the SS and the police,

> if [...] the necessities of the blood, the being, and the man are different, and cannot be avoided during war, then you are bound to tell your men that they may only be responsive to a liaison that they can account for to Germany, to their own blood, and to their future child.[8]

Himmler acted on the assumption that male sexual lust in times of war was unavoidable and that satisfying soldiers' heterosexual desires would be beneficial to the war effort. Indeed several Nazi authorities emphasized soldiers' need for regular heterosexual activity as an outlet for their allegedly uncontainable sexual drives and to improve their military performance.[9] Their phrasing often revealed a blatant pride in the virility and potency of German men. Heterosexual activity was interpreted as a symbol of national masculinity and military strength. Indeed, the 'sexual surrender' of enemy women was generally considered to be one form of conquest of the other nation.[10]

During the racist War of Annihilation, these images of soldierly sexuality and sexual surrender contradicted the Nazi idea of 'racial hygiene'.

Himmler addressed this conflict by appealing to the 'racial awareness' (*Rassebewußtsein*) of individual soldiers. Members of the Wehrmacht, SS, and police should only consider pursuing sexual encounters with women deemed worthy of being the mother of a German child. Himmler knew, however, that clear-cut, permanently fixed criteria for the evaluation of 'racial value' did not exist,[11] conceding that it would be 'pure coincidence whether the girl a soldier gets attached to is pure-bred or unfit'.[12] Himmler's appeal to 'racial awareness' was thus mainly a disciplinary threat, reminding individual soldiers that any transgression of these expectations could lead to punishment.

Wehrmacht, SS, and civil occupation authorities chose different ways to deal with the contradictions that characterized sexual politics during the 'racial war in the East' (*Rassenkrieg im Osten*). The following analysis will explore these regulation-efforts in light of conflicting racial, sexual, and military aims. The first section will focus on sexual torture, rape, and gang rape. Did the fact that German men raped women who were considered to be 'racially inferior' present a serious problem to the Nazi authorities? The second part will turn towards sexual enslavement and military as well as civil prostitution. Did Nazi ideas of 'racial hygiene' play a significant role in the establishment of military brothels and the organization of controlled access to civil prostitution? The third part will focus on consensual relations. Did military and civil authorities generally ban consensual relations between German men and Soviet women?[13]

In conclusion, Himmler's elaborations on the responsibility of the individual German man 'towards Germany, his blood, and his future child' will be reconsidered to highlight the ambiguities of the Nazi category of race in relation to sexual politics at the Eastern front. These ambiguities, however, did not cause visible confusion among German men stationed in the Soviet Union. On the contrary, this article argues that it was precisely the combination of strict orders, ideological contradictions, and practical ambivalence that contributed to the maintenance of state power in a rather uncontrollable territory.

Sexual torture, rape, and gang rape

On 7 January 1942, the People's Commissioner of Foreign Affairs of the Soviet Union, Vyacheslav M. Molotov, published an account of eyewitness testimonies, which during the Nuremberg War Crimes Trials became known as the Molotov Note. On several pages, the document testifies to different forms of sexual violence committed by German men:

> In the city of Lvov [Ukraine; RM], 32 women working in a garment factory were first violated and then murdered by the German storm troopers. [...]
>
> Near the town of Borissov in Belorussia, 75 women and girls attempting to flee at the approach of the German troops fell into their hands. The Germans first raped and then savagely murdered 36 of their number. By order of a German named Hummer, the soldiers marched L.I. Melchukova, a 16-year-old-girl, into the forest, where they raped her. A little later, some other women who had also been dragged into the forest saw some boards near the trees and the dying Melchukova nailed to the boards. The Germans had cut off her breast in the presence of these women, among whom were V.I. Alperenko and V.H. Bereznikova.[14]

Rape, gang rape, and sexual torture were forms of violence that accompanied the brutal German war in Eastern Europe. As the Molotov Note documents, the rape of a woman could end with her murder.[15] Furthermore, some sources indicate that the murder of a woman was sometimes followed by the sexual abuse of her dead body.[16] As Gaby Zipfel has pointed out, the merging of male sexual lust and deadly violence in combat situations is not out of the ordinary. Threatened by the possibility of their own death, men 'reaffirm their sexual potency and their capacity to overcome fear'.[17]

Other testimonies support the descriptions of rape and sexual torture presented in the Molotov note. German men occasionally cut off a woman's breast, which resulted in her very painful death. The technique of putting a woman up on a board, naked, for everybody to see, did not only mean physical torture. In the moment the woman confronted her death, the perpetrators took away her privacy and her feminine identity. In addition, they terrorized the local population who had to watch or overhear details about the victim's humiliation and murder.[18] Sexual torture thus functioned as a direct threat, an expression of power, and a form of communication between occupiers and occupied. Indeed, as Ruth Seifert has pointed out, the sexual violation of women in times of war is not only an act directed against an individual woman. It also carries a 'message from men to men', meaning that one group is no longer able to protect 'their' women. In this respect, sexual violence by the victors symbolizes both the military defeat and humiliation of the male population.[19]

German men furthermore used sexual violence as an instrument during interrogations.[20] In her war memories, the Russian teacher Genia Demianova describes her capture on 5 August 1941 in the Russian city Pskov. After she failed to escape, the commanding officer tortured her with a whip and brutally raped her. According to her account, the sergeant boasted about his sexual success afterwards:

> There is a roar of cheering, the clinking of many glasses. The sergeant is standing in the open doorway: 'The wild cat is tamed,' he is saying. 'Boys, she was a virgin. What do you say to that?'

> Another burst of cheering, then he closes the door. But I am not left alone for long. The others came in. Ten, a hundred, a thousand, one after another. The[y] flung themselves upon me, digging into my wounds while they defiled me. [...]

> Then everything passed. The Germans kept coming, spitting obscene words towards me, guffawing as they tortured me.[21]

Genia Demianova was kept in a school building and sexually enslaved for several days after her initial violation. Her account intensely points to the fact that gang rapes in times of war were frequently carried out in a hierarchical order. The highest-ranking officer is the first to enter the woman's body. The subordinate soldiers respect his performance and wait their turn. In general, the men in the most powerful positions decide who the next rapist will be. In the life-threatening situation of combat, when men are extremely dependent on one another, gang rapes confirm the inextricable bonds between them and the reliability of their hierarchies. With a mixture of lust and willingness to destroy, the men meet after one another in the body of a woman. In this process, they reaffirm their masculinity and sexual potency.[22]

German men did not only exercise sexual violence in the combat zone. Rape was a form of aggression that structured the everyday life of occupation in the military rear. Numerous reports document that women constantly anticipated becoming victims of rape. They fled their homes, lived in permanent hiding-places and disguised themselves.[23] German men raped girls who were less than 10 years and women who were more than 80 years old.[24] They chose women whom Nazi 'racial hygiene' categorized as 'ethnic German' (*volksdeutsch*) or 'Slavic' as well as women whom they despised as Jews.[25] Sometimes the perpetrators selected their victims randomly; at other times a man would seek out a specific woman whom he had known or heard about before. Sometimes the rapists acted spontaneously; at other times they systematically planned their crime beforehand.[26] Various reports also suggest that Germans involved the local population in finding and providing women. Local men either were forced or decided of their own accord to participate in rounding up women.[27]

The Nazi authorities knew about these crimes. In rather curt language, often in the form of a list, local military commanders or civil bureaucrats reported cases of rape and gang rape among incidents of looting, cattle theft, and excessive consumption of alcohol.[28] On 10 August 1941, not even two months after the German invasion of the Soviet Union, the command of the 9th Army reported that the number of sexual crimes in the combat zone had risen significantly.[29] In response, military commanders issued guidelines in which they urged the soldiers to exercise 'restraint with respect to the other sex'. They demanded rigorous action against German soldiers' 'running wild and lack of discipline [*Verwilderung und Undisziplin*]'.[30]

In the everyday situation of war and occupation, however, rigorous action was rarely taken. Compared to desertion, unauthorized leave, self-mutilation (*Selbstverstümmelung*), or sedition of military strength (*Zersetzung der Wehrkraft*), the Wehrmacht did not assess sexual violence as a 'primary crime'.[31] Narratives of former soldiers indicate that a rapist could become subject to disciplinary action by his commanding officer, and a number of soldiers were court-martialed. In general, however, disciplinary consequences seem to have been the exception. Unreported cases were certainly much more numerous.

As Birgit Beck has demonstrated, military judges in the occupied territories of the Soviet Union imposed comparatively light sentences in cases of rape. While soldiers sentenced as sex offenders at the Western front often remained in prison for many years, their counterparts at the Eastern front usually escaped with sentences between a couple months and two years. This difference was mainly due to the methods of racial warfare specific to the Eastern front. The Barbarossa Decree from 13 May 1941, which regulated the activities of German court-martials in 'the East', had established that no criminal offenses committed by German soldiers against Soviet civilians were to be punished. Exceptions should only be made when military discipline or the security of the troops required it, for instance, in the case of 'serious actions that are caused by a lack of self-restraint'.[32] Sexual violence in combat, however, was seldom regarded as 'serious action', and even less so if the victim was designated as 'racially inferior'. In accordance, rapists were not punished for harming the 'gender honor' (*Geschlechtsehre*) of a woman, let alone for violating her physiological and psychological integrity. Rather, the final verdicts in rape cases usually elaborated that the defendant had harmed the reputation of the Wehrmacht.[33]

The fear that the reputation of the Wehrmacht could be jeopardized by sexual violence also became an issue of institutional rivalry. On 10 August 1943, the general office of the Wehrmacht sent a letter to SS-Obergruppenführer Karl Wolf, which listed numerous cases of rape by members of the SS. Due to the constant threat of rape, the local population would flee their homes and frequently join the partisans. Since the non-Germans, the letter continued, could not distinguish an SS officer from a Wehrmacht soldier, this behavior by the SS risked casting a bad light onto the Wehrmacht, harming military strategy and endangering the German victory.[34]

In fact, leaders of the SS and police did deal with sexual violence committed by their men. The documentary paper trail indicates that members of the SS were known to rape women regarded as 'racially inferior'.[35] At a conference of Supreme Judges of the SS and Police courts in Poland and the 'occupied Eastern territories' in May 1943, the topic discussed at greatest length was referred to as 'undesirable sexual intercourse'. According to the minutes of this meeting, SS-Sturmbannführer Heinz from the SS and Police Court in Kiev assumed that at least 50 percent of all members of the SS and the police violated the 'ban on undesirable sexual intercourse with ethnically alien women'. Since it was not in the interest of the judges to sentence more than half of the SS and policemen in 'the East', all participants finally agreed to advise Reichsführer-SS Heinrich Himmler to abolish the ban.[36]

In short, German men – members of the Wehrmacht, the SS, and the police – exercised sexual violence under various circumstances and in different ways. They raped women during battles and massacres, in the military rear and in the everyday situation of occupation. They exercised sexual torture as a means to terrorize their enemies and as an instrument in interrogation. Many of the victims of these crimes were women deemed 'racially inferior' or 'undesirable'. On the whole, Nazi authorities silently accepted these forms of violence as a normal aspect or product of warfare. The belief that soldiers needed heterosexual satisfaction and that the conquest of an enemy nation was accompanied by its 'sexual surrender' trumped the fear of racial transgression. Nevertheless, some cases of rape and gang rape were brought to trial. If a man was convicted, however, it was mainly due to matters of military discipline and military reputation. That German men chose 'ethnically alien women' or 'women of alien races' as objects of their desire seldom provoked special attention.

Sexual enslavement, military and civil prostitution

In July 1940, supreme commander Walther von Brauchitsch argued for the establishment of military brothels in order to prevent the spread of sexually transmitted diseases, a rise of the number of rapes in the German occupied zones, and an increase of homosexual activity within the military units:

> The longer the stay of German troops in the occupied territories will last, the more orderly and peace-like the conditions are under which the soldier lives and performs his duty, the more the sexual question, in all its circumstances and implications, requires serious attention. [...] Due to the diversified natures of men, it is inescapable that there will be tensions and necessities on the sexual field here and there, which we can and shall not close our eyes to.[37]

Von Brauchitsch defined soldierly sexuality as a part of military politics. He assumed that men would accumulate unfulfilled sexual lust if they had no opportunity to engage in sexual activity. Sooner or later, these drives would need to be released. If no 'normal' sexual outlets existed, men would turn towards sexual violence or homosexual activities. A similar view was reflected in military jurisdiction. In April 1944, a soldier was convicted for the attempted rape of two Latvian women. The judges explicitly stated that the defendant could have released his 'sexual needs' (*sexuelle Nöte*) by other means, for instance in one of the Wehrmacht-controlled brothels. Consequently, he would not have needed to rape:

> Roughly speaking, it cannot be said that the defendant has acted due to a sexual emergency [*sexueller Notstand*]. In Riga the Wehrmacht has established disinfection facilities [*Sanierungsanstalten*]. Furthermore, as in all big cities, the soldier can easily exercise sexual intercourse in Riga.[38]

The logic behind this line of reasoning was based on the assumption that 'typically' sexual violence lust and homosexual desire would only emerge in cases in which opportunities for allegedly normal heterosexual activity did not exist. Von Brauchitsch and the military judges thus negated that sexual violence was an aspect of belligerence with its own motives and functions. Furthermore, they rejected the idea that homosexual desire and practices could constitute normal forms of desire and identity.

In accordance with this position, the Wehrmacht had already established military brothels and organized controlled access to local brothels in occupied France and Poland.[39] In September 1942 Field Marshal Wilhelm Keitel (OKW) supported the establishment of brothels in the 'occupied Eastern territories'. The controlled access to heterosexual services was supposed to ensure military discipline and prevent sexually transmitted diseases and the 'siring of racially mixed bastards that are of no interest for Germany'.[40]

The idea that the soldiers needed an outlet for their sexual drives was, however, disputed. Others envisioned the strong soldier to be in control of his sexual urges. A letter with reference to 'Party and Wehrmacht in the General Government and their Executive Functions' from August 1944 held the view that 'brothels have no right to existence. They are feeble concessions to impulse-driven human beings, and typical for the spirit of the rear [*Etappengeist*].'[41] In this view, images of the 'racially aware Aryan master', which were shaped by conceptions of manliness, focusing on a mature character, controlled will, and sexual self-restraint, obviously contradicted the dominant idea of the aggressive and sexually active soldier.[42] Indeed, Hitler himself had originally opposed prostitution, perceiving it as a major cause of Germany's decline.[43] In the course of the war, however, sex was increasingly considered to be 'the underlying fuel of the military machine'. As Annette Timm has argued, 'the expression of male sexuality was not a matter of individual pleasure but of the nation's military strength'.[44]

Consequently, the OKW established a system of officially regulated prostitution in Poland and the occupied territories of the Soviet Union. The organization of this system, however, varied from region to region. It depended on the location, the strategies of the occupation politics, the degree of collaboration with the local authorities, and last but not least on whether such a system had existed prior to the German occupation. In Riga, Latvia, for instance, the sanitation officer found it comparatively easy to establish brothels because there had been a long-standing system of regulated prostitution in that city prior to World War II. As was done earlier in France, the Wehrmacht took over already existing brothels or employed existing prostitution structures.[45] In other parts of the Soviet Union, however, there were no easily visible and accessible prostitution structures and, as a result, the Wehrmacht worked to establish new brothels.[46] On 20 March 1942, the chief sanitation officer at the Army High Command (*Heeresarzt beim Oberkommando des Heeres*) noted that the amount of uncontrolled prostitution in Russia had grown tremendously. There were many secret brothels in larger cities. The number of cases of sexually transmitted disease was reported to be very high. In response, the chief sanitation officer issued a directive titled 'prostitution and brothels in the occupied territory of Sovietrussia', which ordered the establishment of medically supervised brothels for the use of German soldiers only. Russian doctors, under the supervision of German sanitation officers, were to conduct all examinations.[47]

In various regions, sanitation officers complained that the demand for sexual services would exceed the available number of prostitutes.[48] In March 1943, the chief sanitation officer reported that the numbers of visitors to the Wehrmacht brothel in Lvov, Ukraine, was so high that during lunch hours and in the evenings the line sometimes stretched down the street. Hence, he concluded that it was absolutely necessary to expand the number of Wehrmacht brothels. At the same time, however, he expressed concern about the Wehrmacht's reputation. He reported a lack of sympathy (*Verständnislosigkeit*) on the part of the civilian population, and concluded that 'in the present condition, the whole business in the Wehrmacht brothel can be declared unworthy of the Wehrmacht'.[49]

Indeed, the existence of Wehrmacht brothels sometimes disturbed the local population and not merely because of the bad impression made by Wehrmacht soldiers standing in line for commercial sex. In fact, local women had to fear for their lives. The doctor Elena Buividaite-Kutorgene from Kovno, Lithuania, recorded in her diary in 1941:

> In the evenings [Kovno] is empty, dark, and fearsome; young women are afraid to go out since it is said that they are picked up and taken to brothels. Such establishments of various sorts have been very carefully organized, for the commanders and for the soldiers.[50]

Several testimonies repeat the belief that local Wehrmacht commanders forced young women and girls to work in the brothels. Fritz Seidler assumes that young women in particular who refused to follow the call to work in Germany were forced to work in a military brothel instead.[51] Sometimes women also volunteered to work in the brothels or sold themselves on the street, calculating that prostitution was preferable to death by hunger and deprivation.[52]

The fact that most of the women in the brothels in the 'occupied Eastern territories' were not what the Nazis themselves would have considered Aryan was at least condoned. Indeed, Himmler had explicitly approved of sexual intercourse with 'ethnically alien women' in 1942 because it allegedly occurred outside the context of personal attachment and reproduction.[53] Sexual intercourse with Jewish women, however, remained strictly forbidden. In his directive on the establishment of brothels from 20 March 1942, the chief sanitation officer at the Army High Command explicitly stipulated that 'Jewesses are to be banned'.[54] Nevertheless, a number of narratives indicate that exceptions to this ban were frequent. Sometimes a woman would hide her Jewish origins, at other times German men picked a Jewish woman despite or even because of her origin.[55]

As Elena Buividaite-Kutorgene pointed out, the Wehrmacht tried to organize separate brothels for officers and privates. In some cases, it also established special brothels for foreign volunteers.[56] As an adjutant of the 'Eastern battalion' (*Ostbatallion*) put it, 'the man who is prepared to die for Germany must also be granted access to the brothels'.[57] In general, military brothels bound the individual man to the army. By establishing brothels, the OKW demonstrated that it spared no effort or expense to facilitate its soldiers' access to sexual experiences without personal risks: military and medical protection were provided, as were consistent prices.[58]

SS-units organized their own form of prostitution, although the documentary paper trail suggests that the SS-leadership did not organize brothels on a larger scale. Instead, various narratives show that SS-members visited the Wehrmacht brothels designated for officers. When the Einsatzgruppe D (*Deployment Group D*, a mobile killing squad of the SS) was stationed in Taganrog, Russia, for an extended period of time, some members of the command established a theatre group. The members of this group were mostly 'pretty Russian women and girls, who supplemented their food rations'. After the show, there was 'dancing, drinking and the girls then somehow came to an agreement.' Secret meeting points outside of the city were arranged for members of the command, houses were seized and caretakers (*Hausmeister*) were appointed in order to 'protect' the women.[59]

In short, military commanders established brothels in order to ensure military discipline, prevent sexually transmitted diseases, and reduce sexual violence as well as homosexual activity. As demonstrated above, many men took advantage of this offer. Others, however, continued to seek unauthorized commercial sex. As Elizabeth Heineman put it, 'sex was negotiated between the state and the men: the state could withhold access to brothels, and men could choose not to visit them'.[60] The prostitute became nearly invisible in this scenario. The fact that German men chose 'ethnically alien women' as prostitutes was at least tolerated. The soldiers' fulfillment of their sexual drives thus surpassed the 'ethnic aim' (*volkstumspolitisches Ziel*) of 'racial pureness'.

Consensual encounters and romantic relations

In the military rear and in occupied areas, German men often stayed in the same region for extended periods of time. They lodged in private homes and operated amidst the local population, which the Wehrmacht employed in various service positions. In this climate of everyday life during occupation, German men and local women developed friendly contacts and intimate relationships. Today, these are mainly interpreted as cases in which young people fell in love with little relation to or even in spite of the situation of war and occupation.[61] This invocation of love outside of or against the political power structures, however, fails to grasp the ways in which love and power are mediated. Paraphrasing Foucault's analysis of modern sexual discourse, sexuality is not opposed to and subversive of power. On the contrary, sexuality is 'a dense transfer point of power, charged with instrumentality'.[62] Similarly, love cannot exist outside of or opposed to power relations. On the contrary, romantic encounters in the occupied territories of the Soviet Union developed particularly due to the climate of war and occupation, and were structured by its special conditions. A German man who developed romantic feelings for a Soviet woman was often attempting to establish an experience 'outside' of combat. A Soviet woman, on the other hand, who engaged in a romance with a German soldier, might have been seeking normalcy within the everyday situation of violence and terror. Indeed, for a woman deemed 'ethnically alien', who constantly endured the threat of sexual violence, developing an intimate relationship with a German could mean becoming an active agent in shaping her own fate.

The OKW tried to prevent these kinds of relationships from developing. On 15 September 1942, Field Marshal Wilhelm Keitel explicated the military concerns:

> According to the existing reports, the lodgings [of German men] next to the civil population in the occupied Eastern territories led to closer contact [*engeren Fühlungnahme*] and to partly steady relationships between German soldiers and local women. Apart from a significant increase of venereal diseases, this situation abets enemy spy activities and leads to a complete blurring of the necessary distance to the people of the occupied Eastern territories.[63]

Keitel feared that consensual relationships – just like sexual violence – would increase sexually transmitted disease, facilitate enemy espionage, damage the alleged German superiority, and harm the reputation of the Wehrmacht. In addition, long-term relations implied a greater risk of soldiers suffering emotional conflicts. Military commanders dreaded the notion that a man who got to know a woman intimately would cease to regard the local people as enemies and would lose sight of the German aims in the war. Furthermore, the OKW feared that a man might experience distress if his sexual encounters in the occupied territory interfered with his sexual relations at home.[64] Indeed, a couple of soldiers in Norway had been known to commit suicide because they felt unable to handle both their families in Germany and their girlfriends and children in Norway.[65]

In order to deal with these concerns, military orders tried to prevent soldiers from developing any sympathy for the population, and, in particular, to dissuade the troops from seeking sexual encounters with Soviet women. The OKW tried to solve the problem of 'fraternization' by ordering the troops to evict all the inhabitants of houses used for accommodation by the soldiers.[66] To increase soldiers' vigilance, the image of the female enemy spy who would take advantage of the friendliness of German men was conjured up. An order of the 18th armored division stated that nearly all of these women were 'Jewish broads' (*Judenweiber*) whose origins could not be distinguished by sight.[67]

In areas where German men and local women worked in direct contact with each other, the army devised special rules of behavior. In March 1942, the Economic Unit East (*Wirtschaftsstab Ost*) reminded its soldiers to treat the female workers with 'strict reserve' (*strengster Zurückhaltung*): 'Drinking together, intimate approaches to local women and girls, dancing with them and granting trips in official vehicles is prohibited in any circumstance.'[68]

The documentary paper trail and oral testimonies indicate, however, that consensual amusements and intimate relationships did not cease to exist. In Andre Kaminski's documentary *Liebe im Vernichtungskrieg* (Love in the War of Annihilation), a Belorussian woman, introduced as Galina, recalls:

> The Germans – really young soldiers – did often visit us. We were then three girls: myself, Luba and Ira. A record player, dances – it was just fun. Around us the war raged, and here there was nevertheless the opportunity to have a little amusement, to have a rest. That was simply pure human.[69]

Her narrative reveals her desire for normalcy, for 'fun', 'simply pure human' in the life-threatening situation 'around us'. At the same time, she seems to justify her contacts with German men by stressing their very young age and their need to rest. Indeed, as Claudia Lenz has pointed out, women who had intimate relations with German men during World War II adapt certain narrative patterns to relate their story.[70] In an attempt to exculpate the women from the constant accusations of collaboration, Galina stresses their youth and naivety and the allegedly apolitical nature of the relationships.

There are other stories of women who were attracted to German men. Some women established regular relationships with German soldiers because they hoped for better living conditions, food rations, or protection. Others developed romantic feelings for 'a good-looking stranger'. In certain situations, even Jewish women wanted to be with a German man.[71] Generally, however, the partners did not speak the same language. Furthermore, the men arrived in uniforms and were equipped with weapons. For the Russian woman, therefore, the decision to develop feelings for a German man always meant getting intimately involved with the occupational power. The political climate could support her decision if the local population regarded the Germans as 'liberators from the Bolsheviks'. At other times, however, the woman made the active decision to collaborate with the enemy.[72]

The civil occupation authorities worried about the political consequences of these relationships. In accordance with the Wehrmacht and the SS, they feared that this would undermine the allegedly superior position of the Germans in relation to the local people. If the manners of German men became too friendly, the occupation regime felt in danger of losing power. At the same time, however, the civil occupation authorities feared that a complete ban of relations between Germans and local women would offend the local population and minimize their willingness to collaborate. On 27 July 1941, the Reich Commissioner for the Ostland (*Reichskommissar für das Ostland*, RKO) observed that the marriage ban for 'Reich German men' and local women would destroy the opportunity 'to lead these people towards the German Volk' (*diese Völker an das deutsche Volk heranzuführen*). Besides, he found it problematic to decorate local men who had volunteered for the Wehrmacht with the 'iron cross' (*Eisernes Kreuz*) to acknowledge that they had risked their lives for Germany, while discriminating against their sisters by deeming them unworthy of marrying a German.[73] Different bureaucrats reacted to this situation in July 1942 by planning a marriage law for German men in the 'Ostland'. Himmler, however, was opposed, arguing that there should not yet, 'after only one year of experience', be any written rules. Still, he conceded that there could be individual exceptions to the marriage ban in Estonia and Latvia. 'Reich German' men should henceforth be able to marry local women after 'racial inspection'.[74] Indeed, even members of the SS applied for marriage permits with women in the Baltic States and the Ukraine.

By the end of 1942, the Nazi authorities expressed a special interest in the children of German men in 'the East'. On 8 September 1942, the commander-in-chief of the 2nd tank division, General Rudolf Schmidt, submitted a report to Hitler in which he estimated the number of 'racially mixed children' (*Mischlingskinder*) expected in 'the East' to be about 1.5 million per year. His estimation was based upon a rather simple mathematical calculation. He assumed that every second of the six million German men stationed in 'the East' had sexual encounters with local women. A pregnancy would be the natural consequence in half of the cases.[75] One week later, on 16 September 1942, Himmler introduced the figure of at least one million 'soldier's children' (*Soldatenkinder*) at the field-headquarters in front of commanders of the SS and police.[76] This idea – that sexual encounters of German men would result in such a high number of children – displayed megalomaniac Nazi fantasies of unlimited potency and appeared as an affirmation of national strength.[77]

If a woman really did become pregnant, she should undergo a 'racial inspection' in order to establish whether she was 'germanizable' (*eindeutschbar*). This included an evaluation of her appearance, character, origins, and sexual history. The Nazi authorities generally believed that Soviet women who were willing to enter into relations with German men would be 'racially undesirable'. In June 1943, Himmler cited Hitler with the statement that 'in 90% of all cases, German men want to marry the most inferior of girls and women that one can imagine in a people'.[78] The particular fact that these women got involved with the enemy made them dubious and 'undesirable'.

In general, every case was decided individually. Above all, the Nazi term 'occupied Eastern territories' comprised a variety of countries, geographical settings, internal political situations, societies, languages, cultures, and historical experiences. The degrees of collaboration with and resistance against the Nazis varied; correspondingly, varying political attitudes towards the Soviet Union and the Red Army existed.[79] In this context, regional military commanders and occupation authorities often failed to keep pace with regulatory changes. Furthermore, they had a certain amount of autonomy, which allowed them to create their own dynamic scope for interpretation and action.[80]

In short, the ambiguity of the racial categories enabled German men to despise and kill Russian women because of their alleged 'racial inferiority', and at the same time consider the objects of their sexual desire to be 'racially valuable'. Indeed, a German man could justify a romance with an 'ethnically alien woman' without questioning his racist ideas. On the other hand, Soviet women who actively engaged in these relations often sought normalcy and an active subject-status in the everyday situation of war and terror. For the Nazi authorities, these long-term sexual encounters presented a threat. They symbolized racial transgression, the failure of the concept of 'racial awareness', and the blurring of the alleged 'German superiority'. Still, long-term relations were not generally banned. In order to remain flexible, Himmler explicitly opposed fixed policies. The case-by-case basis in which 'undesirable' relationships, engagements, and marriage permits were dealt with, and the decisions that were ultimately reached regarding them, depended on varying and shifting rationales.

Conclusion

When Heinrich Himmler insisted on 16 September 1942 that the individual man in 'the East' must only 'be responsive to a liaison that he can account for to Germany, to his blood, and to his future child', he conceded that the Nazi categories for assessing the 'racial value' of a woman were vague. In the very same speech he expressed his concern that 'it is pure coincidence whether the girl a soldier gets attached to is purebred or unfit'. If the woman became pregnant, according to his logic, she would have to undergo a 'racial inspection'. If she was to be considered 'racially valuable', 'there [was] no harm done: the soldier [had] behaved like a real man'. On the contrary, if the woman were considered 'racially inferior', the man was to be severely punished.[81]

Himmler's approach exemplifies the way Wehrmacht, SS, and civil occupation authorities sought to discipline the desire of German men with regard to (a) the 'racial awareness' of 'superior Aryans' and (b) the 'racial purity' of potential offspring. During the racist War of Annihilation, however, the ideal of the 'racially aware Aryan men' – who did not desire women deemed 'racially inferior' or at least exercised self-restraint – came into conflict with the dominant belief that the victorious German combatants needed to act upon their virile sexual drives. In addition, Wehrmacht, SS, and civil occupation authorities had to concede that 'racial value' was a highly ambiguous and contested category.

Consequently, neither the civil occupation authorities nor the Wehrmacht or the SS enforced a strict ban on 'undesirable sexual intercourse'. Only a relatively small number of men were actually punished for transgressing racial boundaries. Rather, regulating directives were issued to establish the threat and possibility of potential punishment. Furthermore, the assessment of any penalty was not regulated according to the initial transgression of 'undesirable sexual intercourse'; rather, the punishment depended on the result of the sexual encounter, i.e., children or sexually transmitted disease.

The ways in which Nazi authorities dealt with sexual violence, prostitution, and consensual encounters varied according to interests, territories, military strategies, occupation politics at different stages of the war and the occupation, and experiences and knowledge of regional commanders. As a result, initial ideological notions of 'racial hygiene' appeared to be permeable, and the megalomaniac Nazi vision of a 'racial restructuring of Europe' was fundamentally challenged. These irritations, however, did not obstruct the brutality of the German politics of colonization, extermination, and 'germanization'. On the contrary, the complex combination of strict rules and regulations, varying individual decisions, and specific policy changes provided the Nazi regime with the opportunity to demonstrate consistent ideas about racial hygiene and, at the same time, to react flexibly and assure the individual German man in 'the East' that he would be supported.

Far from destabilizing Nazi power or disrupting the pursuit of the war of annihilation, the ambiguities and flexibility of the system served precisely to facilitate its maintenance. In the light of recent research on National Socialism and the German war and occupation in 'the East', the gap between the clear-cut images of racist ideology and the more messy reality of everyday practices may seem hardly surprising. Birthe Kundrus, for instance, has demonstrated that on the home front, the enforcement of regulations to control sexual encounters between foreign forced laborers and German men and women 'varied over time and from place to place, depending upon the circumstances'.[82] Doris Bergen, Gerhard Wolf, and others have shown that the Nazi criteria for the assessment of 'racial value' in the occupied territories of Poland and the Soviet Union were ambiguous and could change according to time, territory, military objectives, and the beliefs and attitudes of the men in charge.[83] What has been largely ignored until today, however, is the place of sex in the German conduct of warfare in 'the East'. Further research is needed to investigate in which ways Nazi understandings of male sexuality, the institutional efforts to control soldierly sexuality, and the different forms of sexual encounters between German soldiers and local women shaped the racist German politics in the occupied territories and the everyday reality of the war.

Notes

Dagmar Herzog, Olaf Kistenmacher, Birthe Kundrus, Susann Lewerenz, Therese Roth, Michael Wildt and Gaby Zipfel offered me valuable comments and inspiring discussions on earlier versions of this chapter – thank you so much!

1. E. Harvey, *Women and the Nazi East: Agents and Witnesses of Germanization* (New Haven and London, 2003), pp. 78ff.; I. Heinemann, *'Rasse, Siedlung, deutsches Blut': Das Rasse- und Siedlungshauptamt der SS und die rassenpolitische Neuordnung Europas* (Göttingen, 2003), pp. 417ff.
2. To gain an insight into the organization of the different Nazi authorities in the occupied territories see W. Lower, 'The "Reibungslose" Holocaust? The German Military and Civilian Implementation of the "Final Solution" in Ukraine, 1941–1944', in G. Feldman and W. Seibel, eds, *Networks of Nazi Persecution: Bureaucracy, Business, and the Organization of the Holocaust* (New York and Oxford, 2006), pp. 236–256.
3. Armeeoberkommando (AOK) 11, Abt. Ic, AO Nr. 2379/41 geh., signed von Manstein, 10 November 1941, printed in *Der Prozeß gegen die Hauptkriegsverbrecher vor dem Internationalen Militärgerichtshof*, Nürnberg 1947–1949 (hereafter IMT), Vol. 3/4, Doc. 4064-PS, 129–132, also quoted in B. Beck, 'Sexual Violence and Its Prosecution by Court Martial of the Wehrmacht', in R. Chickering and S. Förster, eds, *A World at Total War: Global Conflict and the Politics of Destruction, 1937–1945* (Cambridge, 2005), pp. 317–331, 329.
4. Der SS-Richter beim RFSS, Schreiben an das Hauptamt SS-Gericht, Betr.: Geschlechtsverkehr von Angehörigen der SS und Polizei mit einer anders rassigen Bevölkerung, 12 November 1941, BArch [Federal Archives, Berlin] NS 7/265, p. 21.
5. Der Chef der Sicherheitspolizei und des SD, Kommandostab, Meldungen aus den besetzten Gebieten der UdSSR, 25 February 1942, USHMM [United States Holocaust Memorial Museum] RG-31.002M Reel 11 3676/4/105, p. 16.
6. B. Beck, *Wehrmacht und sexuelle Gewalt: Sexualverbrechen vor deutschen Militärgerichten 1939–1945* (Paderborn, Munich, Vienna and Zurich, 2004); D. Snyder, *Sex Crimes under the Wehrmacht* (Lincoln and London, 2007), pp. 135ff.; W. J. Gertjejanssen, Victims, Heroes, Survivors: Sexual Violence on the Eastern Front during World War II. Ph.D. dissertation (University of Minnesota, 2004); F. Seidler, *Prostitution, Homosexualität, Selbstverstümmelung: Probleme der deutschen Sanitätsführung 1939–1945* (Neckargemünd, 1977), pp. 135ff.
7. R. Müller, 'Liebe im Vernichtungskrieg: Geschlechtergeschichtliche Aspekte des Einsatzes deutscher Soldaten im Rußlandkrieg 1941–1944', in F. Becker,

T. Großbölting, A. Owzar, and R. Schlögl, eds, *Politische Gewalt in der Moderne: Festschrift für Hans-Ulrich Thamer* (Münster, 2003), pp. 239–267; A. Kaminski, *Liebe im Vernichtungskrieg. Die Frauen im Osten und die deutsche Besatzungsmacht*, TV Documentary, first broadcasted on 20 May 2002, on Arte.

8. Rede Himmlers am 16 September 1942 auf der SS- und Polizeiführer-Tagung in der Feldkommandostelle Hegewald bei Shitomir, BArch NS 19/4009, 78–127,
p. 125.

9. Beck, 2004, pp. 272ff.; A. Timm, 'Sex with a Purpose: Prostitution, Venereal Disease, and Militarized Masculinity in the Third Reich', *Journal of the History of Sexuality*, 11 (2002), 223–255, 253ff.; I. Meinen, *Wehrmacht und Prostitution im besetzten Frankreich* (Bremen, 2002), pp. 72ff.

10. B. Kundrus, 'Forbidden Company: Romantic Relationships between Germans and Foreigners, 1939–1945', *Journal of the History of Sexuality*, 11 (2002), 201–222, 204–205, 221.

11. See among others C. Essner, *Die 'Nürnberger Gesetze' oder Die Verwaltung des Rassenwahns 1933–1945* (Paderborn, Munich, Vienna, and Zürich, 2004); D. Bergen, 'Sex, Blood and Vulnerability: Women Outsiders in German Occupied Europe', in R. Gellately and N. Stoltzfus, eds, *Social Outsiders in Nazi Germany* (Princeton, 2001), pp. 273–293; Heinemann, 2003, pp. 476ff.

12. Rede Himmlers am 16 September 1942 auf der SS- und Polizeiführer-Tagung in der Feldkommandostelle in Hegewald bei Shitomir, BArch NS 19/4009, 78–127, p. 92.

13. Sexual violence, prostitution and consensual relations could merge. Some women, for instance, were sexually enslaved in military brothels. Others agreed to a relation with a German man in exchange for food. This article nevertheless differentiates these forms of sexual encounters in order to analyse the Nazi efforts of regulation. Sexual politics concerning other forms of sexual activity, i.e., homosexuality, sexual violence against children, sexual desire for animals and autoerotic practices, will not be discussed here.

14. IMT, Vol. VII, pp. 502–503. Birgit Beck has discussed the reliability of these reports that did not distinguish between regular soldiers and members of the SS (Beck, 2005, p. 320). At any rate, they provide a picture of various forms of sexual violence committed by German men in Eastern Europe, and thus present a starting point for further research.

15. Gaby Zipfel has pointed out that men might be ashamed of their experience of sexual pleasure in the act of violence. She suggests that rape victims are frequently killed after being raped, because their tormenters have exposed themselves to them (G. Zipfel, ' "Blood, Sperm, and Tears": Sexual Violence in War', *Eurozine*, 11 (2001), http://www.eurozine.com/articles/2001-11-29-zipfel-en.html, downloaded 10 January 2007).

16. Beck, 2004, p. 234.

17. Zipfel, 2001.

18. On the essential function of the 'third party', the spectators of violence, see J. P. Reemtsma, 'Die Natur der Gewalt als Problem der Soziologie. Eröffnungsvortrag auf dem 33. Kongress der Deutschen Gesellschaft für Soziologie in Kassel, 9. Oktober 2006', *Mittelweg*, 36, 5 (2006), 2–25.

19. R. Seifert, 'Krieg und Vergewaltigung. Ansätze zu einer Analyse', in A. Stiglmayer, ed., *Massenvergewaltigungen. Der Krieg gegen die Frauen* (Frankfurt am Main, 1993), pp. 87–112, 94.

20. H. Amesberger, K. Auer and B. Halbmeyer, *Sexualisierte Gewalt. Weibliche Erfahrungen in NS-Konzentrationslagern* (Wien, 2004), pp. 53ff.

21. G. Demianova, *Comrade Genia: The Story of a Victim of German Bestiality in Russia Told by Herself* (London, 1941), pp. 54–59.

22. Seifert, 1993, pp. 87–88; R. Pohl, *Feindbild Frau: Männliche Sexualität, Gewalt und die Abwehr des Weiblichen* (Hannover, 2004), pp. 478ff. This process of male bonding includes homoerotic elements, which are denied and negated.

23. Gertjejanssen, 2004, pp. 267ff., 274ff.

24. Beck, 2004, pp. 198–199; Gertjejannssen, 2004, pp. 293–294.

25. On the rape of Jewish women see, e.g., H. Heer, 'Killing Fields. Die Wehrmacht und der Holocaust', in H. Heer and K. Naumann, eds, *Vernichtungskrieg. Verbrechen der Wehrmacht 1941 bis 1944* (Hamburg, 1995), pp. 57–77, 64; F. Ni Aolain, 'Sex-based Violence and the Holocaust: A Reevaluation of Harms and Rights in International Law', *Yale Journal of Law and Feminism*, 12 (2000), 43–85; Gertjejannssen, 2004, pp. 285ff., 303ff.

26. Beck, 2004, pp. 219ff.

27. For some examples see Milizionäre der Machniwski Miliz, Rapport an den Vorgesetzten der ukrainischen Miliz, Winniza, 30 October 1941, Übersetzung weitergeleitet vom Vorsitzenden der Winnizer Gebietsverwaltung an den SD, USHMM RG-31.011M Reel 1 P-1311c/1c/2 (03 September 1941–18 November 1941), pp. 12–13; R. L. Bogomolnaya, *Wartime Experiences in Lithuania* (London and Portland, 2000), pp. 31, 45.

28. For examples see Hamburger Institut für Sozialforschung, ed., *Vernichtungskrieg. Verbrechen der Wehrmacht 1941–1944. Exhibition Catalogue* (Hamburg, 1996), p. 100; H. Heer, 'Die Logik des Vernichtungskrieges. Wehrmacht und Partisanenkampf', in Heer and Naumann, eds, 1995, pp. 104–138, 122; H. Krausnick and H. Wilhelm, eds, *Die Truppe des Weltanschauungskrieges. Die Einsatzgruppen der Sicherheitspolizei und des SD 1938–1942* (Stuttgart, 1981), p. 486.

29. AOK 9, Anweisung, Betr.: Überwachung der Disziplin, 10 August 1941, NARA [National Archives and Record Administration] RG 242/314/679, p. 649, also quoted in C. Rass, *'Menschenmaterial': Deutsche Soldaten an der Ostfront. Innenansichten einer Infanteriedivision 1939–1945* (Paderborn, 2003), p. 268.

30. AOK 11, Abt. Ic, AO Nr. 2379/41 geh., gez. von Manstein, 10 November 1941, printed in: IMT, Vol. 3/4, Doc. 4064-PS, pp. 129–132, also quoted in Beck, 2005, p. 329.

31. Beck, 2004, p. 327.

32. Beck, 2005, pp. 326ff.

33. Beck, 2004, pp. 277–278, 247 ff.; Snyder, 2007, pp. xii, 138ff.

34. Chef des Allgemeinen Wehrmachtsamts im Oberkommando der Wehrmacht, Schreiben an SS-Obergruppenführer Wolff, 02 August 1943, BArch NS 19/3717, Vol. 10, 38–42.

35. A. Angrick, *Besatzungspolitik und Massenmord. Die Einsatzgruppe D in der südlichen Sowjetunion 1941–1943* (Hamburg, 2003), pp. 359, 450; K. Mallmann, V. Rieß and W. Pyta, eds, *Deutscher Osten 1939–1945: Der Weltanschauungskrieg in Photos und Texten* (Darmstadt, 2003), p. 93; H. Wilhelm, 'Die Einsatzgruppe A der Sicherheitspolizei des SD 1941/42: Eine exemplarische Studie', in Krausnick und Wilhelm, eds, 1981, pp. 281–636, 480.

36. Richtertagung in München am 07 May 1943, Bericht und Vermerk zu diversen Besprechungspunkten, BArch NS 7/13 1–21, pp. 7–9.

37. Anl. 1 zu OKH, 06 September 1941, Betr.: Selbstzucht, BA-MA [Bundesarchiv-Militärarchiv Freiburg] H 20/825; Oberkommando des Heeres, von Brauchitsch, 31 July 1940, BA-MA RH 53-7/v. 233a/167, also quoted in Beck, 2004, pp. 107f.

38. Gericht der Wehrmachts-Ortskommandantur Riga/264, Feldurteil, 13 April 1944, BA-ZNS [Bundesarchiv-Zentralnachweisstelle Kornelimünster] 31–38, p. 37, also quoted in Beck, 2004, p. 273. On the military procedures of disinfection see Seidler, 1977, pp. 107ff.

39. Gertjejanssen, 2004, pp. 169ff.; Meinen, 2002, pp. 17ff.

40. Oberkommando der Wehrmacht, Keitel, Betrifft: Verkehr des deutschen Soldaten mit der Zivilbevölkerung in den besetzten Ostgebieten, 12 September 1942, Abschrift, BA-MA, RH 26-6/67.

41. Partei und Wehrmacht im Generalgouvernement und ihre Führungsaufgaben, 24 August 1944, BArch NS 55/26, pp. 1499–1506. For a similar line of reasoning see also Militärärztliche Akademie Berlin, Gutachten Löhe an Lehrgruppe C, 09 January 1945, BA-MA H 20/447.

42. On the ideal of aristocratic manhood in Nazi ideology see P. Diehl, *Macht – Mythos – Utopie: Die Körperbilder der SS-Männer* (Berlin, 2005), pp. 162ff.

43. J. Roos, 'Backlash against Prostitutes' Rights: Origins and Dynamics of Nazi Prostitution Policies', *Journal of the History of Sexuality*, 11 (2002), 67–94, 67; Meinen, 2002, p. 72.

44. Timm, 2002, pp. 253f.

45. Der Beratende Hygieniker beim Heeres-Sanitätsinspekteur, gez. Zeiss, Schreiben an den Beratenden Hygieniker des Feld- und Ersatzheeres, Berlin, 10 February 1943, NARA RG 242 T 78/189, pp. 1247–1248.

46. Gertjejannssen, 2004, pp. 169ff.; Seidler, 1977, pp. 138–139.

47. Heeresarzt im OKH, gez. Dr Hanloser: Prostitution und Bordellwesen im besetzten Gebiet in Sowjetrußland, 20 March 1942, BA-MA H 20/825, also quoted in Seidler, 1977, p. 139.

48. Gertjejannssen, 2004, pp. 198f.; F. Vossler, *Propaganda in die eigene Truppe: Die Truppenbetreuung in der Wehrmacht 1939–1945* (Paderborn, 2005), pp. 356f.

49. Leitender San.-Offizier, OFK 365, Az. 49s (I/F), Monatsbericht, geheim, Anlage 3 zu OFK 365 Ia Nr 1286/43, pp. 1–2, Lemberg, 15 March 1943, NARA RG 242/501/217, p. 338.

50. Quoted in I. Ehrenburg and V. Grossmann, *The Complete Black Book of Russian Jewry* (New Brunswick and London, 2002 [1944]), p. 365.

51. Seidler, 1977, p. 154.

52. Ibid., p. 138; Vossler, 2005, p. 353.

53. RKF Himmler an SS-Obergruppenführer Friedrich Wilhelm Krüger, Betrifft: Geschlechtsverkehr von Angehörigen der SS und Polizei mit Frauen einer andersrassigen Bevölkerung, 30 June 1942, BArch NS 19/1913, 3–4, p. 4, also printed in H. Heiber, ed., *Reichsführer! Briefe an und von Himmler* (München, 1970), pp. 156–157, Doc. 120. Himmler referred to brothels in the *Generalgouvernement* (Poland). However, the establishment of brothels in the *Reichskommissariat Ostland* and the *Reichskommissariat Ukraine* suggest a similar attitude.

54. Heeresarzt im OKH, gez. Dr Hanloser, Prostitution und Bordellwesen im besetzten Gebiet in Sowjetrußland, 20 March 1942, BA-MA H 20/825.

55. Gertjejannssen, 2003, pp. 191ff.; Vossler, 2005.

56. Der Heeresgruppenarzt beim Oberkommando Heeresgruppe, Betr.: Bordelle für Osttruppen, 28 April 1944, BA-MA RH 36/v 491, also quoted in Seidler, 1977, p. 183. For more information on the 'Eastern troops' of the Wehrmacht compare R. Thurston, 'Cauldrons of Loyalty and Betrayal: Soviet Soldiers' Behavior', in R. Thurston and B. Bonwetsch, eds, *The People's War: Responses to World War II in the Soviet Union* (Urbana and Chicago, 2000), 235–257, 242.

57. Aktennotiz, 06 December 1943, UAD, 8/4, 19, quoted in M. Plassmann, 'Wehrmachtsbordelle: Anmerkungen zu einem Quellenfund im Universitätsarchiv Düsseldorf', *Militärgeschichtliche Zeitschrift*, 62 (2003), 157–173, 162.

58. Meinen, 2002, p. 75.

59. Schreiben von Dr Görz und RA Dr Aschenauer, grüne Kladde, unpaginiert, BDC-SSO Seetzen, BA-MA, N 642/ Box 29, also quoted in Angrick, 2003, pp. 447–448.

60. E. D. Heineman, 'Sexuality and Nazism: The Doubly Unspeakable?', *Journal of the History of Sexuality*, 11 (2002), 22–66, 54.

61. E. Drolshagen, *Nicht ungeschoren davonkommen: Die Geliebten der Wehrmachtssoldaten im besetzten Europa* (Munich, 2000); Kaminski, 2002; Müller, 2003.

62. M. Foucault, *History of Sexuality* (New York, 1985), p. 103.

63. OKW, gez. Keitel, Erlass, Betr.: Unerwünschter Verkehr deutscher Soldaten mit Einwohnern in den besetzten Ostgebieten, 15 September 1942, Abschrift, BArch NS 19/1691, p. 1.

64. On sexual politics at the home-front see D. Herzog, *Sex after Fascism: Memory and Morality in Twentieth-Century Germany* (Princeton and Oxfordshire, 2005).

65. K. Olsen, *Vater: Deutscher. Das Schicksal der norwegischen Lebensbornkinder und ihrer Mütter von 1940 bis heute* (Frankfurt am Main and New York, 2002), pp. 25–26, 123.

66. O. Bartov, *The Eastern Front, 1941–1945: German Troops and the Barbarisation of Warfare* (Houndmills, Basingstoke, Hampshire and London, 1985), pp. 126ff.

67. Quoted in O. Bartov, *Hitlers Wehrmacht. Soldaten, Fanatismus und die Brutalisierung des Krieges* (Reinbek, 1995), pp. 145–146.

68. Wirtschaftsstab Ost, Besondere Anordnungen Nr. 61, 05 March 1942, BA-MA, RW 31/141, also quoted in Müller, 2003, p. 246.

69. Quoted in Kaminski, 2002; Müller, 2003, p. 251.

70. C. Lenz, *Haushaltspflicht und Widerstand. Erzählungen norwegischer Frauen über die deutsche Besatzung 1940–1945 im Lichte nationaler Vergangenheitskonstruktionen* (Tübingen, 2003), pp. 224ff.

71. See among others Z. Jasinska, *Der Krieg, die Liebe und das Leben. Eine polnische Jüdin unter Deutschen* (Berlin, 1998).

72. Fabrice Virgili has demonstrated that French women who decided to get involved with German men were often excluded and attacked as collaborators, by their families and immediate surroundings as well as by political institutions (F. V. Fabrice, *Shorn Women: Gender and Punishment in Liberation France* [Oxford and New York, 2002]).

73. Müller, 2003, p. 250.

74. Brief RFSS, Himmler, an SS-Obergruppenführer Gottlob Berger, Betr: Zu Ihren Aktennotizen, Reval, 28 July 1942, BArch NS 19/1772, p. 5. In the process of 'racial inspection', the women, as opposed to the men, were subject to an assessment of their sexual history (Bergen, 2001, p. 285).

75. Schmidt's report is among others mentioned in Persönliche Handakte Major Hans von Payr zu Enn und Caldiff, Oberkommando der Wehrmacht/ Wehrwirtschafts- und Rüstungsamt (OKW), Notiz, 18 September 1942, Betrifft: Vorsorgliche Erfassung von zusätzlichen Arbeitskräften, BA-MA RW 19/473. See also Beck, 2004, p. 212; Heinemann, 2003, p. 528; C. Gerlach, *Kalkulierte Morde. Die deutsche Wirtschafts- und Vernichtungspolitik in Weißrußland 1941 bis 1944* (Hamburg, 1999), p. 1080.

76. Rede Himmlers am 16 September 1942 auf der SS- und Polizeiführer-Tagung in der Feldkommandostelle in Hegewald bei Shitomir, BArch NS 19/4009, 78–127, p. 88. See also *Der Dienstkalender Heinrich Himmlers 1941/42*. Edited, commented and introduced by P. Witte, M. Wildt, M. Voigt, D. Pohl, P. Klein, C. Gerlach, C. Dieckmann and A. Angrick (Hamburg, 1999), p. 548; Bericht über Himmlers Rede vom 16 September 1942 vor den Polizeiführern, enthalten in "Besichtigungsfahrt nach der Ukraine (Rußland-Süd)", BArch NS 2/82, p. 221.

77. R. Mühlhäuser, 'Between Extermination and Germanization: Children of German Men in the "Occupied Eastern Territories", 1942–1945', in K. Ericsson and E. Simonsen, eds, *Children of World War II: A Hidden Enemy Legacy* (Oxford and New York, 2005), pp. 167–189. For a general introduction on reproductive policies in the German occupied territories see G. Lilienthal, *Der 'Lebensborn e.V.': Ein Instrument nationalsozialistischer Rassenpolitik*, 2nd revised edn (Frankfurt am Main, 2003).

78. RFSS, Himmler, Niederschrift über Besprechung mit dem Führer zur Heirat von Wehrmachtsangehörigen mit Angehörigen der artverwandten germanischen Völker, 17 June 1943, BArch NS 19/2706, p. 1. For similar lines of reasoning see Müller, 2003, pp. 256f.

79. G. Ueberschär and W. Wette, eds, *'Unternehmen Barbarossa': Der deutsche Überfall auf die Sowjetunion 1941* (Paderborn, 1984), p. 312.

80. Hamburger Institut für Sozialforschung, 2002, pp. 579ff.; J. P. Reemtsma, 'Über den Begriff "Handlungsspielräume"', *Mittelweg*, 36, 6 (2002), 5–23.

81. Rede Himmlers am 16 September 1942 auf der SS- und Polizeiführer-Tagung in der Feldkommandostelle in Hegewald bei Shitomir, BArch NS 19/4009, 78–127, p. 124.

82. Kundrus, 2002, p. 222.

83. Bergen, 2001; G. Wolf, 'Rassische Utopien und ökonomische Zwänge: die rassischen Selektionen polnischer Arbeitskräfte durch die SS in den Lagern der Umwandererzentralstelle', in A. Jah; C. Kopke, A. Korb and A. Stiller, eds, *Nationalsozialistische Lager. Neue Beiträge zur NS-Verfolgungs- und Vernichtungspolitik und zur Gedenkstättenpädagogik* (Münster and Ulm, 2006), pp. 125–148.

8
Sexual Abuse of Jewish Women in Auschwitz-Birkenau

Na'ama Shik

For the love of my father Zeev and my mother Hava, Who went through this hell and remain human beings

> I have returned
> From a world beyond knowledge
> And now must unlearn
> For otherwise I clearly see
> I can no longer live.

Charlotte Delbo, Auschwitz and After[1]

Introduction

Is it possible for us to understand Auschwitz? Can we use our own language to delve into the history of the camp and, in particular, into the sexual exploitation of Jewish women in the camp? Is it appropriate for a historian to try and decipher the reality she wishes to describe? Are the well-established rules and methodologies of historical inquiry sufficient? Can the experiences of these women be recounted by scholars who did not stumble out of their shattered realities, who did not experience the extreme loss, all the more incomprehensible as it involved loss of a sense of self? Is it not preferable to leave the camp behind, to let the wounds heal and the screams be cried out, and to allow death to perish?

In his book, *Nazi Germany and the Jews*, Saul Friedländer wrote:

> From the moment the victims were engulfed in the process leading to the 'Final Solution', their collective life – after a short period of enhanced cohesion – started to disintegrate. Soon this collective

history merged with the history of the administrative and murderous measures of their extermination, and with its abstract statistical expression. The only concrete history that can be retrieved remains that carried by personal stories. From the stage of collective disintegration to that of deportation and death, this history, in order to be written at all, has to be represented as the integrated narration of individual fates.[2]

In his film *Shoah*, Claude Lanzmann interviews Raul Hilberg, who makes an important point. As if aware of the limitations of his, indeed anybody's, ability to encompass the farthest reaches of Holocaust study, Hilberg states,

> In all of my work I have never begun by asking the big questions, because I was always afraid that I would come up with small answers; and I have preferred to address these things which are minutiae or details in order that I might then be able to put together in a gestalt a picture which, if not an explanation, is at least a description, a more full description, of what transpired.[3]

The object of this article is not to suggest a new interpretation of Nazism or the Holocaust, but to explore a single place and theme within both. It is not, as a matter of course, a comprehensive representation, nor is it beyond contestation. I attempt to reveal the female experience of sexual exploitation in Auschwitz, from 1942 when the first Jewish women set foot in the camp, until liberation in 1945, as it is depicted in autobiographical literature and testimonies. The work presented here is drawn from writings produced in the immediate aftermath; it can be no more than a referred sound, an echo of an echo.

The definition of sexual exploitation used here is broad. It includes both physical and verbal abuse. Although rape did take place in Auschwitz-Birkenau, it was rare. However, a wide range of forms of sexual exploitation certainly occurred in the camp: verbal sexual harassment,[4] sexual assaults, prostitution in exchange for food, cases of attempts to force women inmates into sexual relations and threats of punishments if they refused. These acts were perpetrated by both men and women, but mainly by men. In addition, at the time of liberation and during the subsequent months, camp survivors suffered from further sexual abuse by Red Army soldiers. Although these soldiers mainly raped non-Jewish German women, in many cases they raped and sexually attacked Jewish survivors as well.

Daily life in Auschwitz was characterized by two different yet interwoven realities. First, the overall human experience, shared by men and women alike, was composed of dehumanization, the shattering of the self through fear, extreme cold, terror, uncertainty, hopelessness, and negation. At its most extreme, this dehumanization transformed a person into a Muselmann, a being described by Isabele Leitner as 'not quite alive yet not quite dead'.[5] The second type of experience was highly gendered. Its roots can be found in female physiology, and at the same time it is inherently connected to the Nazi worldview. Nazi ideology had a conflicting attitude toward Jewish women's sexuality and motherhood. On the one hand, Jewish women underwent a process of desexualization in addition to the dehumanization. The Nazis annulled the essence of women's biology and personality. On the other hand, the female body remained a sexual object – a fact evinced, as we will see, by a diversity of sexually exploitative practices. In other words, in Auschwitz the Jewish female body became matter only, matter bereft of humanity but nonetheless having sexual traits and the ideological–physical threat of reproductive capabilities. Gender differences in Auschwitz-Birkenau remained visible in and on the body.

Recognizing this fact while writing the history of the female body in Auschwitz does not imply an essentialist analysis nor does it treat physiology as fate. It does offer a historical analysis avoided so far by mainstream historiography. Utilizing a gendered analysis (both attending to the different socialization processes of men and women and to the specific ways female physiology functioned in the camps) we find gender-based differences associated in particular with the selection process and food procurement. However, it is important to note here that even in dealing with female physiology, we have to remember the sociological meanings and frameworks into which assumptions about gender differences fit. The term 'cultural body' may help to express the distinctive aspects of this phenomenon. Menses, pregnancy, sexual abuse, attitudes toward hair and hygiene: none of these occurred in a vacuum. Instead, they were part of complex social relationships, hierarchies, and processes through which yet further meanings were circulated and reinforced.

This article is based on testimonies and memoirs. In general, besides the inevitable differences among individual writers and those giving testimony, such as their sensitivity and sensibilities, their ability to assess the situation, their language, their background, we can identify important similarities in the 'first wave'[6] of autobiographical publications that appeared between 1945 and 1950, which are of particular significance to this research. Contrary to widespread perception, and despite the almost complete absence of women from the historiography of the Holocaust in the decades following the war, a relatively considerable number of testimonies and memoirs by women survivors were published immediately after the war. Notwithstanding these contributions, Holocaust memory and research were subsequently for long shaped by books largely written by and about men.[7]

The first wave of writings and testimonies, by both men and women, constitutes, in my opinion, a unique historical source of great importance. In them, the horrors, difficulties, and various abuses appear in a far more blatant and less 'literary' manner than in later writings. For example, this corpus of texts reveals a variety of forms of abuse that occurred in Auschwitz, including sexual abuse and cases of 'prostitution' among female and male prisoners, usually in exchange for food or other means of survival. Writing and publishing these early testimonies, survivors felt less exposed to the 'public' or to their later families. They were also less exposed to the memory of the Holocaust as it would subsequently be shaped, as articulated by Imre Kertesz:

> The survivor is taught how he has to think about what he has experienced, regardless of whether or to what extent this 'thinking-about' is consistent with his real experiences. The authentic witness is or will soon be perceived as being in the way, and will have to be shoved aside like the obstacle he is ... We, the victims, will appear as the truly incorrigible, irreconcilable ones, as the anti-historical reactionaries in the exact sense of the word, and in the end it will seem like a technical mishap, an accident, that some of us still survived.[8]

Some methodological remarks

We can see that in the last ten years mostly female, but also male, Holocaust researchers dealing with women and the Holocaust have begun to address the subject of sexual abuse during the Holocaust. Indeed, this trend appears to be growing. Yet most researchers have limited their discussion to a narrow source base, while at the same time the research is somehow eclectic in that it tends to deal with 'all' the cases of sexual abuse which occurred during different stages of the Holocaust and in various locations, and simultaneously does not always make a clear distinction between German and non-German perpetrators.[9]

Sexual abuse in the concentration and extermination camps has been approached on two non-parallel tracks of research. The first approach was prevalent until the beginning of the third millennium but is still used by some today. It concludes that there is little evidence of harsh sexual abuse, particularly of incidents of rape, in the various camps. Scholars taking this position argue, correctly, that this is mainly due to strict prohibitions in Nazi ideology, in short, the interdiction against sexual relations, by consent or by force, between members of the 'supreme race' and inferior races, particularly Jews. To engage in such relations was considered a crime of 'race defilement' [*Rassenschande*]. In their book, *Women in the Holocaust*, first published in 1998, Dalia Ofer and Lenore J. Weitzman assert that

> The last distinction in German treatment of men and women – ironically, a clear violation of German policy – was that Jewish women were more likely than men to be subjected to sexual harassment and rape. Although the incidence of rape by the Nazis appears to have been rare – or at least that is our impression, based on the diaries and testimonies we have read – it is clear that many Jewish women were terrorized by rumors of rape.[10]

Ofer and Weitzman also state

> a number of testimonies report systematic sexual assaults on Jewish women in specific localities. Survivors of the Skarzysko camp, for example, reported several sexual assaults and brutal rapes by German commanders even though Germans were prohibited from such 'racial shame'.[11]

We will return to this important note later in this chapter.

Marlene Heinemann asserts that 'rape did occur in ghettos and even some camps despite subsequent punishment...but, the most universal form of sexual assault on women appears to have been verbal abuse...'.[12] Sybil Milton mentions the mythologizing of survivor sexual behavior: 'A popular postwar myth, sometimes exploited and sensationalized, held that Jewish women were forced to serve as prostitutes in the SS bordellos and were frequently raped. Although such cases did undoubtedly occur, it was not the norm and reflects a macabre postwar misuse of the Holocaust for popular titillation'.[13] She cites Auschwitz survivor Kitty Hart, 'who calls these sexual fantasies of postwar literature and television: "ridiculous misconceptions"'.[14] Vera Laska argues that

Considering the tens of thousands of women incarcerated in the camps, rape by the SS was relatively rare. While it is a fact that the SS could – and did – do as they pleased with any female inmate, raping them was not their preference. First of all, most of these women looked unattractive, without hair, dirty, smelly. Second, if caught in intercourse with an inmate, the SS were punished, usually by being shipped to the Russian front, and most SS cherished their camp job which was a sinecure with power. If caught in the act with a Jewess, they could be shot for defiling the master race.[15]

The second approach to studying sexual abuse in Nazi camps has emerged over the last few years and asserts quite an opposing argument: harsh sexual abuse, including many cases of rape, did in fact take place in various Nazi camps. These researchers believe that the lack of evidence for this can be explained by the reluctance of female survivors to talk about these experiences.[16] For example, Jonathan Friedman argues that he has found much more evidence of sexual assault than other scholars have: 'Shoah Foundation testimonies of women who were victims of specific acts of sexual abuse are numerous and geographically diverse ... Moreover, incidents of sexual assault and rape occurred in diverse settings – in the ghettos, in camps, and in hiding places ... '.[17] Talking about the camps, however, he says,

> Ironically, in the sample of testimonies I viewed that relate stories of rape in the camps, I have fewer first hand accounts from women. That does not mean, of course, that witnesses outnumbered actual victims ... it is more likely that once the Shoah Foundation catalogues more testimonies, more victims' accounts will emerge.[18]

In the introduction to her book about Jewish women in the Ravensbrück concentration camp, Rochelle Saidel wrote:

> Fear of rape and sexual abuse was another issue that affected the women in the camp. The racial laws enacted in Germany in 1935, which made it illegal for 'Aryans' to have sexual relation with Jews, should have protected Jewish women against rape and forced prostitution. However, there is evidence in historical accounts and testimonies that these laws were often broken. Most women survivors do not talk about their own sexual exploitation, but some of them tell stories of their comrades' suffering.[19]

She adds, 'No woman I interviewed told me that she was raped, although several said they knew about the rape of other women. While I cannot provide personal testimony from survivors for specific cases of rape at Ravensbrück, it is more than likely that there was rape and fear of rape'.[20] Myrna Goldenberg agrees, writing that rape of Jewish women in the camps did happen, even though supporting evidence is rare: 'Though we might expect otherwise because rape was a serious racial purity issue, rape happened, but was and, to some extent, still is ignored or neglected...nevertheless, Jewish women were raped by Jewish and non-Jewish men in ghettos and camps though evidence to substantiate such occurrences is usually anecdotal'.[21]

Doris L. Bergen can be placed somewhere in between. In her article 'Sexual Violence in the Holocaust: Unique and Typical?', she asserts that 'Nazi ideology...did not constitute a barrier to violence of sexual nature...Instead, ideology shaped the forms that sexual violence took'.[22] Bergen suggests that to understand sexual violence we need to include in the term more than rape.[23] She also asserts that

> at least in certain times and places, the prohibition against sexual relations between people defined as Jews and those classified as Aryans was ignored or defied.... Doubtless many unsanctioned acts of rape occurred: but given that Aryan men could be punished for sexual relations with women from groups labeled 'undesirable', they had extra incentive to destroy evidence of their transgressions by killing their victims.[24]

Nonetheless, toward the end of her article, she says that Nazi ideology marked Gypsies and above all Jews for annihilation and that this shaped the patterns of sexual abuse which did not include mass rape and prostitution of these women. Instead, 'Nazi leaders and propagandists worked to discourage German killers and their henchmen from considering women from the groups marked for destruction as objects of sexual desire'.[25] And she concludes that 'rape by Germans was more common among women from those groups targeted for enslavement – above all, Slavs – than among those slated for total destruction'.[26]

In addition, some recent studies invoke what they call 'tacit consent' among Holocaust survivors unwilling to talk about the subject. These scholars assert that harsh cases of sexual abuse, including rape, did happen in camps, and they object to the myth that there was no significant sexual abuse in the camps. Here, for example, is a quote from an article published in June 2006 in an Israeli newspaper. Entitled 'To Break the Tacit Consent', the article was an interview with a PhD student investigating the subject of women, sexuality, and the Holocaust.[27] The PhD student, Esti Dror, discusses assaults, including crimes of 'race defilement', inflicted by SS men on Jewish prisoners, even as she states that one of the main problems of her dissertation project is to find a Holocaust survivor who will break 'this tacit consent'.[28]

In my opinion, however, this second, more recent approach reveals a distinctively new mythologization of and fascination with the subject of sexual violence. Unfortunately, though perhaps inevitably, the discourse on women's history in Auschwitz-Birkenau is not completely free of the desire to grab attention and garner high 'ratings'.[29] Several aspects of the second approach are deeply problematic. This is not least because different kinds of sexual abuse are apparently being confused in scholars' reading of testimonies and memoirs. These testimonies and memoirs, for instance, include mention of cases of rape that were mainly perpetrated by non-Germans. Moreover, far from being silent out of 'tacit consent', Jewish women as well as men, in the immediate aftermath, *did* talk about these cases. It is thus quite misleading to say that there was an overall 'tacit consent' to remain silent about the subjects of rape and abuse.[30]

Furthermore, in testimonies and autobiographical literature specifically from the early period of 1945–1950, we find repeated mention of horrible atrocities, acts, and experiences which have to be located in the 'gray zone' of ambiguity and complexity with respect to the issues of voluntarism and coercion. Assuming that 'tacit consent' exists now regarding sexual abuse does not provide us with a sufficient answer as to why Holocaust survivors were able to talk about these 'gray zone' events in early testimonies and in autobiographical literature. My own research suggests that the 'truth' is, maybe as always, somewhere in the midst of the two prevailing paradigms. As previously mentioned, earlier research often did not give sufficient emphasis to the particularly relevant sources of 'first-wave' testimonies and autobiographies, often lacked methodological sophistication, and did not clearly enough differentiate between sexual abuse perpetrated by Germans on Jewish men and women and sexual abuse perpetrated by non-Germans.[31]

In my research I have examined hundreds of testimonies and dozens of autobiographical texts. The testimonies were taken from the Yad Vashem archives which contain the following collections: the Yad Vashem testimony collection; the full Zich collection; the YIVO collection; the Munchen collection; the Boder collection; the Hungarian collection and more. This corpus of primary sources can deepen our knowledge of sexual abuse in the camps significantly.

Sexual abuse in Auschwitz

Many of the cases of physical sexual exploitation by the SS and by prisoners in positions of authority took place when prisoners first entered the camp, as they passed through inspection, selection, and in particular, the 'sauna', where new prisoners were led after they had 'passed' selection. Here, still under the trauma and the shock of their first encounter with the camp, men and women were forced to undress, their head and body hair was shaved, they had to go through a disinfection process, they received the prisoner's uniform, and their camp number was tattooed on their body. Many Jewish women who arrived in Auschwitz were transferred there after only a few weeks in ghettos or transitional camps, meaning that they were still relatively robust and attractive.[32] To SS men it was a particular pleasure to come to the 'sauna' to jeer and humiliate them. Although both men and women went through the 'sauna', there were some significant differences between their experiences. First and foremost, men mainly undressed in front of other men, while most women also had to undress in front of men. More often than not, women found themselves utterly exposed and surrounded by men who made fun of their bodies, their breasts, and their genitalia, sometimes by 'playing' with their nipples and touching other intimate parts of their bodies.

Verbal abuse and physical humiliation

Gisella Perl describes the morbid sexual excitement the SS guards exhibited as women passed through the sauna and were humiliated in it: 'The first room into which we stepped was filled with young SS men. Their eyes shone with expectation, their ape-like movements betrayed an unhealthy, abnormal sexual excitement'.[33] While most men describe this process purely in terms of dehumanization,[34] Perl adds a gender-specific dimension of sexual exploitation and abuse.[35] She also describes how after liberation when she was living in New York, she would be reminded of the sauna in Auschwitz – 'the Auschwitz beauty parlor' – whenever she would pass a beauty parlor. The aim of the sauna was, of course, the opposite of a regular beauty parlor: here the aim was to remove any remnants of beauty the women retained. Ada Halperin describes how the SS men used to mock the women in different ways while they were naked in the sauna. In one scene she describes how one SS man opened the sauna door while the women were naked, put his motorbike under the water in order to wash it with them, while he and his friends stood there and verbally abused them.[36] Hela Tischauer, who arrived at Auschwitz from Czechoslovakia in the second transport of Jewish women in March 1942, wrote about the sauna: 'There came in at that time the Lager leader...and many others whose names are today not known to me...and to inspect us like cattle. It was going on like a cattle show. They turned us here and there, right and left...'.[37] Ada Levi from Bonn was sent to Auschwitz from Terezin on 28 October 1944. She tells about the humiliation of standing naked in front of a 'herd' of SS men:

> We were led to a block, there wait for us SS men and SS women armed with cudgels and yelling at us: 'Strip!' We took off our coats and stood there looking helpless at each other. Then again that scream: 'Strip!' Yes, to strip naked, totally naked in front of this herd of animals....[38]

Physical abuse

Many women survivors refer to the verbal and physical abuse that they suffered during the passage through the sauna. Eva Schloss, who arrived at the camp from Holland at the age of 15, wrote,

> From time to time SS officers came in, walked around the room, and jeered at the sight of our naked bodies. It amused them to pinch the buttocks of the women who were young and pretty. When one of the men passed beside me and pinched my buttocks I felt really humiliated.[39]

In her testimony that was given in Yad Vashem in 1988, Tova Berger recalls,

> They told us to get undressed and they shaved us. They shaved my beautiful blonde hair and my two sisters' hair and we were standing naked before the soldiers and for me it was a shock because I was a religious girl. I never was undressed in front of a man and they made all kind of dirty jokes about our bodies and they looked at us and I was standing there shivering, naked, without hair on my body, and I was exposed. I felt like an animal...and the way they treated us already there was so terrible, then I said, 'Where is G-d? Where is G-d?'....[40]

Elsa (Frishman) Glieck, who arrived in Auschwitz in May 1942 with the first transports of women from Czechoslovakia, talks about the devastating physical examination the women with her underwent:

> After the roll-call we, who arrived last, were led back to the 'revier', where we stood in rows, and each time they ordered a certain number of women to go to the back of the 'revier'... the women who arrived first, had already passed us with their heads shaved and wearing striped clothes. The expression on their faces was one of terror. They told us that they had been examined in intimate places with rods, and many said this had caused them to bleed. Later rumors reached us that the SS guards took statistics on how many of the Slovakian prisoners were still virgins.[41]

Lucia Bibs from Corfu, Greece, tells of the so-called 'gynecological checks' that the SS performed on Jewish women during the passage through the sauna: 'After that they cut our hair. Cut our hair all over our bodies. They balded us from head to foot. Then they check what in this hole what in the other hole, everything... We started to cry'.[42]

Attempts at physical abuse by female Kapos

Even though most of the cases of physical abuse were performed by men on women, we can also find cases of female guards who tried to abuse the female prisoners. Halina Birenbaum, who was 13 when she arrived at Auschwitz from Majdanek, describes her Kapo's attempts to turn her into her sex slave in exchange for different benefits, mainly extra food rations. Birenbaum refused.[43] Many survivors refer to the infamous SS woman Irma Grese. Grese was 'well known' for her cruelty and for the fact that she was bi-sexual. While we can find reference to her in many testimonies and memoirs, some survivors 'dedicate' to her full chapters in their memoirs. Olga Lengyel, for example, called one chapter of her book, 'The "Angel of Death" the "Grand Selector"'. In one part she described how Grese used to choose her victims: 'Those who, despite hunger and torture, still showed a glimmer of their former physical beauty were the first to be taken. They were Irma Grese's special targets'.[44] In the chapter 'Irma Grese and Chicha', Isabella Leitner described how Grese used to choose the most beautiful prisoners and give them special 'attention'.[45] Gisela Perl described Grese's sexual perversion:

> One day she happened to visit the hospital while I was performing an operation on a young woman's breast, cut open by whipping

and subsequently infected...Irma Grese put down her whip...and watched me plunge my knife into the infected breast which spurted blood and pus in every direction...Irma Grese was enjoying the sight of this human suffering. Her tense body swung back and forth in a revealing, rhythmical motion. Her cheeks were flushed and her wide-open eyes had the rigid, staring look of complete sexual paroxysm.[46]

Rape

Laura Varon, a Jewish woman from Rhodes, describes how she and her friends were raped by SS guards in Auschwitz. Her testimony is one of very few on this subject. She writes, 'And all of a sudden, the door opened and three Nazis came and they dragged us on the floor, they violated us, sexually violated us. They smelled like beer, you know. They raped us...'.[47] Zofia Minc's testimony describes a blatant attempt at rape:

During the break I was called to the shift commander. I went into Richter's office...He ordered me to sit in the armchair and began explaining to me what an honor it was for me to be found attractive by a German, an SS man, a member of the supreme race. The German grew angry at my long silence, and shouted: 'Strip!' I was trembling, no, this I would not do, let him kill me! He jumped on me brutally and began tearing my clothes. I defended myself with all my might. I almost had to submit, but suddenly the door creaked. Richter jumped behind the desk and I moved in the direction of the exit. The woman in charge came in, looked at me with a strange gaze and ordered me to get back to work.[48]

Raya Kagan, who arrived to the camp from France in early 1942 tells of the so-called 'gynecological checks' that the SS performed in Jewish women during the passage through the Sauna, which were then followed by rape: 'The prisoners were forced to take off their clothes. The SS men shamelessly observed the women's naked bodies and mocked and cursed them. Then they also performed "gynecological checks" on them. The Hitler perpetrators checked the young women and then raped them'.[49]

As previously mentioned, apart from such rare exceptions, cases of rape were unusual in Auschwitz. This does not mean that Jewish women were not raped during the Holocaust, but rather that probably most rapes were performed by non-Germans, including Russians, Ukrainians, Hungarians, Romanians, Lithuanians, and others. Nonetheless, as we can see in this volume, mass rapes and gang rapes did happen in the Soviet Union between the years 1942–1945, and they were performed by SS, Wehrmacht soldiers, and police units, mostly on non-Jewish women but they include Jewish women too.[50] Here we have to take into consideration that, in my opinion, there was a big difference between the situation of sexual exploitation in 'organized-industrial' places of incarceration, like extermination and concentration camps and sub-camps and the 'barbaric front' of the East. In these 'organized-industrial' places we can find two main characteristics which are extremely important to my argument: In them it was much easier to enforce the 'Rassenschande' restrictions. Since we are talking here about very organized places, it was also much more 'complicated' to ignore these restrictions and even to find a 'one-on-one' 'opportunity' without someone noticing it. Moreover, we have to take here into consideration the fact that the East, according to Nazi ideology, was considered to be a 'barbaric' place without laws and full of people of an 'inferior race'. Along with the fact that it was literally easier at the front to get away without punishment if a German violated the 'Rassenschande' restrictions, the whole ideological and psychological environment of the Eastern front made it easier to ignore these restrictions from the soldiers' as well as the commanders' point of view.

Sex in exchange for a chance at survival

A second factor underlying sexual exploitation is bound up with the power hierarchy of the camps, which, in most cases, was gender-based. Sexual exploitation is often a result of unequal power. In Auschwitz the contrast of absolute power and complete powerlessness led to a dual system of exploitation. On the one hand, at the top of the camp hierarchy were the Nazis, the undisputed lords, whose position allowed them to engage in abusive sexual acts. On the other hand, there was a second power system consisting of the male and female prisoners themselves. Prisoners who had survived for a comparatively long time and had become camp veterans engaged in exploitation because of the relative power they had accumulated. These were prisoners who managed to integrate better in the work commando, find additional sources of food, link up with powerful forces in the camp, or organize themselves in various support groups. For reasons having to do with the camp's chronological development and because of the physical structure of the camp, these prisoners in positions of power were usually male and were able to sexually exploit women. Furthermore, it should be recalled that only the women's camp had authority figures of both sexes, which increased opportunities for exploitation of the female prisoners; in the men's camp, the SS and other authority figures were always men.

Regarding the prisoners' power structure, it should be pointed out that one of the explanations for the SS's success in controlling such a large number of prisoners with relatively few personnel is the fact that the camp was actually run by privileged prisoners, usually criminal Germans ('green triangles') and Poles.[51] The SS itself determined the policy, arrangements, and methods of punishment, but between the SS and the general prisoner population were the appointed prisoners. These male or female prisoners enforced disciplinary rules, carried out – and sometimes delegated – punishments, were responsible for marching the prisoners out and placing them in position for roll-calls, supervised the prisoners during work, etc. Therefore considerable power was concentrated in the hands of the privileged prisoners, which in many cases increased their potential to survive. In small camps their main privilege was the right to obtain additional food. In larger camps senior prisoner position-holders obtained many additional benefits including alcoholic drinks, clean, well-fitting clothes, a separate corner in the residential hut, and the satisfaction of their various cravings – singers and 'entertainers' who helped them pass the time enjoyably, cooks who prepared delicacies for them, and boys who satisfied their sexual desires. More than in the other camps, these practices were prominent in Auschwitz. In this camp, where extermination was carried out with industrial efficiency and where the Nazis' regime of terror reached its furthermost extremes, the relative abundance of property accumulated by privileged prisoners was particularly conspicuous. It was said of many of them that they attained a status and enjoyed a life of luxury they never experienced when they were free.

Whereas many women, often regardless of their age, suffered from sexually exploitative practices closely linked to the power structures in Auschwitz, such cases were relatively rare in the men's camps and were essentially confined to a very limited group of boys. While this is not the focus of this essay, I will survey it briefly. We recall that most children under the age of 16 were sent directly to the gas chambers upon their arrival. There were, however, exceptional cases in which boys between the ages of 12 and 16 managed to enter the camp as prisoners, in most cases because they looked older than their age, or because they were given the potentially lifesaving advice by members of the 'Canada Kommando',[52] to say that they were older than they actually were during the selection. Many of these boys worked in what was known as 'the school for builders' in Birkenau and were housed in the 'youth block' or in one of the blocks in Auschwitz I. Others were part of the general prisoner population. The lives of these young boys were as difficult as those of the other prisoners in the camp, but in addition to the 'regular' horrors of the camp, they also suffered from sexual exploitation. They were turned into 'pipels' or 'sex slaves' by veteran prisoners who were usually non-Jewish, political or criminal prisoners. In their discussion of the subject, Kraus and Kulka state explicitly, 'they were exposed to a special danger from the German Kapos who needed boys to satisfy their sexual perversions, the intensity of which intensified during the years of their imprisonment'.[53] Tomas Geva, a Berlin Jew who arrived in Auschwitz as a 13-year-old boy describes in his book many cases of sexual exploitation directed against the boys:

> 'I can no longer allow myself to help you without asking for something in return. You know that not only are we longing for our women, we hardly remember their pleasures.' He locked the door and began unbuttoning his trousers... I simply sat there without moving, without showing a single sign of agreement... 'Never mind, I'll find many others...'.[54]

Scholars researching this phenomenon have determined that while sex in exchange for a chance of survival was sometimes part of the men's experiences, it does not feature prominently in their books. They also tend to note that where it did occur, it generally was voluntary and involved homosexual relations between a younger and an older person – a 'pipel' and a Kapo. Attention should be directed to the problematic nature of the assertion that this usually involved 'voluntary' sexual relations. In view of the fact that we are talking about sexual relations in exchange for an increased chance of survival, that is to say, as a survival practice, it is difficult to term these 'consensual sexual relations'. The fact that these sexual relations occurred between an adolescent boy and an adult Kapo or veteran prisoner with senior status, reinforces the coercive aspect.

Many testimonies and memoirs that were published during the first wave include mention of what I call 'sex in exchange for food'. In most cases, 'sex in exchange for food' was a life or death decision.[55] Women inmates who did not manage to find any other way to obtain the additional food, which was essential for their survival, were constrained to 'sell' their bodies for food.[56] Gisella Perl describes such cases:

> These men were trusted old prisoners who knew everything there was to know about camp life, had connections in the crematories and were masters at 'organizing'. Their full pockets made them the Don Juans of Camp C. They chose their women among the youngest, the prettiest, the least emaciated prisoners and in a few seconds the deal was closed. Openly, shamelessly, the dirty, diseased bodies clung together...and the piece of bread, the comb, the little knife wandered from the pocket of the man into the greedy hands of the woman. ...Our SS guards knew very well what was going on in the latrine. They even knew who was whose 'kochana' (lover), and were much amused by it all.[57]

In the following case, a Polish inmate demands Perl's body in return for a piece of string that she needs desperately:

> I stopped beside him...He looked me over from head to foot, carefully, then grabbed me by the shoulder and hissed in my ear: 'I don't want your bread...I want you...you...Hurry up...hurry up...' he said hoarsely. His hand, filthy with the human filth he was working in, reached out for my womanhood, rudely, insistently.[58]

Margalit Nagel-Gross laconically, and in no uncertain terms, describes being aware of this practice. According to her, it was widespread and accepted, an inherent part of the camp's organizational system:

> So, they 'organized'...together with the 'organizational' method, I should mention those who were called Kochanita (in Polish – lover [the translator]). Nearly every girl had a Polish lover, or an Aryan lover (Volksdeutscher – not a member of the SS or the Party [N.S.]). A Jewish lover did not enter into consideration, because he had nothing, for after all 'love follows the stomach'. Any fellow, as ugly, stupid, and anti-Semitic as he might be, was suitable to be a lover.[59]

In a chapter titled 'A Proposal in Auschwitz', Olga Lengyel, a Jewish doctor from Cluj, is describing how a Polish prisoner offers her food and a shawl, for free. But after a few days the next scene is happening: 'He stood close to me. Then, as though talking to himself, he said: "It's a strange thing, there is something very desirable about you". I felt his arm around my waist. His other hand touched me and began to

fondle my breast. My world fell to pieces'.[60] And yet, Lengyel understands that she will have, somehow, to obtain more food beside the
official ration in order to survive, so she goes to the black market in the
washroom, where she discovers exactly the same thing: 'I decided to go
the washroom where I had heard that the men … occasionally shared
their food with the women … The scene inside was demoralizing … The
place was crowded. Men and women huddled together in every corner
of the room. Couples pressed against one another … '.[61] After that she
'understood' that the first 'proposal' she had received could be considered rather 'generous': 'I learned afterwards that his was the finest style
of love-making in Auschwitz. The ordinary approach was much more
crude and to the point … '.[62]

Tadeusz Borowski offers a male viewpoint on this practice:

> My comrades and I laid a roof over the shack of every block elder
> in the Persian Market … we used 'organized' tar-boards and melted
> 'organized' tar, and for every roll of tar-board, every bucket of tar, an
> elder had to pay. She had to pay the Kapo, the Kommandoführer, the
> kommando 'bigwigs'. She could pay in various ways: with gold, food,
> the women of her block, or with her own body. It depended … A few
> women were usually wearing sheer stockings. Any one of them could
> be had for a piece of bright silk or a shiny trinket. Since time began,
> never has there been such an easy market for female flesh![63]

The interesting point here, which has also been neglected in past
research, is that since the mid-sixties, more or less, such descriptions
of cases of sexual exploitation involving the obtaining of food, are
almost absent from testimonies and memoirs by women as well as men.
Why? As we know, even in present-day, non-wartime conditions, many
women refrain from reporting sexual abuse. The sense of shame and the
feelings of guilt that, tragically, and characteristically, are experienced by
victims are especially strong in cases of a sexual nature. The same was
true for female survivors of the camps, although in their cases there were
some additional variables: the guilt felt by so many survivors for the
fact that they, and not others, had survived. In addition, 'accusations'
came up, tacit or explicit, that were directed against female survivors,
which attributed their survival to their having sold their bodies. Here,
for example, is what Ruth Bondy wrote:

> In Prague, upon my return from the camp, the Gentiles expressed
> only wonder mixed with displeasure: Jewish property had been
> entrusted to the care of many of them. The Jews had disappeared, the

objects had remained – and, suddenly, there appear before us ghosts to remind us of the forgotten. However, here, in Israel, the Jews also wanted to know: How did you stay alive? What did you have to do in order to survive? And in their eyes, a glimmer of suspicion: Kapo? Prostitute?[64]

This helps to explain why early testimonies and memoirs, written *tabula rasa* – that is when the shock and trauma were still immediate and the survivors were not yet influenced by the reading of Holocaust research or about the experiences of others – do recount incidents of sexual abuse, whereas later publications do not. Survivors writing in the early years were less exposed to social judgments and charges hurled at them, including the concept that the Jews went 'like sheep to the slaughter', or the accusation regarding the use of feminine sexuality for the purpose of survival. It seems that the women who wrote the initial memoirs and testimonies cited above did not suffer the inhibitions in entering the 'public sphere'[65] that later kept other survivors from sharing their stories.[66] There are a number of explanations for this. Most were prisoners who had occupied relatively good positions in the life of the camp, and could, as a result, to some extent influence their fate and that of other prisoners. This fact prevented them from becoming what Primo Levi called 'The Drowned',[67] and afforded them a wider vantage point from which to observe the life of the camp, as well as the ability to preserve a certain 'inner freedom' which enabled more 'healthy' survival because they retained a feeling of relative choice.[68] These were women who had also been involved in the public sphere before the war.[69] All these factors contributed to diminishing the feelings of shame and guilt that overwhelmed most survivors, even to the extent that the writers do not mention 'reasons' for writing their memoirs. Another possible explanation for the profusion of women's memoirs appearing during this early period could be that according to traditional social conceptions, women were more easily understood to be 'victims', so post-war society was more 'prepared' to accept their stories of victimization, as opposed to those recounted by men who were more immediately and traditionally connected to notions of resistance.

More than other experiences, the sexual exploitation suffered by female inmates in Auschwitz points to the fact that as Jews and as women they had to contend with a 'double risk' in their struggle for survival. On the one hand, they suffered as Jewish inmates in Auschwitz-Birkenau, with all the difficulties this entailed. On the other hand, despite the annulment of their bodies which was centered on their physiological capacity to give birth, they remained 'temporary' and available sexual entities, objects whose lives and bodies were accessible both to the German staff and, to some extent, to male inmates, mainly the non-Jewish ones, in the camp. To these men, a female Jewish inmate ceased to be a 'human woman', and became a wide-open physical site that possessed the external signs of female sexuality, but contained no humanity. With regard to survival strategies of female inmates, it can be seen that, in a way that perhaps may be termed 'tragic', some internalized the conditions of camp life, and found that their sexuality could play an essential part in their struggle to survive. This was principally true with regard to practices of sex in exchange for food. While the extreme hunger in Auschwitz-Birkenau was a shared reality for both male and female inmates, women found themselves contending with it differently from men.

While it was difficult, in fact impossible, to resist sexual exploitation by Germans, sexual abuse by male inmates generally occurred with the women's 'consent' and on the woman's 'initiative'. In my humble opinion, it was this motif of 'choice' that made the post-war world's reaction more difficult for female inmates, arousing pangs of conscience and loss of self-esteem for many years afterward. This is another reason why stories of sexual abuse appear less frequently in women's autobiographical works after the first wave of publications.

Conclusions: A body that is all flesh

Jean Améry, the Jewish philosopher and Auschwitz survivor, wrote that National Socialism bore the stamp of sadism, not only the stamp of totalitarianism. Here Améry adopted the definition of the anthropologist, thinker, and author Georges Bataille who wrote, 'Sadism is to be understood not in the light of sexual pathology but rather in that of existential psychology, in which it appears as the radical negation of the other, as the denial of the social principle as well as the reality principle'. Améry himself wrote,

> A world in which torture, destruction, and death triumph obviously cannot exist. But the sadist does not care about the continued existence of the world. On the contrary: he wants to nullify this world, and by negating his fellow man, who also in an entirely specific sense is 'hell' for him, he wants to realize his own total sovereignty. The

fellow man is transformed into flesh, and in this transformation he is already brought to the edge of death…he is driven beyond the border of death into Nothingness.[70]

Améry confirms in direct language what the autobiographies and testimonies I have examined reveal in sometimes indirect ways. Nazis radically negated the Other, in particular the Jewish Other. This Other, in the reality of the camp, became mere flesh, driven to the threshold of death. But on the way to death, the Other was forced through a long process of transformation from a member of the human race – a person that thinks, feels, and lives – into a sub-human consisting only of an empty shell of flesh.

This description emphasizes the importance of the subject of the body in my research. As I see it, the body, and in this case the female body, was one of the major sites of struggle in Auschwitz-Birkenau. A key conclusion of this essay is that a considerable difference between the female and male experiences in the camp stemmed from ideological, physical, and cultural definitions that determined gender relations. While the dehumanization process also applied to men, for women it was coupled with the Nazi's dual view of the female Jewish body. On one hand, it had to be exterminated because of its capacity to bear (Jewish) children. On the other hand, after its humanity, psyche, and individuality had been taken from it, the Jewish female body remained a wide-open sexual vessel, and it was permissible to exploit it and to sow destruction in it. Giuliana Tedeschi's book, among others, illustrates how, after a short stay in the camp, the women inmates began internalizing these Nazi conceptions. In one of her narrations, which read as though they have been drawn directly from Nazi ideology, she describes how Jewish women were transformed into empty shells of flesh: 'Bodies, bodies, bodies, many unattractive, many no longer young, some flabby and limp, most imperfect, disproportioned. Crude mass. We all belong to this flesh heap, and we all feel alien to it'.[71]

In one of her amazingly powerful passages, Charlotte Delbo, a French author and survivor of the camp, wrote that in Auschwitz-Birkenau mothers ceased being mothers and became only bodies, losing the diversity of physiological-ideological elements that connect motherhood with gender. They internalized the divide created by the Nazis between women and femininity, between women and the capacity to reproduce, and between motherhood and protection: 'My mother/ she was hands, a face/ They made our mothers strip in front of us/ Here mothers are no longer mothers to their children'.[72] And Gisella Perl wrote: 'Here I was only a shadow without identity, alive only by the power of suffering'.[73]

This discussion of the physical experience of Jewish women need not lead to essentialism and to the claim, as has been made in past research, that women adopted 'feminine' survival strategies using their sexual characteristics. The distinctiveness of the female experience in Auschwitz-Birkenau stemmed from a combination of conceptions in Nazi ideology regarding Jewish women's femininity and sexuality, together with actual female physiology, the female 'cultural body', and the specific situation of women in the camp. Charlotte Delbo wrote about the 'fragmenting reality'[74] of the camp – a reality that fragments the personality and leaves the body as the principal tool of struggle and survival. The centrality of the body in the camp was an essential part of the female experience and of the means used by women to try to survive. The female 'cultural body' is also an essential element in the question about differences between women's experience and the male body and experience in Auschwitz. In the reality of the camps, Jewish female inmates, like their male counterparts, inevitably internalized whatever conceptions the Nazi guards and other prisoners formed about them. This dynamic contributed to the complex relations that existed between torturers and tortured, and between body and soul.

Notes

This paper is based on my PhD dissertation which is written under the guidance of Prof. Shulamit Volkov at Tel Aviv University. From the bottom of my heart, I want to thank Prof. Volkov for her bright and original guidance and for her warmth and kindness toward me. An earlier version of this paper was published in German as 'Weibliche Erfahrung in Auschwitz-Birkenau' in G. Bock, Ed., *Genozid und Geschlecht. Jüdische Frauen im nationalsozialistischen Lagersystem* (Frankfurt/New York, 2005), pp. 103–122. I thank Prof. Bock for her permission to use this article for the revised version as it is presented here, and for being so supportive and so generous with me during the years.

1. C. Delbo, *Auschwitz and After* (New York and London, 1995), p. 230.
2. S. Friedländer, *Nazi Germany and the Jews. The Years of Persecution, 1933–1939* (New York, 1997), p. 5.
3. R. Hilberg quoted in C. Lanzmann, *Shoah: An Oral History of the Holocaust. The Complete Text of the Film* (New York, 1985), p. 70.
4. It is important to note, as Marlene Heinemann argues, that verbal sexual humiliation, which is considered a minor form of sexual exploitation, wounded a woman's sexual identity and thus sped up the destruction of her self-esteem. *Gender and Destiny: Women Writers and the Holocaust* (Westport, 1986), p. 29.
5. I. Leitner, *Fragments of Isabella: A Memoir of Auschwitz* (New York, 1978), p. 46. For an interesting discussion about the 'Muselmann' see: G. Agamben, *Remnants of Auschwitz* (New York, 1999), pp. 41–86.

6. In my opinion it is possible to map four 'waves': 1945–1950; 1950–1962; 1962 to the late 1980s; and the last wave which continues on today. For the first wave publications, see P. S. Goldwasser, *Four Black Notebooks* (Jerusalem, 2005) (Originally 1945) [Polish and Hebrew]; M. Nagel-Goss, *Three Years in Auschwitz-Birkenau* (Israel, 2003) (Originally 1945) [Hungarian and Hebrew]; G. Tedeschi, *Questo povero corpo* (Milano, 1946); O. Lengyel, *Five Chimneys* (Chicago, 1947); L. Millu, *Il fumo di Birkenau* (Milano, 1947); R. Kagan, *Hell's Office Women (Oswiencm Chronicle)* (Palestine, 1947) [Hebrew]; and G. Perl, *I Was a Doctor in Auschwitz* (New York, 1948). We also need to note here the following books that were written immediately after the war but were published only a few decades later: Leitner, *Fragments of Isabella*, 1978; Delbo, *Auschwitz and After*, 1995.

   To these we have to add about 80–100 testimonies that were submitted between the years 1945 and 1947.
7. See for example the books of Primo Levi, Jean Amery, Tadeusz Borowski.
8. I. Kertész, 'Who owns Auschwitz?', *Zionism and Socialism*, October 1999, Tel Aviv [Hebrew], p. 28.
9. See, for example, Heinemann, *Gender and Destiny*, 1986, pp. 27–33; M. Goldenberg, 'Lessons Learned from Gentle Heroism: Women's Holocaust Narratives', *The Annals of the American Academy of Political and Social Science*, 548 (November 1996), pp. 81–86.
10. D. Ofer and L. J. Weitzman, *Women in the Holocaust* (New Haven and London, 1998), pp. 7–8.
11. Ibid., p. 8.
12. Heinemann, *Gender and Destiny*, 1986, p. 16.
13. S. Milton, 'Women and the Holocaust: The Case of German and German-Jewish Women', in C. Rittner and J. K. Roth, eds, *Different Voices: Women and the Holocaust* (Minnesota, 1993), pp. 230–231.
14. Ibid., p. 231.
15. V. Laska, 'Women and the Holocaust: The Case of German and German-Jewish Women', in C. Rittner and J. K. Roth, eds, *Different Voices: Women and the Holocaust* (Minnesota, 1993), p. 265.
16. Although this is beyond the scope of this article, it is a connected theme, so I would like to say a few words about the 'common knowledge' in Israel about sexual abuse. Especially in Israel, but also in other places, we can find the alleged knowledge that Jewish women 'served' as whores for the SS and for German soldiers in some camps and on the Eastern front. As far as I can say, and after deep researching in this area, these things did not happen, at least not in a formal organized systematic way, mainly because of the *Rassenschande* policies mentioned above.
17. J. C. Friedman, *Speaking the Unspeakable. Essays on Sexuality, Gender, and Holocaust Survivor Memory* (Maryland, 2002), p. 54.
18. Ibid., p. 57.
19. R. G. Saidel, *The Jewish Women of Ravensbrück Concentration Camp* (Wisconsin, 2004), p. 23.
20. Ibid., p. 212.
21. M. Goldenberg, 'Sex, Rape, and Survival: Jewish Women and the Holocaust', on the internet in: *Women and the Holocaust – Scholarly Essays*.

22. D. L. Bergen, 'Sexual Violence in the Holocaust: Unique and Typical?', in *Lessons and Legacies: The Holocaust in International Perspective*, Volume VII, Dagmar Herzog, Ed. (Evanston, IL, 2006), p. 180.

23. Ibid., p. 180.

24. Ibid., pp. 186–187.

25. Ibid., p. 189.

26. Ibid., p. 191.

27. M. Peer, 'To Break the Tacit Consent', *Hdaf Hayarok*, 15 June 2006, Tel Aviv, pp. 20–22 [Hebrew].

28. Ibid., p. 21.

29. There is certainly a thoughtful analysis of the popular fascination with sexuality, especially women's sexuality, during the Holocaust. See, for example, the classic work on the subject: S. Friedlander, *Reflections on Nazism: An Essay on Kitsch and Death* (Bloomington, IN, 1982). See also the article of R. Scherr, 'The Uses of Memory and Abuses of Fiction: Sexuality in Holocaust Film, Fiction, and Memoir', in E. R. Baer and M. Goldenberg, eds, *Experience and Expression. Women, the Nazis, and the Holocaust* (Michigan, 2003), pp. 278–297. J. L. Jacobs, 'Women, Genocide, and Memory. The Ethics of Feminist Ethnography in Holocaust Research', in *Gender & Society*, 18 (2004), 223–238. See also notes 5–6 above. The crucial point is that in the last few years we also find this 'Kitsch and Death' approach, one which is not based on historical facts, appearing not just in popular culture but also within historical research.

30. I found only one testimony that tells the story of a young Jewish girl from Poland who was terribly abused, beaten, and tattooed on her body and head for full humiliation by Germans while she was in the ghetto. The file is marked 'confidential – not to be published'. Yad Vashem Archives.

31. See, for example, these testimonies: Hanna Rothe Magid testimony. Rothe Magid recounts how she was gang raped by Polish students after she ran from the Aktion that occurred in the Legionowo ghetto. Yad Vashem Archives, O.3/1570, 1960 [Polish]; Meir Robinstein testimony. Robinstein tells how his wife was raped and murdered by Poles. Yad Vashem Archives, O.3/868, 1958 [Yiddish]; Ivi Bert testimony. Bert describes how she was gang raped by Red Army soldiers after her liberation. Yad Vashem Archives, O.3/7812, 1995 [Hungarian]; Ita Shmulevski testimony. Shmulevski tells about being sexually harassed by a Hungarian guard. Yad Vashem Archives, V.T/1584, 1997 [Hebrew]; Vera Veresh testimony. Veresh was a virgin when she was raped by a Hungarian soldier. Yad Vashem Archives, O.3/1950, 1946 [Hungarian]; Naomi Donat testimony. Donat was raped by a Hungarian policeman. Yad Vashem Archives, O.33.C/3521, 1995 [Hebrew]; Brina Levin Fridmann testimony. Levin Fridmann talks about Jewish girls who were raped and then murdered by Lithuanians. Yad Vashem Archives, O.3/12674, 2006 [Henrew]; Yehodit Zik Finkel testimony. Zik Finkel was sexually abused by the Polish farmer who owned the house she was hidden in. Yad Vashem Archives, O.3/12630, 2005 [Hebrew]; Sonia Perminger testimony. Perminger Fridmann talks about Jewish girls who were raped and then murdered by Lithuanians. Yad Vashem Archives, O.33.C/4235, 1995 [Hebrew]; Soria Shlomovitzch testimony. Shlomovitzch recounts how the owner of the house where she was hidden in Belgium tried to rape her. Yad Vashem Archives, O.69/354, 1981

[English]; Edith Wollf testimony. Wollf describes how a Yugoslavian who cooperated with the Nazis tried to rape her. Yad Vashem Archives, O.3/6275, 1991 [Hebrew]; Yulan Petrover testimony. Petrover tells how a Hungarian soldier raped and then murdered her sister. Yad Vashem Archives, O.69/43, 1981 [English]. Two stories concern German perpetrators: Zofia Minc testimony. Minc tells how an SS officer tried to rape her in Auschwitz. Yad Vashem Archives, M.49.E-Zih/2504, 1947 [Polish]; Hela Shmolivtz testimony. Shmolivtz describes how German police men raped her in the police station in Dambrowa Gornicza, Poland. Yad Vashem Archives, O.3/5596, 1989 [Hebrew].

32. Unlike, for example, Jewish women who arrived after a long incarceration in the ghettos in Poland.

33. Perl, *I Was a Doctor in Auschwitz*, 1948, p. 43.

34. See, for example, Primo Levi's description of the Sauna:

> Imagine now a man who is deprived of everyone he loves, and at the same time of his house, his habits, his clothes, in short, of everything he possesses: he will be a hollow man, reduced to suffering and needs, forgetful of dignity and restraint, for he who loses all often easily loses himself. He will be a man whose life or death can be lightly decided with no sense of human affinity, in the most fortunate of cases, on the basis of a pure judgment of utility. It is in this way that one can understand the double sense of the term 'extermination camp', and it is now clear what we seek to express with the phrase: 'to lie on the bottom'.

P. Levi, *Survival in Auschwitz* (New York, 1971), p. 23.

35. Though it is not the subject of this article, it is worth adding here that when recounting their experiences in the sauna, women speak much more than men about the great pain of losing their hair.

36. Ada Halperin testimony, Yad Vashem Archives, 31 January 1994, p. 31 [Hebrew].

37. H. Tischauer testimony, Yad Vashem Archives, O.36/42, 23 September 1946, p. 11 [English].

38. Ada Levi testimony, Yad Vashem Archives, O.2/202, The Wiener Library, 17 July 1946, p. 4 [English].

39. E. Schloss, *Eva's Story* (New York, 1988).

40. Tova Berger testimony.

41. Elsa [Frishman] Glieck, *Three Years in Auschwitz-Birkenau*, Self Publication, No year was mentioned, 1995, Israel, p. 5 [Hebrew].

42. Lucia Bibs testimony, Yad Vashem Archives, O.3/7972, 25 May 1965, p. 6 [Hebrew].

43. H. Birenbaum, *Hope Is the Last to Die: A Coming of Age Under Nazi Terror* (New York, London, 1971), pp. 90–92.

44. Lengyel, *Five Chimneys*, 1947, pp. 103–104.

45. Leitner, *Fragments of Isabella*, 1978, pp. 50–54.

46. Perl, *I Was a Doctor in Auschwitz*, 1948, pp. 61–62.

47. Laura Varon testimony, Yad Vashem Archives, Jerusalem., VT 1390, 14 November 1996, p. 21.

48. Zofia Minc testimony. Yad Vashem Archives (taken from the ZIH collection), M.49.E-ZIH/2504, 1947, p. 4 [Polish].

49. R. Kagan, *Hell's Office Women (Oswiencm Chronicle)* (Palestine, 1947), p. 51 [Hebrew].
50. See, for example, the very important and illuminating article by Regina Mühlhäuser in this volume: 'Between "Racial Awareness" and Fantasies of Potency: Nazi Sexual Politics in the occupied territories of the Soviet Union, 1942–1945.'
51. See D. Czech, 'The Auschwitz Prisoners Administration', in Y. Gutman and M. Berenbaum, eds, *Anatomy of the Auschwitz Death Camp* (Bloomington, 1994), pp. 363–378. In 1940 the SS team in Auschwitz contained only 500 people. In 1941 the number grew to 700, and in 1942 it contained about 2000. In April 1944 it was 2950, and in August it grew again to 3342 people. On 15 January 1945 it contained about 4480 people, among them 71 women. Over the years of the camp existence, between 7000 and 7200 SS served in it. A. Lasik, 'Historical-Sociological Profile of the Aushcwitz SS', in Gutman and Berenbaum, eds, *Anatomy of the Auschwitz Death Camp*, 1994, pp. 271–287.
52. The name 'Canada' was coined by the prisoners to describe the area where they were forced to sort the Jewish property. The official name was Effektenlager Kommando. Their other 'job' was to stand on the ramp during the selections.
53. O. Kraus and E. Kulka, *The Mills of Death Auschwitz* (Jerusalem, 1960), p. 105 [Hebrew].
54. T. Geva, *Guns & Barbed Wire. A Child Survives the Holocaust* (Jerusalem, 2003), p. 85 [Hebrew].
55. See in this context also: Jozefina Szepper-Mazowiecka testimony. Yad Vashem Archives (taken from the Tenenbaum-Marzic Archives, The Underground Archives in Bialystok Ghetto), M.11/180, 9 January 1946, no page was mentioned [Polish-Hebrew]; Review of the sexual aspects of life in the Blizin and Auschwitz camps, Yad Vashem Archives (taken from the ZIH collection), M.49.E-ZIH/1456, 4 November 1946, no page was mentioned, [Yiddish]. In her book, *Values and Violence in Auschwitz – Sociological Analysis*, Anna Pawelczynska, does refer to the subject, but without any references: '...paid prostitution existed in the camp and the choice of erotic partners was dictated by one's ability to pay – either in the form of help in gaining a better place in the camp structure or, at each visit in the form of food or better clothes'. A. Pawelczynska, *Values and Violence in Auschwitz – Sociological Analysis* (Berkeley, 1979) (Originally Warsaw, 1973), p. 99.
56. In her article 'The Unethical and the Unspeakable', Joan Ringelheim cites Auschwitz survivor Ilona Karmel: 'In Poland, both in ghettos and camps, sexuality was a means of buying protection from the Jewish policemen and others who had means and power'. See M. J. Ringelheim, 'The Unethical and the Unspeakable: Women and the Holocaust', *Simon Wiesenthal Center Annual*, 7 (September 1983), p. 6.
57. Perl, *I Was a Doctor in Auschwitz*, 1948, pp. 78–79.
58. Ibid., p. 58.
59. Nagel-Gross, *Three Years*, 2003 (Originally 1945), p. 28.
60. Lengyel, *Five Chimneys*, 1947, p. 60.
61. Ibid., pp. 61–62.

62. Ibid., pp. 60–61.
63. T. Borowski, *This Way for the Gas, Ladies and Gentlemen* (U.S.A., 1967) (Original 1947), pp. 86–93.
64. R. Bondy, *Whole Fracture* (Tel Aviv, 1997), p. 44 [Hebrew].
65. There were, of course, exceptions. As was mentioned, Charlotte Delbo and Isabella Leitner finished writing their memoirs immediately after the war but did not publish them until the 1960s and 1970s. These writers expressed the fear that their books were not good enough to be published in the public sphere. See, for example, L. L. Langer, 'Introduction', in *Delbo, Auschwitz and After*, 1995, p. xvi.
66. See, for example, Heinemann, *Gender and Destiny*, 1986, pp. 1–12.
67. P. Levi, *Survival in Auschwitz* (New York, 1971), p. 79.
68. Pawelczynska, *Values and Violence in Auschwitz – Sociological Analysis*, 1979, p. 127.
69. For example, Gisella Perl was a medical doctor before her incarceration as well as during the period of her imprisonment, as was Olga Lengyel, who was also part of the camp underground; Ra'aya Kagan worked in politics; Liana Milo-Milol was a journalist, a teacher and activist in the anti-Fascist movement in Italy; Lutiana Nisim was a medical doctor and a partisan.
70. J. Améry, *At the Mind's Limits. Contemplations by a Survivor on Auschwitz and Its Realities* (Bloomington, 1988), p. 52.
71. Tedeschi, *Questo povero corpo*, 2000 (Originally 1946), p. 36.
72. Delbo, *Auschwitz and After*, 1995, pp. 11–12.
73. Perl, *I Was a Doctor in Auschwitz*, 1948, p. 56.
74. Delbo, *Auschwitz and After*, 1995, p. 12.

9
Sexual Violence in the Algerian War

Raphaëlle Branche

English-language historians have argued that the category of gender is particularly useful and relevant for understanding the violence of war,[1] with rape now clearly identified as a 'gendered war crime'.[2] Very few French historians of the modern period, however, have examined past conflicts from a gender-based perspective. Still, times are changing and analyses of rape and sexual violence, and, more generally, a gender-based approach to wars are becoming less and less unusual in French historical studies.[3]

Whether ignored or concealed, for a long time rapes were simply left out of most war narratives. Except for a few cases in which rape was massive and widespread, as in Nanking in 1937, in Berlin in 1945, or, more recently, in the former Yugoslavia, rapes were often simply not taken into account in historical narratives.[4] The paucity of attention is in part due to the difficulty of marshalling evidence. Rapes are, of course, not easy subjects for historians to document. Victims often kept quiet, making it harder to distinguish the rapes from the everyday violence inherent in every war. The rare instances when rapes were the object of disciplinary measures, judicial sentences provide particularly rich and accurate sources. The judicial qualification, the prosecution, and the reparation may be stages in the victims' self-reconstruction process as well as stages in the way official institutions (army, police, justice) take rape into account.[5]

With regard to the French–Algerian war (1954–1962), the Justice Department Archives contain files concerning rapes. But, at that time, the military's own justice system was in charge of any judicial problem concerning a member of the Army; case files are therefore rather thin.[6] Still, they remain the first place to look for evidence about the reality of wartime rapes. Due to restrictions on access, however, military justice files are (for the time being) totally inaccessible to the researcher. Furthermore, an amnesty linked to the cease-fire agreement banned any judicial investigation or suit against a French soldier or an Algerian fighter. This has made historians' work more difficult. The amnesty wiped away any sentence pronounced before 19 March 1962 and henceforth forbade mentioning sentences or judicial investigations. All these reasons help explain why, until now, judicial archives have been underutilized by historians.

We have to compensate for this silence from the justice system. Other sources allow historians to map the outlines of the violence, most notably those found in military archives: disciplinary measures, reports on rapes, and notes show that rapes happened, and happened repeatedly. It will come as no surprise that political and military authorities did not pay much attention. Nor did Algerian nationalists make reference to rapes when they denounced French military tactics. This might explain why the political authorities never demanded a thorough report on the overall subject or on any specific cases. The fact that both sides turned a blind eye further contributed to burying evidence of rapes within the more general phenomenon of anonymous violence.

And yet the sexual violence against Algerian women does have several specificities, which also, moreover, allow historians to offer a more nuanced analysis of what was at stake in this war. Private sources are very useful: written or oral testimonies by former perpetrators, victims, or bystanders sometimes mention the rapes; soldiers' diaries and chaplains' reports written during the war itself describe them; in Algeria, some men and women have written about this deeply personal wound. The sources, in sum, are diverse, and this diversity of the points of view (official sources throwing light on and supplementing private sources) makes a historical investigation possible – despite the fact that the violence of rape was silenced, and silenced repeatedly: by the victims, by the soldiers, and by their superiors.

What French authorities called the 'events' in Algeria was a war, which, one way or another, implicated the whole population. Women were a prime target for the 'psychological action' that the French army organized, which aimed to make Algeria French by winning over Algeria's women. They were also victims of the French army and police forces. If women were at first relatively spared by the violence committed during 'operations to maintain order', they became suspected where men were caught dressed in feminine clothes. In Collo (North-Eastern part of the Constantinois), in 1958, soldiers were told not to 'neglect Muslim women' and to 'frisk them'. The commander in chief in 1956, general Lorillot, had already asked the *Ministre Résidant* (i.e. Minister for Algeria), Robert Lacoste, to recruit female soldiers 'so that Muslim women arrested as suspects could be frisked immediately'.[7] A female social worker from Algiers, Simone, remembers being summoned by the police in May 1956 and taken to the Casbah with other colleagues to frisk women.[8] Very few of her colleagues, as she remembers it, refused such requests. Nevertheless there were never enough women to fill this role, especially in the countryside and rural villages.

Frisking Algerian women meant patting down their clothes. But it could also mean making them lift up their dress. Verifying women's genitals (to guarantee that a man was not wearing female clothing) was also done literally. In addition, their pubic 'hairiness' was checked. Women whose husbands were in the *maquis* were indeed suspected of maintaining contact with them; a shaved pubis was considered as undeniable proof that a woman had recently engaged in sexual intercourse. Thus checking pubic hairs became an activity of intelligence gathering.[9]

Yet, Algerian women's involvement in the liberation struggle was, at first, poorly understood by the French Army. Women fighters in the *maquis* were a small minority; according to Djamila Amrane,[10] who wrote the first important study on the subject, there were about 2000. Most of them were very young women, with more than half of them under 20 years, and 90 percent under 30. Alongside these 'fighters',[11] however, women played many other roles. It was women, overwhelmingly, who took charge of health care and supplying food and shelter. The French tendency to ignore their presence, in contrast to the close scrutiny to which Algerian men were subjected, led the National Liberation Front (FLN) to recruit women as 'agents de liaison'. The Front was not especially in favour of their presence amongst fighters. Instead, it encouraged them to take part in the civil organization of the Algerian people – a structure within which the supply problem became more and more important as the French Army destroyed more and more *maquis*. According to Djamila Amrane and other scholars, this led to new behaviours since supplying food was a traditional male task: the war drove the men out of the villages and the women, in addition to their traditional task of preparing the food, were now also in charge of buying it.

Thus, over the course of the war, the position of women became more and more crucial. All-female cells were organized within the nationalist organization in charge of the Algerian population, the *nizâm*. These cells were eventually dismantled by the French: the military archives show that, as the French army made progress in the struggle against the fighters from the ALN (National Liberation Army), it increasingly went after non-combatant elements of the organization. The French Army progressively acknowledged that Algerian women, too, were its enemies. Within a few years, they changed from being objects – merely part of the landscape, typical, exotic, but not politically implicated in what was happening – to being subjects in the eyes of the French Army. From the moment French officials realized that women might be acting against the French, they were subjected to the same treatment as the men. They were identified, watched, and arrested for what they were doing (or supposedly doing), no longer only seen as wives, mothers, or sisters of men or as bystanders to the acts of some men. At the beginning of 1959, General Massu, one of the most important French generals, commander of one-third of Northern Algeria's territory, gave the order to pay particular attention to women, who were 'currently the object of recruiting attempt by the rebels'.[12] The military units' diaries are unequivocal. At the beginning of the war, to shoot at a woman was still considered a blunder, and a soldier could be blamed for it. But from 1959–1960 on, it was considered to be an act of war. As women started to be considered enemies of France, they were exposed to a larger spectrum of violence. The number of women stopped, arrested, questioned, tortured, imprisoned, put under house arrest, or executed grew. By the end of 1957, a section dedicated to the internment of all female prisoners was created in the camp of Tefeschoun. Before their arrival at Tefeschoun, they often suffered violence when being arrested or during their detention in military centres. This violence had a clearly sexual cast: breasts were burned, electrodes were introduced into the vagina.

Military authorities considered rape a banal form of torture, useful for making prisoners (male or female) talk, or to terrorize them.[13] Violent penetration, often using a piece of wood, a bottle, etc., was frequent. The genitals were a preferred site for inflicting violence, such as when electric shocks were applied. The sex organs were the entry point for pain. This pain was immediate, but it could also be permanent, though invisible, meant to hurt not just the victims but their close relatives as well. Men, of course, could also be subjected to rape, but its symbolic signification, which is part of its criminal efficiency, was greater for a woman, because it could directly threaten her position within her family as mother of her husband's children.[14]

Military men committed sexual violence against women during their detention as well. Many testimonials describe this violence, as compared to the very small number that mention how some soldiers offered protection from such assaults. A male nurse in Southern Algeria remembers a very beautiful young woman who sought refuge in his unit: 'A shelter had to be provided for the girl.... The only possibility was for her to take shelter in the ambulance, to put the doors against the wall so that the men could not come inside, and then to lock the doors'.[15] The level of protection gives an idea of what the male nurse and the unit's doctor feared might happen. Aware of his comrades' sexual frustration and of their obsession with brothels, another soldier, Ugo Ianucci, noted on several occasions his comrades' temptation to submit the 'fellouzes' women' arrested to sexual slavery. Eventually, they achieved their goal. He tried to talk with the soldiers and recorded – disappointed – their discussion: 'We agree with you, Ugo. It is *dégueulasse* [disgusting] what we've done. But that's the way war is. Think of the fels' women that cut our pals' balls off'. 'It's always the same "logic"', is Ugo Ianucci's comment on that. Racism and balls overflowed, indeed.[16]

It apparently seemed obvious everywhere: Algerian women were women who could be raped. That is what a priest recorded in 1956 in reference to several military districts where 'rape has become a method for pacification'.[17] The diary of the writer Mouloud Feraoun offers important clues on the subject: rape became a systematic form of violence in Kabylie, especially during the huge military operations engaged in by General Challe over the summer of 1959. This case is extreme. Most of the rapes committed during the French–Algerian War by French soldiers were committed in a much more common and less systematic way.

It is possible to identify two general categories of rape: rapes with premeditation and opportunistic rapes. Rapes of the first type were often committed at night by a small group of soldiers. It is likely that other soldiers remained unaware of these crimes. The exception to this was when the victim complained about it or when – and several records of disciplinary measures taken provide evidence of this phenomenon – the soldiers were found guilty of deserting their post while they were committing the assault. We also have evidence that some chiefs did authorize their men, implicitly or explicitly, to go into supposedly 'rebel' villages or *mechtas*. A former conscript remembers a routine patrol taken by the intelligence officer 'for his men to sow their oats'.[18] Another quoted his commando's leader: 'you are allowed to rape but do it discreetly'.[19] In these instances, rape became part of a more general violence owing to the war.

Yet most of the rapes committed during this war were directly linked to the pursuit of military operations, albeit to contingent events rather than choice of tactics. Rape was a collective form of violence, with the other soldiers watching while the rapists acted.[20] Men, following one another on the women's bodies, also used their weapons to threaten them. In addition to the rape, the raped woman or her relatives were often subjected to other forms of violence. Their experience of this type of behaviour rendered inhabitants of Kabylie resigned to their fate, as Mouloud Feraoun recorded: 'When the [French] military men drove the people out of their home, cooped them up outside of their village in order to search their houses, [people of Kabylie] knew that the genitals of their girls and wives would be frisked as well'.[21] The commander of East Algeria confirmed and bemoaned this fact in a note: 'Robberies, violence, rapes, and so on' are usually committed when the army is checking the population, 'be it in the villages and mechtas of the forbidden zones or in the urban centers'.[22]

The available evidence does allow us to know that not every woman arrested was raped. Similarly, the fact that torture was widespread in Algeria does not mean that prisoners were systematically raped. Diversity is a recurrent characteristic of this kaleidoscopic war, where evidence of real humanity and extreme brutality could be very close, manifested within a distance of a few kilometres or over the course of a few months. Nevertheless rape was unquestionably a favourite form of torture when the prisoner was a woman, whether she was a convicted 'terrorist', a fighter in the *maquis*, or merely suspected of being associated with the 'rebellion'. What defined how the French pursued this war was that the primary target was not the combatants of the *maquis* or soldiers in the 'frontier army' (massed on the borders with Tunisia and Morocco), but the Algerian population. It was this that gave rape its particular role.

Rape is a violent act where the male organ is a means – although it is possible to use an object as well – yet where hurting the female organ is not the ultimate aim. It is the woman herself who is to be hurt. Though desire is involved, it is less an emanation of sexual desire than a will to power and a desire to humiliate. Through the knocked-about, violated, raped woman, military men targeted her family, her village, and every community to which she belonged, including the most important: the Algerian people. The orders given by the FLN to the Kabyle women bear witness to this fact. In Mouloud Feraoun's account, they were instructed that they must not let the enemy understand that 'the living flesh of the Kabyle soul' has been hurt.[23] This formulation reflects the shared understanding of the psychological or mental dimension of this physical violence. The logic of rape here is precisely the same as the logic of torture.[24]

Yet raping women was not exactly the same. Alongside the suffering that each rape inflicted on an individual, rape during this war imposed another level of suffering on local communities, assaulting values particularly fundamental to these groups, whether family, clan, village, or neighbourhood. As Germaine Tillion put it in 1966, referring to the whole Mediterranean basin, 'it is a fact that a collective and individual over-touchiness goes along, still nowadays, with a certain ideal of virile brutality, whose complement is a dramatization of the feminine virtue. They both fit in with a bloodthirsty familial pride, whose projection lies in two myths: ascendancy and descent'.[25] In this context, rape had yet another additional import: Rape was also an attack on the sexual order that, in Algeria, was premised on the capacity of men to defend women's virginity or purity, i.e. to guarantee paternity.

This order is based on the Muslim religion, a religion – as Mohammed Hocine Benkheira has put it – entirely implicated 'in the sexual relationship, in the regulation of this relationship'.[26] Well-ordered sex refers to human relationship – compared to animals – and to social relationship in a politically ordered world. It is basic and cardinal in the Kabyle culture as well, as Mouloud Feraoun, once again, overdramatizes: 'All the people who know share their shame and anger... for they see it is the biggest crime and know that what makes them Kabyle, their customs, their raison d'être has always been this taboo, this respect for the sanctity of women's bodies'.[27] And paradoxically, French colonialism had contributed to this importance of Kabyle traditions embedded in Islamic rules or virtues.[28]

Another aspect that gave rape its criminal specificity in this context is that it left the perpetrator feeling innocent and the victim ashamed.[29] It was not only a taint hushed up by Algerian women but also an injury which men, too, needed to conceal, since it signalled their impotence, their failure to protect their women, the keystone of male authority and honour.[30] Beyond the women, rape worked symbolically to castrate the men, to quote Gerda Lerner.[31] It is then possible to see the rapes committed during the French–Algerian war as political violence: they are, ultimately, men's business. In territory that, for over a century, was officially defined as extensions of France, three 'departments' of France, the rapes still resonated with the symbolic weight of the rape of Algeria's conquest: they represent the way in which 'possessing a body means to possess a human being'.[32] As Susan Brownmiller overstated it in 1975, yet not without insight, rape is the conqueror's act par excellence: a sign of victory and, for the defeated country, a profound humiliation. However, in the French–Algerian war, the rapes were often perpetrated with the material comfort of an occupation army, whose means were much wider than those of its enemies. The rapes here were not part of an invasion but part of a political will to remain indefinitely in Algeria.

What happened then with the children? French public opinion was confronted a few years ago with the reality of rapes during the French–Algerian war through the judicial action of one man, Mohamed Garne. His mother, Kheïra Garne, then aged 16, was raped by soldiers in charge of guarding the concentration camp of Teniet-el-Haad, Western Algeria, in 1959. They apparently tried to induce an abortion by beating her several times on her belly. Yet the young woman gave birth to a boy, who was taken in charge by nuns and then, after six months, given to a childminder and definitively taken from his mother. The efforts by rapist soldiers to induce abortions were mirrored, documents suggest, on the Algerian side. The ethnologist Camille Lacoste-Dujardin reported such behaviour among the Iflissen, a group living in the North of Tigzirt, in 1969:

> Kabyle honor, although awfully demanding and rigid when women were in question, do not hold violated women responsible for the results of this war of terror. They choose to forget. Not only do the husbands not seek to divorce and the young women marry quickly, but efforts are made to induce an abortion, so no victim will have to bear a child due to these rapes.[33]

Talking to Djamila Amrane, also a veteran from the war, Mimi ben Mohamed remembers more dramatic propositions:

> Fahia [Hermouche] and I kept bringing up the topic of rape. Our people, at first, they didn't want to believe it. Later, they knew. All these pregnancies, what are we going to do with them? Then commander Si Lakhdar, maybe because of his youth, said: 'ok, we kill the babies'. We said: 'No, this is not possible, we cannot kill innocent people. These children have nothing to do with it; nor do the women, since they have been forced. It is not possible simply to destroy a child like that, it would be a crime. And in fact they did not do it, they kept all these children. Husbands did not want them but they kept them in the end. There were troubles but everybody understood'.[34]

In the end, some children were abandoned or taken care of by charities. Others were kept within the families and the villages that decided to heal these wounds collectively. But this was not decided without suffering and discussing. Thanks to these testimonies and others, little by little, some light has been shed on the topic. Yet, on several points, darkness and silence remain – they are even stronger on rapes committed by the Algerian fighters.

Studying how sexual violence against women is perpetrated leads to some understanding of their logics – which is not necessarily the same as the agents' intentional strategy. Unlike the war in former Yugoslavia, there was no systematic and planned use of rapes linked to official projects of 'ethnic cleansing'. Until now, no archive allows us to argue that rape was used politically or strategically in order to strengthen French authority in Algeria. No text has been found that recommends rape or authorizes soldiers to rape. Unlike torture, no justification ever appears, at least on the surface, in official instructions. Rape remained totally forbidden in the French army. A few centuries ago, Grotius could write that some civilized nations, even if they did not authorize rape, might find it 'understandable' in wartime. But times have changed and, during the French–Algerian war, no jurist advanced such an argument.[35] When military authorities were notified, rapes seem to have been punished and the rapists brought before military courts. In every case, among the few well-known inquiries about rapes, the perpetrators were not just charged, but punished – which stands in sharp contrast to the military's response to claims and evidence of torture.

There were, however, very few rapes brought to the attention of military authorities. In addition to the silence of Algerians, officers were not always in a hurry to punish the rapists serving under them. It is obvious that, further down the chain of command, among the officers and non-coms directly in contact with the rapists and their comrades, many chose not to make punishing this violence a priority. Indeed, the fact that most soldiers served in small and isolated units, involved in a mostly static war, makes it easy to conclude that impunity concerning rapes was almost total during this war.

Within these groups of men, 'where virile values are amplified',[36] rape offered an opportunity for a violent yet safe confrontation between a man's self image and the Other's image. The confrontation led to a virile man and a conquered woman. Virility is a key dimension of this violence, aggravated by the ordinary racism to which Algerians were subjected. As the war increasingly lowered inhibitions, it gave rape an opportunity to expand. At that time, indeed, rape was still considered by many French men as a 'compelling impulse', 'expression of the man's nature', indeed an act whose criminal or transgressive feature was not obvious in every case to the man himself.[37] According to such received ideas, rape would involve sexual desire, and rape would be the sign of male sexual impulses impossible to control. Such an understanding works to erase the dimension of domination, a valence yet particularly important in colonial wartime.

Draftees serving in Algeria grew up in a world where being a man, to a great extent, meant having a sexuality where the feminine and the masculine are confronted, for the benefit of the man. Leaving for Algeria, they wore proudly on their chest 'good for girls' or 'girl ready' badges (*bons pour le service*). This shows the persistence in French society of a vision of the draft, of military service, as a rite of passage into manhood.[38] The war gave these young men the opportunity to assert their virile identity on a daily basis through the violence, the weapons, and the exaltation of strength.

According to Anne-Marie Sohn's works on the first half of the twentieth century, French justice showed indulgence towards gang rapists in peacetime, as if gang rapes were considered to be 'a normal sowing of oats for young men, even a demonstration of virility'.[39] These collective rapes (only 9 percent of the rapes prosecuted) were usually committed under the command of a leader, who might be the only one to rape the victim as the others stood watch or took part in holding the woman down. Such a structure is very close to that of the rapes committed during the French–Algerian war, where the gang rape might have strengthened the primary group's cohesion – the group that the war created out of young men, forced to live together over long months.[40] This dimension explains why some of them boasted to their comrades about rape, presenting the crime as an act of glory, a violent certificate of virile identity.

Military men in Algeria certainly knew that rape was forbidden, and the fear of being punished might have narrowed the scope of this violence. At the same time, the exceptional state of wartime led some men to fabricate new norms of behaviour, distinct from ordinary civilian life and freed from its most fundamental codes. Some military men might have let rapes happen, even committed them, because they came to see the victims less as fellow human beings but instead as wholly different – i.e. women, Algerians and enemies.

Notes

This essay is in large part a translation of R. Branche, 'Des viols pendant la guerre d'Algérie', *Vingtième Siècle, Revue d'histoire*, 75 (Juillet–Septembre 2002), 123–132. I thank Todd Shepard who has been so helpful with this translation.

  1. A. L. Barstow, ed., *War's Dirty Secret: Rape, Prostitution, and Other Crimes against Women* (Cleveland, 2000), p. 257 and C. O. N. Moser and F. C. Clark

(dir.), *Victims, Perpetrators or Actors? Gender, Armed Conflict and Political Violence* (London and New York, 2001), p. 243.

2. R. Copelon, 'Gendered War Crimes: Reconceptualizing Rape in Time of War', in J. Peters and A. Wolper, eds, *Women's Rights, Human Rights* (New York, 1995), p. 372. However, the newer emphasis on 'gender' should not cause us to downplay the *sexual* specificity of this violence.

3. S. Audoin-Rouzeau, *L'enfant de l'ennemi (1914–1918)* (Paris, 1995), p. 222; G. Vigarello, *Histoire du viol, XIX–XXᵉ* (Paris, 1998), p. 358; J. Martin, 'Violences sexuelles, étude des archives, pratiques de l'histoire', *Annales HSS*, 3 (Mai–Juin 1996), 643–661.

4. The rapes committed by the Red Army while conquering Eastern Europe and Germany have been studied by some historians. See N. M. Naimark, *The Russians in Germany. A History of the Soviet Zone of Occupation, 1945–1949* (Boston, 1995); A. Grossman, 'A Question of Silence: The Rape of German Women by Occupation Soldiers', in R. G. Moeller, ed., *West Germany under Construction: Politics, Society and Culture in the Adenauer Era* (Ann Arbor, 1997); J. Mark, 'Remembering Rape; Divided Social Memory and the Red Army in Hungary, 1944–1945', *Past and Present*, 188 (August 2005). About the massacre of Nanking by the Japanese Army in 1937 and the central place of rapes in the violence and its memory, see D. Yang, 'Convergence or Divergence?: Recent Historical Writings on the Rape of Nanjing', *American Historical Review*, 104, 3 (June 1999), 842–865; and M. Yamamoto, 'History and Historiography of the Rape of Nanking' (PhD, Tuscaloosa, Alabama, 1998). As an introduction to a historical study of the more recent conflict in former Yugoslavia, see R. Van Boeschoten, 'The Trauma of War Rape: A Comparative View on the Bosnian Conflict and The Greek Civil War', *History and Anthropology*, 14, 1 (2003).

5. Elisabeth Jean Wood has provided important reflections on the variations in sexual violence in wartime ('Variation in Sexual Violence during War', *Politics and Society*, 34, 3 (September 2006). As a political scientist, she has underlined the need for comparative study but also the difficulty in building a general framework of understanding. By focusing on particular cases and providing a close scrutiny of the historical specificities, historians have a key role to play in improving collective reflection. This is all the more true for the complex and contested history of colonialism and its violences.

6. S. Thénault, *Une drôle de justice. Les magistrats dans la guerre d'Algérie* (Paris, 2001), p. 347.

7. Note by the commander of Collo' sector, July 1958 (SHD, 1H 4402/2∗). Letter to Robert Lacoste, 3 August 1956 (SHD, 1H 4026/3∗).

8. Interview with Simone, January 1999.

9. L. Devred, *Une certaine présence. Au nom de l'épikié* (Paris, 1997), p. 255; and R. Trouchaud, *Haine et passion en Kabylie, en hommage à tous les combattants d'AFN* (Nîmes, 1994), pp. 137, 157.

10. D. Amrane, *Les Femmes algériennes dans la guerre* (Paris, 1991), p. 218; and 'Les femmes face à la violence dans la guerre de libération', *Confluences. Méditerranée*, 17 (1996), 87–96.

11. 'Fighter' is the way they are described until now ('mudjahidate') but the reality needs to be studied very precisely for, apparently, they were almost everywhere forbidden to carry weapons. See R. Seferdjeli, 'The French Army and Muslim Women during the Algerian War', *Hawwa: Journal of Women in the Middle East and Islamic World*, 3, 1 (2005), 40–78.

12. 'Ne pas négliger les femmes, parmi lesquelles le rebelle fait actuellement un effort de recrutement'. Annexe n. 1 to the 24 February 1959 directive, 10 March 1959, later published in *La Revue Historique des Armées*, 3 (1995), 52–54.

13. D. Blatt, 'Recognizing Rape as Method of Torture', *Review of Law and Social Change*, 19, 4 (1992), 821–865.

14. See V. Nahoum-Grappe and B. Allen, *Rape Warfare: The Hidden Genocide in Bosnia-Herzegovina and Croatia* (Minneapolis, 1996), p. 180; and V. Nahoum-Grappe, *CLIO. Histoire, Femmes et Sociétés*, 5 (1997), 163–175.

15. Interview with Jean Suaud, February 2000.

16. U. Iannucci, 'Soldat dans les gorges de Palestro', *Journal de guerre* (August 2001), 73, 99. The diary was written in November 1959.

17. Letter from minister Muller to minister Cabrol, 6 July 1956 about the Bougie sector (SHD, 1K 625/31∗), quoted by X. Boniface, 'L'Aumônerie militaire française, 1914–1962', Thesis (University of Lille-III, 1997), p. 486.

18. Interview with Jean-Louis Gérard, February 1999.

19. 'Vous pouvez violer, mais faites-ça discrètement'. B. Rey, *Les égorgeurs* (Paris, 1961), p. 19.

20. U. Iannucci, op. cit., November 1959.

21. M. Feraoun, *Journal 1955–1962* (Paris, 1962, 2nd edn 1994), p. 348, entry for 20 February 1959.

22. Note by General Gilles (commander of the CAC), 1 July 1958, 1H 2579/2∗.

23. Ils ont expliqué 'texte du Coran à l'appui, que leur combat à elles consistait précisément à accepter l'outrage des soldats, non à le rechercher spécialement, à le subir et à s'en moquer. [. . .] Au surplus, il est recommandé de ne pas parler de ces choses, de ne pas laisser croire à l'ennemi qu'il a touché la chair vive de l'âme kabyle si l'on peut dire, de se comporter en vrai patriote qui subordonne tout à la libération de la patrie enchaînée'. M. Feraoun, op. cit., 20 February 1959.

24. R. Branche, *La Torture et l'armée pendant la guerre d'Algérie* (Paris, 2001), p. 461.

25. 'C'est un fait qu'une susceptibilité collective et individuelle exacerbée accompagne partout, aujourd'hui encore, un certain idéal de brutalité virile, dont le complément est une dramatisation de la vertu féminine. Ils s'intègrent l'un et l'autre dans un orgueil familial qui s'abreuve de sang et se projette hors de soi sur deux mythes: l'ascendance, la descendance'. G. Tillion, *Le Harem et les cousins* (Paris, 1966), pp. 67, 218.

26. 'Tout entier dans la relation sexuelle, dans la régulation de cette relation'. M. H. Benkheira, 'Allah, ses hommes et leurs femmes: notes sur le dispositif de sexualité en islam', *Peuples méditerranéens*, 35 (October–December 1983), 35–46.

27. 'Tous ceux qui savent partagent leur honte et leur colère (. . .) parce qu'ils considèrent cela comme le plus grand des crimes et que de tout temps leurs mœurs, leurs lois, leur raison d'être, en tant que Kabyles reposent sur

cet interdit, ce sacro-saint respect qui doit préserver la femme'. Mouloud Feraoun is overwhelmed when he adds: 'Il est fort douteux qu'une intrusion aussi brutale dans des mœurs anachroniques pour mettre un peuple arriéré au diapason du monde moderne, aide à l'avènement de cette fraternité humaine à laquelle rêve M. Guy Mollet et que M. Lacoste s'efforce de réaliser' (8 January 1957).

28. In Algeria, Muslims endured social, economic, and political inequalities as members of the native population. But this was not the case for the other religious groups. Algerian Jews, in particular, enjoyed full citizenship since 1870. They were given full citizenship collectively and without being asked individually. By contrast, a Muslim had to apply for citizenship individually, and this process would also lead him to give up his Muslim judicial status. Therefore, being a Muslim and being a native became more related and also meant being discriminated against specifically. The role of Islam in the resistance against the French had been very important already at the beginning of the colonization. It stayed so until the end and was part of the birth of the concept of the Algerian nation from the end of the nineteenth century and even more from the 1920s and 1930s on. See J. McDougall, *History and the Culture of Nationalism in Algeria* (Cambridge, 2006), p. 266.

29. S. Brownmiller, *Against Our Will: Men, Women and Rape* (New York, 1993), p. 472.

30. See G. Tillion, *Le Harem et les cousins*, op. cit.; R. Jamous, 'Interdit, violence et baraka. Le problème de la souveraineté dans le Maroc traditionnel', in E. Gellner, ed., *Islam, société et communauté. Anthropologies du Maghreb* (Paris, 1981), p. 163; 'Le corps dominé des femmes ou la valeur de la virginité', in M. Gadant, ed., *Le nationalisme algérien et les femmes* (Paris, 1995), pp. 302, 245–268.

31. G. Lerner, *The Creation of Patriarchy* (New York, 1986), pp. 80, 318.

32. 'Possession d'un corps devenue celle d'un être', 'maintien du violé en situation de dominé'. G. Vigarello, *Histoire du viol, XIX–XXe*, op. cit., p. 262.

33. C. Lacoste-Dujardin, *Opération 'oiseau bleu': Des Kabyles, des ethnologues et la guerre d'Algérie* (Paris, 1997), p. 308.

34. 'Fahia [Hermouche] et moi avions posé le problème du viol. Les nôtres, au début, ils ne voulaient pas le croire. Bon après, ils savaient. Toutes ces grossesses qu'allons-nous en faire? Alors le commandant Si Lakhdar, peut-être parce qu'il était jeune, a dit: "Bon, on tue les bébés". Nous avons dit: "Non, ce n'est pas possible, on ne peut tuer des innocents. Les gosses n'y sont pour rien et les femmes non plus, puisqu'elles ont été obligées. Ce n'est pas possible de détruire un enfant comme çà, ce serait un crime". Effectivement, ils ne l'ont pas fait, ils ont gardé tous ces enfants. Les maris n'en voulaient pas, mais finalement ils les ont gardés. Il y a eu des difficultés, mais chacun a compris...' D. Amrane, *Des Femmes dans la guerre d'Algérie*, op. cit., p. 47.

35. H. Grotius, *Le droit de la guerre et de la paix* (Bâle, 1746), tome 2, p. 263. (The 1st edn appeared in 1625. Quoted by G. Vigarello, *Histoire du viol, XIX–XXe*, op. cit.

36. 'Lieux d'exacerbation des valeurs viriles'. S. Audoin-Rouzeau, *L'enfant de l'ennemi (1914–1918)*, op. cit., p. 77.

37. A. Sohn, *Du premier baiser à l'alcôve. La sexualité des Français au quotidien (1850–1950)* (Paris, 1996), p. 310.
38. O. Roynette, *'Bons pour le service'. L'expérience de la caserne en France à la fin du XIXe siècle* (Paris, 2000), p. 458.
39. 'Un défoulement normal de la jeunesse, voire une démonstration de virilité'. A. Sohn, *Du premier baiser à l'alcôve*, op. cit., p. 305.
40. See in this contest also A. Parrot, *Coping with Date Rape and Acquaintance Rape* (New York, 1999), p. 190; S. K. Ward, et al., *Acquaintance and Date Rape: An Annotated Bibliography* (Westport, CT, 1994), p. 218.

10
The 'Sum of Such Actions': Investigating Mass Rape in Bosnia-Herzegovina through a Case Study of Foca

Teresa Iacobelli

Rape has always accompanied war. In the twentieth century alone there have been numerous examples occurring in countries as diverse as China, Germany, India and Rwanda.[1] Believing it to be a natural consequence of conflict, military historians have tended to ignore that rape is also a weapon of war. This belief has prevented historians from looking seriously at the act of rape, both its meanings and its consequences. As it became clear in the war in Bosnia-Herzegovina in the 1990s, rape is more than a by-product of war: the act itself provides a vital function in the destruction and disgrace of an enemy. However, what has not been as clear in the Balkans is the exact nature of the rapes which did occur there. Were the rapes perpetrated against Bosnian Muslims and Croats the result of an intentional and systemic policy ordered by Bosnian Serbian command, or were they random acts by soldiers, militias and a few sadistic leaders at the local level? This paper will attempt to answer this question through a case study of the Bosnian city of Foca, an area which first became synonymous with mass rape in 1992. By focusing on this singular example I will attempt both to contextualize mass rape and to answer some broader questions regarding its use in the former Yugoslavia. I will seek to determine why mass rape happened and how it came to be seen as a legitimate weapon of war in Bosnia-Herzegovina. Finally, I will address the experience of mass rape in Foca to determine whether there was an organized policy of its use, and if so, whether this was a reflection of a policy of mass rape incited by Serbian command throughout Bosnia.

In order to have an understanding of the incidence of rape and ethnic cleansing which occurred throughout the Balkans in the 1990s, it is first necessary to provide some background on the conflict. The Balkan crisis is essentially the story of the disintegration of Yugoslavia which had included the republics of Croatia, Bosnia-Herzegovina, Montenegro, Macedonia, Slovenia and Serbia, as well as the two provinces of Kosovo and Vojvodina. This paper will focus solely on the rapes of Muslim women during the war within Bosnia-Herzegovina. This particular conflict lasted from April 1992 to November 1995 and it stands out as the epicentre of mass rape during the wars of Yugoslav succession. It is my contention that in Bosnia systemic and highly organized rape orchestrated by Bosnian Serbian command facilitated a program of terror, as well as a program of genocide.

The roots of the Balkan conflict are still hotly debated. At the outset of the war the popular representation by the Western media of the Balkans, and particularly Bosnia-Herzegovina, was as a powder keg of ethnic rivalries waiting to explode. Bosnia was referred to in the popular press as 'one of the most ethnically muddled states in Europe'.[2] Blaine Harden of *The Washington Post* went on to say that 'What makes Bosnia's mixture of peoples so volatile is that Muslims, Serbs and Croats live together in the same streets and apartment buildings in many cities and towns'.[3] True, Bosnia-Herzegovina did have what was considered to be an ethnically diverse population, being 44 per cent Bosnian Muslim, 31 per cent Orthodox Serbian and 17 per cent Roman Catholic Croatian according to a 1991 census report.[4] But reports such as Harden's presented this diversity in such a way as to make it a foregone conclusion that civil war was imminent for the area, ignoring a post-Second World War atmosphere of peaceful co-existence that existed especially within Bosnia's cosmopolitan cities. The fact was that, regardless of how statistics were divided, there was more that united Bosnians than what set them apart. For the majority of Bosnia's Muslims, their religious identity was secondary to their identity as Europeans. Muslims and Christians dressed and spoke similarly, and by 1991, 18.6 per cent of Bosnian marriages were described as 'inter-ethnic'.[5]

Regardless or ignorant of these facts, journalists and statesmen alike portrayed the war in Bosnia as an inevitable outcome arising out of centuries of ethnic rivalries.[6] Scholars and journalists pulled out their history books, thumbing through them for possible seeds to the present crisis. Writing in the summer of 1992 journalist Thomas Butler concluded that '[t]he fundamental cause of Yugoslavia's terrible calamity is not just recent history…Today's horrors are woven from strands of nothing less than the entire tapestry of history since the 6th-century Slavic invasion of the Balkans, with the subsequent division of Croats and Serbs between Catholicism and Orthodoxy and eventually Islam'.[7] Such explanations were useful exercises in avoiding an assignment of blame in the tense climate, as well as precluding the rest of the world from having to really understand, let alone intervene, in the conflict. However, the problem with such explanations is that they were both patronizing and inaccurate.

While it is true that the Balkans had a history of ethnic conflicts, ancient hatreds did not lie at the root causes to the Bosnian conflict in 1992. By this I do not mean to suggest that history is unimportant in the Balkans, for it most certainly is; however, I do mean to suggest that history was not the determining factor in the war. Rather, the war in Bosnia-Herzegovina was artificially constructed by political leaders for political goals, and to achieve these goals leaders relied upon the manipulation of history. As Tim Judah, who was the Balkans correspondent for *The Times* and *The Economist*, and author of *The Serbs* writes, 'The Serbs went to war because they were led into it by their leaders. But these leaders drew on the malign threads of their people's history to bind them and pull them into war'.[8]

Serbian leaders recalled both ancient grievances and the more recent memories of the Second World War. Popular terms of the past such as *Chetnik* and *Ustasha*[9] were brought back into the popular lexicon, as were nationalist symbols. At times the Serbian leadership portrayed, and the media often reinforced, the idea of the Balkan crisis as merely a continuation of old antagonisms from the Second World War. However, as Judah writes,

> It is true that between 1941 and 1945 hundreds of thousands of Yugoslavs died at the hands of other Yugoslavs; like the rest of Europe, however, they lived at peace with one another for the next forty-five years. It was the conjunction of historical circumstances, personalities, arrogance and misjudgements which led to the war, and it is important to keep in mind that the Serbs, as a people, are no different from anyone else in Europe ... The Serbs were misled but they were not sheep. Supremely confident of victory, too many were happy to be misled.[10]

Rather than the amending of old grievances, the goals of Serbian leadership were nationalistic and focused on the conquest of land in order to form a greater Serbia. Led by Serbian President Slobodan Milosevic, the nationalist agenda gained momentum throughout the 1980s with the crumbling of communism and the death of Yugoslavia's communist strong-arm leader Josip Broz Tito (1892–1980). Milosevic's agenda was supported throughout Serbia by leading academics, religious figures and the Serbian media.[11]

The ties that bound Yugoslavia began to unravel in 1991 with declaration of independence by both Slovenia and Croatia. Conflicts with Serbia followed, which Bosnia-Herzegovina literally stood in the middle of. Situated between Croatia and Serbia, Bosnia became the next target of Serbian aggression and expansionist goals. On 3 March 1992, following a positive referendum vote, Bosnians declared their wish to remain multi-ethnic and independent. Unwilling to accept these results, an attack by Serbia followed, as did a policy of ethnic cleansing.

Ethnic cleansing was a phrase first used by the international community to describe the events in the former Yugoslavia, without having to use the more loaded term of genocide. Ethnic cleansing was described in part by the United Nations as 'Massive violations of human rights and international humanitarian law … used deliberately to achieve ethnically homogenous areas'.[12] Abuses in Bosnia clearly shaded into one another, at times overlapping between ethnic cleansing and outright genocide, which I would describe as the intended destruction of a particular group, both physically and culturally. In the case of Bosnian Muslim women, they were specifically targeted by Serbian military forces in an intentional policy of genocidal rape meant to destroy the Muslim community of the nation. Genocidal rape operated by three methods. First, public rapes were meant to cause terror in Bosnian communities, inciting Muslims to leave with the desire never to return. While this function most certainly meets the criteria of ethnic cleansing, I would argue that the intent of public rapes also met the United Nations definition of genocide in that they 'caus[ed] serious bodily and mental harm to members of a [specific] group'.[13] Second, the rapes were genocidal in that they were used as a means of torture prior to eventual murder. Finally, a policy of forced impregnation was clearly genocidal, as it was meant to control the reproduction of Muslims and strengthen the Serbian population.[14] At this point it is important to interject a crucial distinction made by Norman Cigar, author of *Genocide in Bosnia*, and that is, '[n]ationalism is not synonymous with genocide nor is it necessarily its cause'.[15] The genocide in Bosnia, which included mass rapes, was not simply the result of sporadic outbursts of frenzied emotion, but 'it was a rational policy, the direct and planned consequence of conscious policy decisions taken by the Serbian establishment in Serbia and Bosnia-Herzegovina'.[16]

Thus, within this atmosphere of intense nationalism and constructed ethnic rhetoric, the siege of Bosnia-Herzegovina began in

April 1992. Among the first to fall to Serbian firepower was the city of Foca and its surrounding villages. Located near the banks of the Drina River, Foca lay in southeast Bosnia, near the border of Montenegro. The pre-war population of the city was approximately 40,000 people of whom 51.6 per cent were identified as Muslims, 45.3 per cent as Serbian and 3.1 per cent as others.[17] Foca had a 500-year-old Islamic presence and was home to 14 mosques in and around the city, including the Aladza (the coloured mosque) known for its exceptional beauty and the Ustikolina, which, built in 1448, was the oldest mosque in Bosnia.[18]

Beginning from the era of the Second World War it is possible to reconstruct a short history of Foca. The war in Yugoslavia was not a singular conflict, but could be characterized more as series of battles waged among different and constantly changing groups. Chetniks, Communist partisans and Ustasha forces were in a constant struggle for power, meaning that at times Serbs fought against Serbs (Partisans vs. Chetniks) and that Muslims played a role in all of the forces, including alignment with the predominantly Serbian Chetniks at times. Throughout Yugoslavia what is clear is that the face of the war differed by region. In the case of Foca, Muslims paid the highest price, experiencing large-scale massacres at the hands of Chetnik forces in 1942 and 1943. In a single incident in January 1943, 9000 Muslims were massacred, 8000 of whom were women, children and the elderly.[19] Incidents such as this encouraged the Muslims of the region to join with the Partisans. As Noel Malcolm, author of *Bosnia: A Short History* writes,

> A terrible system of mutually fueled enmities was now at work. The more Muslims there were joining Partisans, the more the Cetniks regarded Muslims as such as their foes; and the worse the killings of Muslims by the Cetniks became, the more likely local Muslims were to cooperate with Partisan, German, Italian or NDH forces against the Cetniks.[20]

Malcolm goes on to conclude that

> Altogether 75,000 Bosnian Muslims are thought to have died in the war: at 8.1 per cent of their total population, this was a higher proportion than that suffered by the Serbs (7.3 per cent), or by any other people except the Jews and the Gypsies. Muslims fought on all sides – Ustasa, German, Cetnik, Partisan – and had been killed by all sides. Many had been killed in Croatian and German death-camps, including Jasenovac, Buchenwald, Dachau, and Auschwitz.[21]

It should be noted for the purpose of this essay that in no account of Foca during the Second World War has there been mention of mass rapes. This leads one to assume that while martial rape may have likely occurred, it was not widespread. Thus, an historical legacy of rape cannot account for Serbian policy decisions in 1992, nor can a motive of revenge. Furthermore, Serbian leadership does not seem to have been influenced by an environment in which rape was common outside of war, a factor which could have made the transition to martial rape an easier one.

The city of Foca, calm in the inter-war years, was to become a flashpoint during the war in Bosnia-Herzegovina in 1992. Foca being among the first cities to fall to the Serbs, journalist Roy Gutman wrote of it that 'what happened there set a pattern for ethnic cleansing in the rest of Bosnia. Foca could be a case study in the role played by civilian politicians in the brutality against the non-Serb population'.[22] Furthermore, Foca provides one of the first and most striking examples of the highly organized regime of mass rape that characterized the Bosnian war.

The siege of Foca began on 7 April 1992 and was successfully completed by the Bosnian Serb Army and the paramilitary forces called in from both Serbia and Montenegro. The occupation was completed in only ten days, ending on 17 April 1992. The villages surrounding the city of Foca continued to be under attack until mid-July of that same year.[23] What appears by all accounts to have been an organized policy of ethnic cleansing took effect almost immediately. Men were separated from women and taken to Foca Kazneno-Popravni Dom (KP Dom Foca), a large prison facility from which many men went 'missing' and are now presumed dead. Women, young children and the elderly were held at a number of detention centres across Foca.

In total, it is estimated that between 20,000 and 50,000 rapes occurred within Bosnia-Herzegovina during the course of the war.[24] An exact number of rapes in Foca specifically cannot be determined from the sources, although charges for the cases of 14 specific victims identified by code names were included in the Foca Indictment.[25] Handed down in June 1996, the Foca Indictment was passed by the International Criminal Tribunal for the former Yugoslavia (ICTY) and was the first such indictment to deal specifically with sexual offences committed in war. It charged eight men with breaches of the Geneva Conventions, including gang rape, torture and sexual enslavement, in the Foca region between 1992 and 1993.

The first rapes in Foca began on 11 April 1992, three days after the initial attack, and they lasted until February 1993. Following the separation by age and sex, women were detained in various houses, apartments and motels throughout Foca. Quickly a regime of torture and gang rape was instituted and participated in by Bosnian Serb soldiers, policemen and members of various paramilitary groups. According to the Foca Indictment, 'Among the purposes of the assaults were to extricate information from the women about the whereabouts of their menfolk and the existence of any armed resistance; to punish and intimidate them; and for reasons based upon discrimination'.[26] According to many victims of these interrogations, more often these were exercises in mock weapon-searches that very quickly developed into rape at gunpoint.[27]

By 3 July 1992, at least 72 Muslim prisoners were being held at the Foca High School. At least 50 of these prisoners were female, some as young as 12 years old, being held for the sole purpose of rape. The high school was under constant patrol by armed Serbian soldiers and members of the local Foca Police who worked in close alliance with the Bosnian Serb army. Detainees at Foca High School reported being raped every night of their detention either at the school, or after being taken to nearby apartments. Perpetrators included members of the military police. Foca High School remained a rape camp until 13 July 1992.[28]

From Foca High School the same victims were then moved to the Partizan Sports Hall which operated as a rape camp from 13 July 1992 to at least 13 August 1992. Located in the centre of Foca, Partizan was only 70 metres from the local police station and clearly visible.[29] Conditions at Partizan were described as brutal, characterized by

Inhumane treatment, unhygienic facilities, overcrowding, starvation, physical and psychological torture, including sexual assaults. There were neither blankets nor towels provided for the detainees. Only a few mattresses were provided for sleeping. Food, allotted on an irregular basis, was meagre. Medical care for the detainees, either on a regular or emergency basis was not authorized. Some women [were] beaten and in need of urgent care. Women bled and suffered pain as a result of sexual abuse. Two women died in Partizan due to beatings inflicted upon them by Serb soldiers.[30]

Like Foca High School, Partizan was constantly guarded by local police. Soldiers freely entered in groups, either to stay for a while or to remove women temporarily from the premises. No attempts were ever made by the guards to stop the soldiers. One victim, identified only as Beba, who fled to Foca after being raped in her own village, and who could view Partizan from where she hid within Foca, reported, 'I saw the same men entering and leaving daily...I can say in Foca there were 50 men involved in rape. They slept during the day and raped at night'.[31] Her story regarding time and numbers corroborates that of the numerous victims at Partizan. Victims reported gang rapes as a daily ritual; some testified to being raped up to 150 times during their two months of detention. These stories were deemed to be entirely credible upon gynae-cological examination. One victim, referred to only as M.C., recalled of one incident on 12 August 1992, 'I counted 29 of them [soldiers]. Then I lost consciousness'.[32]

Detainees from Partizan Sports Hall were released on 13 August 1992 and were immediately deported to Montenegro. Here, for the first time, victims finally received medical care. Examinations showed that some victims, as a result of their experiences, suffered long-term physical dam-age such as the inability to ever bear children; all women suffered some degree of psychological trauma.[33]

What must be remembered is that the detainees from Foca High School and Partizan Sports Hall represent only a small portion of Foca's total rape victims. Many more women experienced sexual assault within their own homes or at small detention centres scattered throughout the area. Others who were held at Partizan were released earlier from the hall, but kept as sexual slaves. Such was the case of a 15-year-old girl identified in the Foca Indictment only as FWS-87. FWS-87 was removed from Partizan on 2 August 1992. She was kept at various houses-turned-brothels until 25 February 1993, where she was repeatedly raped and forced to perform chores. The victim was eventually sold to two Montenegrin soldiers for 500 Deutschmarks.[34] Furthermore, included in the Foca Indictment are not only those rapes which occurred in Foca proper, but those that occurred in the surrounding villages as well. For example, Alexandra Stiglmayer, author and freelance correspondent in Bosnia-Herzegovina, wrote that four women whom she interviewed from the small town of Miljevina, just outside Foca, reported that of the approximately 100 Muslim women who chose to stay in Miljevina, all had experienced at least one rape.[35]

Today, Foca is an example of a successful campaign of ethnic cleans-ing. Twenty thousand Muslims were expelled from the city.[36] A NATO-led stabilization force attempted in November 2000 to reintroduce some refugees who had fled during the war, but this proved to be largely unsuccessful.[37]

In light of the incidents which occurred in Foca, it is now my inten-tion to determine whether the accounts reflect an actual policy of rape instituted by Serbian command. Croatian author Slavenka Drakulic writes of Foca that '[r]ape was generally encouraged as a highly efficient method of achieving one key aim of the Bosnian Serb army: frightening and humiliating civilian Muslims'. She goes on to say, '[b]ut there appears to have been no specific order to rape'.[38] Yet, in the absence of a 'smoking gun' can a policy still be proven? In my view, given the pattern and the nature of actions carried out in Foca, it can.

Following the successful siege of Foca, power was concentrated into the hands of three key men at the local level. These men were Vojislav Maksimovic and Peter Cancar, who were both responsible for organizing the military campaign, and most importantly, Velibor Ostojic, who was a minister in Bosnian Serb leader Radovan Karadzic's government.[39] All three men were included in Karadzic's inner circle and were said to have maintained close contact with him throughout the occupation of Foca. Journalist Roy Gutman's sources also confirm that Ostojic made frequent trips to Pale, where Karadzic maintained his own headquarters.[40] It is believed that from these frequent meetings and from a number of other conversations which took place during the siege resulted the decisions to call in paramilitary troops, to destroy Muslim cultural sites, to establish both rape and concentration camps and to ethnically cleanse Foca of its non-Serb population.[41]

As indicated, the chain of command also included the local police, who actively participated in both the siege and the rapes of Foca. According to the ICTY,

> During the take-over and the arrest of the non-Serb population, there was a close alliance between the Foca police (hereinafter, SUP) and the Serb forces. The arms and uniforms for the Serb soldiers were distributed from the SUP building. Serb soldiers were constantly going in and out of the SUP building and started their wave of arrests from there.[42]

Dragan Gagovic, who was chief of police at the time, recommended both Foca High School and Partizan Sports Hall as appropriate rape camps. He also personally visited Partizan and could both see and hear what was happening there from his SUP headquarters. Finally, according to the indictment against him,

> Around 16 July 1992, a group of detainees from the Partizan Sports Hall, went to the SUP building and informed Dragan Gagovic about the constant sexual assault of women in the detention facility. On or around 17 July 1992, Dragan Gagovic personally raped one of the women who, on the previous day, had complained about the incidences of sexual assaults.[43]

What occurred in Foca at the Partizan Sports Hall was an exercise in public rape and public humiliation. Knowledge was widespread and acts were by no means the result of ad hoc individual actions. According to 'Azra', a 20-year-old who was detained and raped in Miljevina,

> 'Responsible people knew exactly what was going on and didn't do anything about it... All they had to do was give two or three of them [rapists] a stiff punishment and it would've stopped. But they never did that; practically speaking it was legal to rape Muslim women and all the rest of it'.[44]

While all of the time denying allegations of systemic and organized rape in Foca throughout 1992, Karadzic and his cohorts did very little to disprove the allegations or to ease international concerns. Foreign journalists and aid organizations were denied access to the city by Serbian forces throughout the spring, and Ostojic refused to answer questions by either phone or fax, referring to the questions on organized rape as 'hypothetical' and thus not worthy of answers.[45] On the other hand, in April 1992 Karadzic denied any knowledge of Partizan and, when asked about a policy of rape, he stated: 'We know of some 18 cases of rape altogether, but this was not organized but done by psychopaths'. He went on to call the rumours of mass rape 'propaganda' by 'Muslim Mullahs'.[46]

Contrary to the denials of Serbian leadership, by 1993 a number of governmental and non-governmental organizations had proven that rape in Bosnia-Herzegovina was widespread. At war's end, in a major legal precedent, the ICTY laid the very first charges which prosecuted rape as a separate crime against humanity. On 26 June 1996, eight men were charged for carrying out martial rapes in Foca.

The eight men charged under the Foca Indictment were what I would term *middle men*. In the indictment, charges were not laid against Ostojic, Maksimovic and Cancar, the main decision-makers in occupied Foca.[47] Charged instead were Dragan Gagovic, Gojko Jankovic, Janko Janjic, Radomir Kovac, Zoran Vukovic, Dragan Zelenovic, Dragoljub Kunarac and Radovan Stankovic. Of these men, six did hold positions of authority, five as sub-commanders of the military police, and Dragan Gagovic who held the highest position as chief of police. Seven of the eight men, including Gagovic and the five sub-commanders, were also paramilitary leaders. Therefore, of the eight men indicted, seven were responsible for the actions of individuals subordinate to them. Only Radovan Stankovic was not responsible for the actions of subordinates, but he was a member of an elite paramilitary unit and charged with running a house in Miljevina where many women were detained and raped.[48]

In reviewing the personal histories of these men what is striking is the banality of their own backgrounds. All were either born in or residents of Foca. Their professions ranged from police commanders (Gagovic) to café owners, waiters and unemployed mechanics. How each man came to organize and supervise as well as commit rape is a disturbing question that was left in the hands of the prosecution of the ICTY. Beginning on the 20 March 2000, Dragolijub Kunarec, Radomir Kovac and Zoran Vukovic were the first men in the Foca Indictment to stand trial. The task before the prosecution 'was to demonstrate that the rapes in the town of Foca were carried out in a systemic and organized fashion'.[49] Prosecution did so by establishing a pattern of events based upon the victims' testimony of repeated gang rapes. Approximately 20 Bosnian women testified before the court, again setting a precedent in a war crimes trial, as this was the first time that testimony of the victims was asked for and considered in a case of rape. On 22 February 2001 Kunarec, Kovac and Vukovic were all found guilty, receiving sentences of 28 years, 20 years and 12 years imprisonment for their crimes.[50] Speaking on the positions held by the convicted, Judge Florence Mumba stated that '[p]olitical leaders and war generals are powerless if ordinary people refuse to carry out criminal activities in the course of the war. Lawless opportunists should expect no mercy, no matter how low their position in the chain of command may be'.[51] Present in the court room as the verdicts were read, special correspondent Slavenka Drakulic wrote: 'Watching them, you understand that war finally boils down to what one individual does to another, to what they did to those girls. In the end, the war is only a sum of such actions'.[52]

Both Mumba's and Drakulic's comments make clear that the existence of a top-down policy of genocidal rape, which both legitimized and accommodated atrocities, does not absolve individuals of responsibility. Power was not, and never is, so centralized. Serbian leadership required the consent of the people. As journalist Peter Maass writes, 'Gaining the support of ordinary people ... is a crucial element in any successful reign of terror. The wavering masses, the silent majority, the good men, they must feel stained by the same blood as the Visigoths who fired the first shots. They must be made into accomplices to the crime'.[53] This was as true for Bosnia as it was for Nazi Germany. While support was initially difficult to gain in the multi-ethnic Bosnia-Herzegovina, owing in part to intense propaganda a significant portion of the

Bosnian Serb population, along with outsiders, did eventually become radicalized enough to either participate in 'preemptive genocide' or to deny outright its existence or stay silent in the face of it.[54]

As for the other men charged in the Foca Indictment, Radovan Stankovic was arrested on 9 July 2002 by French and German SFOR troops, and his case was handed over to the State Court of Bosnia-Herzegovina. On 14 November 2006 Stankovic was given a prison sentence of 16 years for crimes against humanity. On appeal, the sentence was increased to 20 years. On 25 May 2007, Stankovic escaped from police custody.[55] Dragan Gagovic was shot dead by French SFOR troops on 13 January 1999. He had remained in Foca and, making no attempts to hide, continued to work as a café owner and a karate instructor. French authorities attempted to arrest him as he returned from a karate competition with a van full of students. Gagovic reportedly steered the automobile into the soldiers and then, according to reports by the Russian newspaper *Izvestia*, French soldiers 'cold-bloodedly shot the driver [Gagovic] dead'.[56] Janko Janjic is also dead, having blown himself up with a hand grenade on 12 October 2000 when German SFOR troops attempted to arrest him in Foca.[57] Gojko Jankovic surrendered to authorities in 2005 and on 16 February 2007 he was handed a 34-year jail term by Bosnia's State Court.[58] Finally, Dragan Zelenovic was arrested in Russia in 2005. He was transferred to the ICTY at The Hague where he pled guilty to seven counts of torture and rape as crimes against humanity. For his participation in these crimes, Zelenovic was sentenced to 15 years imprisonment.[59]

While the international community, symbolized by the ICTY, has definitively decided that organized mass rape did occur in Foca, does this automatically indicate a policy of mass rape throughout Bosnia-Herzegovina? No, the evidence which emerges from one city cannot speak for the entire country, but the evidence collected from across many towns and villages, and the conclusive findings from both governmental and non-governmental organizations, does suggest a calculated and widespread systemic policy of rape driven by Bosnian Serbian leadership. Early in the war the Western media, along with national governments, were reluctant to label the Serbian actions in Bosnia as systemic. In the summer of 1992, journalist Peter Maass wrote: 'accounts indicate that the waves of arrests, beatings and executions in Bosnia – while widespread and brutal – are not systemic or carefully planned. Rather, the refugee accounts portray ad hoc campaigns of terror that vary from city to city'.[60] By 1995, after four years of brutal fighting and four years worth of documented cases of rape and other atrocities, the media had made significant shifts in its opinion.

Documentation and proof of a policy has come from a variety of sources. First, statements from the perpetrators themselves indicate that they were acting on superior orders. Vojislav Seselj, who led a Serbian paramilitary group known as the *White Eagles*, stated in a 1995 *Washington Post* article that 'Milosevic didn't sign any of the orders himself but they came from his security chiefs. He is directly responsible'. Going on to talk about those Serbs accused of war crimes, Seselj stated that 'if these men go The Hague they will say where their orders came from – Slobodan Milosevic'.[61] Claims such as this were corroborated by numerous victims who have said that they were told by their own rapists that there were orders to commit the crime. 'Mirsada,' a 23-year-old victim of rape from the town of Brezovo Polje, stated that a man who abducted her had said, 'We have orders to rape the girls', going on to say that he was 'ashamed to be a Serb...everything that is going on is a war crime'.[62] Testimony from aid workers on the ground also proved useful in establishing the systemic nature of the rapes. Selma Hecimovic, a worker in Zenica, Bosnia, who documented testimony from rape victims and organized refugee resettlement projects, stated emphatically that '[t]his has gone further than a "war crime", this is not a war crime any more but an attempt to destroy a whole people. This isn't the kind of rape that is the consequence of any war, this is organized rape, a stage in a programme'.[63] In an interview with journalist Roy Gutman, Dr. Melika Kreitmayer, who worked with a large number of rape victims from Brezovo Polje, stated: 'My impression is that someone had an order to rape the girls'. Gutman goes on to say that '[s]he cited as proof that some young women said they had been taken to a house and not raped but were instructed to tell others that they had been raped'.[64]

In fact, the pattern of abuse which occurred in Brezovo Polje closely mirrors the experience in Foca, as well as in numerous other towns and villages across Bosnia-Herzegovina. Women were initially raped in their own homes, at times in front of family members. According to one unnamed victim,

A man broke into our house and raped me...My husband had to watch while I was raped. I have a four-year-old daughter; she saw the rape. There was no way I could avoid it; he would have killed both of us. He just said, 'Your husband has to watch'.[65]

Once occupation was secured, the town's inhabitants were separated according to age and gender. Men were taken to detention centres such as the KP Dom in Foca or the infamous Omarska, located outside of Prijedor. Women, children and the elderly were transported to alternative locations, where again a group of women would be selected for rape. Referring to this first phase of occupation, Todd Salzman, author of 'Rape Camps, Forced Impregnation, and Ethnic Cleansing' writes that '[t]he psychological impact of such atrocities is evident. Through fear and intimidation, victims and witnesses would be hesitant to return to the scene of such events'.[66]

From this initial phase onwards it was common for women to experience frequent changes in their location. Upon initial separation from the men, women would be held in what were termed *refugee collection centres*. Here women were often taken away to be raped, or raped in front of other detainees. Gang rapes and other forms of physical torture were widely reported in such settings. In the case of Foca, the initial site of detention or refugee collection centre was *Buk Bijela*. *Buk Bijela* was initially created as military headquarters and barracks for Bosnian Serb and paramilitary soldiers after the siege of Foca, but it was turned into a temporary holding centre for Muslim civilians in July 1992. At *Buk Bijela* women were separated from children and made to suffer interrogations which turned into violent gang rapes. Victims included girls as young as 15.[67]

The final phase of detention which consistently speaks of the victims' experiences across Bosnia is the detention at both brothels and rape camps. In the case of brothels, women were usually kept at abandoned houses and used as sexual slaves. Captured war criminal Radovan Stankovic was accused of running one such brothel in Miljevina. Known as *Karaman's House* (the owner of the home being Nusret Karaman, a Muslim living in Germany) this brothel held at least nine women from August to October 1992. Detainees were as young as 12 and 14, and in addition to being subjected to repeated rapes during the course of their stay, they were also forced to perform household chores. According to the Foca Indictment, 'At Karaman's house, the detainees constantly feared for their lives. If any woman refused to obey orders, she would be beaten. Soldiers often told the women that they would be killed after the soldiers were finished with them because they knew too much'.[68] Rape camps, on the other hand, were established in locations such as abandoned hotels, restaurants and gymnasiums and held a greater number of women. As in brothels, women in rape camps were again detained for long periods of time and subjected to repeated torture, rape and sexual slavery. Partizan Sports Hall serves as the obvious example of a rape camp in the case of Foca, but such camps existed throughout Bosnia-Herzegovina, identified by names such as *Restaurant Sonja* (Vogosca) and *Vilena Vlas* (Visegrad).

Incidents which occurred at these rape camps also follow some typical patterns suggesting that they were run according to a Serbian policy. Foremost in suggesting that rape was being intentionally used by Serbian command in order to perpetrate genocide is testimony pointing to a policy of forced impregnation. Numerous accounts from victims reveal a Serbian intent to impregnate women. Victims scattered in various locations have testified that their rapists told them that they were to give birth to Serbian children. Ifeta, who suffered rape at a camp in Prijedor, states, 'while they were doing it [raping her] they said I was going to have a baby by them and that it'd be an honor for a Muslim woman to give birth to a Serbian kid'.[69] In the case of Foca, the indictment lists numerous accounts by victims which attest to similar statements. A policy of forced impregnation is also suggested by the fact that women who did become pregnant were held until an abortion was no longer an option. Kadira, a 40 year old Bosnian Muslim who was taken from her village and detained at a camp in Doboj, states that

> Women who got pregnant, they had to stay there for seven or eight months so they could give birth to a Serbian kid. They had their gynaecologists there to examine the women. The pregnant ones were separated off from us and had special privileges...Only when a woman's in her seventh month, when she can't do anything about it anymore, then she's released.

And those that did not get pregnant? Kadira recalled that '[t]hey beat the women who didn't get pregnant, especially the younger women; they were supposed to confess what contraceptives they were using'.[70] A policy of forced impregnation to enact genocide seems almost contradictory, but within the Balkan culture this policy made perfect sense. Todd Salzman argues that Serbian culture is based on a 'patriarchal myth' which believes that a child's identity is determined by that of the father. This proved important in the Bosnian conflict as this myth is also accepted within the Muslim and Catholic cultures. Thus, a child which results from a Serbian rape will always be considered Serbian, not only by the perpetrator, but also by the victim and her community.[71]

Further reinforcing the idea of an organized policy of rape is that, according to author Norman M. Naimark, '[r]ape camps received logistical and financial support from branches of the Bosnian Serb government'.[72] Only with these financial resources could local rape camps operate for months on end and only with organizational support could camps quickly dissolve themselves and successfully relocate once they had been discovered by international organizations. Reports from aid organizations such as Human Rights Watch and the United Nations 'indicate that the research, planning, and coordination of rape camps was a systemic policy of the Serbian government and military forces with the explicit intention of creating an ethnically pure state'.[73]

Also indicative of an official policy is the widespread toleration of the rapes. As it was shown in the case of Foca, the occurrences at Partizan were clearly visible to authorities. If authorities were not participating in the rapes themselves, they certainly made no attempts in Foca to stop them either. This toleration of rape was found to be widespread throughout Bosnia-Herzegovina. Commanders in rape camps did little to stop the practice of rape or to punish those subordinates who participated in it. The international community did believe that the commanders had the power to exercise such authority. The UN Commission of Experts found that following an explosion of media attention on mass rape in January and February 1993, the reported number of cases began to drop dramatically. Citing this correlation between media scrutiny and the decreasing number of reported rape cases, the UN Commission speculated that it 'would indicate that the commanders could control the alleged perpetrators if they wanted to. This could lead to the conclusion that there was an overriding policy advocating the use of rape as a method of "ethnic cleansing", rather than a policy of omission, tolerating the widespread commission of rape'.[74]

The final significant factor in the suggestion of an organized policy of mass rape is the document known as the RAM plan. Numerous eyewitness accounts attest to the existence of such a document believed to have been written in 1991. The plan, drawn up by the Yugoslav National Army (JNA), contains details for the planned military conquest of Bosnia-Herzegovina. All accounts of the plan claim that it also sets forward a process of removing Muslims from Bosnia-Herzegovina by various tactics including organized rape. The RAM plan apparently indicated that Muslim morale could be effectively weakened by the raping of Muslim women, including minors.[75] Another key piece of evidence indicated in *Rape Warfare* by Beverly Allen is a letter from the commander of the third battalion of the Serb army to the chief of the secret police in Belgrade in which he states that

Sixteen hundred and eighty Muslim women of ages ranging from twelve to sixty are now gathered in the centres for displaced persons in our territory. A large number of these are pregnant, especially those ranging in age from fifteen to thirty years. In the estimation of Bosko Kelevic and Smiljan Geric, the psychological effect is strong, and therefore we must continue [the practice of genocidal rape].[76]

Such documents present a convincing argument when it comes proving a top-down directed policy of rape.

Confronted with the issue of an organized mass rape, Bosnian Serbian leadership consistently denied allegations. When asked about the rapes of Muslim women for example, General Mladic, commander of the Bosnian Serb Army, crudely stated: 'We Serbs are too picky to do such things'.[77] From the onset of the war, Serbian leadership took no responsibility for alleged atrocities. In the spring of 1992 Radovan Karadzic stated that 'We can affirm with certainty that our army defended our people and their borders in a model manner and that it did not commit a single crime, rape or attack against civilians'.[78] Asked about a policy of ethnic cleansing, and faced with the streams of Muslim refugees, Karadzic instead used the term *ethnic transfer* and stated that there was no policy, and that Muslims were leaving of their own accord as they no longer felt comfortable in the now Serbian territory. These denials trickled down to low level officials as well. In the town of Visegrad where Muslim homes and mosques were burned to the ground, the local Serbian mayor stated, 'I don't know what you mean by "ethnic cleansing"! The Muslims left voluntarily. We even supplied the buses. We didn't force them to leave, I swear'.[79] Oftentimes Serbian denials were backtracked and forced to adjust to the increasing international awareness and proof of war crimes. While the existence of concentration camps was initially denied outright by Karadzic, he later amended his denial to an admission of camps, but stated that they were only prison camps and not for the purpose of extermination.[80] These outright denials certainly extended to the issue of rape as well. Karadzic maintained that there was no evidence to prove the claims of mass rape, and he called the accusations 'a horrible lie', going on to say, 'Our generals are extremely sensitive about moral behaviour'.[81] More often accusations of rape were blamed on Muslim propaganda and the desire of Muslim women to cover up their own immodest behavior. Accusations were regarded as attempts to slander the character of the Serbian soldier. As one paramilitary leader reasoned in 1993, if the 'Serbs had raped so many Muslim women, when would they have had time to win the war in Bosnia-Herzegovina'.[82]

Despite such denials, investigations conducted during the course of the war and following its end have proved that various wartime atrocities, including mass rape, were most likely the result of a purposeful policy. Between the established patterns of abuse that were mirrored from town to town across Bosnia; between both victim and perpetrator testimony; between the sheer numbers of reported rape cases; and from information regarding Serbian military goals and directives at the outset of the war, the existence of a policy of mass rape is a difficult argument to deny. Mass rape fit perfectly into the Serbian war aims of increasing their own population and driving Muslims out of their land in the pursuit of a greater Serbia. Rape proved a decisive factor in provoking fear and intimidation, and in destroying the social fabric of the Bosnian Muslim community. And as the international community largely fell silent, mass rape proved to be largely successful. Foca is only one of many Bosnian towns that changed in both name and character, cleansed of its multi-ethnicity. What occurred against Bosnian Muslims was no accident, and it was not random; it was deliberate and calculated, and it was genocide. While there may be no smoking gun, there is proof enough of a policy of mass rape and proof that Serbian command legitimized the use of rape as a weapon of war.

Notes

1. In 1937–1938, Japanese troops raped approximately 50,000 women in Nanking, China. Historians argue that the rapes do not appear to have been ordered and may have been motivated by the desire to show domination. In this regard the rapes were largely unsuccessful, as coupled with the murder of 300,000 Chinese, the rapes contributed to increased rebellion, rather than submission. J. S. Goldstein, *War and Gender: How Gender Shapes the War System and Vice Versa* (New York, 2001), pp. 366–368. In 1945, 2 million German women were raped by Red Army soldiers advancing into Berlin. Historians agree that revenge was the motivation for these rapes, and while not explicitly ordered, the rapes appear to have been officially sanctioned. L. Morrow, 'Unspeakable', *Time* (22 February 1993) and S. Brownmiller, *Against Our Will: Men, Women and Rape* (New York, 1975), pp. 66–67. In 1947–1948, an estimated 75,000 women were raped during the India/Pakistan partition. Women were abducted and raped by men of differing religions. Rapes occurred by all sides, Muslims, Hindus and Sikhs. In response many women were martyred, either by killing themselves or being killed by men of their own religious background. U. Butalia, 'A Question of Silence: Partition, Women and the State', *Gender and Catastrophe*, ed. R. Lentin (New York, 1997), pp. 91–99. Finally, in 1994, an untold number of

rapes occurred in the Rwandan genocide. Both Tutsi and sympathetic Hutu women were the victims of Hutu violence. This was a clear case of genocidal rape, perpetrated along tribal lines. It is estimated that 800,000 persons died over the course of 100 days in the Rwandan genocide. 'Shattered Lives: Sexual Violence during the Rwandan Genocide and Its Aftermath', Human Rights Watch (September 1996) http://hrw.org/reports/1996/Rwanda.htm (8 April 2004).

2. B. Harden, 'In Bosnia, "It is Very Ugly, Very Sad What is Happening"', *The Washington Post* (13 April 1992), A16.
3. Harden, *The Washington Post*, A16.
4. N. Cigar, *Genocide in Bosnia: The Policy of 'Ethnic Cleansing'* (College Station,TX, 1995), p. 5. Census statistics also confirmed in *The Washington Post*.
5. P. Maass, *Love Thy Neighbor: A Story of War* (New York, 1996), p. 27.
6. For a thorough review of the opinions of policy makers regarding the Bosnian conflict, see chapter 8 'The Denial Syndrome: The Victims and Bystanders' in N. Cigar's *Genocide in Bosnia*; 'In Plain View' by R. Ali and L. Lifschultz in *Why Bosnia?: Writings on the Balkan War* (Stoney Creek: Connecticut, 1993), as well as contemporary newspaper articles which reflected the views of leading statesmen such as U.S. Secretary of State Warren Christopher, negotiators Lord Owen and Cyrus Vance and Canadian Major-General Lewis MacKenzie, Chief of Staff of the UNPROFOR mission in Sarajevo.
7. T. Butler, 'The Ends of History: Balkan Culture and Catastrophe', *The Washington Post* (30 August 1992), C3.
8. T. Judah, *The Serbs: History, Myth and the Destruction of Yugoslavia*, 2nd edn (New Haven, 2000), p. xi.
9. Popularized during the Second World War, broadly speaking, Ustasha referred to Croatian nationalists, while Chetnik was a term applied to Serbian guerilla fighters. In the most recent conflict the terms were used largely as derogatory labels, although some Serbian paramilitary troops referred to themselves as Chetniks. Information derived from A. Callmard, *Investigating Women's Rights Violations in Armed Conflict* (Canada, 2001).
10. Judah, *The Serbs*, p. xiii.
11. For greater insight into the Serbian nationalist agenda, see the Serbian Academy of Arts and Sciences (SANU) Memorandum of 1986. A key document of the nationalist agenda, it articulated the sentiments of Serbian academics, outlined injustices against Serbians and committed support for a strong Serbia over a unified Yugoslavia. Document can be found at http:www.haverford.edu/relg/sells/reports/memorandumSANU.htm.
12. T. Mazowiecki, Special Rapporteur to the United Nations Commission on Human Rights, 'Situation of Human Rights in the Territory of the Former Yugoslavia', UN Doc. E/CN.4/1993/50 (1993) http://www.haverford.edu/relg/sells/reports/mazowiecki_10feb93.htm.
13. United Nations Convention on the Prevention and Punishment of the Crime of Genocide (9 December 1948) http://www.unchr.ch/html/menu3/b/p_genoci.htm.
14. Criteria and definition of genocidal rape derived from, B. Allen, *Rape Warfare: The Hidden Genocide in Bosnia-Herzegovina and Croatia* (Minneapolis, 1996), p. ii.

15. Cigar, *Genocide in Bosnia*, p. 5.
16. Ibid., p. 4. Also see F. Hartmann's 'Bosnia', in *Crimes of War: What the Public Should Know*, ed., R. Gutman and D. Rieff (New York, 1999) for a discussion of this topic and K. Doubt's article 'On the Latent Function of Ethnic Cleansing in Bosnia' which discusses why the policy of ethnic cleansing was far more brutal in Bosnia than in other parts of the former Yugoslavia, found at http://www.haverford.edu/relg/sells/WitnessDoubtLatent.html.
17. Indictment: Gagovic & Others ('Foca') (26 June 1996) http://www.haverford. edu/relg/sells/indictments/gagovic.html (8 January 2004), 7.
18. R. Gutman, 'Unholy War: Serbs Target Culture and Heritage of Bosnia's Muslims' (2 September 1992), *A Witness to Genocide: 1993 Pulitzer Prize-Winning Dispatches on the 'Ethnic Cleansing' of Bosnia* (Toronto, 1993), p. 79. All 14 mosques in and around Foca were destroyed during the course of the siege. For further reading on the cultural destruction of Bosnia refer to *Killing Memory: Bosnia's Cultural Heritage and its Destruction* by A. J. Riedlmayer (film).
19. N. Malcolm, *Bosnia: A Short History* (Washington Square: New York, 1994), p. 188. Judah, *The Serbs*, p. 121.
20. Malcolm, *Bosnia: A Short History*, p. 188.
21. Ibid., p. 192. For a more complete history of Yugoslavia in the Second World War refer to chapter 13 'Bosnian and the Second World War, 1941–1945' in *Bosnia: A Short History* and chapter 7 'We Chose the Heavenly Kingdom' in *The Serbs*.
22. Gutman, 'Three Who Planned Rape and Murder: Leader's Inner Circle Set up Rape Camp in Muslim Town' (19 April 1993), *A Witness to Genocide*, p. 160.
23. Indictment: Gagovic & Others ('Foca'), 8.
24. Note that exact figure cannot be known; figure of 20,000 is taken from the European Union Commission, and 50,000 is an estimation by the Bosnian Government. Goldstein, *War and Gender*, p. 363.
25. Indictment: Gagovic & Others ('Foca'), 3.
26. Ibid, 2.
27. Gutman, 'A Daily Ritual of Sex Abuse' (19 April 1993) *A Witness to Genocide*, p. 165.
28. Second Part of the Indictment against Gagovic & Others: The Charges http://www.haverford.edu/relg/sells/indictments/gagovic2.html (8 January 2004), 3. For an explanation on what constituted a rape camp, refer to A. Stiglmayers's article 'The Rapes in Bosnia-Herzegovina', in *Mass Rape: The War against Women in Bosnia-Herzegovina*, ed. A. Stiglmayer (Lincoln: Nebraska, 1994), pp. 115–131.
29. Second Part of the Indictment against Gagovic & Others 7.
30. Ibid.
31. Gutman, 'A Daily Ritual of Sex Abuse', p. 164.
32. Ibid, p. 166. For further information on the significance of gang rape in Bosnia-Herzegovina refer to E. Hague's article 'Rape, Power and Masculinity: The Construction of Gender and National Identities in the War in Bosnia-Herzegovina' found in *Gender and Catastrophe*.
33. Second Part of the Indictment against Gagovic & Others 8.
34. Indictment against Gagovic & Others ('Foca'), 4. What happened to FWS-87 in the period between her sale and becoming a witness at the ICTY is unclear.

It appears that the Montenegrins did not purchase her to save her, as she was taken to Montenegro on numerous occasions by her Serbian captors for the sole purpose of rape. The sale appears to have been another phase in her torture, and it is unclear when she was eventually freed.

35. Stiglmayer, *Mass Rape*, p. 104.
36. Cigar, *Genocide in Bosnia*, p. 61 and 'Bosnia and Hercegovina: A Closed Dark Place', Human Rights Watch http:www.hrw.org/reports98/foca/ (3 August 2007).
37. 'Bosnian Muslim Refugees Return', *BBC News* (25 November 2004) http://news.bbc.co.uk/1/hi/world/europe/1040529.stm (21 January 2004).
38. S. Drakulic, 'Viewpoint: Foca's Everyday Rapists', *Women, State, Culture...* (29 June 2001) http://k.mihalec.tripod.com (12 January 2003).
39. Gutman, 'Three Who Planned Rape and Murder', p. 157.
40. Ibid, p. 159.
41. Ibid, p. 158.
42. Indictment against Gagovic & Others ('Foca'), 8.
43. Ibid, 10.
44. Stiglmayer, *Mass Rape*, p. 110.
45. Gutman, 'Three Who Planned Rape and Murder', p. 159.
46. Ibid, p. 158.
47. Radovan Karadzic was indicted for war crimes, including rape, by the International Court on 24 July 1995; a warrant for his arrest was issued on 11 July 1996. Karadzic was arrested by Serbian security officials on 21 July 2008 and is to be transferred to The United Nation War Crimes Tribunal at The Hague to stand trial.
48. Indictment Against Gagovic & Others ('Foca'), 8–9.
49. 'Rape: A Crime against Humanity', *BBC News Online: World: Europe* (22 February 2001) http://news.bbc.co.uk/1/low/world/europe/1184763.stm (3 January 2004).
50. 'UN Tribunal Jails Serbs for Sex Crimes', *Southeast European Times* (22 February 2001) http://www.setimes.com/htm12/english/3290.htm (3 January 2004).
51. Drakulic 'Viewpoint: Foca's Everyday Rapists'.
52. Ibid.
53. Maass, *Love Thy Neighbor*, p. 112.
54. Serbian leaders took control over the media and constantly reinforced the idea that an independent Bosnia would result in the victimization of Serbians within Bosnia's borders. Serbians were constantly encouraged to take offensive actions and participate in 'preemptive genocide' as a means to saving themselves. In reality, there was never any indication that Bosnian Muslims planned either an aggressive takeover of Bosnia or atrocities against its Serbian population. In 1992, Muslims in Bosnia's Government 'believed in a pluralistic country, refrained from creating an army (or acquiring weapons) and repeatedly pledged to defend minority rights'. Maass, *Love Thy Neighbor*, p. 28. The term 'preemptive genocide' is derived from Maass, *Love Thy Neighbor*, p. 88.
55. 'Radovan Stankovic', Trial Watch http:www.trial-ch.org/en/trial-watch/profile/db/legal-procedures/radovan_stankovic_466.html (3 August 2007).

56. E. Guseinov, 'French Soldiers Shoot a Bosnian Serb Leader', *Izvestia* (13 January 1999), 3.
57. D. Dardic and I. Gajic, 'Death Rather Than Extradition' (18 October 2000) http://free.freespeech.org/ex-yupress/reporter/reporter61.html (10 March 2004).
58. 'Gojko Jankovic' Trial Watch http://www.trial-ch.org/en/trial-watch/profile/db/legal-procedures/gojko_jankovic_503.html (3 August 2007).
59. 'Summary of Sentencing Judgment for Dragan Zelenovic' United Nations (4 April 2007) http://www.un.org/icty/pressreal/2007/pr1152e-summary.htm (3 August 2007).
60. P. Maass, 'Refugees Give Accounts of Random Serb Terror', *The Washington Post* (5 August 1992), A27. Maass's 1996 book, *Love Thy Neighbor* reveals a very different outlook on the war and its systemic atrocities.
61. J. Pomfret, 'Atrocities Leave Thirst for Vengeance in the Balkans', *The Washington Post* (18 December 1995), A17. Further testimony from perpetrators can be found in A. Stiglmayer's 'The Rapes in Bosnia-Herzegovina', pp. 147–161.
62. Gutman, 'The Rapes of Bosnia: We Want the World to Know' (23 August 1992), p. 68.
63. E. Vulliamy, *Seasons in Hell: Understanding Bosnia's War* (New York, 1994), p. 201.
64. Gutman, 'The Rapes of Bosnia', p. 69.
65. K. D. Askin, *War Crimes against Women: Prosecution in International War Crimes Tribunals* (The Hague, 1997), p. 265.
66. T. Salzman, 'Rape Camps, Forced Impregnation, and Ethnic Cleansing: Religious, Cultural and Ethical Responses to Rape Victims in the Former Yugoslavia', *War's Dirty Secret: Rape, Prostitution and Other Crimes against Women*, ed. A. L. Barstow (Cleveland, 2000), pp. 72–73.
67. A complete description of *Buk Bijela* and the testimony of its victims can be found in the Second Part of the Indictment against Gagovic & Others, 1–2.
68. Third Part of the Indictment Against Gagovic & Others http://www.haverford.edu/relg/sells/indictments/gagovic3.html (8 January 2004), 7.
69. Stiglmayer, *Mass Rape*, p. 118.
70. Ibid, p. 119.
71. Salzman, *War's Dirty Secret*, pp. 78–79.
72. N. M. Naimark, *Fires of Hatred: Ethnic Cleansing in Twentieth-Century Europe* (Cambridge, 2001), pp. 169–170.
73. Salzman, *War's Dirty Secret*, p. 71.
74. Ibid. It should be noted that this conclusion is speculative, and that the decrease in rapes could mirror a number of other factors including the possibility that the media may have stopped reporting on the rapes and moved on to other stories (as they have been known to do), or victims could have been silenced by their own perpetrators who may have increasingly threatened their victims as their own actions became more public. Perpetrators' threats could also have reflected a growing fear of retribution from the international community, as the first rumblings of an international war crimes tribunal began to circulate in early 1993. Ibid, p. 72.
75. Ibid, pp. 70–71.

76. Allen, *Rape Warfare*, p. 59. Brackets found in Allen.
77. Naimark, *Fires of Hatred*, p. 169.
78. Cigar, *Genocide in Bosnia*, p. 88.
79. Ibid.
80. Ibid, p. 90.
81. Ibid, p. 91.
82. Ibid, p. 92.

Index